THE
ART OF
THE
INTERVIEW

OTHER BOOKS BY LAWRENCE GROBEL

Conversations with Capote

The Hustons: The Life and Times of a Hollywood Dynasty

Conversations with Brando

Talking with Michener

Above the Line: Conversations About the Movies

Endangered Species: Writers Talk About Their Craft, Their Visions, Their Lives

Climbing Higher (with Montel Williams)

LAWRENCE GROBEL

 THREE RIVERS PRESS • NEW YORK

THE ART OF THE INTERVIEW

LESSONS FROM A MASTER OF THE CRAFT

070.4
Grobel

Published by Three Rivers Press, New York, New York.

Member of the Crown Publishing Group, a division of
Random House, Inc.

www.crownpublishing.com

THREE RIVERS PRESS and the Tugboat design are registered trademarks
of Random House, Inc.

Printed in the United States of America

DESIGN BY ELINA D. NUDELMAN

Library of Congress Cataloging-in-Publication Data

Grobel, Lawrence.

The art of the interview : lessons from a master of the craft /
Lawrence Grobel.—1st ed.

   Includes bibliographical references and index.

   (trade pbk.)

 1. Interviewing in journalism.   2. Interviewing in mass media.   I. Title.

  PN4784.I6G76 2004

   070.4—dc22   2004004664

ISBN 1-4000-5071-5

10 9 8 7 6 5 4 3 2 1

First Edition

ACKNOWLEDGMENTS

An acknowledgment is not a dedication, though in this case it could be, for there have been some special people who I would like to single out. There are the editors at *Newsday* (Stan Green, Lou Schwartz) who got me started interviewing "household names" back in the early seventies. There is *Playboy*, which has allowed the space for this form to flourish (thanks Hef, and Christie); and my current editor there, Steve Randall, who understands what it is we do. There is Anne Volokh at *Movieline's Hollywood Life*, who also recognizes that interviews can peel away the layers to get to the core of those whom some believe have none. There are the editors and writers who contributed so thoughtfully to Chapters 6 and 7. There is Tom Wortham, chairman of UCLA's English department, who thought this subject worthy of five upper-division credits and gave me the freedom to turn a seminar into a textbook. There is my agent, Noah Lukeman, who has written two writing books himself and has renewed my faith in the mercurial business of agenting. My editor, Carrie Thornton, who never threatened my life as I fought her on changes and who showed impressive patience and good taste from start to finish. The book cover designer Mary

Schuck. Elliott Gould and Al Pacino, whose friendship demonstrates uncanny trust in a journalist. And Diane Keaton, who insists that we never do an interview so we can remain friends. There is J. P. Donleavy, a writer I've read and admired since my college years, who took time out of his own writing and farming life to pen a rare foreword. My wife Hiromi, who has heard all these stories and more and still sleeps with me. My daughters Maya and Hana, who can't quite figure out how talking to people for a living can actually provide for a living. Zachary Intrater, whose love of words and appetite for books has made him a reliable resource and near Zen master. And there is every person who sat across from me as I recorded their words. Thank you all.

CONTENTS

FOREWORD BY J. P. DONLEAVY   xv

PROLOGUE
AN ENCYCLOPEDIC APPROACH   1

INTRODUCTION
ROBERT MITCHUM, ADOLPH EICHMANN, SEXUAL REPRESSION, AND FINDING ONE'S VOICE. DON'T ASK. OR DO.   15

1
KINDS OF INTERVIEWS   31
Print. Books. Radio. Documentaries. Television.

2
GETTING THERE   63
What happens after you've got the assignment? Publicists. Researching and preparing questions. Convincing a subject to sit with you. Changing a reluctant subject's mind. Learning to be patient. Becoming a chameleon and an actor. Behaving differently with different subjects. Be Educated. Be Current. Knowing when to be forceful. Those dumb questions. When an editor wants you, but the subject prefers someone he knows. Bringing the caviar.

3

YOU'RE THERE, NOW WHAT?   123

Learning to deal with your nerves. Talking to "stars" and experts. Getting your subject to open up: Knowing when to delve into a person's fears and anxieties, traumas, and financial affairs. Getting them to trust you. When to be an "equal" and when not to be. Maintain control. Relying on your personality. Getting beyond the plug: You've let them promote, now it's your turn. Recognizing good copy when you hear it. Zero in on specifics. Going with the unexpected. Burying oneself in chauvinism. The battle of the sexes. Searching one's past for clues. The problem with parents. Parents and their children. Nightmares: When it just isn't working. Asking the tough questions. Avoiding confrontations until the end. Dealing with subjects who treat you badly. Nobel Prize winners. Don't overlook asides. Knowing when enough's enough.

4

I DON'T WANT TO TALK ABOUT THAT!   195

Jack Nicholson. Anjelica Huston. Dylan McDermott. Jodie Foster. Harrison Ford. James A. Michener. Norman Mailer. Saul Bellow. Al Pacino. Sharon Stone. Truman Capote. Oliver Stone. Marlon Brando. Robert De Niro.

5

STRUCTURE: WHEN THE TALK STOPS   220

Editing raw transcripts. How to start: The Importance of a good beginning. Endings. The meat in between.

6

EDITORS ON EDITING AND EXPECTATIONS   252

Stephen Randall *(Playboy)*, Peter Bloch *(Penthouse)*, Andrew Essex *(Details)*, Heidi Parker *(Movieline ∕ Hollywood Life, Playboy)*, Barry Golson *(TV Guide, Yahoo)*, Bill Newcott *(AARP the Magazine)*, Janice Min *(Us)*, Will Dana *(Rolling Stone)*.

7
OTHER VOICES/OTHER WRITERS   293

Kevin Cook, Claudia Dreifus, Michael Fleming, Kristine
McKenna, Steve Pond, David Rensin, Diane Shah, David Sheff.

8
THE INTERVIEWER INTERVIEWED   345

APPENDIX 1
DREW BARRYMORE QUESTIONS   367

APPENDIX 2
ON THE ROAD WITH THE ANGRIEST MAN
IN AMERICA   379

SOURCES   451

INDEX   453

FOREWORD

J. P. DONLEAVY

If ever the words "matter of fact" come to mean anything, they do with a low-key vengeance mean something blunt and to the point in Larry Grobel's *The Art of the Interview.* Which at the least, is a one-hundred-thousand-word definition in depth of the meaning, if it has any, of celebrity and fame. And in summing it all up, it would nearly teach you a lesson: Don't try to be famous, you'll regret it. But in spite of such implied advice, there's not in this treatise a recluse to be seen or mentioned anywhere. There are instead even interviews of the interviewers. And you begin to get an idea of when you're famous, what the smart thing is

to say in order to stay that way. All communicated by one of the specialists analyzing his subjects inside out, from their youth onward and into the flowering of their careers. Their motives exposed which first ignited them to achieve their notability. Except there is a catch. To be a subject for Larry Grobel to make you in depth more famous, you've already got to be pretty famous.

Now then. As someone who is normally racked with humility, and also just about the world's worst interviewee, writing this foreword I find myself both puzzled and flattered. But I was, in fact, once actually interviewed by Larry Grobel. The interview being for *Newsday* and which was never published in that periodical but was to appear later in Larry's book *Endangered Species,* which gives the best indication of where one might languish today, shovel in hand, knee-deep in my bogs watching my cattle and hoping to God someone might point and say:

"Hey, I know who you are."

Ah, but forget all that old sorrowful self-deprecating stuff, which all strikes me as a matter of false self-effacement. One accepts the fact that except in avoiding danger, it's a strong human trait not to want to be ignored. Even in writing this I'm depending upon someone somewhere having heard of me. So, being best known for being unknown, how have I qualified for the attention of Larry Grobel in the first place. I simply can only conjecture it must have been from his reading one of or all of my novels and helping to contribute to every writer's dream, that someone somewhere will open up one of their books and get hooked, to read on. And then tell somebody else he likes to do the same. In any event, one always remained aware that one of the most used expressions in the United States, if not spoken, was then thought and which pervades all conversational confrontation.

"What the hell use are you to me."

This remark did not seem to be in effect when Larry Grobel first came into my ken, now many years ago. Paying me a visit to interview me in the rather large house I live in, isolated out in the midlands of Westmeath. A house, as it happens, whose fame now somewhat rests as much upon the fact that James Joyce was here as that I am here.

And then some years later didn't one day dawn out in these isolated midlands, when you mildly assume that maybe the world does give a good goddamn that you are languishing where you are. And present the occasion when a letter arrived from Hollywood. The place from which all writers want to hear from. Because it can mean the biggest bucks he will ever know in his life. And what they wanted to do was to option the film rights of *The Ginger Man* and *A Fairy Tale of New York,* two of my earliest novels. The gentleman's name signed to the letter was none other than Larry Grobel.

Like all presumably serious novelists, one was suspicious of the movie industry, especially as so many adaptations of novels did not please nor represent an author's intention. A script perhaps going through a dozen writers and as many drafts and driven in that many different directions by that many opinions. Nor was an author who tended to treat the making of a film as an art form encouraged.

I was less than tempted to get involved with Hollywood other than as an observer. But my son Philip, who had some knowledge of the film business, dutifully read the letter and said I should look into it. When I asked him why, he said these people whom Larry was then representing must have a large cash flow, which makes them capable of what they want to do. Plus somewhere along the line, following a number of fruitless back-and-forth communications, my second wife, who knew a little bit about the Hollywood scene, intervened and took it upon herself to inform Larry Grobel that "if you're going to get anywhere with that old curmudgeon you're best advised to simply get him on a plane and fly him out to Hollywood."

And presto, first class they did.

I can't recall Larry's position exactly at that time except that he represented the film department of Katz-Gallin and seemed to know who numerous people were across the nation. Actors, producers, managers, agents, and moguls in the movie industry and political figures as well as a few titans of literature. He seemed, in his very well-bred, somewhat shy manner, not particularly in the business of interviewing celebrity subjects, nor did he mind shunning the hot-spot places of Hollywood and throughout, was dutifully looking after me.

It was during these visits to Los Angeles that Larry revealed another aspect of himself. Sensitive to my eccentric interest in the dead of Hollywood as they reside in their final resting places and joining me to explore the haunting quality possessed by Hollywood's socially taboo spots. And about which few in Hollywood wanted to know. We had formed a comfortable comradeship and he had no inhibitions in heading straight out as we did to its cemeteries. The astonishing Forest Lawn a prime target. This strange refuge for the dead with its landscape, and its massive mausoleum, in itself an architectural monument worthy of note. But it was on this same visit to Hollywood that one of the Hollywood living was given some attention. An old Trinity College/Dublin acquaintance and later a friend of mine was wrapping up a film he had recently made, and was holding a party. Knowing the ins and outs of the geographical Hollywood landscape, Larry volunteered to take me there.

On the way Larry pointed out where some famed figures of literary importance had lived, such as Scott Fitzgerald. But when it came time to finding out the whereabouts of the address at which my old pal was holding his party we had a lot of detouring to do up and down blind alleys. Larry was totally mystified as we searched, that this old friend of mine was indeed a fabled Hollywood legend himself, the film director George Roy Hill. That he was to be finally found celebrating with his cast in a modest bungalow in an anonymous twisting little street somewhere hidden in the suburban reaches of Hollywood simply nonplussed Larry. And was no surprise to me. As we finally after many a false turn located the address and approached the little secluded house, I sensed Larry very quietly surprised at the lack of flashbulbs, journalists, limousines, or any other evidence of notoriety of any description. Meanwhile, explaining to Larry that George was a very curious fish indeed and was in effect a recluse who rarely, as far as I knew, ever gave interviews or dined out in expensive restaurants. But Larry did immediately understand, and delved into the mystery of this affair as he had on our tour of cemeteries and mortuaries, exhibiting all the signs and instincts of being a true writer smelling out as best he could the bizarre.

Before I left Hollywood and its cemeteries, it was also at this time that Larry brought me to meet another famed figure who would be classified as a celebrity, namely Hugh Hefner, who resided in his Playboy Mansion surrounded by swimming pools, lawns, exotic fish, attractive ladies, and even a private emporium full of pinball machines in which Larry and I were delighted to enter and where one could play free of charge to one's heart's content. Mr Hefner himself in our meeting, albeit brief, was wearing his silk pajamas and turned out to be a shyly introspective gentleman. And it seemed very appropriate that Larry, connected with *Playboy,* set forth to become one of the world's greatest interviewers. Featuring finally, as was the case, Marlon Brando, in a famed interview in *Playboy* magazine and which later was published in book form and a copy sent to me. I left the book for my son Philip to read on his bedside table when he was to arrive in Ireland visiting. Thinking that perhaps he wouldn't bother reading such an interview, I was fascinated to find he had and to be able to ask him what he thought of Mr Brando, and I quote:

"Marlon Brando is simply the most intelligent man in the United States."

It was in fact from Philip's remark that I realised that Larry Grobel had the ability, in whatever regard such is required, to elicit from people a profound element, should they possess such, and Larry himself would have to be regarded as the most intelligent interviewer in the United States. A fact that this present volume brilliantly and fascinatingly demonstrates. And as Larry tells it, *The Art of the Interview* speaks for itself. And it's happened. The interviewers have become as or more famous than their subjects.

—J. P. Donleavy. 2004

I WANT YOU OUT OF HERE! AND I WANT THOSE GODDAMN TAPES!

—Coach Bob Knight

AN ENCYCLOPEDIC APPROACH

I became a partner in their own understanding of themselves.

—GAY TALESE

Not long ago I found myself among ten invited guests at a dinner party at Steve Martin's house. I've gotten to know Martin since his Wild and Crazy days as a stand-up comedian, before he started appearing in movies. First came a *Playboy* interview, then one for a magazine I had to use a pseudonym for, and then one for *Movieline*. After those, he came to my house for dinner, then to a class I teach at UCLA, and we've stayed in casual touch ever since. Joyce Carol Oates and her husband, Ray Smith, were at the dinner, as were David Mamet and his wife, and two poets, Susan Wheeler and Carol Muske-Dukes. When Oates was asked her connection to

Steve, she said it was through me, and that I had interviewed her for *Playboy* some years back. She then spoke about what I do, and that led to a lively conversation around the table about the nature of being on both sides of an interview. At one point Carol Muske-Dukes said, "I don't see all that much difference in interviews I read, they all seem the same to me." I bristled slightly, but I didn't want to try and defend the uniqueness of certain interviews at that time. Instead, I told them how selling encyclopedias during a summer between my freshman and sophomore college years taught me how to get people's attention, how to focus, and, though I didn't know it then, how to be a good interviewer. Mamet, who wrote a classic screenplay on the salesman's life *(Glengarry Glen Ross),* and who had a penchant for writing about cons *(The Spanish Prisoner, House of Games)* was all ears. So were the others. Martin, I think, fiddled with the idea of sticking a fork in his eye, but remembered *Bedtime Story* and didn't want to repeat himself.

To start a book about the art and craft of interviewing by relating my tale of how I learned how to pitch the *Collier's Encyclopedia* to strangers in their homes in Queens, Bedford-Stuyvesant, and Long Island may seem a little strange, but bear with me. There's a moral to this story. In fact, more than one.

MY FRIEND JOHNNY had worked for Collier's the summer before and was very successful at it. I had helped him learn the "pitch" then, but it never occurred to me that I might want to try it until he made the suggestion. The fact that he averaged nearly $200 a week, back in the mid-1960s, greatly encouraged me.

So I went to the Long Island office of *Collier's Encyclopedia* and sat in a small room along with about ten other people, when Morty walked in.

"Well, let's get down to business," he said. "None of you know what this is all about, except that you answered the ad in the newspaper promising you some money each week if you're sincere and dedicated, right?"

Right? Wrong—I knew what it was about, but none of these other guys did. I had a friend in the business; they came in response to an ad. That's why they all looked so apprehensive—they didn't know what they were getting into. There were no women because the ad specifically asked for men.

"Our work is special—some might even say it's not work at all. It involves learning and education, and you won't be selling a product. This you must believe, because if you think you're about to become a salesman, forget it, you can leave right now."

This Morty, boy, he had his shtick down pat. He was the sales manager, and Johnny had told me he was worth $20,000 a year (remember, this was when that seemed a decent amount of money) and would probably become the district manager before the end of the summer. He had a law degree and had passed the bar, but actually found the book business more lucrative.

"What we're dealing with is encyclopedias—but we're not in the business of selling them. The encyclopedia we're working for cannot be bought in any book or department store [what good encyclopedia can?] and our job here is, believe it or not, to actually give them away." Morty paused to let this important fabrication sink in. "That's right, you're all going to play summer Santa Claus. It's as simple as Simon himself."

Morty looked at our faces. Those who weren't smiling weren't going to get through the next three days—Morty knew that. It was his business to know—to size up a potential salesman the way he had learned to size up prospective customers. In this business, you didn't waste time spoon-feeding and coaxing the unsure. The training period lasted only three intense days; after that you were assigned to a group and taken to an area in Queens or Long Island and put out for five hours on your own. In such work, the only way you really learn is by doing. Those who can't do, learn that, too. Not everyone can give away encyclopedias for $365 a set.

What Morty and his field managers tried to stress was that in working for Collier's everybody made money and no one, including the lucky recipients of the books, came out holding the short end of the proverbial stick. For every set of books we managed to place (the word *sell* was strictly forbidden), the commission would be $87.50 up to the first ten sets, $97.50 for the next ten, and a free set of books after placing twenty sets (which you would probably sell and keep the entire $365). The hours we worked were between 5 and 10 P.M., because that's when most couples were home, and you wanted to talk to both husband and wife, so they couldn't use each other as an excuse for canceling. The field manager, who drove you to your territory each evening, received $10 for every set you placed, the sales manager, $20, the district and regional managers, God knows how much. When you subtracted all these commissions, those free books were worth about $150 less than what the people who accepted them ended up paying.

How did free books wind up costing nearly $400? A good question. The answer, as Morty would have said, is as simple as Simon himself. And as deceiving as Morty himself.

You see, the sales pitch that we were expected to learn was prepared for the company by a well-known university's psychology department. It took eighty minutes from start to finish, and if you managed to make it all the way through, your chances of getting a set of signatures on the bottom of that contract were better than one in three. But if closing the deal was tricky, by far the most difficult part of the job was getting into the house itself. You couldn't give away free books until you managed to get through the door.

During the three days of training, we were made to believe that working for Collier's was like playing at being God. We weren't tricking anybody into something phony and we weren't promising anything we couldn't deliver. Encyclopedias, after all, aren't a bad thing. They are true books of facts and knowledge. They are an investment in education, just as college is. They are good to have around when you have a question that you can't answer off-the-cuff (why the sky is blue; why people get depressed).

Our training didn't stress getting through the door very much—simply because there is no sure method of getting through a door of some strange house when, for all the house owner knows, you might be harboring a submachine gun in your attaché case. Fear plays a large role in the minds of suburban homeowners, and when the doorbell rings at night and the person outside is unknown and uninvited, people think twice before they let you in.

What we did learn was how to make a pitch. First, we had to assure the homeowners we weren't selling encyclopedias. We did this by convincing them the books weren't on sale in the open market. Then we told them we were authorized to place a free set of books in a few homes in the area in return for two things:

1. A letter from the family getting the books, written six months after they had received them, saying what they thought of Collier's. They could say anything they wanted—they weren't expected to say they loved the encyclopedia if they didn't, even if they did get them for nothing. We promised that the books wouldn't be taken back, no matter what they wrote. (This letter was a gimmick, naturally; it wasn't really followed up, and letters from those who remembered to write probably were read with amusement.)

2. The other thing asked was that they show good faith in accepting the encyclopedias by keeping them up to date by purchasing a yearbook and subscribing to the library service the company offered. Obviously, if they were unwilling to keep the books up to date for at least ten years, then they were not worthy of getting the free books in the first place. This part of the pitch was to make them feel guilty if they refused to update them, but it was also the part where the money came in, so the library service was added to entice those who wanted more than just "something for nothing." With that service, we would tell them, you could get answers and information to anything under the sun—for the ridiculously low price of $36.50 a year, and that included the yearbook, too. *But,* we would caution, our voices lowering to a manly whisper, this service could only be guaranteed at that price for the first ten years. After that, they would have to pay what everyone who went out and bought the books (once they went on sale) paid—*double* the price just quoted.

By the time you got around to talking about yearbooks and library services, you had already shown the lucky couple what the entire set would look like (you carried in your attaché case an accordion-like mock-up of the books), as well as a sample volume of the entire set condensed, showing them the various topics, the pretty color pages, the fine gloss of the paper, and the strength of the binding.

It all sounded so easy, I couldn't wait to get out there. I had spent hours practicing the pitch before a mirror. During the training I got to stand before the others and sell them on the fine points of investing in their children's future ("Sure, you can use the set today, no problem, but what about five years from now, when your son is old enough to look up things for himself—he's not going to want a dated encyclopedia. Times change so rapidly, one day we're on the moon, the next, on Mars—you can't go out and buy a new encyclopedia every year now, can you? Of course not; so, the only way to keep them from becoming dated is . . ."). I felt confident, I knew the material, I wanted to get out there and make money being a nice guy. At $87.50 a set, I only had to place one set a day and—bingo!—$437.50 a week. Not bad for a summer job.

But the calculating and dreaming ended just hours after Alan, my field manager, put me out in what he called "virgin territory" somewhere on the South Shore of Suffolk County. I never would have believed how unfriendly people could be if I hadn't been out there knocking on door after door, unable to sneak even a shoelace through: "What do you want?" "We don't want any." "Are you the babysitter, where have you been?"

What was wrong? My hair was cut short, my tie was straight, I looked presentable. The problem, I soon realized, was that I looked like a salesman. When I wasn't. If only they knew I was *giving* books away *free*!

For the first three days in the field, I couldn't get past a single door, with one exception—and she was alone, not dressed, and willing to listen but not, I was sure, buy. "Stay awhile," she said,

"My husband won't be home for hours." "No girl is worth eighty-seven dollars and fifty cents," I mumbled. "What?" she asked. "Nothing, just a motto I learned during training," I said and walked out, more depressed than ever.

Some time after ten, often closer to eleven, Alan would drive up to the streetlight or mailbox meeting place. I'd throw my attaché case in the trunk and report on how I did. It was one of the rules of our team that nothing would be discussed inside the car—which made sense. Imagine one guy placing three sets, about to burst with the excitement of having made $262.50 in one night, sitting next to a guy who couldn't even get a foot through a door.

After my third unsuccessful night, I was retrained. What that means is they were allowing me one last chance before suggesting that giving away free encyclopedias wasn't my line. They put me out with one of their top salesmen, Jim, and it was through him that I learned how to get into houses.

Jim would throw his case behind the nearest bush and knock briskly at a door. When the lady of the house answered, he'd smile, look at the blank pad in his hand, and ask if she ever ate Jell-O. She would be thrown by such a question and he'd begin this incredible Jell-O routine. He never mentioned encyclopedias or anything that sounded like a salesman's pitch. What an eye-opener! He did what I had never thought of doing—he talked nonsense until he convinced them to let him in so he could check and see for himself if they had any Jell-O in their cabinets or refrigerator. If they did, he promised a free quarter. If they didn't, he'd tell them they were the only people on the block who didn't eat Jell-O. He'd tell them anything, whatever popped into his head, to get into that house and get them listening.

He would even rearrange furniture once inside, usually moving a chair from the kitchen to the living room, telling me later that if they allowed him to do that, then he knew he was home safe, because a man's home was his castle, and by changing the layout of his house, you've altered his comfort level. In effect, you've taken control.

Jim only placed one set of books that night, but that was one more than I had in three nights. I mapped out my strategy and the next day I was ready.

The first house I attempted I managed to place a set of books. I felt terrific. After hiding my attaché case, I had knocked on the door, and when the husband answered I told him I was a sportswriter for my college newspaper doing a survey on the attitude of Long Islanders toward the Los Angeles Dodgers and San Francisco Giants: Did he regard them as traitors? And did he find himself leaning toward the Yankees and Mets because he favored hometown teams? The guy just happened to be an old Brooklyn Dodger fanatic and we got to talking about Duke Snider and Pee Wee Reese for a half hour before I told him what a lucky man he was about to be. By the time his wife had joined us, he and I were beer-drinking buddies, and when I explained that I was new at my job and was supposed to select only certain kinds of families for these free books—ones who liked children and read newspapers—they assured me they were just the people I was looking for.

"No money involved, eh?" my buddy asked me.

"Not for the encyclopedia," I answered.

"Unbelievable," he marveled.

"Yes," I said, "it is."

I was a little nervous about presenting the closing pitch where the money was mentioned, but somehow it came off well. I explained to him that he could pay for the yearbook and library service in daily ice cream or cigarette money. The ice cream money came out to ten cents a day for ten years, the cigarette money worked out to a little over three years (these were the days when a pack of cigarettes cost considerably less than they do today). There really was no ten-cent payment plan, but it made the payment seem minuscule, and the first inclination of most people was to go for that one. Which was why we carried in our cases poster-size pictures of the dictionary or atlas, the junior Great Books, and the beautiful finished or unfinished, light walnut or dark mahogany bookcase, all of which they would get, along with a little toy bank that changed dates after their quarters dropped in, if they took the cigarette plan. "We can offer all this to you at no extra cost because by taking the three-year plan you're saving the company an extra seven years of bookkeeping."

He really believed in keeping things up to date and thought it was reasonable enough to pay no more than a pack of cigarettes a day for the next three years. "I've been wanting to give up smoking for years, ha-ha."

"Right on, ha-ha," I said.

"Listen to him," his wife said. "Mister two-pack-a-day Joe."

"Two packs!" I said, picking up the unexpected cue. "Why, you could get *two* free sets of encyclopedias and live ten years longer."

"Hey, har-har, how about that," he said. We laughed, they signed, he happily gave me the required $10 cash deposit; I was out the door and on the street before they could think about it.

There is no feeling in the world like that of a salesman who has placed his first order and knows he's X amount of dollars richer. The mind does incredible calculations concerning time and money: new bank accounts, sports cars, trips abroad, all sorts of ways to invest the money that will be pouring in as you talk your way through home after home. The feeling can actually lead to a momentum, which it did in my case, and I managed to get into three more homes that night and place a second set of books. Hot damn! I was on my way.

My opening pitch became more and more absurd as I went from door to door. Sometimes I'd say I was doing a magazine survey, other times I'd ask if they had problems with junk mail. If the lady of the house answered, I'd open with something about cosmetics or the high cost of food and what did she think of it. If her husband answered, I'd try the sports bit, or else politics:

Who would you vote for? Who did you vote for? Would you change your mind now? If a child answered the door, I'd tell him or her to open it and then get his or her mother or father—that way I'd already be in the house when they arrived. And if a grandmother opened up, that would be the best of all, just a glass of water as a request and in you'd be.

Once inside, the trick is to get them thinking positively, get them shaking their heads yes—no matter what ridiculous questions you have to ask. Talk about ice cream, then ask: You do like ice cream, *don't you?* Television: Do you ever watch television? Weather: Isn't the rain good for the lawn? Isn't it terrible, this rain, ruining a perfectly good day? Is that yellow globe up in the sky called the sun? Do you like money? Would you like to make more money? Do you have any hobbies? (Find out what they are; you'll use them later on when you tell them how the library service can provide information dealing with whatever hobbies they might have mentioned—guppy breeding, glue sniffing, stamps, barbed-wire collecting, whatever.) Keep them nodding their heads. If one is more agreeable than the other, work on the other: "Your wife says she likes children, but you seem a bit skeptical, sir, is it that you don't like children? You were once a child yourself, ha-ha—*weren't you?*" "Ma'am, you looked doubtful when I said you seemed to be an artistic family—now surely you can't tell me you're uninterested in art when you have that fine Rockwell print Scotch-taped to the wall over there?" Yes yes yes yes yes yes yes yes . . . the more the merrier, because when the clincher comes, they'll be so conditioned to saying yes that they'll (hopefully) just keep on nodding as you slip them the contract and click the ballpoint into writing position.

Every encyclopedia "giver" is guaranteed to have funny stories. One incident I'll never forget happened in Queens. I was demonstrating the sturdiness of the binding to this young Puerto Rican couple. We had been taught to hold up a single page of the same volume and shake it, showing how it wouldn't tear from the binding because it wasn't glued in like Brand X, but carefully stitched together. I made the mistake of gripping the page in my fist instead of holding it loosely and just as I shook the book over their new coffee table the page ripped and the volume went crashing through the table, shattered glass sprinkling all over the carpet. I was on the phone to Morty before they had a chance to recover and the company covered the damages.

In some houses I walked in on arguments and was asked to settle some question that was bound to put me on the wrong side of either husband or wife. One Jewish mother tried to fix me up with her niece, and one lonely man tried to fix me up with himself. In certain areas of Queens, junkies approached me for a fix and young girls for an evening of sweet delights ("No girl is worth eighty-seven dollars and fifty cents, no girl is worth eighty-seven dollars and fifty cents," I forced myself to utter.)

I found myself getting to the library service part of the pitch and promising the people it could do anything. Blueprints for a new house? A store? Just write the service. Build a rocket to the moon? Collier's can help. Want to rob a bank? Sure, ask the library service for a layout. Anything you want to know, the library service is there, with some of the best minds in the country, ready to answer your requests. (Morty told me, later on, that if a third of the people who subscribed actually used the service, it would put Collier's out of business. I didn't doubt him.)

The most depressing family I pitched was at a home where a four-year-old boy came running to answer my knock . . . and kept running until he hit the screen door and fell backward. "My boy is retarded," the father said to me. "If you can make him understand one thing from those books, I'll buy them right now."

I might still be selling encyclopedias if it weren't for two things: my conscience, and the fact that of the thirteen sets of books I placed in the two weeks I worked, I only got paid for six. The other seven canceled on me. The first week, I didn't believe the customers had backed out of their orders; I thought Morty and company were stealing my hard-earned commissions. I had been expecting a check for $525 and got one for $175. Morty never told me about the cancellations, and when I questioned him he just said I'd better tone down my library service bit or people might start suing.

The second week my check was larger, but still half of what I had expected. I saw that there was money to be made, and I knew if I kept at it I'd keep making it . . . but it just didn't seem right. What we were doing was selling prestige and dreams: better education, advanced learning, unanswered questions answered. It wouldn't have been bad if we admitted to selling them, but working on the "something-for-nothing" premise seemed just another version of "never give a sucker an even break."

What I didn't realize then, but do now, is that those two summer weeks knocking on doors and entering into the lives of strangers taught me lessons I would use when I knocked at the doors of African sculptors, race-car drivers, movie stars, novelists, politicians, and Nobel laureates. What I learned is that to talk to people, especially people you are meeting for the first time, you need to be prepared and you need to have confidence. You need to know how to open a conversation. How to carry it forward. How to lead. How to ad lib. How to listen. How to be a chameleon and submerge your ego. How to make people comfortable. How to act and how to react to situations. How to be in control. How to keep things positive. How to stay on top of current events. How to ask offbeat questions. How to close.

"Giving away" encyclopedias also gave me stories to tell at dinner parties and during lulls in one-on-one conversations. And stories are what you want to get from interviews. Because when a person has a good story to tell that you can use, people will read it.

This book is filled with stories. Many of them are told to illustrate some point or another. But even if you aren't inspired to purchase a tape recorder and start asking questions of friends, family, neighbors, or movie stars, you may think differently the next time you pick up a newspaper, magazine, or watch *Nightline, Dateline, Primetime Thursday, Beyond the Glory, On the Record,* or *60 Minutes.* At the very least, if you're ever at a dinner party and some poet says all interviews seem the same to her, you can respond, "That's because you never sold encyclopedias when you were in college."

INTRODUCTION

ROBERT MITCHUM, ADOLPH EICHMANN, SEXUAL REPRESSION, AND FINDING ONE'S VOICE. DON'T ASK. OR DO.

> Making interviews is not easy at all. People think it's easy. It's stupid to think it's easy.

—ORIANA FALLACI

Robert Mitchum was, in the words of the late George C. Scott, the only real tough guy in the movie business. Coming from Scott, whose manic escapades were well documented, that remark gave me pause when Mitchum's publicist called me to meet with his client on the set of *That Championship Season* in 1982. I had already interviewed Marlon Brando, Al Pacino, Scott, and Henry Fonda for *Playboy* and Mitchum was next. He was the kind of guy other guys liked to read about—once arrested for vagrancy in Savannah, Georgia, only to escape from a chain gang after six days; arrested again for marijuana possession in 1948, serving sixty days, allowing pictures of him mopping the jailhouse floor to keep his mug in the public's eye. He had worked his way up from jobs as a ditch-digger, a coal miner, a deckhand, and a pro boxer to movie star, giving chilling performances as a psychopathic preacher in *The Night of the Hunter* and as a crazed ex-con in the original *Cape Fear.* By the time I went to meet him he had appeared in ninety-five films, playing everything, he once said, "except midgets and women." He was someone the magazine had been after for decades and they were very anxious to get his story, in his words, on tape and in print.

But Mitchum wasn't sure he wanted to cooperate. So my meeting with him was just to get acquainted. No tape recorder, no notes, no questions.

I hung around the set all morning as his publicist stood restlessly next to me. When they broke for lunch I followed him to the star's trailer. Mitchum wasn't very friendly. He sat eating a sandwich, downing a drink, and never offered me anything more than a nod.

"So," I began, "you obviously don't like doing interviews."

He chewed his sandwich.

"I can understand that. But we're glad you're finally coming around to doing this one."

He took a swallow of his drink.

"I was with Brando on his island," I said, figuring if any name was worth dropping it was that one. "It took him awhile to get comfortable, but once we started we went for a solid week."

Mitchum grunted.

"When you're ready to do this, I'll be so prepared you won't be bored. There's a hell of a lot to talk about."

He turned his head behind him. Was he even listening? In exasperation I just flat out asked him if he wanted to do this interview.

"Not really," he said.

I'd never run into a situation like this. I'd been with actors who were reluctant to talk and who avoided interviews as much as they could, folks like Brando, Pacino, Barbra Streisand, Warren Beatty. But once these stars agreed to it they at least made an effort. Mitchum was as incorrigible as he could be. So I decided to make him an offer:

"Mister Mitchum, I've never done this before but I can see we're not going to get very far this way. What if we tape an hour and see how it goes? If you don't feel comfortable after that I'll give you the tape and my word that I won't write anything about you."

"That's the problem," he said, "it's that first hour."

"Well, that's why I'm here," I said. "I'm only doing my job."

"That's what Eichmann said."

"Excuse me?"

"You're just doing your job—what Eichmann said."

"Are you comparing doing a *Playboy* interview with what Adolf Eichmann did to the Jews?" I asked.

"Same thing," he said.

Now it was my turn to chew this over. Only I had no sandwich to bite into, no drink to wash down the bitter taste in my mouth. "Your publicist knows where to reach me," I finally said as I stood up. And walked out.

My editors weren't too happy to hear this story and very disappointed that Robert Mitchum would not be appearing in their pages. I wasn't too happy, either—until this time I considered what I did for a living something special. I was talking to iconic, often reclusive celebrities and getting them to open up for a public eager to hear what they had to say. Mitchum didn't hide his contempt for journalists. I remember going to dinner with Al Pacino that night. He asked me how it went with Mitchum and I told him. Pacino was appalled and said he had no right to behave that way or say what he said. "You're the guy who did Brando, for God's sake, who does he think he is?"

I never got the chance to probe Robert Mitchum and find out who he was, and I always felt it was his loss. For the thing about in-depth interviews is that they are revealing, they often give an accurate word portrait of the subject, and they are lasting. They are as much a part of the personality profile of an actor as any of his or her movies. And they aren't easy to do.

A good interview appears seamless, as if the conversation actually happened the way you read it. But in truth, it often takes many sittings in various settings to get the words on tape, and then once those tapes are transcribed it takes days or weeks of intense concentration to index and edit them. Some of the more than four dozen *Playboy* interviews I've done have run well over five hundred pages of transcript. Reducing that by 90 percent is a monumental task—it involves reading every word spoken, highlighting the most interesting sections, making notes of what was said where, then reshaping it to make it appear that it all happened in one sitting. Putting together a good interview involves many skills: One must be able to converse like a talk-show host, think like a writer, understand subtext like a psychiatrist, have an ear like a musician, be able to select the best parts like a book editor, and know how to piece it together dramatically like a playwright.

I never really thought about the many facets of interviewing until I was asked to teach a course about it at UCLA a few years ago. The chairman of the English department discovered that I had graduated from UCLA in the late sixties with a degree in English and had somehow figured out a way to survive without becoming an English teacher. There were fourteen hundred English majors at the university, he told me, and he was concerned about their survival once they received their diplomas. Could I offer a seminar on the art of surviving in the real world?

At first I thought of doing a course called "The Freelancer's Guide to the Universe: How to Survive a B.A. in English." Then I went more literary: "From the *Tao Te Ching* to T. S. Eliot's *Four Quartets*." Then I thought about taking students on the road with Jack Kerouac, Augie March, Ken Kesey and the Merry Pranksters, Tom Wolfe, and William Vollmann. I mapped out six completely different courses, all journeys toward the path of surviving in a world that gets more complex and terrifying yearly. And then I thought about putting together a course where I might actually know what I was talking about. How did interviewing relate to life skills? That's when I came up with the talking, listening, thinking, analyzing, selecting, and editing segments that all good interviewers incorporate, whether they realize it or not.

But was I ready to offer such a course? Did I really want to pass on all that I had learned over three decades so that these young graduates could enter the marketplace and, if they took my advice, wind up replacing me? Because when you're first starting out, I would tell them, if you show enough confidence in yourself that you'd be willing to work for very low wages, or even for nothing, just to prove what you can do, you might pick up some assignments. If it isn't going to cost an editor to see what you're capable of doing, then you have a shot at impressing him or her.

Well, I figured, what the hell, I haven't discovered the fountain of youth yet. The gray in my beard doesn't excite editors half my age to assign me interviews with Eminem or Britney Spears or the Olsen twins. Twenty years ago I was asked by a publisher if I wanted to write a book about interviewing and I wasn't ready. Now I am.

I didn't know I was until I started teaching. I keep the seminar limited to sixteen students each quarter, all of whom have to write an essay on why they want to be in such a class. The answers are varied enough to make it interesting. Though I bring in people for them to interview—writers, actors, directors, producers, athletes, TV personalities, publicists, agents, publishers—the focus is not on becoming a journalist but rather on developing skills that can help them in any endeavor whatsoever. I wind up not just with English and writing majors but students who have ambitions to continue their education in medicine, business, film, history, and law; who will go on to work in rehab programs, or join Americorps or the Peace Corps.

It is inspiring. Challenging. Fun. We read interviews in magazines and books, we watch and analyze TV interviews, we study good writers who write insightful prose. Because every interview needs setting up, it's important to know how to write descriptively. Questions have to be concise, not rambling. Answers need to be edited to cut out the boring parts. Though the majority of interviews I do are with celebrities, no one should be expected to have such a narrow focus, because there are only so many celebrities to go around. There are far more noncelebrities to interview and write about. So while my examples are mostly with recognizable names, what we learn applies to anyone and everyone out there. Because the process is the same, whether you're preparing to interview Tom Cruise or Tim Pruise, if you haven't done the legwork, you aren't going to get much out of the person. Interviewing is really an equal opportunity job. What you put into it is in direct proportion to what you will get out of it.

And what I discovered my students got out of it made me realize that there really are life skills that can be learned. Among the assignments I give them—interview each other, interview two guests, interview someone who is doing what they would like to do upon graduation—the outside interview is the most challenging and the most rewarding. If a student hopes to go to law school, I suggest that she interview the dean of one of the law schools she would like to attend. If someone wants to be a director, there are plenty of film directors in L.A. to talk to. Naturally, interviewing someone in a position to hire or remember you can be nerve racking if you aren't prepared. But that's my job, to help prepare them. And more often than not the results are positive. I know this because I get to read their papers, and then when the class is over I hear from many of them. I didn't intend on quoting former students when I started this book; it feels a bit too much like providing testimonials for a product I'm selling. So my apologies in advance. But my intention is really to emphasize the broad range of applications in which interviewing can be used. The bulk of this book will be illustrating how to talk to people in the news, but the majority of readers who might pick up this book will not be interviewing celebrities. My hope is that if you follow the guidelines and read between the celebrity lines you will get out of this what you need to be able to hold your own in conversation with anyone. At least, that's what some of my students have been telling me. Here's what I mean:

"Your class wasn't about meeting celebrities," one student e-mailed me. "It was about learning how to communicate. It was about confronting new comfort levels. It was about self-confidence."

"I know I have a long way to go," another wrote, "but this class has pointed out my deficiencies as well as helped provide solutions to the problems I struggle with and questions I have. For me, the course was largely about humanity, and in the process of studying individual perspectives I learned a lot about myself."

One student went for a job interview at an advertising firm in Phoenix, Arizona. She wasn't there to interview the media director, but to be interviewed by him. But she applied the techniques she learned and wrote to tell me: "I researched the company and put together all these questions about the company, the advertising business, the man's own success, my future, networking practices, etc. I was essentially interviewing *him* because I was the one who wanted something out of it. So I took it like a magazine interview! We ended up talking for over an hour. At the end he said I was one of the most prepared interviewees he had come across. He was really impressed because I asked questions about his answers and challenged him to really think about what he was saying. There was no lapse in conversation. I always had a question on the backburner. He also said I was one of the least nervous people he had interviewed.

"When I signed up for your class I really wanted to learn some things that would help me in my pursuit of a career in advertising and PR, and it has tremendously. I know I will never be a journalist or a writer; I am absolutely horrible at the editing process. But your class gave me the skills necessary to handle any type of interview. Even if I don't get the right contact this time, I have the confidence to keep trying."

Another student described her current job: "I'm working right now as a Case Manager at a Homeless Youth Drop-In

Center. It's a day community center where the homeless can come in to access services. I'm actually doing case management at two different ones, full-time at one and part-time at another. At my part-time job, I coordinate the Needle Exchange program we have there. The agency is an HIV Community Center, so we do harm reduction. One of our specializations in prevention programs is offering clean syringes to IV/IM users. It's all been an interesting ride for me. I've gotten to know a lot of junkies and tweakers, and I'm learning so much about drug use. Remember how I was so curious to ask Anthony Kiedis all those questions about his former addiction when he came to the class? Well, the curiosity never burned out. This part of my job keeps things exciting and novel for me, but it's also depressing in a way. Sometimes I feel like I'm a journalist b/c of all the insane people I meet at work. Since they're all still young (under twenty-five), they're not fully crazy yet, but I see a lot of them in the beginning stages of schizophrenia. And case management is a little like interviewing. When I conduct a psychosocial assessment on a client, I have to ask a lot of personal questions about their background and lifestyle. And I have to be inconspicuous, yet effective about the assessment so that they don't get paranoid that I'm documenting their lives. Documentation is basically what I'm doing. I use a lot of the interviewing skills that I learned from your class in this job. The lead-in and follow-up questions are significant parts of my case management."

And then there was this, from a shy young woman whose work was always meticulous and sound: "There's something about the interview process that doesn't make you feel so small or alone anymore. At the risk of sounding like Mrs. Dalloway, to me, it's a way that lets you feel connected to someone who may have seemed unapproachable or incomprehensible. In the process of teaching us how to articulate someone else's voice, you've helped me to develop my own."

Perhaps this is the answer to the question, why write this book? I don't think most people who consider the craft of interviewing believe it will lead to self-discovery, but when you start doing this, that's exactly what can happen. Because you begin to learn about yourself: about your abilities and your limitations. For me, it's been a journey into the unknown, because no matter how many people I interview, I never know what to expect.

When I first met Jean-Claude Van Damme at his home in the San Fernando Valley in the summer of 1994, the temperature was over a hundred degrees and he was floating on a rubber raft in his swimming pool. "Take off your shirt, come on in," he said. I wasn't prepared to begin our interview floating in his pool but I was game, and rested my tape recorder carefully on my chest as we got to feel each other out. My willingness to do that made him like me, and he invited me to continue our talks in Pittsburgh, where he was going to make his next movie. There we talked after he was finished shooting, usually beginning at 10 P.M., smoking expensive cigars and drinking premium wines in his hotel room until two or three in the morning.

To interview opera star Luciano Pavarotti I went to New York, Chicago, and San Francisco, where he performed at the opera houses and spoke with me late at night, after the operas. With Dolly Parton, I traveled through West Virginia on her private bus, talking as we rode and then in motel rooms after her performances. I've played paddle tennis with Al Pacino, sailed and played chess with Marlon Brando on his island in Tahiti, played basketball with Elliott Gould, boxed with Lucia Rijker, been lassoed by Kiefer Sutherland, kissed by Halle Berry, fed sushi by Nicole Kidman, eaten turkey sausages with Robert Evans and a cheap sandwich with Bruce Willis. I've traveled twelve hours in a car with Bob Knight a month after he was fired from Indiana University, spent a few days with newly elected governor Jesse Ventura as he adjusted to his office, and hung out with Anthony Kiedis while he and the other members of the Red Hot Chili Peppers were putting together their record *By the Way*.

Because Christian Slater lived near me in the Hollywood Hills, I was able to walk to his house and see his private world as we spoke inside his inner sanctum, where models of *Star Trek* spacecraft and figurines filled shelves and hung from the ceiling. And when stars don't want their homes written about or they want to get out of the hotels they may be staying at, they often come to my house to be interviewed. Such has been the case with Kidman, Berry, Sutherland, Marlon Brando, Jon Voight, Angelina Jolie, Kim Basinger, Cameron Diaz, Alec Baldwin, Kurt Russell, Sharon Stone, Bridget Fonda, Annette Bening, Patty Hearst, and Harrison Ford. My kids have gotten used to seeing such people sitting in our living room or shooting hoops in our backyard. It's all part of the job—one must be prepared to be a host, to share food, to entertain with stories, to basically do anything and everything to make the subject feel comfortable, to put them at ease, so that when you turn on that tape recorder and begin asking questions they feel like they're talking to a friend. It's not always easy to be such a chameleon, but that is what a good interviewer must be.

Preparing for an interview varies, depending on whom one is preparing for. Stars like Anthony Hopkins, Harvey Keitel, Goldie Hawn, and Clint Eastwood have been around a lot longer than Kate Hudson, Hugh Jackman, Heath Ledger, Christina Ricci, or James Franco, and there is obviously a greater body of work to see, more profiles to read in books and magazines, more people to talk with who have worked with them. The younger stars are still experiencing the first bloom of fame—they often are riding a wave that hasn't yet come to shore, they feel invincible, and they have a great deal of optimism. Older stars who have been around a lot longer have usually experienced the ups and downs of stardom, they've reached the heights of fame, they've fallen from those heights, they've carried pictures, and they've also begun taking cameo roles if something strikes their fancy. They are less optimistic, more realistic about the fickleness of celebrity, and have a certain refreshing cynicism that comes from experience. Some of these younger stars are making far more money than De Niro or Hopkins did when they were starting out and that affects their behavior. It can lead to insecurities if you feel you're not worth the millions being offered, or it can separate you from your youth. Older stars are often more savvy as to how the game works. But all of them, young and old, are living unreal lives: they're catered to, looked after, pampered. It takes a lot of character for them to see through that fantasy. It's that kind of character one should look for when reading interviews with them.

I find it necessary to see and read everything about the people I'm preparing to interview, so that when we finally meet I probably know more about them than they remember themselves. I feel confident when I'm prepared, and that confidence is critical, for if they sense I'm well prepared, they also know that I've taken them seriously, and if my questions can be challenging and interesting for them, then they can start to enjoy the process.

Every interviewer is different when it comes to asking questions. Some just prepare note cards with topics to discuss. I prefer to write my questions, sometimes as many as five hundred. That doesn't mean I will ask them all, but I know that there are areas I want to cover, and if our conversation doesn't flow, then I have these written questions to fall back on. If, however, some question stirs a person's memory and we go off on a tangent, I like to go with that, because that's often where the best material comes from—the unexpected.

Sometimes you find yourself in a position of asking a question that your subject has obviously heard many times before. If you have the right tone and if your face reflects true interest, it's still possible to get a serious response. For example, before his marriage to Annette Bening, I was with Warren Beatty when he was living in the penthouse apartment at the Beverly Wilshire Hotel. He had three different phone lines and all of them kept ringing, different women wanting to know what he was doing in an hour. He somehow managed to juggle all of these women's desires and still talk to me. (Dustin Hoffman once noted that he was with Beatty in the hotel's lobby discussing politics when a beautiful woman walked by. Hoffman barely noticed her, but Beatty, who didn't know her, shot his arm out and caught the woman mid-arm. He didn't say a word to her, just continued talking to Hoffman, who had completely lost his concentration. Beatty put up his other hand, indicating to the woman that he would be with her shortly, and finished his conversation with Hoffman.) As I sat with Beatty and saw how he kept so much action afloat I got a firsthand glimpse into his fabled lifestyle. I had read about him, but now I was witnessing it. In the middle of one of our interrupted conversations I couldn't help myself, I just looked at him and asked, "What's it like being Warren Beatty?" He looked back at me and for a moment was about to give some flip answer, but he saw that I was serious. What was it like? "I've been asked that by a hundred people," he said, "but I have a feeling you really want to know." He was right. I really did. And he told me.

When I was with Barbra Streisand, I wound up seeing her over a period of nine months—by far the longest time I've ever spent doing one magazine interview. I made the mistake of telling her that I wouldn't turn in my copy until we both agreed we were finished talking. Now, had I said that to almost anyone else, I would have been finished in one or two sessions. But Streisand is a perfectionist. Whenever I asked her a question that had even the nuance of being critical, she would take the question apart to see if it was fair to have asked it.

For instance, she carefully dissected the words *control* and *power* each time I used them. She didn't like the word power because it reminded her of Hitler, and she felt *control* had "negative implications." If I asked her why she insisted on having control over everything she was involved in, she would answer, "First, let's clarify the word *insist,*" which she didn't like because she felt that to insist is not a part of the creative process. As for *control,* she thought it was too broad a term and narrowed it to "artistic responsibility," elaborating: "If you mean that I am completely dedicated and care deeply about carrying out a total vision of a project—yes, that's true." If I asked her about her ego, she would challenge that with the question "What is conceit and what is ego? And why are they being put down?" Then she'd go on to examine it in detail.

Interviewing someone like Streisand can be both an exhilarating and a draining experience. The interviewer must always be mentally alert, ready to challenge a thought and be challenged in return. It's really a very subtle (and sometimes not so subtle) battle going on between subject and interrogator, and the best interviews give you a sense not only who the subject is, but also who that anonymous person on the other side of the tape recorder is as well.

CELEBRITY INTERVIEWING is a special type of interviewing. You have to jump through far more hoops to get to the celebrity; you have to deal with agents, publicists, personal assistants. And none of that is fun. Everyone who works for a celebrity believes their job is crucial, and they demand proper respect. You may think you're dealing with a PR flack, but that publicist sees herself as the last barrier between her client and the hungry, career-threatening masses. There are, of course, other types of interviews—such as research to write a profile or general article, for background sources, oral histories, material for ghostwriters, on stage in front of an audience, radio, television, documentaries, biographies—but the one thing all interviews have in common is that the person asking the questions should be prepared. And should be sensitive toward the subject, famous or not, and aware of how delicate asking probing questions can be.

I once took a short trip with a friend whom I always suspected had a repressed secret life, so he surprised me when he challenged me to interview him on the drive from L.A. to La Jolla. "Why would you want me to do that?" I asked.

"Because you're the pro," he said, "you talk to all the stars. Let's see what you can do with me."

"Nah," I declined, "it wouldn't be fair. You're a novice, you wouldn't be able to handle it."

"Try me."

"Forget it, you'd be crying after three questions."

"Ask me three questions then."

"Please, let's not go there. It's a beautiful day, let's just enjoy the ride."

"C'mon, do it. I'll bet you lunch you can't make me cry."

"Because you'll avoid answering."

"No, I'll answer any question you ask me honestly."

"You better be careful what you ask for, you may regret it."

"You ask, I'll answer, and then you'll take me to lunch."

"Have you ever wanted to dress in women's clothing?" I asked him.

"What kind of question is that?" he snapped.

"See, forget it, it's stupid. Interviewing's not a game where you make the rules."

"OK . . . OK," he said, then paused. "Yes, I have. I've even done it." And then he proceeded to tell me all the times he snuck into his mother's closet when he was a boy, and how he tried putting on makeup as well. The makeup was a bonus answer—it was going to be my second question. But he started to unravel with just this one question—which was way more than I anticipated. I didn't want to hear all the things he started to tell me. When he finished he was sweating. "OK, ask me another," he said, his voice an octave higher, his teeth clenched.

"Nah, forget it," I said. "I'll take you to lunch."

"Ask me!"

I took a deep breath. Did I really want to go there with him? Did I want to expose him to himself? This was beginning to border on the sadistic and I didn't want to go any further, but he kept insisting. I began to think that he had a subconscious need to unburden himself, and somehow I was the unlucky player to get this out in the open.

"C'mon, ask!" he demanded.

So I did. "Have you ever had any kind of anal sex?"

"You bastard!" he said, struggling with whether to answer or throw me out of the car. But he had promised to be honest and he started in, again, with stories I don't need to relate here. Other than to note that his tears started flowing shortly after the torrent of pent-up emotions were unloaded in that car. I knew it was a mistake to play this game with him. I wasn't really interviewing him; it was more like Truth or Dare, long before Madonna popularized it. And it ended a friendship.

There was, admittedly, a cruelty to the questions—and that isn't what one does in an interview. One must spend hours talking to someone before broaching the subject of cross-dressing and sexual repression. To throw it out there so completely out of any context had shock value. He wasn't expecting it, and he felt compelled to tell the truth, even though the truth would separate us forever. Because we weren't just casual acquaintances meeting for the first time with a tape recorder between us—we were actually on our way to witness the marriage of a mutual friend.

Why tell the story then? Because it illustrates what an interview is not, and that is, it is not just a series of tough, pointblank questions. An interview is more like a massage: You cover the entire body, you find knots and work those out. It's like a dance, where you lead and your subject hopefully follows (and, at times, the subject leads, and you follow until you can regain control).

So, be careful what you ask people. You may be surprised by their answers.

1. KINDS OF INTERVIEWS

PRINT. BOOKS. RADIO. DOCUMENTARIES.
TELEVISION.

> A good interview should have the character of a good novel.

—HARRISON SALISBURY

It's hard to imagine how a non-fiction book, newspaper, magazine, or radio or television talk show or news show could exist without interviews. One person asking another a question in search of an answer, looking for information, or an anecdote, or some shared gossip. An interview is the interaction between people. Most are one-on-one, but there are roundtable interviews and group interviews. I once interviewed a high school marching band inside their school gym—I'd ask a question and point to someone, or someone would raise a hand to respond. Another time I interviewed two dozen performance artists in my living room, feeling very much the performer as I tried to ask provocative questions to already provocative artists.

The work of interviewers is everywhere.

Pumla Gobodo-Madikizela, a clinical psychologist, wrote a book called *A Human Being Died That Night: A South African Story of Forgiveness.* She went to Pretoria Prison to interview Eugene de Kock in 1997 for his role in the killing of three black policemen who had died when a bomb exploded in their car. De Kock was a reviled man: He had led a death squad and had tortured black South Africans. She spent six months interviewing de Kock, and then she interviewed the family of victims to prepare them for testifying at the Truth and Reconciliation trials. Her task could not have been an easy one.

Barry Mile's biography of Allen Ginsberg, Gerald Clarke's of Truman Capote, and Ted Morgan's of William S. Burroughs could not have existed without the interviews these writers did as part of their research. Each had access to his subject, as well as to the people who knew their subject. On the other hand, Richard Ellman never interviewed Oscar Wilde or James Joyce, A. Scott Berg never personally spoke with Max Perkins, Samuel Goldwyn, or Charles Lindbergh, Norman Mailer never talked to Gary Gilmore, David King Dunaway didn't know Aldous Huxley, Albrecht Folsing didn't interview Albert Einstein, Jeffrey Meyers didn't live at the time of Joseph Conrad, nor Neil Baldwin when he wrote about Thomas Edison. And yet these writers wrote biographies of these subjects, using whatever interviews and articles that existed about them, and talking to people who could enhance their portraits of them.

One could list practically every biography ever written and make the same point: that even if the subject lived a thousand years ago, there is only so much research one can do before feeling the need to talk to someone about that subject—a scholar, a friend, an enemy, anyone who has passion about or insight into the person one is trying to uncover. And that need to talk is a need to interview. Can you imagine a Studs Terkel book that didn't involve his asking questions and someone providing answers? To get the story right, one must know what to ask, how to ask, and how to listen to the answers. Without the inclusion of well-done interviews, you'd still have fiction, sitcoms, dramas, and music, but when it comes to nonfiction, so-called reality TV, and National Public Radio there would be very little to read, watch, or listen to.

PRINT

The most in-depth interviews usually appear in print: in newspapers, magazines, books, or online. Makes sense: Print allows more space than radio or television. You can condense most TV interviews into a few paragraphs of print. As you will see in other chapters of this book, there is more to a printed interview than transcribing what has been said and handing it to your editor. Just as most writing involves rewriting, *all* interviews demand editing. Words, sentences, and paragraphs will have to be moved around, cleaned up, reduced, or deleted. And almost all interviews done these days in any medium are recorded for the simple reason that the technology exists and legal departments demand accuracy.

When Norman Mailer was asked how he felt about being interviewed, he said he always sat down with a general sense of woe, because "the interviewer serves up one percent of himself in the questions and the man who answers has to give back ninety-nine percent. I feel exploited the moment I step into an interview. Of course, once in a while there is such a thing as a good interview; but even then, the tape recorder eats up half the mood. It isn't the interview I really dislike so much as the tape recorder."

Truman Capote hated tape recorders and told me he never worked with one (though I suspect his aversion might have had something to do with a general antipathy to electronics, a fear of pressing the wrong button—Play instead of Record). When he was conducting his interviews for *In Cold Blood,* or when he interviewed Marlon Brando in Japan during the making of *Sayonara,* he relied on his memory. He said he would go back to his room and write down everything that his subjects said, filling filing cabinets with his notes and research. He was meticulous, he was slow (it took him a year to write the Brando profile), but he had a good ear, and few complained that he misquoted them.

Lillian Ross prefers to "listen carefully and take notes." Nicholas Pileggi and Thomas Morgan also don't like tape recorders.

For Pileggi, who wrote the book *Wise Guy: Life in a Mafia Family* (which was the basis for Martin Scorsese's *GoodFellas*) and worked for *Esquire* and *New York,* "the problem with a tape recorder is that it exhausts you. It's stronger than you are. It throws all that stuff back at you in exactly the same way. And if you try to fast-forward it, you feel you've missed something. Before you know it, you're going bananas and you're spending all your time with the tape recorder."

Morgan, who has published nonfiction and fiction, and wrote for *Harper's, Look, Esquire,* and *Holiday,* feels it's inhibiting. "The interviewee is inhibited by the fact that he's on record in a way that he doesn't feel when you're sitting there scribbling away. Part of that, of course, is understandable because he can always say, 'You got it down wrong.'"

Exactly. I once did a story about mail-order entrepreneurs and spoke to the owner of a business who proudly showed me a book he published for 60 cents and sold for $9. When the article came out, he called my editor and denied he had said the things I had him saying. I was in Florida on another assignment when my editor called to warn me: "He's threatening to sue us." "Let him," I said, "it's all on tape." The businessman must have had a lapse of memory and forgot that I was recording our conversation, because once he was reminded he withdrew his complaints.

A similar thing happened some years later when I interviewed Vincent Bugliosi for *Playboy.* This was after O. J. Simpson had apparently gotten away with murder (or so many people, including Bugliosi, thought) and the former L.A. prosecutor had a lot to say about that and other matters. But while the interview was still in galleys Bugliosi managed to obtain a copy and let the powers that be at the magazine know that he didn't say any of the things I had him saying. He was so upset that he crossed out most of the interview and rewrote his answers. My editor called to ask me if everything I had Bugliosi saying was on tape. I said it was. He then told me what Bugliosi had done and I said that if Bugliosi was allowed to change our interview then I wanted my name removed (this had already happened once before, I later found out, when Bugliosi was interviewed by David Sheff and Sheff had his name removed from the final piece). In the end, *Playboy* published the interview as I had given it to them. I never heard from Bugliosi, and if I was ever asked to interview him again, I would politely decline.

The first celebrity I ever interviewed, Mae West, wouldn't let me use a tape recorder. When I took it out, I might just as well have unzipped my fly—the look of shock on her face was that succinct. "Oh no, oh no, you can't use that, put it away."

"But this is an interview," I stammered. My first such interview for *Newsday*'s Sunday magazine. "Don't you want me to be accurate?"

"I once allowed one of those to be used," she told me in that famous nasal tone, "and the reporter made a record out of it. I won't let that happen again."

"Can I sign something that says I won't turn our conversation into a record?" I asked. She had caught me completely off guard with her insistence that there be no recording of our interview.

"Just put it away," she said, "and ask me your questions."

Luckily I had taken a pad with me, because I filled it up that day. I worked through the night to try and get her voice right when I wrote the story.

Ray Stark, who produced four of John Huston's movies, also had an aversion to having his voice captured on tape. When I went to talk to him about *The Night of the Iguana, Reflections in a Golden Eye, Fat City,* and *Annie* for my book *The Hustons,* he looked at my tape recorder as if it was rotted meat. "I can use a pad," I told him, "but I don't understand why you wouldn't want to insure being quoted accurately."

"I just don't like those things," he said. But after he warmed up to talking he allowed me to turn it on.

Ava Gardner, who was in *The Night of the Iguana,* also hated tape recorders. When I went to see her in London she told me she couldn't talk with a tape recorder on the coffee table between us. It made her too self-conscious. So I put the machine under the table, out of her sight, and that seemed to work.

Three people I've interviewed pulled out tape recorders of their own: Jerry Lewis, George C. Scott, and Elizabeth Hurley. They didn't trust journalists and felt they were misquoted in the past. "I do this because I've been fucked," Lewis told me. "And I don't like getting fucked by reporters." Hurley said after being involved in a lawsuit against a tabloid she was under instruction from her lawyer to record everything she said to the media. Scott never gave a reason for his taping; he just turned his machine on, then drank his Bloody Marys and forgot all about it. He never turned the tape over or bothered changing tapes during the many hours we spent on two coasts talking.

THOUGH I RESPECT the work of Capote, Pileggi, and Morgan, I don't agree with them about tape recorders. I also don't think a good journalist should solely rely on them. When I was writing articles for *Newsday*'s Sunday magazine in the early seventies, I interviewed a man named Slim Hennicke for a piece about the history of aviation on Long Island. Hennicke was a barnstorming pilot at the turn of the twentieth century, and he had wonderful tales of parachuting from biplanes holding on to a billowing piece of canvas and then passing a hat around to the spectators after he had safely landed. His basement was crammed with aviation memorabilia, and we spoke for a few hours among his busts of Lindbergh and Clarence Chamberlin, among the wooden propellers and leather helmets and rusted engines that flew those historic planes. When we broke for lunch I went across the street to a diner and checked my equipment. I discovered that my tape recorder had not recorded a single word Hennicke had spoken. What I learned was that before a battery went completely dead it could still generate enough power to turn a tape, but not enough to record anything. I didn't think I could ever replicate what Hennicke had told me from memory, so when I returned I just started asking him questions similar to the ones he had already answered. Fortunately, Hennicke was an old man who enjoyed his stories and didn't mind repeating them.

After that experience I made sure I used two tape recorders on every interview and that I put in new batteries each time.

Recording conversations can provide a false sense of security if the tape recorder malfunctions, if the tape itself gets stuck, if the batteries die—but assuming it works, then it allows you to concentrate more on what is being said, and to respond, without having to look up from your notebook as you try to write down everything that is being said. Still, it's a good idea to jot down phrases as you listen, especially if the person you're talking with likes to jump from subject to subject. That way you can look down at your notes and refer back to something you heard but might want to delve deeper into.

My advice when it comes to tape recorders is to use two and to try to get the older metal ones instead of the newer plastic ones. I've found that the plastic ones record the humming of the machine itself, and the metal ones sound clearer. I also prefer the microcassette recorders to the regular cassettes because they are less obtrusive, take up less space when you're doing long interviews and are using four or five tapes (doubled if you're using two machines), and the better machines like the Olympus 100 or 200 record just as well as the larger ones. I also like to use ninety-minute tapes on the slower speed, which allows me to record three hours on one tape. (I've yet to find a digital tape recorder that can distinguish and translate two voices into text when downloaded into a computer, but when that time comes it will eliminate transcribing and save one a lot of time and money!)

One last tip: Turn on the tape recorder as soon as you can. This is contrary to what *New Yorker* writer Ken Auletta believes.

He prefers not to open his notepad or turn on a tape recorder right away; instead, he likes to "just talk to people a little bit. Create a sense that you're not going to exploit them." I do understand what Auletta means. But my experiences have taught me that if I don't get the tape recorder on the table right away, I've lost immediate control of the interview, and it can take days before I get it back.

When I went to Marlon Brando's island, every time I tried to pull out the tape recorder he said, "Later." After three days of walking and talking I was getting frustrated because he wasn't allowing me to record anything. So finally I just took it out and turned it on as we sat propped against his thatched hut looking out at the sea. That's when he looked at me and observed that sometimes the best conversations happen in silence. And for the next thirty minutes, that's what I recorded!

When I first went to New York to interview Al Pacino, I took out my tape recorders right after I walked through his apartment door. "Why don't we wait awhile with that?" he said. Rather than put them away, I said, "Why don't I just put them on and we try to forget about them?" He shrugged. "OK, I guess you know what you're doing."

It may seem like a technical matter whether to record a conversation or take notes instead, and, if recording, knowing when to turn it on, but it's one of those subtle things that sets the tone for all that follows. If you just take the recorder out, turn it on, and then start talking, you've established that you know what you're doing without asking for permission and allowing your subject a choice. The real trick is to make the person forget all about the tape recorder, which may be easier than making him forget that you're taking notes. Either way, it's all about taking control. If you give in at the beginning, it's going to be a long way back to equal.

BOOKS

You'd think that interviews would be mostly tied to nonfiction, but good fiction writers also often need to understand what their characters are thinking, how their jobs work, and motivations. Novelists who write about crime, like Elmore Leonard or James Ellroy, do the legwork or have researchers who talk to criminals, lawyers, judges, and jailers; those who write about social issues, like John Updike or Joyce Carol Oates, must also listen carefully to people who tell stories that eventually wind up in their fiction. For historical writers, like Gore Vidal or Howard Fast, what our forefathers said becomes fodder for their fiction.

As for nonfiction writers, if you are lucky enough to write someone's biography, you must have the material. That involves interviewing that person—a process that can take months, and sometimes years. One prepares for this the way one does for an extensive magazine interview: by doing research. Since the subject is cooperating, you should be able to get additional help from the people he or she has dealt with. When John Huston agreed to my doing a book about his family, the first thing I asked for was his address books; the second, a letter from him saying that the people in those books should cooperate with me.

He had different address books for different countries, and along with that letter, they proved invaluable. Here's the letter Huston provided.

Dear Larry:

From what you have been telling me, it is clear you are proceeding with full intent to root out the corners of my life. I understand that your goal is a detailed portrait of my family, commencing with my father and ending with a look at the most recent generations of Hustons. For the in-betweens you have my full support to contact those of my friends and associates whom you feel

*will be useful to your task. I trust they will offer a true memory and
fresh perspective to the telling of my past years.*

Best of luck with your work.

Sincerely,
John Huston

Without that letter, reclusive and media-shy people like Ava
Gardner, Paul Newman, Olivia de Havilland, Roman Polanski,
First Lady Nancy Reagan, and probably dozens of others
would never have consented to see me. And the fact that Huston wrote that they should talk honestly ("offer a true memory
and fresh perspective") opened up the floodgates for some of
them. I don't know how many times I heard: "I can't believe
John wants us to tell the *truth!* I never thought I would tell
these stories!"

When Montel Williams asked me in the summer of 2003 to
work with him on a book about his life after being diagnosed
with MS in 1999, I felt the subject was important, but I had no
idea the hell Williams had gone through until we started talking.
When he mentioned that he had attempted suicide, I knew that
there was going to be some high drama in this book, but I had
to draw it out of him. It was one thing for him to say he was suicidal, another for him to recall all the details, and still another to
convince him to reveal what his memory could unlock. Each
day that we talked brought new questions that I would come up
with, and over the next few weeks we'd go deeper and deeper
until we both felt drained by the experience. But that was only
the beginning for me: I had to take all that talk and divide it into
chapters and find his voice, not mine, in the narrative that
became *Climbing Higher.*

Then there are those subjects who want a book but aren't
ready to reveal themselves. This is a problem. I've been involved
with four major stars and two behind-the-scenes talents who
hired me to help them write their books, and all six didn't make

it past the proposal. One was afraid of opening up the can of worms that led to his being incarcerated. Another spoke freely of his early problems with his mother and with some revealing anecdotes of sexual perversity, but when he read what he had said he backed away from it. Another, a famous singer, didn't want to talk about his failed marriage or his dope smoking or his early connection with the mob, and as we tried to talk around these subjects he realized that he really shouldn't be trying to write a book that left out as much as it was going to include. One company man was passed over for the presidency of his company and he was far more bitter about it than he thought—which he discovered when he read what he had to say and then decided to shut down. Another Hollywood figure wanted to write a book but didn't want to violate any confidences he had with former clients. Since he managed some of the most recognizable names in show business, he didn't have much of a story to tell if he left them out of it. It was like Elliott Gould once telling me he wanted to write a book, but he wanted to leave his first wife, Barbra Streisand, out of it. I told him he couldn't do that; it would be like Hugh Hefner writing his memoirs but leaving out the sex.

But when the subject is ready and you happen to be the one chosen to work with him or her, it can be a worthwhile, challenging endeavor. There are writers who have made good livings helping people like James Earl Jones, Chris Rock, Jackie Chan, Sophia Loren, Tim Allen, Richard Pryor, Ava Gardner, Henry Fonda, and Marlon Brando write their autobiographies. They may rarely reach the realm of literature, but match a good story with a good storyteller and hope that your agent was sharp enough to include you in a percentage of the royalties.

RADIO

In March 2003, I was invited to conduct a "master class" in interviewing and also to appear on a panel about Truman Capote, along with George Plimpton and Dick Cavett at the seventeenth annual Tennessee Williams Festival in New Orleans. After the class, Fred Kasten, the program director of WWNO, the National Public Radio affiliate, interviewed me. He set up his DAT recorder in an upstairs library and began by asking me when I started writing. I told him about the time when I was ten years old and faked being a reporter on my elementary school paper so that I could find out about the history of the oldest house in the area where we lived in Jericho, on Long Island. Then I spoke about all the rejected poetry I had submitted to national magazines when I was thirteen, and winning a *Newsday* American history essay contest when I was fifteen. As I talked I wondered why he was letting me go on—I knew this wasn't the material he was after. But Kasten, who has been in radio for twenty years, was patient. He let me talk, and afterward I asked him about his technique.

He said that he often began his interviews chronologically, even though he knew that the early years hardly got used, because he was allowing his subject's voice to warm up. "With radio, you get to present the voices of these people, which tell as much about them as the words that they use," he said. "You try to get people to get inside their own heads. People who have been interviewed a lot are pretty well rehearsed with their early years. But I ask about that anyway just to relax them and get them talking. I look to hear their true voice and not their canned speech."

I wondered how long he allowed someone to talk before cutting in with a question, or with some vocal attempt to change the subject. He told me that Ira Glass gave him advice about that which he's used ever since. "Ira Glass did a lot of editing in the newsroom for NPR before he started doing *This American Life,* and his rule is forty-five seconds. You can have a single voice speak for forty-five seconds, then you have to interrupt it with something, to let that idea soak in and move to the next one. I applied that technique and my work improved."

David Isay, whose work at NPR has garnered him Polk and Peabody Awards, doesn't hold to that forty-five-second rule. "I don't agree with Ira," Isay said when I called to talk to him about his methods, "but that's his style. I've had people talk for seven or eight minutes, as long as it's interesting. But I believe in radio that less is more. In a print story you can introduce something complicated, you can digress and come back; but with radio, we're on a clock. If you confuse someone for an instant, you've lost them. Every second has to be paced right and perfect. On public radio we do eight-, twelve-, or twenty-two-minute pieces. Twenty-two minutes is the longest. I imagine when I'm doing a radio story that I'm lifting up the listener from behind and carrying him through the twenty-two minutes or however long it is and then dropping him down without him even knowing that he was carried. If there's any error or if something's confusing, it won't happen. A radio story is a very linear thing; you can't be too complicated. You've got to lose yourself in it. I can tell pretty fast whether someone is going to be good or not. If they're not, it's like landing a plane—I'm trying to land that plane as quickly as I can and get out of there."

Isay is known for his extended pieces on prisons and ghettos, his American Folklife Radio Project, and his ten-part series on old Yiddish radio broadcasts. "The research that I do is exhaustive. I've read, talked to, and have learned everything that is humanly possible to know about a specific subject before I go in and start reporting it. I go completely over the top. I always write a page worth of questions. Errol Morris, who did the documentary *The Thin Blue Line,* breaks people down. He does twenty-four-hour interviews with people. For me, what makes a piece is a combination of what's being said, how it's being said, the energy—all these factors that go into making a tape electric. Which would be the equivalent in print of a good quote. There's a very fast decline after an hour and fifteen minutes of interviewing, so I try to get in everything I can in that period.

"Also, the people I interview usually haven't been interviewed before; they're not really hiding anything. I'm not dealing with famous people. The question I'm always asking is, how does it make you feel?

"I won't interview somebody if I don't think it's a positive thing for them. I refuse to let anybody discuss what we're going to talk about before turning on the tape recorder. My mantra is full disclosure and complete honesty with subjects at all times."

As with most good interviewers, Isay has developed his ear to pick up on those golden quotes that you can almost see running as headlines in print or as something that will stick in one's mind when heard over the radio. "I can see the sparks coming out of people's mouths. It's an electric thing," he says. "What makes a radio interview stand out is emotional content. Capturing a real, authentic moment—it could be tears, it could be funny, just feelings that are evoked. Radio is a medium for telling emotional stories.

"My work is my life. It's twenty-four hours a day. Much of my self-revelation happens in my work. When I'm in an interview, listening is a pretty intense thing, especially when you're talking to someone who hasn't been interviewed or hasn't been able to tell their story before. It's a pretty profound bond that forms. I'm like a laser beam; I'm so focused when I'm listening, it's exhausting. After I'm done it's like having run a marathon; I'm totally wasted."

Isay, who fell into radio when he was a twenty-two-year-old medical student, may have given up becoming a doctor to do his radio interviews, but he still thinks along medical lines. "I think of these radio interviews like doing surgery—I know I need to get the liver out, I go in, cut 'em open, look for that organ, slice it, and take it out. I'm not going to leave until I get it. Once I get it, I protect my tapes like I'm carrying diamonds. I don't let them leave my body."

SUSAN STAMBERG is the person everyone else at NPR looks up to with admiration and awe. She began there in 1972 and served as host of *All Things Considered* for fourteen years before branching out to other NPR shows like *Morning Edition* and *Weekend Edition*. She estimates that she's interviewed twenty thousand people in her thirty years in public radio. When asked where NPR stood in the media spectrum, she answered: "At the top. Our big disadvantage is that you can't wrap fish in us. People say that if TV had been invented first, everyone would be talking about this new invention—radio. It's walkable, pocket-able and you don't have to sit and look at it all day."

DOCUMENTARIES

There was a movie that came and went in 2003 which I thought deserved more attention than it received. It was called *Interview with the Assassin,* and from the moment I realized who the assassin was supposed to be I marveled that it hadn't been done before. The majority of people in America believe that Lee Harvey Oswald was not the lone assassin of President John F. Kennedy in November 1963. Conspiracy theories include communists, fascists, anti-Castro exiles, the FBI, the CIA, certain Southern congressmen, even the vice president at the time. There are hundreds of books on the subject. Oliver Stone dealt with it in his film *JFK.* But it was Neil Burger who came up with the idea for this mock documentary: What if the second assassin, who fired his shots from behind the fence on the grassy knoll in front of Kennedy's open car, was still alive and wanted to confess? What if he was living in a quiet suburban neighborhood and the guy living across the street happened to be an out-of-work cameraman? Anne Rice came up with her brilliant idea of interviewing a vampire; Burger's idea was to interview the man who could prove Kennedy's assassination was a conspiracy. And it was done as an interview. A man whose confession would be filmed and documented. It was a perfect illustration of a remark filmmaker Jean-Luc Godard once made: "In filmmaking you can either start with fiction or documentary. But whichever you start with, you inevitably find the other."

There were 541 documentary films submitted to the 2004

Sundance Film Festival, and 40 were selected. A lot more than that were shot for industrial, commercial, and artistic purposes. Documentaries often include interviews. Errol Morris's *Fog of War* consists of a straight-on interview with former secretary of defense Robert McNamara. Andrew Jarecki's *Capturing the Friedmans* includes interviews with various family members in an attempt to understand what happened to the head of the Friedman household. Michael Moore has used his offbeat interviewing techniques to ambush GM executives or NRA president Charlton Heston in his award-winning documentaries *Roger & Me* and *Bowling for Columbine*. Depending on the filmmaker, the interviews conducted might be well researched or spontaneous. Sometimes the filmmaker isn't after an in-depth response but a good visual. Sometimes it's as effective to have a person not answer as it is to have someone go on and on about a subject. Because documentaries, like television, are visual experiences. You watch and form opinions as much by a person's body language as you do from what is spoken. If a person looks into the camera and says something like "I did not have sex with that woman," it might become a signature statement that gets repeated for years if that person is later proved to have been lying. If a person says, "I shot the president," and then sets out to prove it, you have to suspend your disbelief until you hear what he has to say, and then decide whether to believe him or not. But it certainly would behoove the interviewer to ask the right questions and know how to follow up if the subject being interviewed is a controversial person or someone who affected history.

Sometimes, however, getting what you're looking for out of any particular filmed interview can be tricky: Your subject may give you only a set amount of time, he might have his own agenda, or he may be unwilling to go in the direction you'd like to cover. Moreover, because you're there with a camera and a crew, the situation doesn't always lend itself toward intimacy.

When Nick Broomfield interviewed Aileen Wuornos for his

two documentaries about her—*Aileen Wuornos: The Selling of a Serial Killer* and *Aileen: The Life and Death of a Serial Killer*—he found the woman sitting on death row awaiting her execution willing to talk to him because she had "a strong agenda, a whole lot of things she passionately wanted to say." Promoting the second documentary, Broomfield told the *L.A. Times* (January 5, 2004) that "it was quite hard to steer the interviews, to get her to talk about things other than her obsession with the police. It's the only film I've done where I felt I was more a conduit than somebody who was deciding the direction."

When writer/director Patty Jenkins was researching *Monster,* the film that would star Charlize Theron as Wuornos, she corresponded with Aileen but decided not to interview her. Jenkins also told the *Times,* "Aileen had an agenda with me as well. And I didn't want to cover the same material as the documentaries had covered: it was a completely different period of time I was covering. I don't know what could have come of an interview. I don't know she would have ever trusted me in that period of time."

Documentarians are faced with numerous obstacles when interviewing. Often the filmmaker isn't an interviewer and spends more time preparing for his shot than for his questions. Because it's a visual medium, you can't expect to film a talking head and keep an audience's interest. You've got to juggle place and setting, the way a subject is lit, and how what is said moves your story forward. When Martin Scorsese got seven directors (including himself) to document *The Blues* for PBS, the challenge for each director was to incorporate the singers' and musicians' music with their words. The same was true for Ken Burns's jazz series, as well as his series on baseball, the Civil War, and Mark Twain. While these documentaries use interviews to help define a point of view, the interviews aren't necessarily the primary focus of the film. That is why it is important to make these interviews as interesting as possible, so that what is said is as riveting as what might be shown (it's common to use talk as a voice-over while illustrating that commentary with moving images). Also, an interview can be used to contradict the image shown—a politician might deny participating in a demonstration and the visual might show him there; a person might be talking about how he was instrumental in cleaning up a river, while the visual can zoom in on the polluted waters.

It's important to remember to ask for your subject's permission on camera to use the interview you're about to do. Also remember that while film is more expensive than tape, it should not prohibit you from getting as much material as you can—just keep the cameras rolling as you ask questions and record the answers. It takes a while for a subject to loosen up before a camera, so do your best to make the person you're about to interview comfortable. Ask easy questions at first, let your subject find his or her voice, and be prepared enough so that you can lead that person in the direction you want. The camera can often pick up telling details, so don't bombard your subject with lengthy questions. Be precise and concise in what you ask. And prepare sensitive questions to bring out as much emotion from your subject as possible. If a tear wells up in someone's eye, the camera will catch it. That tear might be as revealing or moving as anything the person has to say.

What you want to avoid when shooting documentaries is the boring interview, the static conversation, the repetitious. You don't want to cut someone off; if a person pauses, let his silence fill the room until he starts talking again. Often that silence can be dramatic. If you've got someone covering a certain topic, there's no need to have it said again by someone else. Know your material. Know what you have . . . and what you need.

TELEVISION

On any given day one can turn on the television and watch someone being interviewed, from early morning until late at night. You can wake up to the *Today* show, *Good Morning America,* or *The Early Show* and watch Matt Lauer and Katie Couric or Diane Sawyer and Charles Gibson. . . . Then come the mid-morning shows, with Regis Philbin, the gals from *The View,* Jenny Jones, and Maury Povich. In the afternoon you can find Ricki Lake, Oprah Winfrey, Montel Williams, Ellen DeGeneres, and Dr. Phil. In the evening you can watch the wonderful old-timers on *60 Minutes,* or those on *Dateline, Primetime,* or *20/20.* On cable there's Larry King, *Hard Ball's* Chris Matthews, Bill O'Reilly, Hannity and Colmes, Jules Asner, Bob Costas, and those characters on *The Best Damn Sports Show, Period.* And after the late news you have Jay Leno, David Letterman, Ted Koppel, Chris Brury, Charlie Rose, Jon Stewart, Conan O'Brien, and Jimmy Kimmel. We certainly can observe a lot of different styles with these TV interviewers. And if you don't like what you see, there's always the satirists: Martin Short's Jimmy Glick, HBO's *Da Ali G Show,* or the late Chris Farley's wonderful sweaty mock interviews still seen on reruns of *Saturday Night Live.* What do any of these TV interviewers have in common with print interviewers? Very little, actually.

Journalist Sydney Schanberg, whose *New York Times* reporting on Cambodia inspired the film *The Killing Fields,* has observed that "what those [cable talk-show hosts] like Tucker Carlson, Chris Matthews and Bill O'Reilly do might be journalism if they did real research. But they don't have the time, and that's not the purpose of the shows. They are not journalists but performers. And a lot of people have begun to mistake performers for journalists."

I learned about television very quickly when I was asked by *Playboy* to try to duplicate the magazine interview on the air. I wound up doing fifty television interviews with people like Miles Davis, Truman Capote, Luciano Pavarotti, Norman Mailer, Betty Friedan, Mamie Van Doren, Marilyn Chambers, Shelley Winters, Natalie Cole, Neil Simon, and Allen Ginsberg. I tried to bring my journalist's sensibility to the endeavor, but inevitably I wound up being called aside by the director, who reminded me that I needed to keep my questions shorter and make them punchier, and to not allow the guest to ramble. In other words, he was listening for sound bites. People who watch TV are not used to rambling conversations that meander around in the wilderness before hitting pay dirt. Alex Haley told wonderful stories about his life and his work, but he was a storyteller and his tales went on for five, six, seven minutes. When it came to editing the piece down to eight total minutes, we didn't use any of those extended stories. The same was true with Allen Ginsberg. He went on about the CIA and the Vietnam War, detailing the behind-the-scenes shenanigans that the general public wasn't hip to, but in the end we used what he had to say about having incestuous feelings toward his father, because that was short and less complicated than his political views.

The first TV interview I did was with the legendary Hollywood photographer George Hurrell in 1982. Here was a man who had given us some of the memorable images of stars like Joan Crawford, Faye Dunaway, Errol Flynn, Greta Garbo, Johnny Weissmuller, and Mae West. We went to his studio, where the two-camera crew set up. There were two chairs in the middle of the studio where Hurrell and I were to sit. Once we were miked, with the cameras behind me, I started asking him questions. After a few minutes, the sound man interrupted us—there was a problem with one of the mikes. He made his adjustments and we started over. Already I was uncomfortable: start over? That wasn't what I was used to. But I did, and two minutes later we were stopped again; this time the lighting guy had to move one of his lights because there was a shadow touching Hurrell. We started again, but we didn't get more than thirty seconds into it when the director came out and said that there was something fuzzy with the picture, the way the camera was positioned Hurrell was just slightly out of focus. So the cameraman and the soundman walked over to Hurrell and *lifted* him in his seat, moving him six inches to the right. I was mortified. This completely knocked me off my stride. I was so sick from the way they treated our guest in his own studio that I slightly threw up into my glass of water. I excused myself, took off my mike, walked over to the director, and whispered, "I don't know what you think you're doing here, but this is too amateurish to continue. I don't want to be interrupted again. Get the lights, the sound, the positions right now and just let the cameras run once we've begun."

I sat back down, apologized to Hurrell, and we did the interview. Afterward, over lunch, I apologized again to Hurrell and he said, "You can't let these things upset you. I've been on movie sets for fifty years and what I've learned in that time is that to the crew, talent is just another prop; talent is furniture, to be moved around."

What I learned from that experience is that in order to do successful TV interviews I must get to know the crew, learn the names of the lighting and sound and camera men, talk to the director, get on the same page. They've got to know how I work, just as I needed to learn from Hurrell how they did.

This didn't help when I went to New York to interview Betty Friedan. We took a room at the Drake Hotel to film this meeting between *Playboy* and the author of *The Feminine Mystique,* one of the inspirational sparks of the women's movement. Our conversation seemed to go without a hitch until I brought up the name of Phyllis Schlafly, whose antifeminist views upset Friedan. "I don't want to talk about her," she said, and started to get up.

"That's OK, we can pass on that, but don't get up because you're miked," I said.

Then I asked her why Schlafly's name so riled her.

This time Friedan stood up, unhooked the mike from her blouse, and said she didn't want to do the interview.

I calmed her a second time and convinced her to put the mike back on. We started to talk about something else when I mentioned that it was interesting that our interview was to appear on the Playboy Channel. As if she wasn't aware of that, Friedan rose a third time—what was she doing talking to *Playboy?* She was a cranky woman who had fought plenty of battles and just didn't have it in her that day to fight another. It was easier for her to walk.

But I insisted that Friedan stay and finish the interview, and somehow she agreed. All this while I was thinking that her standing up to leave three times would make for good television. We went through a few reel changes until five o'clock, when the director told me that the crew would have to be paid overtime if we continued, and he wanted to wrap it up. I told him I needed another fifteen minutes because I didn't have an ending. He didn't want to put another reel in the camera. I didn't know him or his crew—I had flown in from L.A. and they were all from New York—but I said he shouldn't worry about the extra cost, I would be responsible. He huddled with his cameraman; they then said go ahead and finish, and I asked Betty Friedan how she wanted to be remembered. A simple question, but this cantankerous woman just softened contemplating her own immortality, and she gave a terrific self-assessment that I knew would work. When she finished, I thanked her and walked her out of the hotel. Then I returned to the room and said to the director, "Boy, I'm glad I insisted on that last reel, that really made this interview work."

He looked at me without a hint of embarrassment and said, "We didn't shoot it."

"What do you mean?" I asked.

"You were making such an issue out of it, I just told the cameraman to say he was rolling. We didn't put any film in the camera."

I was furious, but what could I do? I had lost my ending. On the plane back I tried to look at the bright side: Friedan had tried to stop the interview three times, she had stood up and walked away, and I had to talk her back into her seat. Maybe that would be enough to make this interview memorable.

But when I returned to L.A. and watched the tape, I saw that each time Friedan stood up and walked away, the camera remained focused on the empty chair. The cameraman never moved his camera, he didn't follow Friedan. None of her ranting visually worked. I was totally disappointed.

Another lesson learned about working in television: When the interview is on your shoulders, don't work with people who won't listen to you. And before you start shooting, make sure your cameraman understands that his camera should always be focused on the subject. If that subject gets up, the camera should stay with her. If the subject moves, so should the camera.

For a while, it seemed like I was always learning something new about television, and it often had to do with the unexpected. I flew into New York again to interview Morgan Fairchild, who was doing a play on Broadway. We had rented the theater where she was working for the morning and had arranged to start the interview at 9 A.M. But at seven I got a call from the producer, who said that Fairchild was sick and couldn't make it. Since we were already set up at the theater and would have to pay the crew and the theater whether we shot her or not, I tried to think of who we might get at the last minute to replace her. I called a friend of mine who worked for ABC and we went through his Rolodex, trying to find a name. We eliminated all women, because women would have to be made up, and there just wasn't enough time. The same was true for most men, but when he mentioned Charles Grodin, I thought he might do it if I could convince him. So I called Grodin at seven-thirty that morning, apologizing profusely, explaining the situation. He agreed to come to the theater by nine, and I was relieved. We had a subject.

But then I began to panic. I wasn't at all prepared to interview him. I knew very little about him, other than he appeared in *Rosemary's Baby, The Heartbreak Kid,* and *Heaven Can Wait,* and as a love object of Miss Piggy in one of the Muppet movies. (This was before he did *Midnight Run* with De Niro and briefly had his own TV talk show.) My mind was fixed on Morgan Fairchild (and on Norman Mailer, whom I was also interviewing soon). So I got to the theater and asked the few crew members what they knew about him. They knew less than I did. When Grodin walked in I thanked him for coming on such incredibly short notice and apologized in advance for my lack of preparation. Then we went to the stage, got miked, and the cameras rolled.

"I've got Morgan Fairchild questions and Norman Mailer questions," I began, trying to ease into this on-the-fly interview. "Which would you like first?"

"I'll take Morgan," Grodin said.

We were off and running . . . but needless to say, it wasn't memorable.

WHAT WAS MEMORABLE, as a story to tell at least, was the time I showed up at a hotel in L.A. to interview Marilyn Chambers, the porn star of *Behind the Green Door*. Chambers was the kind of person I thought should be interviewed on the Playboy Channel. The questions I prepared to ask her were unlike any I had written before, having to do with sexual positions, number of men at one time, the taste of European versus American versus Asian semen. I figured if you're going to interview a porn star, then get into the porn!

What I wasn't prepared for was the extra person in the room—the soundman, carrying a boom mike. "What's this?" I asked the director.

"We want to shoot this one with the boom," he said.

"What's wrong with the lapel mikes? They're easier . . . and the room is small, the guy is right next to us, he's in our line of vision, it's distracting."

"Yeah, that's OK, let's try it this way this time."

"I don't like it," I said. "There's got to be a reason you're using him."

The director took me aside and whispered, "Look, the last time Marilyn Chambers did a radio interview, she went down on the interviewer."

"Yeah, so?" I asked.

"We thought she might do it again, and if you were miked, it wouldn't be as easy."

"This is television, not radio," I said. "People can see it. And how do you even know they weren't faking it on radio? She's not going to do that."

"You never know."

"But I do know that I'm married, I've got a kid. Even if she wanted to, do you think I'd let her?"

He looked at me like I had just asked him the dumbest question he had ever been asked. It had never occurred to him that if Marilyn Chambers wanted to demonstrate her oral techniques on camera that I would not be a willing, nay ecstatic, participant!

Needless to say, we did the interview. Hugh Hefner saw it and thought it was too shocking to air and insisted we reedit it. And, other than ask the kind of questions that shocked Hefner, I did nothing that would embarrass my wife.

WRITER ORIANA FALLACI doesn't like TV journalists, "because TV journalism produces mindless interviewers." She's only partially correct. There are some exceptions.

One of the best television interviewers I've seen is someone who, for reasons that are beyond my comprehension, is not currently working in television: Roy Firestone. I've watched him go from CBS local news to ESPN, where he started the *Up Close* conversations, and then was moved to doing one-hour specials. His forte is interviewing athletes, and he's won six Emmys and seven Ace Awards talking to over four thousand of them. It never gets easy because athletes aren't often articulate. They're usually young, gifted, semi-educated, and millionaires. They don't need to be hassled while revealing themselves on camera. Yet Firestone has managed to help many of these young Adonises find their emotional center. He's even parodied himself in the film *Jerry Maguire,* when Cuba Gooding sits down with him and says, "You ain't gonna make me cry!" And, of course, Firestone does.

What's his secret? How does Firestone find the vulnerable person behind the hero's façade?

"There are very few good interviewers in sports," according to Firestone. "Most people have this perfunctory approach, they fall into: 'How are you feeling now? You must feel great.' Most sports interviewers are very matter-of-fact. That's never been interesting to me. I'm not interested in the technique of an athlete. I'm interested in the roads they have traveled to get where they are. I try to find the crossroads, the turmoil, the strangeness, the vagaries, the nooks and crannies of people's lives. How people carry themselves in a room, how they approach what they do. I'm interested in weakness instead of strength, I'm fascinated by obsessions, about race relations and how we get along as people. A lot of the critics don't see the human side of what I do, but my heart is what drives my interviews. I think I get to the heart of the individual. Sugar Ray Leonard talking about infidelity, Lyle Alzado talking about his impending death, Wade Boggs talking about his mother's passing, Arthur Ashe about the love he had for his daughter. I'm also interested in the rapport between parents and children: Frank Barkley talking about his son Charles; Magic talking about his father. I've been called the Barbara Walters of sports because so many athletes have shed tears on my show. One year I interviewed sixty-five athletes and one out of every four cried. Mickey Mantle, George Brett, Magic Johnson, Dennis Rodman about his little girl, Emmitt Smith about the paraplegic grandmother who raised him. It's mostly about family, but isn't that ultimately what you want to know about an athlete, what makes him tick? One of the most profound lines was the simplest ever delivered on our show, when Washington Bullets coach Wes Unseld said,

'The best thing my father ever did was love my mother.' That got me. It's certainly not a Mike Wallace or Larry King approach. It's just different."

Bob Costas believes Firestone's great strength is his empathy. "People know that he has a good heart," Costas says, "his objective is not to screw them. He's not trying to play a game of gotcha with his guests." What Costas most admires in his friend and colleague is Firestone's willingness to "ask the question that goes beyond the basic research to try and get some insight into the person. Asking Pete Rose what he would be like as a woman is not specifically a Pete Rose–type question, but it's one of those things where you say, 'Whoa!' Roy's willing to take a big swing." (Rose's answer to Firestone's question: "I think I'd be a very ugly woman!")

While waiting to decide if he will continue in television or do his brand of soul-searching on radio or the Internet, Firestone's got a story for every sports figure he's interviewed or tried to land. He's as hardworking and dedicated as any athlete he has ever profiled, and that includes the great ones. He's his own one-man show. He reads voraciously, watches every clip and event pertaining to who he is preparing to interview, writes his own questions, introductions, and afterthoughts. He does his own negotiations with the agents and managers and entourages who surround the big-buck athletes. He works on the editing, he listens in his car to tapes of his interviews, he's always trying to improve himself. "I've never been a prima donna," he says between phone calls and faxes. "I get my fingernails dirty every day."

Why he prefers television over print when it comes to interviewing is because of the performance aspect of it. "You don't see the person getting emotional in print, they are a lot more composed. But people get worked up on camera because it's a moment, it's being taped, people are watching it, everyone is paying attention, listening. I've had maybe twenty-five people cry while I interviewed them and I don't think they would have done it for print."

Watching those who have replaced him on ESPN, one can only wonder what the folks who run the network are thinking.

"Because the pressure is on the sports talk people to come up with the best and the brightest—Shaq, Kobe, Allan Iverson, Barry Bonds—the sports interviewer's job is becoming more difficult," Firestone says. "I've had to reinvent myself because the athletes are changing—they don't want to come into the studio anymore to be interviewed. Virtually anybody of any real quality—you absolutely have to go to them, if they'll even do it. And the only way they'll do it is it's got to be made as easy as possible for them. And the future of these interviews seems grim because more celebrities are going to say the heck with us interviewers and refer fans to their own websites on the Internet."

NOT ALL INTERVIEWS aim at the jugular, or try to create controversy, or attempt to bring out one's emotions. While Firestone has had to deal with the idiosyncrasies of producers who feel they know more than he does even though they've never conducted an interview themselves, there are people like Connie Martinson, whose literary interviews appear on government and public broadcasting channels, who don't have to put up with the whims and judgments of those who prefer the common denominator to the one-of-a-kind.

The soft-spoken Wellesley-educated Martinson is one of the most solid interviewers on television. If her show, *Connie Martinson Talks Books,* doesn't appear in your local *TV Guide,* you can catch it in public libraries throughout the country. Martinson has been talking to writers about their works for three decades, and writers like to do her show because she is prepared. Unlike the majority of radio and TV interviewers, who have read the inside dust jacket flap to get some idea of what a book is about, Martinson will have read the book. She will have marked it up. Post-it notes will be sticking out of various pages. And she will refer to them. So, instead of the writer being asked to describe the contents of his book, Martinson will be more specific: She will touch on the details that demonstrate what a good reader she is, and she will bring out the best in the writer—once he recovers his speech, because usually the writer is flabbergasted that someone on television has actually read his work. Martinson never attempts to embarrass her guests; she is there to spend a half hour having an intelligent, literate conversation that she shares with her audience. When she asks the author to sign her book when it's over, he inevitably writes a big thank-you to her. Because she represents the ideal reader.

Another low-key TV interviewer is C-SPAN's Brian Lamb, whose show *Booknotes* has become a favorite for nonfiction writers. "We're not trying to get them to cry here," Lamb told reporter Sylvia A. Smith of the *Journal Gazette*. "I'm just trying to get to the person without being emotional about it." How Lamb gets to the writers he interviews is by first reading the books they've written and then keeping his questions short and to the point. "In this crazy television business," he said, "people think they have to ask the intellectual, erudite question that's going to make them look so bright. I don't care whether people think I'm bright or not. This is not a show done for intellectuals. A lot of people started to hear me ask some very basic questions and they'd say, 'Oh, my goodness, why is he asking those stupid questions?'"

His response? "I want to know the answer."

What Lamb has learned, having interviewed more than eight hundred authors, is that most interviewers in television "abhor a vacuum. Commercial television doesn't allow them to have a pause. Interviewers are almost trained putting words in people's mouths. They ask closed questions. They say to the guest: You think that George Bush is a great president, don't you? Well, we have just the opposite approach: What kind of president do you think George Bush is? That person can take that anywhere they want to. You're not prejudicing their answer. You're not forcing them to say, 'No, I don't think he's a great president.' It flows. They're not used to that."

SOLID, STALWART INTERVIEWERS like Lamb and Martinson aren't TV savvy enough to land jobs on commercial television. Most smart interviewers don't have whatever it is that the camera seems to love. Katie Couric is cute and effusive; Diane Sawyer is sweet but deceptive—she will go after you with kindness and sincerity; Oprah Winfrey and Barbara Walters are larger-than-life; Jay Leno and David Letterman are comedians who get to play around with guests. Larry King, Charlie Rose, Ted Koppel, Tim Russert, and the cast of *60 Minutes* aren't very exciting, but they're survivors; they've been around a long time, and we've gotten used to them. King is like some uncle who sits across from his subject suppressing any pride he might have that he gets people on his show who don't enjoy baring their souls to a TV audience. Ted Koppel is the schoolmaster who has the smarts to keep you from going off track or telling lies. Tim Russert chairs *Meet the Press* and is knowledgeable enough to ask the right questions to the politicians who sit across from him. Charlie Rose manages to land interesting guests, but in his enthusiasm to get some points across he at times steps over the line of interviewer and often winds up answering questions he asks before his subject has a chance to do so.

But television has the added dimension of being visual. How you look is often as important as what you say. You see Matt Lauer with his shaved head and you either get past it or you don't. Maria Shriver's cheekbones start protruding and you can't help but notice. Oprah puts on weight, she takes it off, she looks cuddly, and you are watching Oprah, you aren't paying as much attention to her guests as you do to her. It's truly reality TV, because people are watching and you have to look good, or interesting. You have to hold your own physically. If your face is broken out and makeup can't hide it, you aren't going to make it on TV. If you have a nervous tic, forget about it. If you're as smart as Stephen Hawking but you suffer from some malady that alters your voice or puts undue attention on you, then consider print.

Nonetheless, we get most of our information from the tube. So if you want to be a TV interviewer:

TAKE ELOCUTION LESSONS.

JOIN DEBATING CLUBS.

LEARN GOOD POSTURE AND POISE.

WORK OUT AT THE GYM.

DRESS WELL.

FIND A GOOD HAIRSTYLIST AND MAKEUP PERSON.

TONE DOWN YOUR GABBY NATURE.

BE PREPARED.

LEARN TO ASK SUCCINCT, TO-THE-POINT QUESTIONS.

UNDERSTAND THE IMPORTANCE OF SOUND BITES.

HAVE AN UNDERSTANDING OF TIME.

DON'T LET YOUR GUESTS RAMBLE, BUT DON'T APPEAR RUDE WHEN YOU CHANGE SUBJECTS.

KNOW THAT UNLESS THE INTERVIEW IS "LIVE" AND YOU'RE ON THE AIR WHEN THE CAMERAS ARE ROLLING, MOST TV INTERVIEWS CAN BE EDITED, AND SO YOU CAN MAKE MISTAKES AND DO ANOTHER TAKE.

In the winter of 1985, I was interviewed by Jane Pauley on *Today* for my book *Conversations with Capote*. Before I flew to New York, I spoke to someone who knew her and he told me to pass on his greetings. I was nervous before doing this interview. Capote had said so many outrageous things that I worried that Pauley might ask me to share some gossip, and what if I got the names wrong? Sure enough, when I sat down with her, we exchanged greetings and I passed on the hellos from my friend.

Her eyes lit up—thank goodness, she knew him. Then she said to me, "I'm just going to start by asking you about Capote's hate list, and you can talk about the people he hated." We had about thirty seconds before the red light came on and Pauley must have seen how the blood in my face began to drain. This was exactly the nightmare question I didn't want to have to deal with on national television. What if I said he hated someone he liked? I looked at Jane Pauley with all the pleading I could muster in my eyes and said, "Why don't you just ask me how I got to know him?" And then the red light went on, she looked into the camera, and began her introduction. It seemed like an eternity before she asked her first question, and, God bless her, she was merciful. When it was over, all I could think was it pays to know someone who knows the person who's about to interview you.

2. GETTING THERE

BEFORE THE INTERVIEW BEGINS YOU HAVE
PEOPLE TO DEAL WITH, RESEARCH TO DO,
QUESTIONS TO PREPARE, AND PATIENCE TO
PRACTICE

Most good interviews revolve around "You've got to be kidding" or "Tell me what you've never told anybody before" or "Why?"

—DIANE SAWYER

If you look at an interview as a step-by-step process, the first step is getting the assignment. Either it's a story idea you've pitched to an editor or an editor has suggested a story or subject to you. If it's not an editor, it might be a producer or a teacher or the subject himself who might want help on a project, but whoever it may be, once you start thinking about a subject, the next step is to get that person to agree to talk with you. And assuming the subject agrees, the step after that is getting prepared for that conversation. That's what this chapter is about.

WHAT HAPPENS AFTER YOU'VE GOT THE ASSIGNMENT?

You're taking a class and the teacher assigns a report. You want to hire a contractor to put on an addition to your home, but you've heard all those exasperating contractor stories and you'd like to find a good one. You're working for the school or local newspaper and the editor asks you to interview a musician who will be appearing in town in a few days.

Now what?

Not a bad idea to get a handle on your story before making the calls. You don't want to do too much, in case the person you want to speak with doesn't have the time or inclination to speak with you, but you want to do something that will at least indicate you know what you're talking about. Because the more you know about someone, the better your chances are of connecting. And the way to find out about someone, or some subject, is to do research. Do a search on the Internet; go to the library; read newspapers and magazines—see what's out there. You're on a hunt, and you need ammunition. Once you have some information, you're ready to call the person you want to speak with. If he's not a celebrity or the CEO of a company, you might be able to reach him directly. Otherwise, you will have to go through a secretary, an assistant, or a publicist. What they will want to know is why you want to talk to their boss or client. If it's an assignment, you want to state that. If it's for your own information, you should be ready to explain your reasons for wanting to take up some of this person's time. Most people, in general, are willing to talk and are often flattered that someone wants to talk to them. The subjects who have publicists, on the other hand, are more selective. Those are the people for whom preparation is essential. If two people are calling that musician to ask for an interview and one of them says, "My editor asked me to do this, but I've never really listened to her CD, could you send one to me?" and the other says, "I'm very excited to be making this call because I've listened to her work and her words and music have touched me deeply," who do you think will get the interview?

I'm always surprised at how unprepared people will be before they request an interview or before they actually go and meet the person they are about to interview. I've done book tours where I've met with newspaper and magazine writers, appeared on radio and television, and have been told, "I haven't had a chance to look through your book yet [let alone read it!] but I thought you could just fill me in on what it's about and how you wrote it. And who's the most interesting person you ever met? And who would you most like to interview?"

(In Norman's Mailer's *The Spooky Art,* he writes: "On a publicity tour . . . you are . . . an object to be manipulated as effectively as possible. The career of media interviewers conceivably rises or falls a little by how well they handle you.

"Moreover, count on it: Three out of four interviewers will not have read your book. That tends to make them ask questions [like]: 'Tell me about your book.' After you've answered that a few times, you begin to feel as if the limousine in which you are traveling is out of gas and you have to push it up the hill.")

For one television segment of which I was the subject, the producer/director/interviewer said he wanted to follow me around for the day. I asked him if he even knew what I did—since a day in my life, unless I was actually going to interview someone, could be about as interesting as watching bamboo grow. He asked me if I could send him some stuff. He didn't live very far from me, so I suggested that he might want to come to my house, get an idea of what he might like to shoot, save time that way, and I'd be happy to give him some material to help him prepare. He thought that was a swell idea, but of course he never showed up until the scheduled date, when he and his crew came and spent an entire morning trying to figure out what to shoot and where. And when we were finally ready to do it, he looked at me and said, "Listen, I didn't have the time to do the research, so I'll ask you some general questions and you can fill in the details. Is that OK?"

Well, no, it's not OK. But it would have to do, because I had only one other choice, and that was to ask them to leave. I knew that the piece he would end up with wouldn't be very good—how could it? He didn't have anything challenging to ask me, he was leaving it up to me to tell some stories, and when you let your subject take control of the content, it's never going to be as stimulating or interesting as when you, the interviewer, are in charge, when you have a direction, when you are prepared.

As Nicholas Pileggi once said: "The most important thing going into an interview is your knowing so much about it that you wouldn't even need the interview."

Adds Barbara Walters: "If you're really going to do an in-depth interview, then you have to know an awful lot about the person, certainly enough to know when he or she isn't telling the truth, isn't telling the whole story."

To Thomas Morgan the biggest mistake an interviewer can make "is the failure to be well enough prepared to know in advance what questions this person must answer."

Diane Sawyer, on the other hand, failed in her interview with John Updike because she was overprepared: "I was in awe, and when you're in awe it's better to underprepare and go simple."

Dick Cavett also felt that "the earliest mistake I made was to be overprepared, and then panicked because I had so much stuff I wasn't going to get to. Suddenly I couldn't focus on anything."

If you read what enough interviewers have to say, you come to the conclusion that there is no one way to do the job. Which is absolutely true. But I'd rather be overprepared than under-prepared. I'm more relaxed and in control when I know where I'm going, and more open to being sidetracked as well.

PUBLICISTS

How do you get to your subject? If it's a businessman, scientist, professor, Realtor, district attorney, athlete, or whoever, the first step is to call his place of business and ask for him. Most likely you will be put through to his secretary or assistant, and you can explain why you want to see him. You can also write a letter to his place of work requesting an interview and then follow it up with a phone call. If it's a writer, you can call her publisher, ask for the publicity department, and talk to someone there.

If it's a movie star (unless it's Marlon Brando, who doesn't retain one) the answer is through the star's publicist. If you don't know who that may be, you call the Screen Actors Guild and ask for that person's agent. Then you call the agency, speak to the agent's assistant, and ask for the name and number of their client's publicist. Then the fun begins.

Publicists become powerful only if they selectively refuse to publicize. . . . The publicist who most fully embodies the role of barrier is Pat Kingsley, the head of PMK/HBH. She represents Tom Cruise, Al Pacino, and Jodie Foster, among many others. . . . Kingsley rebuffs media requests so often and with such zeal that she is known as Dr. No. "Pat Kingsley cares nothing about journalism," Lynn Hirschberg, a contributing writer for the Times Magazine, *says. "She would give Annie Liebovitz days"—to shoot the star's photos—"and give you an hour."*

"The public is not nearly as curious about stars as the press is," Kingsley said. "They just like to see nice pictures. So two hours, total, should be sufficient for a profile—but I usually say an hour and a half. Some writers like to get close and nail the celebrity. Not on my watch!"

—*Tad Friend,* The New Yorker, *September 23, 2002*

The culture now depends so heavily on spin, puffery and the exultation of personalities. These guys are the disseminators, dealing in a strange currency. They don't just promote a star. They're ecclesiastical figures for the whole infotainment culture.

—*Jon Robin Baitz, playwright and screenwriter* (People I Know)

Publicists have achieved an unfortunate power in the industry. If the actor is a big star, the publicist can determine whether or not you will ever get to see his/her client. They will also set the parameters of the interview, the time you will have, and make sure you do not have any direct contact with their client until the appointed hour. The publicist acts as a barrier to the journalist. She is the keeper of the gate, the bouncer at the door, the pit bull at your ankle. She is being paid by the client, not by you, and if you write something that upsets her client, she may lose that client. She doesn't want that to happen. You are a nuisance to her. If you work for a major publication, you may be a necessary nuisance, but a nuisance nonetheless. And if you've written bad things about other people, she may call your editor and say that her client doesn't want to talk to you. If the editor wants that star badly enough, he may agree to assign another writer. For a *Rolling Stone* interview a few years ago, Tom Cruise apparently rejected fourteen writers before settling on the one who eventually did a nice, soft piece about him.

It shouldn't be that way. The editor should stick with his writer . . . but landing an interview with a major star helps sell magazines, and editors, like publicists, understand the bottom line. This leaves writers in a bad position. If you want to be true to your profession, you want to write a story without turning it into a puff piece. But if you go after the truth, and the truth is uncomfortable to the subject, it might hurt you later on. There is no easy solution to this. That is why I prefer the Q&A format over the profile for movie stars. In a profile, it's easy to color the piece with your perceptions: If someone is setting fire to a toilet and you happen to be there, that makes for a colorful story in your article. It's fun to write, but it will most likely make that person sorry he ever talked to you, and the next time you call that publicist to get to another of her clients, it isn't going to be easy. In a Q&A, you can ask the question about why was the toilet set on fire, and allow the person to answer—and you're not interjecting your Freudian thoughts on the matter, you're allowing the subject to finesse it or bury himself.

Of course, you still have to get past the publicist to reach the star.

LET ME SHARE with you an example of a writer's nightmare dealing with trying to land an interview with someone I'd already done before. When Minnesota governor Jesse Ventura announced in the summer of 2002 that he wouldn't seek reelection, I called my editor at *Playboy* and said, "Let's see if he'll talk with us again." My editor agreed. Our first interview with the governor, which ran in November 1999, may have had something to do with why he wasn't running again—after it came out, his statewide approval rating dropped twenty points, from 70 percent to 50 percent. The reason was his big mouth: He said things about religion and fat people and women in the Navy that created a media storm that didn't settle down for a month. He never denied saying any of those things, but he felt that because *Playboy* had released the interview to the Associated Press a week before the magazine came out, the quotes were taken out of context, and there was no full interview yet to see the framework of his responses.

So I called his director of communications, and made my pitch: the governor's leaving office, he doesn't have to worry about a constituency any longer, he can be free to say the things he may have been holding back while in office, and he might find the publicity useful in whatever new endeavors he has planned. The director of communications brought it up to the governor, and Ventura said yes, but not until he left office. So I waited until January 2003 and called the communications guy, who said that the governor had hired a Hollywood agent and that was the person I now had to deal with. I called the agent and he said this request was new to him, he'd have to speak with Ventura and get back to me. But this agent wasn't very big on getting back, so after waiting a week, I called again. He was out of the office, his assistant said, but he'd take a message. The next day the assistant called me to say that the agent would be calling that afternoon. He didn't call. Over the next month I made dozens of calls and was told on every occasion that he was either out of his office or was sick. So I contacted the director of communications again, even though he was no longer working for Ventura. He said that I wasn't the only one complaining about Ventura's new agent and promised to get a message to his former boss. The message that came back to me was: deal with the agent.

After a few more efforts, I was told by the agent's assistant that the matter had been turned over to Ventura's new Hollywood publicist. So I called her. She was friendly, but not "up to speed." I told her that we were on a deadline, that the July issue was being held for this interview, which we needed to get done by the end of February, so that I could meet my March 5 deadline (the July issue comes out a month early, and the magazine needs copy three months in advance). She said that the governor was concerned about being taken out of context and what could we promise to ensure that that wouldn't happen again? I said I could ask my editor about not releasing it to the Associated Press a week early and that should solve that problem. As for what the columnists picked up, there was nothing one could do about that, but at least the entire interview would be on the newsstands when anything was quoted from it. Then she said she wanted to make sure there was a cover line with Ventura's name on it and I said that should not be a problem, the last time we ran the interview with him *Playboy* used the cover line "The next President? Jesse 'The Interview' Ventura."

"I want to speak with your editor, to go over all of this," the publicist said. So I gave her his phone number and she said she'd call that afternoon. She didn't, and I suggested to my editor that he call her. He did, but she didn't answer. He called the next day, she didn't answer. He called me, and I called her, spoke with her assistant, but she didn't answer. On the third day, my editor called her, and later he told me that she started to yell at him for six minutes. She was screaming that she couldn't be harassed like this, couldn't be pressured, and my editor was confused. She was the one who wanted to speak to him, all he was doing was responding to that request. He also had a deadline coming up in two weeks and needed to know if he should find a replacement for the July issue. When he explained this to her she claimed she knew nothing of a deadline.

When my editor told me this, I said she was not being forth-right, that I had explained to her about the July issue coming out in June, we had even discussed a cover line, and that with the governor's new job at MSNBC about to start, the timing couldn't be better: He would have had a few months to settle into being a talk-show host and either he would have an audi-ence or would need one, and since *Playboy* reached a much larger audience than MSNBC (four hundred thousand in prime time as compared to 3 million *Playboy* readers, and three times as many who see each issue) it was a win-win situation for Ventura.

I then was pointed toward the director of communications at MSNBC. He responded immediately. He thought a *Playboy* interview should go to the top of the list of requests he was get-ting from the media to talk to MSNBC's new talk-show host. He called me and I explained what was going on and he said, "You don't have to sell me on this. He should do it. It's just that the deadline is short because he's on vacation for the next week and a half." That still left half a week, I noted, and with the movie summer blockbusters there might be an interview with some movie star scheduled for August, so we could lose the window of opportunity we had with the July issue. The MSNBC guy understood, but he needed to talk with Ventura, and then with his agent and publicist to make sure everyone was on the same page. And with Ventura sunning himself some-where warm, this would just have to wait until he returned.

All this just to get a couple of hours with the man who was a former wrestler, former mayor, former governor, and would most likely be a former talk-show host six months down the line. You can see how exasperating dealing with publicists can be. And for someone doing this as a freelancer, how much unpaid time it can take up. Because in the end, if Ventura wasn't willing to sit down and talk as soon as he returned from vaca-tion, and if *Playboy* decided that it didn't want to run an inter-view with him in the fall because he would be old news, then this whole effort to get to him would come to naught, and my time would be worth the same thing.

In the end, I never interviewed Ventura again. The war in Iraq postponed his entry into TV talk land, and he just faded as an in-demand celebrity. He had become yesterday's news.

THERE ONCE WAS a time, some years back, when writers didn't have to deal with publicists the way they do today. Now, if you want to interview Jodie Foster, her publicist may tell you, as she told me, that there are two areas that are off-limits: her sexuality and John Hinckley. If you accept those conditions, you can talk to Jodie. If you don't, you can't. Simple. And if you accept and then renege, well, Jodie will handle it herself, and then she will let her publicist know that those areas were broached. Do you think that publicist will be getting more clients?

As a side note, this isn't just a writer's nightmare—photographers, too, must deal with publicists and their demands. In a December 2001 syndicated column, Liz Smith wrote about "the drill" if you want to put Jennifer Aniston on a magazine cover. "You must get the dreaded PR titan Stephen Huvane to talk to you in the first place—just so he can say, 'No way; nothing doing.' (Huvane has replaced Pat Kingsley and Nancy Seltzer as the most feared flack in Hollywood.) But just in case Huvane softens up, you must then promise not to publish a smiling photo of Aniston. She isn't crazy about her teeth showing. And no profiles. Aniston doesn't like the way her nose looks from the side. There will be absolutely nothing doing if her hair in any way resembles the hair of her TV character, Rachel [in *Friends*]. What Aniston really likes is a picture of herself smirking slightly. She likes to smirk."

This doesn't mean you have to be a stooge. It just means you have to figure out clever ways of asking your questions and obtaining interesting answers. It's a challenge, really. When I finally got to see Barbra Streisand, after more than a year of trying, I was no longer dealing with her publicist—in fact, I insisted that I deal directly with her.

She was, at the time, working on *A Star Is Born* with Kris Kristofferson. The director, Frank Pierson, wasn't enjoying his dealings with his star and her producer/boyfriend Jon Peters, and before the picture was finished he wrote an article that appeared as a cover story for *New York* magazine under the headline "My Battles with Barbra and Jon." This so angered Streisand that she decided to respond, in print, and since I had been after her for both *Playboy* and *Newsday*'s Sunday magazine, her people called me and told me to come to the Todd-AO studio in Hollywood to meet her. I did, and when she appeared, followed by her entourage of five people, she came right up to me and, without even a hello, asked, "Why does the press hate me?" I took a step back and ran off a list of reasons. Behind her I heard a collective gasp. No one, apparently, talked to Streisand so bluntly. Streisand, though, eyed me anew and instructed me to follow her into the screening room, where we then sat in two plush leather chairs and watched a rough cut of her movie. When it was over she turned to me and asked, "Well?"

To which I replied, "You're going to make a lot of money."

My answer apparently met her approval and she told me to call her publicist to arrange for a time for us to talk. "Look, Barbra," I said, "it's taken me over a year to get this far. I don't want to start calling your publicist every week asking for a date. If you really want to do this, give me your number and I'll call you directly."

Streisand thought about this a while then carefully wrote her phone number on a tiny corner of a yellow pad, ripped the piece off, and handed it to me. I called the next day and we arranged a time to begin the interview.

When I arrived at her Holmby Hills house, she came down the stairs and handed me two sheets of paper. "Here," she said, "sign this and we can begin."

I looked at what she wanted me to sign. It was a letter to her, supposedly written by me, saying that she had the right to all the material that resulted from our interview—that she could edit it, stop it, own the tapes, and had approval of the final draft. I told her I couldn't sign such a letter.

"What do you mean, everybody who talks to me signs," she said.

"Well, first, I didn't write this letter, your lawyer did. Second, I've never given away control of an interview. Third, you're asking for too much. Fourth, if I did sign this, then I'm signing away my rights as a journalist and am becoming more of a secretary. Fifth, you're castrating me before we even begin. Sixth, you see yourself as an artist, and I consider what I do an art as well. To sign that letter takes away my art. I'd rather not do the interview."

We sat in her living room at an impasse. She wasn't happy, but neither was I. This was a very important interview for me—it was my first for *Playboy*—and I was ready to give it up on principles that I felt strongly about. After about ten minutes Streisand made a decision: the lawyer's letter in my name would not be signed. We moved to a couch in front of a fireplace and I took out my tape recorders. Then the phone rang.

It was her lawyer, asking if I had signed. No, Streisand answered, I hadn't, and she was going ahead with the interview, anyway.

The phone rang a second time.

It was Jon Peters, asking the same question and getting the same answer.

It rang a third time.

It was her manager. "Did he sign?" "No." "What do you mean, he has to sign!" "You talk to him," Streisand said, and handed me the phone.

I put the phone to my ear and heard, *"I don't want to fucking talk to him!"*

I handed it back to Streisand. "He doesn't want to talk to me," I said.

And that's how our interview, which turned into a nine-month marathon, began.

SOME YEARS LATER I interviewed Barbara Walters and was able to confirm that when Streisand said that everybody signs, she wasn't kidding. Streisand was the subject of Barbara Walters's first prime-time television special, and the only reason Streisand agreed to do it was because Walters allowed her to retain editorial control. When I asked Walters about this, she said: "I'd never done a special before; nobody had ever done them on prime time. Streisand's then-agent called me and said that Streisand and Jon Peters would talk to me, but that she wanted editorial control. I had just come to ABC. As it turned out, it was so difficult [dealing with Streisand] that we said we would never, under any circumstance, give away any control again. And we haven't."

STREISAND'S PUBLICIST at the time was someone who had also represented Frank Sinatra. For years I had tried to interview Sinatra, but never got anywhere. The publicist would put me off. Realizing he wasn't going to let me in, I tried to go around him. I wrote a letter to Sinatra's lawyer. He sent it to the publicist, who called me. "You think you can get to Frank Sinatra without me? Well, good luck. And don't bother trying through me again." He was angry, he was flexing his muscles, and I never got to talk to Sinatra.

Something similar happened with Al Pacino. When he was making the third *Godfather,* every magazine wanted an interview with him. I was contacted by a few different editors, who knew that I had written about him in the past and that I had developed a friendship with him. (This is a very tricky issue: journalists shouldn't befriend their subjects. But sometimes it happens. When it does, it's always best to let editors know about it, so they can decide whether they still want you to write the piece.) One of the editors was at *Entertainment Weekly,* which had just launched and felt it needed to scoop some of the other magazines to show it had arrived and could compete. *Entertainment Weekly* offered to pay me twice as much as any other publication had offered, but I didn't think Pacino wanted to be bothered doing any publicity at all, so I didn't say anything to him. Then I happened to go to New York and spent time with Pacino. On the way to his dentist, he mentioned that he had to get back at a certain time because he was meeting a writer for *Interview* magazine. "Al," I said, "you're doing publicity? If you're going to talk to them, I've got a half dozen requests from magazines that want you."

"Who's offering you the most money?" he asked.

"Entertainment Weekly," I said. "They want a cover story."

"So, go with them."

I contacted *EW* and let them know, and a contract was soon in my hands. Then, about a week later, I got an angry call from Pacino's publicist. She was just furious that I was doing this story for this new publication without having gone through her. "Why didn't you tell me about this?" she asked.

"I thought Al would," I said.

"It's not up to him to tell me, it's up to you."

"No, it isn't," I said. "I'm not your client, he is."

"Just because you're friends, you can't go around me like this," she said. "My job is to plan a strategy for him. You know he doesn't do very much, and this is not the right place for him at this time. If you think you can do this, then just wait until you want to see any of my clients that are not your friend."

This was not a fun conversation. It got uglier. I felt that Pacino was doing me a favor, but now it was backfiring. I had committed to writing the story, I didn't want to back out of it, but I knew that I had made an enemy. His publicist was one of the most powerful people in Hollywood.

In the end, I wrote the piece, Pacino posed for the cover, it was a good picture, he liked it, and when I happened to be at his publicist's office some time later I noticed that she had it framed on her wall.

IN THE FALL of 2001, before Halle Berry won her Oscar for her performance in *Monster's Ball,* I interviewed her for *Movieline.* She came to my house, we talked for nearly five hours, and after the story appeared Halle sent me flowers from London, where she was filming *Die Another Day,* along with a very nice note. Up until that time, Berry wasn't being taken as seriously as she took herself, and her publicist told me that the story might have been helpful in her pursuit of the Oscar. I had no thoughts one way or the other about that—I had just found, from my research, that Berry was a fascinating character: She grew up as an overachiever who had won beauty contests, excelled in school, but came from a broken, at times abusive home. She had suffered from diabetes without knowing it; she had been beaten by men, had a bad first marriage to a professional ballplayer, and fought against great odds to bring the story of another black woman, Dorothy Dandridge, to television. Halle Berry was a survivor, someone who had suffered through prejudice, who had yet to learn about relationships, had received bad press for leaving the scene of an accident, but who had a great belief in herself.

So when *Playboy* wanted me to interview her for the January 2003 issue, I didn't think I'd run into much resistance from her publicist. But this was after Berry had won her Oscar, and the rules had changed. Berry was more in demand, and her publicist was juggling all the media requests to get to her. She was also working on two new films and trying to keep a marriage going (the *Enquirer* had reported that her husband, Eric Benet, was in a rehab facility suffering from a sex addiction). The days of her driving herself to a journalist's house for a leisurely afternoon chat were over. Now one was lucky to get any solid block of time with her.

For months the publicist tried to fit me into her client's busy schedule. My own deadline was mid-September, and each time it looked like a date would be set, it would be canceled. Halle was in London, Halle was in Vancouver. When she was in between sets and in L.A., the publicist promised I'd see her then. But that didn't happen. And when I would finally get to see her, the publicist said, it could only be for two hours. Remembering how easy Halle was to talk with, and how much she seemed to enjoy talking, I wrote her publicist an e-mail asking for more time:

"All I try to do is the best job I can. A very rushed conversation isn't much fun for anyone—not for me asking the questions and always having to look at my watch, cutting off answers etc; and not for the person being asked the questions, having to look into the eyes of her interviewer who is always thinking ahead and not in the moment, knowing the clock is ticking. I view this particular interview as part of a historical record, there's more of an art to it than to many of the others. That is why I try to get a little more time . . . just so the talk can be more relaxed than rushed. I think you understand."

But the publicist didn't understand. As far as she was concerned, I was lucky if I got two hours with her golden client. And I would have to fly up to Vancouver, where she was filming the sequel to *X-Men,* to see her.

So I made my arrangements, booked a flight, a hotel, a car for the following week, and had to cancel everything when I heard Berry's schedule had changed: I had to fly up the next day to see her. That, of course, wound up costing *Playboy* more money.

When I got to Vancouver I had a message to call Berry's publicist. She said she had "good news and bad news." I sighed. This good news/bad news routine was starting to wear me down. It was the fourth time she used it on me: good news—Halle will do it; bad news—not for a while. Good news—Halle will be back in L.A., and do it then; bad news—only two hours. Good news—Halle might be able to give more time; bad news—has to be done in Vancouver after my deadline. Good news—Halle can do it at the end of August; bad news—back to two hours. Good news—Halle has the whole day to give you; bad news— you have to be there tomorrow because of a change in her film schedule. And this time, the bad news was that we were back to the two-hour limit and we had to start at 10 A.M. the next morning because she had to work in the afternoon. And the good news? That she was doing it at all!

So that night I went to dinner and took my questions with me. I eliminated 40 of the 160 I had prepared, hoping that if I could get in a question a minute, I could do this thing. (To think that years ago I turned down the chance to interview Sophia Loren for *Playboy* because she could *only* guarantee me six hours!)

The next morning I arrived fifteen minutes early at the house in North Vancouver where Halle was staying. The photographer and his two assistants were setting up in the living room and the publicist was there to make sure that at the stroke of noon I was to say my good-byes. Halle came down on time and spent the first fifteen minutes posing for the pictures that would run in the magazine. Figuring I was losing my time with this, I started asking her simple questions, like whether she preferred working in Canada for the sequel to *X-Men* or in England, where she had done the Bond film, *Die Another Day.* When Halle hesitated, the photographer, a native of Vancouver, prompted her: "You've got to say Canada!" Then I asked Halle who was her favorite James Bond. The photographer answered first: "You've got to say Connery!" Realizing that I was working with an imbecile photographer who didn't understand that he was there to take pictures and not to answer my questions, I leaned over and whispered ever-so politely, "Shut up." Then I smiled at Halle and listened to her praise her costar, Pierce Brosnan.

Most of the time when I interview someone, we're alone. That's the way I prefer it. But sometimes you can't control the circumstances. The first time I interviewed Halle Berry we were alone; the second time, her publicist was not going to allow the kind of time we had the first time. And she wasn't going to leave us alone. She sat on the steps that led to the living room where we talked. And when I brought up the sensitive subject of her cheating husband, Halle spoke about the rawness of this twist in her marriage, but then her publicist appeared and said, in no uncertain terms, that Halle had answered the question, and that I should move on. The publicist's behavior was clearly out of order, and unnecessary. Halle knew how to defend herself, she was charming and vulnerable and adept at getting her points across. In fact, my instinct was to ask Halle follow-up questions about this sensitive subject, just because her publicist interrupted us. My feeling is if a star needs a publicist to help her through an interview, she probably shouldn't bother doing interviews, because obviously there is something to hide.

Because I had interviewed Halle before, we were able to cut down the small talk and get right to the questions I wanted to cover, so it was possible to get the interview done in two hours—but had that been the first time I met her I doubt if we would have gotten very far. And then at the end of 2002 I saw the glut of cover stories her publicist had arranged for her: *Vogue, Essence, Cosmopolitan, Entertainment Weekly*. Our *Playboy* interview was just one of dozens of pieces that appeared. And then there were all the television shows, the appearances on Larry King and CNN's *People in the News*, the spots on *Entertainment Tonight* and *Access Hollywood*, and all those local showbiz bits. It seemed like overkill for a movie in which she wasn't even the main star. Why weren't these stories spread out more? Why did Halle Berry need so much publicity? I don't know the answer to that, but I do better understand why her publicist wasn't allowing any more than two hours at a crack with her client. Because she was just lining up those interviews, one after the other. And, perhaps, in that way drowning out any substance with the gush of media she was able to generate. In the end, it all became just a blur. Halle Berry was everywhere.

So, what does one learn from this? For one thing, dealing with publicists is a bitch. Their job is to protect their clients. They are very often overprotective. They can be frustrating to deal with. But you mustn't let them get to you. Eventually, one hopes, the client will get so bored with having to do puff pieces with journalists who have made so many agreements that they might snap out of it and let their publicists know that they don't need to be so protected. One hopes . . . but realistically, you just have to do the best you can within the limits of time and subject matter. You've got to figure out ways of getting a subject to open up by coming up with offbeat questions that might stimulate an original line of thinking. And if ever you need a reason to be thankful for not having to interview the very famous or the highly celebrated, this may be it: You don't have to negotiate with a publicist; you don't have to go in with your hands tied. Of course, you're also not going to sit knee-to-knee with Halle Berry, but that's not the reason you're in this in the first place, is it?

RESEARCHING AND PREPARING QUESTIONS

There are many ways to be well informed, but it boils down to this: research. Depending on who you are preparing to interview, you must read whatever books that your subject has written, or contributed to, or have been written about him, or are about topics that relate to him. You must see that person's movies, read the articles, read the reviews, talk to people who have worked with that person. For businesspeople, read the company's annual report, read the business section of the newspaper, know the history of the company as well as the way the current market is shifting. For scientists, historians, geologists, mathematicians, and others in the academic world, learn what you can about their expertise, read articles or books about their interests (for a geologist, it can't hurt to read some of John McPhee's books; for a mathematician, there are many nontechnical books that will get you thinking about numbers and concepts). When I prepared to interview Linus Pauling I knew I couldn't grasp the chemistry that led him to figure out the general theory of anesthesia, but I could read his book *No More War!* and I could ask him layman's questions about the importance of his work, and how he was able to combine his scientific passions with his deep sense of civil disobedience.

For actors, go online and read what has been written about them, see their movies, watch their TV shows, read reviews of their work (especially the critical ones), go to the library and ask the librarian what they might have about the person. On my bookshelves I have dozens of biographies about stars, books about eras (like *Easy Riders, Raging Bulls, The Gross, The Grove Book of Hollywood, Reel Power, Hollywood Remembered*), all of Pauline Kael's books, as well as collected reviews, profiles, or essays by John Simon, Terence Rafferty, James Agee, Dwight Macdonald, Stanley Kaufman, Lillian Ross, Andrew Sarris, Rex Reed, Tom Burke, Richard Schickel, Roger Ebert, François Truffaut, Kenneth Tynan, Alexander Walker, and David Mamet. Books of gossip like *Inside People, Dish, Fame.* Film guides like David Thomson's *Biographical Dictionary of Film,* Ephraim Katz's *Film Encyclopedia,* Leonard Maltin's *Movie Encyclopedia.* When I'm interviewing someone in the movie business, I go through all these books' indexes, looking to see if my subject is mentioned.

For writers you have to read what they have written and see what interests them. For Elmore Leonard, I read fourteen of his novels; for Joyce Carol Oates, I tried to read different genres— her essays, her poems, her short stories, plays, and novels. For Saul Bellow, I reread books I had read when I was younger, like *Henderson the Rain King, The Adventures of Augie March,* and a half dozen others; I also read his essays, and all the books I could find about him. For Truman Capote, I read all of his books, and many of the articles that were written about him. For James A.

Michener, who wrote one-thousand-page novels, I selected a few from his early years, a few from his middle years, and some of his more current work. When I went to see him, he said he had only one day to give me. I told him I had prepared fifty-six pages of single-spaced questions—all culled from my readings. He suggested we begin at eight the next morning, and we did . . . and talked until ten in the evening. He invited me to return the next day at eight, and we did it again. And again the third day. And the fourth. And by the evening of the fifth day I was exhausted, and Michener was finally ready to return to the novel he had been writing when I had interrupted him.

When Fox Sports TV reporter Jeanne Zelasko was asked to work the Daytona 500 she wasn't sure why her boss thought she could handle it, since she didn't know anything about NASCAR. She had two weeks to prepare. "The first thing I did after arriving at Daytona was go to a bookstore," she said. "I read every book I could find on NASCAR, including *NASCAR for Dummies.*" Her research led her to a whole new world, where the participants were accessible and the reporting exciting. "Working the pits is like working the postgame of a major event," she said. "It's a real adrenaline rush. Only you get that rush four or five times rather than just once because you have four or five pit stops to cover."

MY WIFE CAN'T STAND the way magazines have begun to overrun our house. Stacks of them appear in closets, in cabinets, on shelves, in boxes stacked in the garage, in our two daughters' rooms now that they've left the house, on the floor of our bedroom, on the unused chairs in our dining room, on each step leading to my upstairs office, and, of course, in the bathrooms. *The New Yorker,* the *Atlantic, Harper's, Rolling Stone, Details, GQ, Esquire, Playboy, Diversion, Movieline's Hollywood Life, Vanity Fair, Spin, Newsweek, The Los Angeles* and *New York Times Sunday Magazines, Entertainment Weekly, ANOTHER,* the *Smithsonian, National Geographic, Interview, Mother Jones, Golf Digest, Maxim,*

Detour—they proliferate like rabbits. And every time I get one of those mailers offering a year's subscription to some magazine for less than a buck a copy, I can't resist. It's all research, I tell my wife, even though she knows I don't have time to read these things. But I do browse through all of them when they arrive, I check out the table of contents, I flip through every page, I note the articles I want to read . . . and then I put them first by my bedside, then move them in stacks to a corner of the room, then downstairs where they are filed separately in different areas of the house. Because I know that when I get an assignment, the first thing I will do is go through all of these magazines to find previous stories about the subject. And what I can't find at home I'll look for at the library or on the Internet.

Take, for example, a 2003 interview I did with Drew Barrymore. When my *Movieline* editor called and asked if I could prepare to talk to her in a week's time, I went and found two previous stories on her in that magazine, a *Rolling Stone* cover story, a piece about her in the late *Talk* magazine, and her *Playboy* interview. That's five major pieces on the then twenty-seven-year-old actress dating from 1998 to 2001. But in the year since those articles appeared Drew married and divorced Tom Green, successfully produced *Charlie's Angels* and a sequel, and had on her plate *Confessions of a Dangerous Mind, Duplex, So Love Returns, Barbarella, A Confederacy of Dunces* . . . so I knew I had to find more updated material.

I was able to pull up several articles off the Internet: "A Whole New Drew" from *Premiere,* "For Real This Time" and "Kidding Aside" from *People Weekly,* "Drew Love" from *Canadian TV Guide,* a short interview that appeared in *FHM,* "Drew Confessions" from *Allure,* "Personal Best" from *Us Weekly,* "The True Drew" from *Rosie* magazine, "This Girl Gets Through Anything" from *YM,* "The Risk It Took for Love" from *Marie Claire,* "The New Drew" from *Harper's Bazaar,* and "Tom, Drew Divvy Up Assets" from *E! Online News.* On a flight to New York I found a left-behind copy of *InStyle* on the seat next to mine that had a short blurb showing Drew and the Silent Movie Theatre in L.A., indicating she was a patron of the place. And in a book review by producer Lynda Obst on the Mollie Gregory book *Women Who Run the Show,* I read these words, which I duly highlighted, cut out, and put in my growing Barrymore file: "I first noticed the sea change [in Hollywood's value system] when I read Drew Barrymore—a woman I know to be smart and ambitious— deny with horror that she was a feminist. The word suddenly had an icky old-fashioned quality that she took for granted. It stunned me."

Now why would I spend so much time reading so many different pieces about this young actress? I'm making an example of Barrymore, but the fact is, no matter who I'm asked to interview or profile, I do the same kind of research, because I want to know everything I can about that person before I start writing my questions. In that way, I stay ahead of the curve, so to speak. I'm not looking to write something that has appeared somewhere else. I'm looking to go the next step, to get as much original material as I can. And the only way I know to do that is to know what's out there.

So I read the newer articles, highlighting whatever I had found that was not in the other articles, and then went through those highlights to form my questions. Let me show you what I mean.

Almost every article about Drew Barrymore contains the same biographical material: her early appearance in *E.T.,* how Steven Spielberg became a father figure to her, the disappearance of her father from her life, her preteen club years with her reckless mother, her early marijuana and cocaine usage, her being put in a mental institution at fourteen, her separation from her mother for over a decade, her first marriage, which lasted less than a month, her being a vegetarian, her getting back to meat, her flashing her boobs to David Letterman. OK, so we know all of that; why rehash it? It's basically unnecessary, because the majority of people who will pick up a movie magazine to read about Drew Barrymore will most likely know most of these details. What they want to know now is what she's been up to lately, where her head is now. But, of course, there are so many interesting details from her past, it's hard to dismiss the opportunity to ask her some questions that may not have been asked before.

So what did I learn from each of the pieces I read that I didn't get from the others?

From *Playboy* I learned that she's the reincarnation of her grandfather John, that her father is both crazy and a genius and a nomad from hell, that the most profound moment of her life was telling her mother she wanted to be an actress when she was three years old. Her drug of choice is comedy, she's made promises she couldn't keep, she's afraid of hygiene and food, she once spit into someone's coffee when she worked as a waitress, and she thinks Adam Sandler is the most amazing person in the world. From different issues of *US,* I learned that when she was in New York to host *Saturday Night Live* she fled the NBC studios upon hearing about the first anthrax cases in the city. Also, her *Bad Girls* director, Jonathan Kaplan, commented that Drew reminded him of Jodie Foster. In *Talk,* the writer considered her the "anti-Jodie." Also in *Talk,* she spoke about sitting on the set of *Charlie's Angels* when then-fiancé Tom Green went in for his operation for testicular cancer. *Talk* filled me in that she loved to read Charles Bukowski and T. S. Eliot and on the fact that Barrymore was the first actress–producer since Streisand and Fonda in the seventies to have made a ton of money by starring in and shaping movies to her own tastes. In the two *Movieline* pieces she spoke of the fire that destroyed her house as something that happened for a spiritual reason. She said she liked to watch old films with her family members in them, that Miramax boss Harvey Weinstein was her mentor, that Madonna was an early role model, that she wants to direct, and that she was going to be a good mother one day. (But that day was still in the distance, according to *Rosie* magazine, where Drew said,

"I'm too selfish now to have children.") *Rosie* also informed me that when she was a child she considered herself "this precocious little brat . . . who thought I knew everything." She went a bit further in *Marie Claire* when she said, "I was a belligerent, horrible little nightmare, totally out of control." From *Rolling Stone* I got that she didn't eat chocolate, feared the ocean, felt crazy inside her head, was profoundly taken by the book *Conversations with God,* and didn't think she was capable of being loved. She did offer a definition of love: "Someone who helps you and you help them . . . and you're just in this wonderment together." She told *Premiere* that her phone doesn't ring much and that she isn't someone who people think to hire. She also said that she and Tom Green were "so meant to be together" and that "the universe doesn't make it difficult for people to meet . . . it's up to you not to fuck it up." She mentioned therapy and that she had never met her half sister. *People Weekly* informed me that Courtney Love's eight-year-old daughter with Kurt Cobain preceded Barrymore down the aisle on her way to marrying Tom and that they installed a huge banner wishing a happy anniversary to a fictitious couple to try to fool the paparazzi. From Canada, *TV Guide* was the only one to report that Drew was deeply hurt by the *Saturday Night Live* send-up of the fire that destroyed their house. *FHM* told me more about what she looks for in a man, and what she found in Tom: "He's funny, extremely understanding, loves to go on adventures, he's kind and a good communicator and inspires me to do good things in life and be a good person." *Allure* reported that at the premiere of *Charlie's Angels* at Buckingham Palace, she sat next to Prince Charles and made him laugh when she grabbed Lucy Liu's boob accidentally. She spoke about the irony of both she and her mother posing in *Playboy* and going out with young musicians in *Marie Claire.* To *YM* she admitted to treating everyone "with a lack of judgment" and crying over a letter of appreciation her partner Nan Juvonen wrote to her. From *Harper's Bazaar* I learned that she yanked her first gray hair and saved it in a Ziploc bag and that she's always trying to make her breasts look smaller. And according to *E! Online News*, Tom Green got the $2 million Studio City house and Drew kept her L.A. pad and a cash payment of $307,603 from her ex to make up the difference.

All the positive talk about Tom and her great love for him made me wonder what went wrong, why did such a great flame burn out so quickly? I knew I'd ask her, but I wanted to have some idea of the answer myself before seeing her. And finally, in the January 12, 2002, issue of *People Weekly*, there was this: "During a Nov. 1 *Tonight Show* appearance Barrymore admitted to being controlling at times in the marriage." I missed that TV appearance, but that's what I was looking for. Tom Green was the one who filed for divorce. The great prankster just couldn't take being under someone else's control. And Drew didn't trust enough, coming from the dysfunctional family she came from, to give up control of any part of her life. Then in *Marie Claire* I found her saying about her attraction to "bad boys," that they validated the fact that she was a bad girl, but what would eventually drive them away is that she'd get in their faces all the time, which made her bad boys claustrophobic. This was an area to explore. This is why one does research.

Because an interview is a pact between you and the subject, your job is to not bore the person you're questioning. You want fresh, alert responses and the best way to ensure that is to ask fresh and probing questions, to go deeper than what she has said in the past. It doesn't matter if it's Drew Barrymore or John Ashcroft, Don DeLillo or Matt Groening—if you're being paid to interview someone, your job is to do the best interview you can, and thus you must read everything available on your subject, you must digest what is said, you must look for nuances, for subtleties, for thoughts hinted at but not fully expressed, and then delve into those areas.

Here's how I do it.

Out of all of my research I began to write my questions, putting them in some kind of order so that when we spoke, I could look under a topic in bold caps and underlined—for instance, **FAMILY** or **RELATIONSHIPS** or **TEEN YEARS**—and have a series of questions that relate to that topic. I've found that when you make order out of chaos it helps move a conversation along, especially if you're limited in time. (Ken Auletta works in a similar fashion. "Generally," he says, "I plan out an interview so certain types of questions are grouped together. That way I'm controlling the rhythm of the interview.")

The questions I prepared for Drew can be found in Appendix 1 at the end of this book, but for this chapter, I will give you some of the questions I wrote after reading the articles mentioned above and Drew's answers, to demonstrate how you turn something someone says into something to further explore.

Once my questions were written and put in an order that seemed to work as an imaginary conversation in my mind, I felt ready to talk to her. There were 158 questions, which usually takes about three hours to ask—my rough estimate is a minute a question, though I find that during the first half hour I ask fewer questions than during the last half hour, when I may say something like "I know our time is short, and I've still got a lot of questions, so let's see how many we can get in." By then we are warmed up, the subject sees what I'm after, that I'm hoping to pry whatever good quotes I can from her. And we're now both working to get through this.

The actual interview with Barrymore took five hours, but for a while I wasn't even sure, after all my preparation, that it was going to happen. It kept getting postponed due to her movie schedule—at first it was going to be on a weekend, then during the week, then when she had a day off when she wasn't going to be traveling. When a date was finally set, her publicist called to say that Drew wanted to see my résumé. I've been doing these interviews for over thirty years, have interviewed Nobel Prize winners, Oscar, Emmy, and Grammy winners, great artists, writers, scientists, and businessmen, and no one had previously asked for my credentials. Drew Barrymore wanted them. So I sent them on and waited to hear if we were still on. Word came back on the day she wanted to see me, and I packed my equipment, printed out the questions, and headed to Sony's studios in Culver City.

We met in her trailer on the lot and in between her filming an action sequence for the *Charlie's Angels* sequel I managed to ask most of my questions. Barrymore's a good interview. She's very quotable, and my editor was satisfied because a lot of what Drew said she had never said before. And that, to me, is how one determines the quality of an interview. How original is it? How thought-provoking? How provocative? How many quotes might be pulled out and reprinted elsewhere?

What were some of the best things she said that day? Well, here you go.

COMMENT

··

A friend had heard Drew talking about her love of the Beatles and had mentioned it to me. I thought it was a good way to ease into our conversation . . . and wound up using what she said near the beginning.

Q: Weren't you on the radio talking about why life is better because of the Beatles?

BARRYMORE: I knew that you were going to be different. Yeah, that's the meaningful stuff in life. Public radio, and trying to save it. Particularly when it has to do with the Beatles. Every month I pick a different Beatle song—right now I'm back on "It's Only Love." But I'm also into "Yes It Is," as well. And the Anthology version of "Mother Nature's Son." There's a weird book called *The Guide to the Advanced Soul*, someone gave it to me many years ago, and if you open it, whatever your problem is there is a passage that will pertain, sort of like a fortune cookie, only more insightful. To me, putting on a Beatles song is like that. Whatever dilemma you're going through, if you put on a Beatles song, they will answer it. I also love that you can make love to their songs, you can drive to them, live, cook, clean, be sad, happy, just all of life works to that music.

Q: Who's comparable to the Beatles for you today?

BARRYMORE: I really love Beck—he's my favorite. He does to me what the Beatles do. I just went and saw both his concerts again. I know his body of work and his lyrics so well. What Beck is doing today is what the Beatles did back then, which is to explore every genre of music—all different instruments, styles, ethnicities, cultures—that blows me away. Beck will do folk, rap, funk, big band, country, weird disco—I love when you can't pigeonhole someone.

COMMENT

The kind of remark that allows you to change the subject smoothly.

Q: That would apply to you as well. Your company's next film is *Duplex*, where you and Ben Stiller attempt to murder an old woman for her house. Sounds like a dark comedy. Do you consider it groundbreaking in any way?

BARRYMORE: I do. On NPR they were talking about how *The Graduate* had changed the Industry in a time when everything was about Westerns and musicals. When I think about my favorite filmmakers—Preston Sturges, Hal Ashby—I think of where are these men and these stories? But they're out there—the Wes Andersons, the Spike Jonzes. There always will be people making incredible films, that are smart, wild, interesting, that stimulate your mind. I still love a broad comedy—I need that stuff like medicine—if I've had a bad day, just give me some Jim Carrey and I'm good to go! Woody Allen is the greatest comedian ever, but his comedy is so smart that I have to know

COMMENT

The question was about her film, but she's chosen to tell us about her favorite film-makers, past and present, and her favorite film, which she then breaks down. So, though she's jumping around here, she provides a lot of information about the films in her life.

the film so well to enjoy it, otherwise I'm going, "My God, last year I didn't understand that reference." *Annie Hall* is my favorite film— it's the most amalgamated film that ever existed. He broke all the rules, he breaks the fourth wall down. It's a comedy, it's a drama, it's about love, life, it's heartbreaking. They don't end up together in the end. It goes backwards, forwards, it's nonlinear, it's narrative. He has the best shot in all of cinema—when they're walking on the beach and it's just the shot of the weeds rustling in the wind and they're not even in the frame, it's just their voices talking. There's no rationality to how he tells the story, it's all over the place—and yet it's completely coherent. It's movies like that that justify why I spend my life in a box trying to go out there and make them.

Q: In an *L.A. Times* book review for the book *Women Who Run the Show*, producer Lynda Obst wrote about the changes in the way young women view feminism: "I first noticed the sea change when I read Drew Barrymore—a woman I know to be smart and ambitious —deny with horror that she was a feminist. The word suddenly had an icky old-fashioned quality that she took for granted. It stunned me." Were you aware that you've stunned producers like Obst?

COMMENT

A catchy pull quote.

BARRYMORE: I wasn't, but now I am. I think every feminist pukes and wants to punch me in the face. When I was growing up feminism had a taste in my mouth that there didn't seem to be that love for men in it. There was a lot of male bashing. I don't like men who suppress women, I'm an equalist. I don't want to think that women are better, or superior. I just want it to be equal. There are two sexes and I don't understand why it should be any other way. But I understand that it took feminists to pave the way for a woman of my age to have the opportunities that I do.

COMMENT

Again, this leads to a way to smoothly transition to another topic, somewhat related.

Q: Speaking of opportunities, where are you with *Barbarella?*

[*She answers, but instead of printing the whole interview, I want to demonstrate transitions here, and show how to build an interview based on new research, getting new insights.*]

ON TOM GREEN

Q: You thought you found it all in Tom: "He's funny, extremely understanding, loves to go on adventures, he's kind and a good communicator and inspires me to do good things in life and be a good person."

BARRYMORE: All true.

Q: So what was missing?

BARRYMORE: [*Long pause, the only time during the interview speech doesn't come quickly*] The ability to see the big picture. Trust in time. It was a big problem for us.

> **COMMENT**
> *A way of indicating this is still a sensitive and emotional subject.*

> **COMMENT**
> *Often people answer in a way that's not satisfactory, so don't be afraid to call them on it, to try and get them to be more explicit.*

Q: That's still abstract. What was the big picture?

BARRYMORE: It's the ability to allow a relaxation that there will be time. We weren't sure how to function in our rela— tionship due to a lack of trust and time.

> **COMMENT**
> *I would still have liked her to give some examples, but this was as much as she was giving up . . . so time to take a different tack.*

Q: You played your relationship out in public. Was that a mistake?

BARRYMORE: Yes.

Q: And will you do it differently in the future?

BARRYMORE: Yes.

Q: Did it become more a performance than a relationship with Tom?

BARRYMORE: It felt like a circus.

COMMENT

This is revealing. It is her marriage she is talking about.

Q: Did he feel the same way, or did he enjoy that?

BARRYMORE: Well, so much of his job was about that. And I played along with it because I thought it was fun and funny. But you always have to remain who you truly are, you can't become another person.

Q: On *The Tonight Show* you admitted to being controlling at times in the marriage. Was that a problem for Tom?

BARRYMORE: It wasn't a problem for me and Tom, I was speaking more about myself. The greatest downfall that I've experienced in relationships is one word: expectations. If you can somehow excoriate the expectations out of things, which is not to say that you don't need things and you don't have hopes. There are specifications and compromises in relationships that people can do to ease each other's fears or the things in their personalities or their pasts that make them who they are:

COMMENT

When the answer isn't clear, keep asking.

there is a way to be gentle about that. But too many expectations just drive people nuts.

Q: And the expectations are . . . that it's going to be perfect? That it's going to be something special?

BARRYMORE: For the most part it's: Do it my way.

COMMENT

Pay dirt!

Q: Your expectations are it's either your way or the highway?

BARRYMORE: And the other person's too. When it comes down to expectations, if you could just keep it to one term, at its core someone's going to do it the way you want them to do it, and that's just not the way people function.

Q: Which makes you irritated, frustrated, angry, temperamental?

COMMENT

I'm trying to get some kind of understanding and closure here. One can only pursue this for so long before moving on.

BARRYMORE: Less and less as I get older, but the other side of me is I want so much to make people happy that I go way out of my way to be a people pleaser, and have in the past forgotten all about my own needs.

COMMENT

Notice the transition from one kind of relationship to another.

Q: Your needs often clashed with your father's, who often wasn't there for you. You've been very open about your disappointment with your father, calling him crazy, a genius, and a nomad from hell. How crazy and what kind of genius?

BARRYMORE: Crazy because he won't accept any responsibility for himself. He only looks to others to take care of him. He's totally obsessed with weird little phobias that cripple his life. Genius because he is incredibly smart about spirituality. And a total genius because he's a fucking mad poet. He says things that I have to go write down. He'll say, "Daughter, I need food." And I'll say, "Oh, are you hungry?" And he'll go, "Hungry? I was hungry since the day I was born!" That's fucking cool, man. He'll talk about the flickering Buddha in the corner, or the bush he's having sex with which quivers when he walks by it. And I'll say to him, "I can't handle you, you're too crazy." But it's all like genius

COMMENT

Drew has often said in interviews that her father was crazy, et cetera, but she has never been specific. Here she gives some details. Doesn't sound that crazy to me . . . until she gets to the bush . . .

poetry. With my dad, he is the only relationship that I've been able to have in my life that is as profound and important to me, but that I've had a total lack of expectations with. When I was a kid I didn't know how to have a lack of expectations, but since I was a teenager I've made total peace with that man. You can't expect anything from him, and whatever little gems you get, you take them, write them down. He's just a mad man who lives out in a world that's interesting and neat to me. But he's not a dad. He'll never provide me with anything. If anything he's a taker, not a giver. But I accept that. My relationship with my mother is different. I had different expectations of her growing up.

Q: Spielberg, who became a father figure, recalled a time when you were six telling him you had a better way of doing a scene in *E.T.* Do you remember that?

BARRYMORE: I don't remember that moment, but I remember most everything about it like it was yesterday. I do remember he would ask me to come up with lines, which was intimidating. But it was like, Okay. I'm sure it was way less intimidating then than it would be now. When Woody Allen asked me to improv I thought I was going to vomit in the corner. But when I was six years old, I was so much more bold. I can't believe the audacity I had when I was a kid. I was so non-self-conscious. I'm way less like that now.

Q: You have a half brother and two half sisters, all older than you. . . . .

BARRYMORE: I have two half sisters? I only know of one.

Q: Blyth and Jessica?

BARRYMORE: I don't know the story of Jessica. I've heard of her.

Q: Who is she?

BARRYMORE: I don't know!

Q: She might be your half sister?

BARRYMORE: It's never really been explained clearly to me. It's not like the family gets together and talks about it.

Q: So the ones you know are Blyth and John?

BARRYMORE: I've never met Blyth.

COMMENT

There is no way to know this without having read about it.

Q: *Bad Girls* director Jonathan Kaplan said that you reminded him of Jodie Foster. In *Talk* magazine they wrote that you were the anti-Jodie. Different people, different perceptions. Who knows you better?

BARRYMORE: I think we are very different. She has had an extraordinary grace about her that I lack. She's had an intelligence and studiousness that I'm too fumbly for. But I do respect her consistency and longevity, and her love of film. The fact that she became a director is a great goal and dream of mine. I've always seen her as a role model. And, by the way, she was the hottest kid ever. You watch her old movies—she was one groovy ass chick.

Q: Do you still have your first gray hair?

BARRYMORE: Yes, I keep it in a plastic bag and wrote on it "My first gray hair," and George Clooney wrote on the other side of it, "And my last." But it wasn't—I'm getting patches of them now. It's freaky. It's like, Oh my God, I'm getting older. I see little wrinkles and things change.

Q: What other things do you save?

COMMENT

I knew about the gray hair, but this follow up gives us more insight into Drew.

BARRYMORE: I save a lot of things. I love saving concert tickets, little photographs that I take, a feather that I'll find on the beach, matchbooks from restaurants, corks from wine bottles on a special night, someone's birthday candles from their cake. If somebody writes me a note, I save it. Especially if it's a lover.

Q: How many years have you been in therapy?

BARRYMORE: Thirteen going on fourteen. I have an incredible therapist now. I never liked going to therapists who were yes-men and who would tell me I was a good person. Fuck that! Tell me what my problem is, I want to fix it, let's have an intellectually stimulating conversation about what I'm not realizing. Show me how to get there. I'm always hesitant about the term self-help because it sounds strange, but furthering your mind and being more self-aware makes you a better person.

Q: Your grandfather is the subject of a famous story—when Raoul Walsh took his body from the morgue and brought it to Errol Flynn's house. Do you know anything about that legend?

BARRYMORE: My dad said it wasn't true, but then he alluded that it was true, so I don't know what to believe. They parodied it in that great movie *S.O.B.* I hope it's true. I hope to God my friends steal my body out of a morgue and throw a party when I'm dead.

COMMENT
....................................➤
Just before I went to interview her a friend of mine reminded me of this incident and wondered whether it was true. I looked up the story in Flynn's My Wicked, Wicked Ways. *Drew's answer gave me my ending. Earlier, when I asked about the Beatles, it was also something a friend mentioned to me. So I got my beginning and ending from friends. It pays to have friends.*

CONVINCING A SUBJECT TO SIT WITH YOU

Between the time the SLA kidnapped her from her Berkeley apartment on February 4, 1974, and her arrest nineteen months later on September 18, 1975, after which she would eventually be sentenced to seven years in prison, Patricia Hearst, granddaughter of William Randolph Hearst, heiress to America's largest privately owned media and land conglomerate, appeared on the covers of *Time* and *Newsweek* (as well as *Rolling Stone, U.S. News & World Report,* and numerous other publications) over a dozen times, setting the record for most covers in the shortest time frame. Her autograph on any of these covers is considered a bit of the Holy Grail among collectors of such things because she refused to sign any of them. I know this because she told me so when I plunked the February 2, 1976, *Newsweek* in front of her one day and asked for her John Hancock. "I don't sign those," she said. "And when people send them to me, which they do all the time, I keep them. I won't return them."

This was one of numerous revelations Ms. Hearst told me when I was with her. And this is how I became the lucky journalist who got *the* Patty Hearst interview for *Playboy* (March 1982) after she had served two years in prison before President Jimmy Carter commuted her sentence.

"Patty Hearst is coming with her husband for breakfast to the mansion," Christie Hefner told me over the phone. "Why don't you join us?"

"You mean to see if she'd agree to do the interview?" I asked.

"You never know," Christie said.

Hearst and Christie Hefner had run into each other in the past. Both were young, media-connected women who could empathize with each other. I was sure when Patty got kidnapped, Christie began thinking about bodyguards.

So I joined them at the Playboy Mansion, home of Papa Hugh and his ever-changing warren of Playmates. Christie resided in Chicago, but was in L.A. on company business. This breakfast was part of that business.

It was 8 A.M. when I walked through the marbled foyer into the dining room where Christie, Patty, and her husband and former bodyguard, Bernie Shaw, were already sitting. Christie made the introductions and I joined in the polite small talk one makes when one has so much more on one's mind to say. After all, here was the young lady who was the subject of one of the greatest FBI manhunts in American history—the Osama bin Laden of her day. After being blindfolded and held in a closet by her kidnappers for fifty-seven days, she decided to join them. She made a tape that was played on every radio and television station, saying, "I have been given the choice of being released in a safe area or joining the forces of the Symbionese Liberation Army and fighting for my freedom and the freedom of all oppressed people. I have chosen to stay and fight. . . . I have been given the name Tania, after a comrade who fought alongside Che [Guevara] in Bolivia. . . . I have learned how vicious the pig really is, and [my] comrades are teaching me to attack with even greater viciousness." Then she and this fervid band of eight revolutionaries proceeded to rob a few banks and accidentally kill an innocent bystander named Myrna Opsahl. They holed up in safe houses in Sacramento, San Francisco, Anaheim, and L.A. until the L.A. police got a tip where they were staying and torched the place, killing most of the members. Hearst and the Harrises (Bill and Emily) escaped incineration that day because they had gone to rob a sporting goods store. For months after that, Hearst believed if she tried to turn herself in she would be killed. The attorney general of the United States said he was convinced she was a terrorist. She figured her parents would want nothing to do with her. So even when she was alone, she didn't think about surfacing. She was, effectively, a prisoner of her own mind, a mind that had been brainwashed into believing that the revolution was the only way to go, and that the cop pigs must be offed.

Where's Patty? became the "Where's Waldo?" of dinner conversations across the country. Everyone, it seemed, had an opinion about her. Was she a victim or a convert? A young vulnerable woman susceptible to being brainwashed by a rowdy band of louts or a spoiled heiress who had found adventure, excitement, and acceptance among a daring group of forward-thinking activists?

And once she was captured and interrogated by psychiatrists, lawyers, and law officials for thousands of hours, what was left of her? Who, really, was she and what had she become?

These were the thoughts going through my mind as I passed the butter, salted my eggs, and talked about the beautiful koi in the pond by the swimming pool. "Speaking of the pool," Hearst said as we finished our coffee, "are we going to do the Jacuzzi?"

"Sure," Christie said. "You'll join us, won't you?" she asked me.

"Of course," I said, feeling just a tad uneasy. I hadn't been prepared for this turn of events. I didn't have a bathing suit with me, and I wasn't sure if one was required. I didn't know the proper etiquette for such a morning dip.

"We can change in the dressing rooms behind the grotto," Christie said. "Larry, there are bins of suits there you can choose from."

So, that was a relief. I didn't want my lack of six-pack abs or anything else to be held against me when I popped the question to Ms. Hearst of whether she would consider spending a couple of days talking to me.

But I was in for a Playboy Mansion lesson: you don't get invited into the storied grotto when your waist is above thirty-two inches. At least that's what the bathing suits in the bin indicated. There must have been three dozen to choose from, and none of them made it past my derriere. My thirty-six-inch waist might as well have been a fat man's forty-four inches. In fact, that's exactly what it should have been when I found the one pair of boxers hidden in the last bin that could wrap around my waist—with eight big inches to spare! Even with the waist strings pulled tight, I had to hold on to the suit to keep it from slipping to my ankles.

"What happened to you?" Patty Hearst asked when I finally made it into the grotto, where the series of Jacuzzis were located. It was like an above-ground cave, with mood lighting and speakers cleverly disguised as faux rocks. The actor Robert

Culp once described this party-favorite site as a "wonderful sybaritic womb."

"I had to make a phone call," I lied, my hand tightly gripping the bathing suit as I eased into the hot water between Christie and Patty.

Whooooooosshhh!!!!

Just as the water rose above my waist so did the suit, like a small parachute.

"What the hell . . . ?" Patty's husband Bernie said, trying to stifle a laugh.

I basically did my Inspector Clouseau best to ignore the five-hundred-pound gorilla in front of us, as I pushed down on the bloated suit to get the water and air out.

"So Patty," I transitioned smoothly, "do you plan on doing any interviews to promote your book?"

And that is how I got Patty Hearst to agree to do the one and only in-depth interview about her ordeal with the SLA, her life as Tania, her life on the lam, her capture, imprisonment, and eventual release.

So if you ever get a call to meet someone in the news, take the meeting. And be open to whatever may happen, keeping one objective in mind: landing the interview.

OF COURSE, it doesn't always work out the way you'd like it to. When the race for the Democratic presidential nomination began to heat up in 2003, I had the opportunity to join a breakfast fund-raiser for North Carolina senator John Edwards. He was the youngest of the potential candidates and *Playboy* had wanted to interview him. But my editor told me that he had turned down the magazine's request. I figured I had nothing to lose by going to the breakfast and speaking to him afterward. When I was introduced to the senator I spoke bluntly:

"I understand you didn't want to do a *Playboy* interview, Senator, but let me tell you why I think you should. You're not the front-runner; there's some question about your inexperience and your youth; you didn't serve in the armed forces and after 9/11 and Iraq, it's evident the country will want to elect a leader who understands the military; only the right wing of the country will get annoyed that you appeared in *Playboy,* but that's not your constituency; and when Jimmy Carter made headlines from his *Playboy* interview, it didn't seem to hurt him—in fact, a lot of young people voted for him because of his honesty, and that may have helped get him elected. It's a risk, but so is running for president. With the size of the potential audience, and the fact that if you're lucky it will get more attention just because it's *Playboy,* it may be a risk worth taking."

It was a mouthful, but I only had a few minutes with the senator and I took my best shot. He said, "I never turned it down, I don't even know about it; that has to do with my communication people."

When I heard that I held out some hope. Over the next few weeks I dealt with many of his people, trying to pin down Edwards. I spoke with two lawyers who gave him advice, a publicist and his assistant, the senator's press secretary, his chief of staff, his communications director, an outside consultant, and a campaign pollster. I was told by one of the lawyers that he would do the interview, and by his press secretary that he wouldn't. I was put on hold, passed from one to another, and finally I realized a John Edwards interview in *Playboy* just wasn't going to happen. What it told me was that Edwards was just another politician who wouldn't challenge his pollsters, who wouldn't take risks early in his campaign (doing a *Playboy* interview is always risky, not just for what might be said, but because certain segments of our society still don't approve of women posing *sans* clothes), and who would not wind up with the nomination in 2004. The one thing about Bush that I wasn't seeing with the Democrats at that time was that Bush was willing to take risks. I didn't like the risks he took, but he gave the impression that he was willing to stand by his decisions. Edwards was showing me that he didn't yet make decisions. It was still all tied up in committee.

WHEN I REFLECT on the number of times I have had to sell myself or the publication I was working for to get an interview, I wonder how on earth I've continued doing this as a profession. In the seventies and eighties it wasn't this hard, unless it was a Brando or a Streisand one was dealing with. But as magazines proliferated, as more and more publications vied to get a certain number of people on their covers, the competition grew. Sometimes it helped when I was "the guy who did Brando" and sometimes it didn't, when the person being wooed was insecure and didn't think he measured up to Brando.

The way I try to convince people to agree to let me interview them is that I let them know that I will be prepared, that I won't waste their time, that I will do my best not only to challenge but to stimulate them. I remember once that Alec Baldwin was on the fence, so he asked to meet me. I went to his trailer on a studio lot and he proceeded to tell me all the things he didn't want to talk about—it was pretty much everything I had hoped to bring up. But what could I do? He was being up front about it: Don't ask me these things, and if you do, then I don't want to do the interview. So I agreed, went home, reworked my questions, went back to see him, and the first thing he said was "That stuff I said yesterday? Forget about it. Ask me anything you want." So I did. And when the piece was published he called me in a rage: "Why did you print that stuff, I told you I didn't want to talk about that stuff!"

AS YOU MAY RECALL with Streisand, it was my appealing to her as a fellow "artist" that finally got her to talk to me without having to sign away ownership of the interview. With Brando, it may have been my liberal politics and the fact that I had been in the Peace Corps, which I told him about when we discussed doing the *Playboy* interview over the phone.

Sometimes you don't have to convince someone, they come to you with a story, but that is very rare. After serving jail time for attacking a police officer, after allegedly attacking a woman he was dating, Christian Slater called me (I had interviewed him once before, and had also talked about him for an *E! True Hollywood Story* on TV) and said he didn't want to have to spend the rest of his life talking about what had happened to him. He wanted to tell his story once and never again. He wanted to tell it in *Rolling Stone,* and would I be interested in doing the interview with him? I called *Rolling Stone,* which said yes, and we did it (see the next chapter). But that's a pretty unusual occurrence. More often, you're making calls, talking to assistants and publicists, making a case for why their client should talk to you.

CHANGING A RELUCTANT SUBJECT'S MIND

What happens after someone has agreed to talk to you, but then at the last minute pulls out? You've done the research, you've written your questions, you've devoted your full attention to the subject for probably weeks, sometimes longer, on this person . . . and suddenly you're told it isn't happening. It's pretty deflating, like discovering that a piece of pottery you've uncovered is a fake or a first edition book you've located after months of searching is a book club edition.

It's happened to me for all different reasons with Alfred Hitchcock, Fred Astaire, Leonard Bernstein, Debra Messing, Robert Zemeckis, Chuck Barris, Johnny Depp, Aretha Franklin, Faye Dunaway, Jennifer Love Hewitt, Jack Nicholson, Colin Farrell, Norman Mailer, Henry Fonda, and Willie Shoemaker. Sometimes a person pulls out because of scheduling problems; sometimes because they realize that the magazine they've agreed to appear in shows naked ladies; sometimes it's because they can't agree on a photographer to shoot their picture; sometimes it's because they're ill, or insecure, or overbooked. And sometimes you never find out.

When this happens, I always make an attempt to convince the person that he or she should reconsider. Often this is a waste of time—usually once someone has made up his mind not to talk to you, that's it. But with three of the above subjects who said no at the last minute, I was able to get them to change their minds.

With Henry Fonda, it was actually his wife, Shirlee, who intervened after her husband had complained that he just wasn't up to talking to anyone about his life. Fonda was ill and slowly dying in 1981 and Shirlee wasn't ready to lose him. She thought that perhaps if I could get him to open up he'd start thinking about his life and about his family, his art, his bees, and hopefully come back to her. She called and asked to see me. "Do you think you could talk to Henry over a period of days, for as long as possible actually?" she wanted to know. "Right now he's not talking at all, but if you could get him to talk for an hour or two each day, it might be very good therapy for him."

This was a first for me. I had never been asked to keep an interview going for as long as possible. Usually it was the opposite. With Fonda, when I arrived he had someone help him out of his chair and he'd walk, slowly, for fifteen or twenty minutes before settling back to talk to me. His voice was hoarse from little use, but his memory was strong, and Shirlee, listening from the kitchen, was pleased to hear her husband's voice again. Even when he sounded cranky and cantankerous. Especially then!

WHEN NORMAN MAILER'S secretary let me know that he wouldn't have the time to see me on his book tour (he was promoting *Ancient Evenings* back in 1983) I was so disappointed that I sent him a $90 telegram (this was before we had faxes and e-mails) that let him know how I had read his writing as a teenager and had always admired the way his mind worked and that I had prepared diligently to talk to him after he had agreed to see me, and that he really shouldn't renege on an agreement. I guess he took pity on this guy who would spend so much on a telegram and relented.

JOCKEY WILLIE SHOEMAKER had agreed to be interviewed and I had done my research and prepared my questions and was about to leave my house to drive down to Del Mar to see him when he called to say that he was thinking about our interview and he just didn't feel he had that much to say. I said that I was just out the door, the drive down would take me about two-and-a-half hours, and if he still felt that way when I got there, I'd turn around and go home. He wasn't expecting that I wouldn't take no for an answer, and agreed, as long as I understood he still didn't want to do the interview. When I got there, he let me in and we talked for a few hours. I went with him to the racetrack to watch him ride (this was in 1982, before his paralyzing car accident), and we went back to his house and talked some more. In the end, when I worked over the material, I realized that there was a reason they called him the Silent Shoe. Because he wasn't very articulate. He answered my questions without supplying the telling details, the wonderful anecdotes. I had to fill those in with my questions, which my editor pointed out to me when he rejected the piece. "The questions are better than the answers," he said. The interview never made it into print.

YOU WIN SOME, you lose some. The Mailer and Fonda interviews were worth the extra effort; with Shoemaker, he was legendary enough to go after, in spite of his reluctance. What I should have done with my time with Shoemaker was turn it into a profile—use only those quotes that were exceptional, and write around them. You can't do anything when you don't have the material, so don't give up on the first no. But you also can't always turn someone around, and if you can't be convincing on your second or third request, best to start looking for another subject.

LEARNING TO BE PATIENT

Marlon Brando once asked me how I could keep on interviewing actors. How much did they really have to say? I've thought about that over the years—after all, once one has interviewed Brando, whom many consider our greatest actor, why continue to talk to actors who are not his equal? This has never bothered me. As John Travolta once told the Actors Studio audience, "People are interesting. You just have to ask them the right questions."

One of the fascinating things I've learned through talking to actors, as well as writers, musicians, and anyone else, is that no one's the same, everyone's got a story to tell, and if you scratch below the surface, the stories are all unique. But you often need patience to find that uniqueness.

I learned patience when I first went to interview Elliott Gould back in 1974.

Gould's publicist asked me to meet him at Elliott's rented house in Beverly Hills at 9 P.M. The publicist and I were there on time but Gould was not. His door was open and we waited inside, but after an hour the publicist said he had some place to go, leaving me alone in the house. Another hour went by before Gould arrived. He turned on the television as I took out my tape recorder and I said that I couldn't record over the TV. "So let's go in the other room and put on Marvin Gaye," he said.

"We can listen to music or we can do this interview, but not both at the same time," I said.

He didn't say anything. I mentioned that I, too, was from Bensonhurst in Brooklyn. He chewed on some peanuts. I knew that he had once been a spokesboy for Fox's U-Bet chocolate syrup and brought it up. "Information," he said. He hadn't apologized for being two hours late and wasn't responding to my attempts to break the ice. He may have been pissed off that I didn't want to compete with the TV or listen to Marvin Gaye, and I didn't really know where to go with him. I asked him how long he lived in his house, whether he ever went back to Brooklyn, what he thought of the Dodgers. He remained unresponsive. Finally I said that maybe it was the wrong time to do this interview, the hour was late, and we could try again another day.

"What do you mean?" he said as if snapping out of a dream. "We're talking, aren't we?"

"I wouldn't exactly call it that."

"You can't just rush into things and expect answers. It takes time. I don't know what you're looking for, what you want to see, but I'm talking to ya and all you've got to do is stay at it. You want some stew?"

"It's almost midnight," I said. "I ate a few hours ago."

"My mother made it. Eat again."

"Does your mother live with you?"

"Does yours?"

"You lived in the same room with your parents until you were eleven, didn't you?" I asked, trying to use the stew as a way into his childhood.

"That's right. We behaved like savage fuckin' animals, trying to act like something that we weren't," he said. "I was caught in the insecurity of thinking that maybe there was something wrong with me. I didn't know enough to be what I was supposed to be. There was no harmony."

"Wasn't that around the time when your name changed from Goldstein to Gould?"

"Yeah, it happened on TV. It was this silly little show, singing and dancing with a group of kids. They said, 'Your name is Gould not Goldstein.' It wasn't even changed legally but that doesn't matter because you are what you're known as, no matter who you are. Sometimes I am Elliott Goldstein. Elliott Goldstein is a lot younger than Elliott Gould, so sometimes I gotta be Elliott Goldstein. Then I say fuck Elliott Goldstein. But sometimes I like being Elliott Goldstein. There's much more I discover about Elliott Goldstein than I do about Elliott Gould. Elliott Gould just works for him."

Somewhere in there is an existential statement about identity and fame that I've yet to decipher, but I was beginning to get the hang of how Gould's mind worked, which was scattered like a running back going left, then right, looking for a little light to go forward. When I tried to dig deeper into this matter of dual identities, he changed direction and decided he didn't really have a split personality. "Elliott Gould, Elliott Goldstein, Elliott Goldstein, Elliott Gould—it's all the same person."

Whoever that person was, I couldn't seem to capture him in words. After our first two-hour session I transcribed the tapes and saw that in cold print it made little sense. I went back a second and a third time and listened to his offbeat answers to my straight questions.

For example when I asked him about the values of those in his industry versus people who have nothing to do with the movies, he boiled it down to one word: greed. "That's what causes distortion and deviation," he said. "The forests are disappearing and life is being eliminated. I see all these science-fiction pictures coming true, with robots governing the finite. We're pretty magnificent . . . and also very corrupt. We're greedy. We kill things. We don't know what to do with ourselves. Yet our potential is so flexible, we can be anything. It took all of this time to get where we are and in the last twenty to fifty years look what has happened. What we're going to have here on earth is going to be very much like what Hitler was devising, in terms of an aspect of humanity other than as a sociopolitical farce of conformity. At that time we will no longer be conscious, we will just be robots, that will be our end. Then we will be the aliens that we all are looking for in the sky. We will become all the things that we're afraid of."

Remember, this was a celebrity interview I was doing. My editors were expecting to read what Elliott Gould thought about once being married to Barbra Streisand, about working with Robert Altman, about *M*A*S*H* and *The Long Goodbye* and being the first American actor to work with Ingmar Bergman. What I was getting was inner and outer space and I was actually encouraging him by attempting to follow his stream-of-consciousness thinking.

"A lot of what you say ties you to humanity," I said. "You don't speak with a lot of I's. Is that a result of analysis?"

"I think there's one I," Gould answered. "There's basically one brain and one life. To be able to be open enough and trust yourself enough to just know that wherever it's at, the information is there. It's like the Universal sign in the movies, or like the belt around Saturn. Whatever information is there, wherever you're at, it all comes to you."

Whatever came to me definitely didn't come through to my *Newsday* editor when he read the copy I sent him. "He sounds too stoned," he said. "We can't run this." I had never failed with an interview before and I didn't want all my time with Gould to go to waste, so I asked to go back one last time and see if I could make it more accessible.

There were two *Playboy* Playmates at his house, along with Jimmy Caan, Warren Berlinger, and four other of Gould's friends. Music was blasting, food was being consumed, the smell of weed was in the air. Elliott was manipulating a pinball machine when I entered and told him that the interview had been rejected but that I was sure we could make it work if we kept talking. "Go ahead, ask me anything," he shouted over the noise in the house. I knew I wasn't going to be able to separate him from the pinball machine, so I just took out my tape recorder and asked him about something I had heard about a film he never completed in 1970 called *A Glimpse of Tiger*. Was it true that Warner Brothers collected a large sum of money on an insurance policy taken out for that film because they claimed Gould was crazy?

"Yeah," he said, never looking away from his pinball game. "I've been thinking about opening up the case and suing for damage, detrimental to my character."

One of Gould's friends heard the topic of conversation and suggested that he not talk about this for the record. But Gould didn't care; if I wanted to know, he'd tell me. I didn't know the details, so I could only ask him broadly what it was all about. And he told me: how David Carradine had introduced him to

LSD, which he began experimenting with. How he would come on the set sucking on a pacifier, or bare-chested with cotton balls attached to his chest, his behavior scaring his costar Kim Darby and confusing his director, Anthony Harvey. Coming off a *Time* magazine cover story and being named the top male box-office attraction that year, Gould also became moody and temperamental. When he told Harvey that he didn't really understand the script as well as Gould did and should let the actors act without his interference, producer Ray Stark hired a few guards to be on the set at all times. When Gould saw the guns holstered around their waists he balked. "Don't ask me to come someplace where somebody is there ready to shoot me with a gun," he protested. "I'm ready to go all the way with your minds, but not with your pistols." He walked off to simmer down, and when he returned and said he was ready to shoot, they told him to forget it. He went to see Stark, whose son had recently died. Stark said to him, "What are you trying to do to me, Elliott? You want to give me a heart attack?" Gould said no, he didn't want anything to happen to him, especially after what had happened to his son. At this Stark got angry and threw a punch at Gould. Stark was a much smaller and older man and Elliott didn't want to fight him, so he stepped away and Stark fell down. But word got out that Gould had struck Stark and that only led to further disharmony. The picture was canceled and the studio got two psychiatrists to testify that Gould was crazy, and on that basis the Fireman's Insurance Fund coughed up a half-million dollars. No one checked with Gould—not even the two psychiatrists. It didn't smell right, but that's the way things go in Hollywood. One day you're on top, the next day you're written off as a bad risk. Elliott Gould didn't work for a major studio for the next four-and-a-half years.

"They stopped the picture after one week!" Gould shouted as everyone in the house suddenly became very quiet. Even the Playmates sensed something heavy was going down. "I was seeing an analyst for six-and-a-half years and they never bothered to talk to him. And that's why I ended up making crummy movies for independent companies, because I couldn't be insured."

With Gould willing to talk about things that actors rarely talk to the press about, I suggested we continue the interview in another room. We went upstairs to his bedroom and I got him to talk about his two marriages, his children, his smoking grass during a *Playboy* interview, all the topics which I knew would satisfy the gossipy needs of my editor.

"You want to go visit Groucho?" he asked, after I had finished asking most of my questions. We left his house and drove to see one of Gould's early idols.

Groucho Marx was sitting up in his bed watching television and ignoring the phone, which was ringing. When we entered he looked at Elliott and told him to answer the phone. "It stopped ringing, Groucho," Gould said. "Answer it anyway," the old vaudevillian said. Elliott lifted the receiver and said, "Hello?" as if he expected someone to actually be on the other end.

When he introduced me, Groucho looked at my beard and said, "You need a shave."

"So do you," Gould said and brought out Groucho's electric razor. He held his friend's pale, stubbly chin with one hand and proceeded to shave him with the other. Groucho seemed pleased. He was eighty-six, frail, with a beret on his head and a wit as sharp as when he performed with his brothers. Elliott was one of the few younger actors who recognized his genius and paid homage to him. No matter how far out Gould might have gone, he came down to earth with Groucho.

Gould, for me, was a learning experience. He let me in in a way that was different from other celebrities I was meeting at the time. He wasn't interested in "information," in talking about things that were already in print, in repeating himself. He had—and still has—an eclectic, iconoclastic, and original mind, and this caused problems for those who didn't want to try to follow what he was thinking. What Gould taught me was to listen carefully. He challenged me the way reading James Joyce challenged me. Gould was the incarnation of stream of consciousness. As he would tell me later, he was taking me to another level, and seeing if I was willing to go there with him. The second article I wrote about him, following this initial five-session interview, was titled "My Friend Elliott Gould."

"That surprised me," he told me twenty-five years later, "because I didn't know we were friends. I guess you saw something I didn't. I was just trying to communicate."

BECOMING A CHAMELEON AND AN ACTOR: BEHAVING DIFFERENTLY WITH DIFFERENT SUBJECTS

There are writers I know who are very uncomfortable interviewing someone. These are introspective people who prefer to work at home and not have to put on a face to meet and talk with strangers. Or they have their own strong egos themselves and they aren't eager to sublimate them for the sake of other, equally strong egos. And one thing you have to be willing to do as an interviewer is to sublimate your ego. As Gay Talese has noted, "It is shifting attention from one's ego and directing it toward someone else, and asking them, 'What is it like to be you?'"

In a 2004 remembrance of his friend John Gregory Dunne, *L.A. Times* writer Tim Rutten quoted Dunne as saying, "The world is fundamentally divided between people who are utterly fascinated with the drama of their own lives and those who are completely uninterested in themselves. I am completely indifferent to the drama of my own life and that indifference has led me to be truly interested in other people and their lives. Every really good reporter I've ever known enjoyed that same liberty—a freedom from self-absorption."

To be a good interviewer, you have to become a chameleon, changing the colors of your personality to fit the mood of the person you are interviewing. This might mean dressing a certain way, or sucking up to someone, or praising with false flattery. There are writers who say they will never do any of this to get their story. All I'll say about that is that when an interviewer can't get his story, he'd better be willing to do what is necessary.

"Interviewing is a social talent," journalist Marie Brenner believes. "You have to be a good listener. You have to not be afraid to speak up and ask very direct questions in a way that doesn't alienate someone. If you'd gone to a lot of parties as a child, you would probably do this pretty well, because of the seduction and the performance and the flirtation and the confidence and esprit that you have to go in with."

For example, when I interviewed Jerry Lewis in 1975, he was such a reluctant character that I interrupted our conversation, basically called a time-out, and told him how, as a child, I had my tonsils removed and was told by my doctor not to try to talk for a few days. But the following day I watched a Martin and Lewis movie on TV and laughed so hard I was sore the rest of the week. This personal story worked wonders with Lewis, whose whole body language changed. Suddenly, I was no longer the enemy, but a friend. It was just a small flattery and I wasn't telling him a lie. I just shared a moment from my past that happened to involve him to obtain the desired result.

When I talked with Cheech and Chong, my references and demeanor were very different than when I sat with Henry Fonda or Linus Pauling. I was an audience for Robin Williams and Sid Caesar, more serious with Saul Bellow and Arthur Miller, flirtatious with Grace Jones and Dolly Parton. When George C. Scott made a pitcher of Bloody Marys, I drank with him. When Kurt Russell tested my mettle by putting me in control of his plane as we flew toward a mountain range, I tried not to let him see me sweat. When Allen Ginsberg kissed me at the Laguna airport, I acted as naturally as I could. When Van Damme brought out his strong cigars, or when certain unnamed subjects offered hits off their joints, I did my best to participate without losing focus. When Al Pacino wanted to hand wrestle or Lucia Rijker wanted to box, I showed I was game. But when Marlon Brando gave me a ham-and-cheese sandwich, I left it on the plate.

I don't eat ham.

BE EDUCATED

Movie critic Joel Siegel tells of meeting Orson Welles in the green room of *Good Morning America* in the early 1980s. Siegel remembered that Welles had played the Shadow on the radio and he asked Welles if he had helped create the character. "I wasn't the first Shadow," Welles told him. "That was Robert Hardy Andrews." Siegel recognized the name and said, "The guy who created Jack Armstrong." Welles was impressed.

"One thing I've learned about doing interviews," Siegel observed in his book *Lessons for Dylan,* "and that's what this was, disguised as casual conversation. It's important to establish early on that you're not a schmuck."

The more you know, the better your interview will turn out. Seems obvious: if you're well read, if you've seen a lot of movies, if you've studied history, have an understanding of science, know something about mechanics and the healing arts, can clean a clogged drain, oil a squeaky screen door, replace a six-foot fluorescent light, shoot a foul shot, serve and volley, hit a baseball, or play backgammon, chess, and poker, that knowledge may come in handy when you're with the person you are interviewing. A young Marlon Brando impressed Tennessee Williams when he replaced the playwright's lightbulb. Want to impress Christopher Walken? Cook him a meal. Sandra Bullock? Show her you understand plumbing. Goldie Hawn? Know something about Eastern philosophies. Diane Keaton? Know about art and photography. Nick Nolte? Show off your green thumb. Dolly Parton? Share your knowledge about ghosts and goblins. Richard Feynman? Bongo drums!

When I found out that both Steve Martin and Oliver Stone liked J. P. Donleavy's novels, I knew that I had something in common to talk with them about. When I read that Drew Barrymore was a big fan of T. S. Eliot's poetry, I wrote questions about the *Four Quartets* to see how serious she really was.

So: Read. Watch. Be curious. Feed your brain. Knowledge is a good thing. You can never know enough.

BE CURRENT

Besides all of the above, it's also important to know what's going on at the moment. If that means learning the box scores or the weekend box-office results or who's watching what according to the Neilson ratings, then do it. If there's a war going on somewhere, or a coup in a foreign country, or a terrorist attack, or a new disease that's causing havoc in certain areas of the world, know about it. It's true; we live in a global village. What happens in the Middle East affects Wall Street; if SARS cannot be contained in China or AIDS in Africa, know enough to be able to talk about it. There is always a place in an interview for up-to-date questions and responses.

After the Oklahoma City bombing, I was interested in what Saul Bellow had to say about the characters of Timothy McVeigh and Terry Nichols. And I tried to tie in one of his works with another mad bomber: "In *Herzog*," I observed, "you described Moses Herzog as a person in a very agitated and almost mad state who is resisting everything, including his own intellectual life. That description could also apply to Ted Kaczynski, the Unabomber."

To which Bellow answered: "Maybe so, but having read Kaczynski's manuscript in the newspapers I would place him intellectually about 170 degrees vertically below Herzog. He just didn't have a mental life worth mentioning. It just shows how you could be a brilliant mathematician and otherwise be a high-IQ moron, which is how I see him."

KNOWING WHEN TO BE FORCEFUL

You ring the bell of the penthouse suite at the Beverly Hills Hotel and Warren Beatty answers the door. He looks at you. You look at him. Everything you've ever read about him has led you to believe he's an extremely reluctant interview. So you've dressed in a way that surprises him: You're wearing an African fugu, a striped oversize cloth that a pregnant woman could wear to cover up her added weight. And when his eyes meet yours, you point at him with your index finger and say, "Warren." He lets you in, and later invites you to stay for dinner.

OR YOU'RE WITH Sandy Gallin, former manager to stars like Dolly Parton, Cher, Michael Jackson, and Florence Henderson. He's agreed to talk about his life but tells you straight out that he's never completed a book and has a four-minute attention span. You say to him, "Turn off your phones and let's sit by the pool," and for the next four hours you talk without any interruptions.

BARBRA STREISAND eyes you warily for the fourth time in four meetings. It's becoming a burden. She's let you in, she's agreed to talk, but she just can't bring herself to relax for the first hour each time you're together. So you say, "Look, Barbra, you're making this too hard. Either trust me or don't. If you can't, I'll stop this and it's over. If you can, then don't make me work so hard to earn your trust each time we meet."

WHEN SHARON STONE is late for your lunch at a San Francisco restaurant of her choosing, you look around and see that it's crowded. Taping your conversation will become a transcriber's nightmare. You ask the maître d' if there's a private room you can use and he kindly takes you to it. But when Stone arrives, she insists on sitting in the main dining area, where she can be seen. You have just met, but you whisper in her ear, "Trust me, I know what I'm doing." Then you turn and start walking to the other room. You're taking a chance with a temperamental diva. If she doesn't follow, you might as well kiss this interview good-bye. But she does. It takes her an hour of pouting before she begins to open up. But it's worth it. You stay there for five hours. She gives you plenty of quotable material.

WITH PATTY HEARST, she doesn't want to admit that she ever liked being Tania, her alter ego who helped rob banks with the SLA. But it's your job to see if it's possible to bring Tania out of her. To get her angry. To get her to say something threatening. She doesn't want to go there, but your questions begin to annoy her. "You must know that when you became Tania you captured the imagination of a lot of people," you say.

To which she gibes, "Maybe you liked it."

"Well," you goad, "she was a symbol of defiance, antagonism, liveliness, antiestablishment at a time when *many* people were feeling that way."

"It amazes me to sit here and hear you say that it was a lively image," she challenges. "It was a terribly violent image. It was the result of a violent kidnapping. Tania never really existed except as a fantasy for most people."

And then her previously simmering anger erupts. "You have a really odd idea about the SLA! You have this romantic notion of what they were like, that it was all one great adventure! You lived it vicariously and it's just too exciting for you and you can hardly control yourself, and it's so disturbing to find out that I don't even think Tania lived except in people's imagination, like yours—and she *still* lives in yours!"

You've done it. You've gotten to her. And when you later ask her if she still likes to hunt and she answers yes—pigs, deer, ducks—you can't help yourself, you wonder aloud what else she might feel satisfied shooting?

"Oh," she says, "maybe you."

And then Patty Hearst adds, "Every hunter will think I'm right. They'll think, Boy, what a jerk she is to talk to this guy!"

YOU MAY HAVE TO act like a jerk at times, or you may have to challenge, tease, coax, or goad your subject into saying something provocative, but that's part of the job description of an interviewer. You have to be willing to think on your feet, to change directions quickly, to demonstrate that you know what you're doing, and to take charge. In this business, first impressions count, so give some thought to how you come across, how you stand, how you smile, how you shake a hand. If your body language spells confidence and your ability to provoke can also be interpreted as playful or sincere or non-threatening, then the force you exert will be accepted for what it is: assurance.

THOSE DUMB QUESTIONS

Don't ever be afraid to ask a dumb or simplistic question. You should never be inhibited by your questions, or intimidated by your subject. As long as you can edit out the dumb question and replace it with one that may be more appropriate, based on the response, it's OK. If no one else is listening, who's going to know?

WHEN AN EDITOR WANTS YOU, BUT THE SUBJECT PREFERS SOMEONE HE KNOWS

Earlier I wrote about publicists who want to choose the writer before agreeing to allow their star clients to talk. But sometimes it's the star who has a writer in mind and won't agree to anyone else. *Playboy* wanted me to interview Johnny Depp when he was working on a film in Ireland. Depp agreed to the interview and I prepared for it, but at the last minute Depp said he wanted another writer. *Playboy* had to make a choice: stick with me, even if it meant losing the interview, or give Depp who he wanted. In years past this was a no-brainer: you didn't allow the lunatics to take over the asylum. You got tough; you didn't let the subject dictate what writer he wanted. Magazines were read for the writers who worked for them. Can you imagine *Esquire* in the 1960s or 1970s telling Norman Mailer or Gay Talese that the subject of a future profile wanted another writer? But those days seem to be very distant today. Magazines compete for their cover subjects. If *Playboy* said no to Depp, then he'd just talk to *GQ* or *Details or Rolling Stone,* all of which had one other advantage over *Playboy:* the cover. *Playboy* rarely puts a guy on the cover.

So Depp got the writer he wanted, and *Playboy* got the interview.

In 2002, *Movieline* wanted me to interview Kevin Spacey. I like Spacey, he's a wonderful actor, a committed individual, and he speaks up for the right causes. But Spacey preferred another writer he had worked with before, and my editor was in the position of sticking with her first choice or capitulating to an actor she wanted for her cover and who would also appear at one of the magazine's events. Guess who didn't interview Spacey?

Just remember that in cases like this, it's not personal. Depp and Spacey never met me, so they weren't rejecting me personally. They just wanted some writer whose work they were familiar with, or who knew them, so they would feel more comfortable. It goes with the territory. Not everyone realizes how much better they'd be served if they had only talked to *you!*

BRINGING THE CAVIAR

When Joan Collins was on the TV drama *Dynasty,* she was hot. Hot enough to be asked to pose nude in *Playboy.* Hot enough to be the subject of a 1984 *Playboy* interview. Hot enough to make unusual demands. The day before I was to go to her house her assistant called and said Ms. Collins would like me to bring a can of beluga caviar and a bottle of Crystal champagne.

"Gee, that sounds like fun," I said, wondering what my editor was going to say about this unexpected $300 expense. "And what will Ms. Collins bring to this party, besides her lovely self?"

"She'll bring the potato," her assistant answered.

AS I SAID in the beginning, it's a step-by-step process. You land the assignment, you do the research, and, if you have to, you bring the champagne and caviar. Why shouldn't an interview start off in a celebratory way?

3. YOU'RE THERE, NOW WHAT?

Looking for Openings in All the Right Places

This is analysis. By the time we're finished, I will be empty and your tape recorder will be full. It's a crazy feeling. I get the feeling when you leave I will be interviewing myself. I had a fantasy the other night that this interview is so great that they no longer want me to act—just do interviews. I thought of us going all over the world doing interviews—we've signed for three interviews a day for six weeks . . .

—AL PACINO

OK, you've got the assignment, you've done your research, you've written your questions, and you've got a date to meet your subject. You're either feeling very jittery and may be losing sleep prior to the big day or you're full of eager anticipation. But one thing is certain: Your mind is focused on the task at hand. All other worldly concerns are put aside. The unpaid bills, the unreturned phone calls, the pressures of a demanding relationship, the sick friend, the winning lottery ticket waiting to be cashed in—all of that is pushed into the recesses of your mind. What's front and center is what's about to take place after you knock on that door and your subject appears. Is he smiling or preoccupied? Does he look at you or through you? Does he glance at his watch or down at your shoes? Is he checking you out as thoroughly as you're giving him the once-over? What happens next?

LEARNING TO DEAL WITH YOUR NERVES

In 1973, when I first started interviewing what *Newsday*'s editor called "household names," I was surprised at how nervous I was. I spent hours rehearsing my questions, like an actor going over his lines. And when I sat down face-to-face with Lucille Ball or Carol Burnett or Cher I felt my body heat up. I tried to ignore the perspiration that dripped down from my forehead. My mouth got very dry. I wanted to appear calm and relaxed, but I could barely get my opening questions out without my voice breaking. I didn't understand why I felt this way: I had my questions, these people were expecting me, I had no ulterior motives. I was just there to record their answers and get out of there.

But instead of tying myself up in knots I decided that if this was the way I felt, I would have to learn to deal with it. Being nervous before an interview isn't any different from being nervous before going on stage or standing at the plate to face a fastball pitcher or taking the SATs or LSATs or MEDCATs. Your nerves are pumping adrenaline through your body. You're taking your situation seriously. You want to do well. You don't want to fail.

What I taught myself to do before facing my subject was to sit in my car and take a few deep breaths. Then I would repeat the mantra I was given when researching an article about Transcendental Meditation. I'd check my equipment, look over my questions, and think of myself as a modern-day gunslinger. My job was to nail my opponent (yes, I began to look at whatever larger-than-life face I was to interview as an opponent). I knew that whomever I was about to interrogate would be evasive and that it would be up to me to get him or her to be forthcoming. I wasn't exactly sure how I was going to do that, but if I wanted to succeed and get more assignments, I had to figure out a path.

There's no patented way to tell you what that path is, because each of us behaves differently in such situations. I know of one *Playboy* interviewer who is so nervous when he goes to talk to someone that he sweats profusely, he uses napkins to wipe his brow, he stutters . . . but he manages to get people to confide in him. I think they feel sorry for him and are trying to calm him down. It's not the way I'd recommend going into battle, but for him, it works.

I also discovered that many stars are nervous when a tape recorder is put on a table and their words are about to be captured. I saw fear in Robert De Niro's face when we first met. I noticed how uncomfortable Al Pacino, Ray Romano, Jack Nicholson, Kim Basinger, and Ava Gardner were. It altered the atmosphere in the room. It was almost as if my nervousness was transferred to them, and thus I felt lighter. Their discomfort calmed me.

It's not a negative thing to be nervous before an interview. You just have to understand your body. Just as public speaking is the number one fear most people have, interviewing someone can also be a fearful prospect, because the person you're going to see is usually more established than you are. They're not coming to get your advice; you're there to hear what they have to say. There's a natural imbalance in the dynamic. What you have to learn is how to turn that around.

The way to calm yourself is to be prepared. Because preparation begets confidence. And confidence emanates outward.

TALKING TO "STARS" AND EXPERTS

While celebrities get a lot of free stuff and perks and get waved at by strangers and asked to sign autographs, they all put their socks on one at a time; they all get headaches and colds; they will all one day be asked to step aside by a paparazzi who doesn't recognize them. Robert Downey Jr. may be an actor's actor, but he's got an addiction problem you don't want to go anywhere near. Winona Ryder may be cute as a button and a mighty fine actress, but she has the same urges we all do when it comes to paying high prices for clothing from Saks that you know isn't worth what they're charging. Marlon Brando might send shivers down the spines of his fellow actors, but he's got a weight problem you wouldn't want to trade his fame or talent for, and family problems you wouldn't wish on your worst enemies.

For every celebrity you can name, dollars to doughnuts they've got problems you wouldn't want to deal with. True, they've also got a lot of money, nice cars, big houses, access to private planes, groupies who throw themselves at them, and magazines who put them, and not you, on their covers. But where are Clark Gable, Marilyn Monroe, Rudolph Valentino, and Humphrey Bogart now? Same place you will be when you die. Either buried underground, or stuck in a wall, or turned to ash.

Try and remember that when you're about to ring a big star or a hotshot expert's doorbell. Try and remember what Shelley wrote in "Ozymandias":

> . . . Two vast and trunkless legs of stone
> Stand in the desert. Near them, on the sand,
> Half sunk, a shattered visage lies. . . .
> And on the pedestal these words appear:
> "My name is Ozymandias, king of kings:
> Look on my works, ye Mighty, and despair!"
> Nothing beside remains. . . .

And then remember what Polonius told his son Laertes : "This above all: to thine own self be true."

For that is advice worth taking. Be yourself. Don't try to be someone you're not. Celebrated people have good shit detectors. They can recognize a phony when they meet one, especially a phony interviewer.

GETTING YOUR SUBJECT TO OPEN UP: KNOWING WHEN TO DELVE INTO A PERSON'S FEARS AND ANXIETIES, TRAUMAS, AND FINANCIAL AFFAIRS

What you will often find, when doing your research, is that the people you are planning to interview have not all been born with silver spoons in their mouths. They have gone through their share of suffering. They have lost a family member, have been the victim of abuse, have witnessed an alcoholic parent attack his spouse, have been on the short end of a pyramid scheme, have flunked out of school, have had to deal with depression . . . in other words, they're human, and many have experienced those slings and arrows of outrageous fortune—and they often don't want to talk about it. But if you know about it, then it's probably something you should be asking about. Depending on how sympathetically and delicately you ask those personal questions will determine whether you're going to get revealing or emotional responses.

Almost everyone I've ever interviewed had something uncomfortable in their past that I knew I had to ask about. And though I may prepare questions about the topic, I never know exactly how I will phrase the questions or at what point during the interview it will come up. But I know that more often than not, the interview will turn on those moments.

When Dylan McDermott was five years old his mother was shot and killed by her boyfriend. It may have been an accident; it may have been a homicide. McDermott has never felt comfortable talking about it. Anjelica Huston was seventeen when her mother drove with a friend through France and lost her life in a car crash. Her mother's death has haunted Anjelica ever since. Elisabeth Shue has never looked deeply inward to open up about the loss of her older brother, who, during a family gathering, jumped out over a lake on a rope and lost his life. Ava Gardner once forgot to meet Howard Hughes at the airport because she wanted to see her ex-husband, Mickey Rooney. When Hughes returned to her apartment he blackened her eye. She picked up a brass bell and knocked out one of his teeth, then grabbed a chair and was going to crush his skull with it when her maid stopped her. Pierce Brosnan lost his first wife to ovarian cancer. James Earl Jones stuttered so badly as a boy that for long periods of time he went silent. Jim Carrey's family lost their home and had to live in a tent. Nick Nolte was arrested for selling false draft cards. Rodney Dangerfield lived most of his life having to deal with undiagnosed depression until the age of seventy-five. Senator John Edwards lost his sixteen-year-old first son when the boy's car overturned, a subject he has never wanted to discuss publicly. James Garner's stepmother constantly humiliated him to the point where Garner almost strangled her. Halle Berry's father often beat his mother and sister and once nearly killed their dog. Jamie Lee Curtis never felt close to her father, Tony, whom she called a ghost. Sally Field went through most of her life without friends. Meryl Streep lost the love of her life, John Cazale, to illness. Sylvester Stallone's father called his son stupid, and put a cage over his bed to keep him locked in his room. Truman Capote's mother would lock him alone in hotel rooms when he was two years old. Anthony Kiedis lost his best friend to a heroin overdose, and then had to battle drug addiction himself. Christian Slater had drug and alcohol problems that landed him in and out of rehab. Alex Haley won a Pulitzer Prize for *Roots,* and then had to face the humiliating charges of plagiarizing sections of his book. Norman Mailer wound up in a mental institution after stabbing his wife at a party. Roman Polanski had to flee America because he didn't want to stand trial for having sex with a minor. Joyce Carol Oates had to deal with a stalker. Bob Knight lost his job as Indiana basketball coach because he violated a zero-tolerance proclamation that he felt ruined his reputation and his life. Harvey Keitel fought his ex-wife, Lorraine Bracco, for custody of their daughter because he feared that Bracco's boyfriend was a child molester.

The examples could go on, but you can see how broaching these subjects would not be easy—and yet, if you ignore them, you're not really doing your job. These are all tough subjects to bring up, and tough questions to ask. You've got to have a feel for the way the conversation is going. You have to figure out some way to ask the meaningful question. You have to listen to the nuances of each conversation, waiting for the right moment, looking for an opening that might come unexpectedly, as it did when Charlie Sheen asked me to turn off my tape recorders in the middle of our interview in 1990. He wanted to ask me how to approach the subject of what happened with his girlfriend and a certain gun accident. I didn't know what he was talking about; it was an incident that I had not uncovered in my research. But here was Sheen, bringing it up. So I said to him that the best way to handle it would be for me to ask him straight up what happened and to let him tell his version of the story. He agreed, I turned on the machines, and got golden material handed back to me. (See how the story played out later in this chapter.)

When a person begins to show vulnerability, don't back away, but go forward. If you miss that window of opportunity it might not come back once the person is more composed and defensive.

But, remember this: the most problematic area you can bring up is not sex or past abuse or rejections but the IRS. I learned this lesson when I was interviewing Warren Beatty. After a few hours at his hotel suite we agreed to continue the interview by phone. The next day I called him and asked about some hundreds of thousands of dollars in back taxes he once owed. I didn't know anything more than what I had read in the paper, but just bringing it up brought the already cautious Beatty to a complete stammer. "Uh, you know, I think . . . can we do this later? I've got to go do something. I'll call you."

But he never did. And I never got through to him again.

So: NEVER start an interview talking about money and taxes. NEVER bring it up halfway through. Wait until you've asked all your other questions before bringing up someone's financial affairs.

GETTING THEM TO TRUST YOU

Understand this: You walk in to meet the person you're about to interview. She looks at you warily. She is about to put her thoughts in your hands. She may have read some of your previous work, but she doesn't know you. She's been burned in the past. She doesn't trust you. It's only natural. You smile. If you have the time, you tell some personal stories. You do what you can to get her to relax. You don't immediately take out your notes, you don't turn on your tape recorder, you just start talking. You try to show her that you're not a monster, not the enemy, not there to make your reputation on her mean-spirited remarks. You're just there to do the best job you can. You want her to work with you, just as she works with her business partner or director. If you can't earn her trust, you might as well get whatever mean-spirited remarks you can, because otherwise, it's going to be bland and boring. And you're not going to get many more assignments.

BACK IN HIS single days, Warren Beatty told me that most journalists who came to interview him had something other than just that interview in mind: They often had a script they wanted him to read, or a physical experience they were hoping to share. Eventually, he became wary of anyone who wanted to talk with him. And he's not alone. Who can blame the journalist who has been writing that screenplay that will catapult him into another tax bracket once a major star is attached? He's got the assignment to interview one of those stars who can change his life and he figures, what the hell, when the interview is done, why not sell him on his script idea?

Of course the star will be polite and say he will read it. He's just spent an hour or two talking to you for some newspaper or magazine piece and he doesn't want to offend you by telling you the truth: that he will not read your script, and that he is peeved that you brought it to him.

On the other hand, if you're a particularly attractive person and the star has nothing scheduled after your interview, who knows? Some old columnists have made a nice living off of tales told about their bedroom romps with Marilyn Monroe or Ava Gardner or Montgomery Clift or Errol Flynn. Whether these stories are true or not, I have no doubt that Beatty was telling me the truth when he said that most writers who came to see him had ulterior motives.

Just keep in mind that the people you're interviewing, unless they've never been interviewed before, are usually savvy. They can smell that perfume or script in your bag the moment you walk through their door. They don't want to hear about some charity event that needs a celebrity's presence, or a book you've written that might sell more with a blurb from them. And if the people you're trying to interview don't trust you, they're not going to feel comfortable around you. You're not going to get very good interviews. And the fantasy of sharing intimate moments once the interview is done, or of sitting in story meetings a few weeks later, will be just that. A fantasy.

So if you want to be earn your subject's trust (which you do, because he'll open up more if he trusts you will know how to deal with sensitive or intimate material), don't go into an interview with a hidden agenda. Don't have ulterior motives. Don't be dishonest with the person you're there to see and with yourself as well. Reporting is an honorable and dignified profession—be proud of what you do. Be proud that an editor has entrusted you to get the story. Do a good job. Let the published interview be your reward—and your ticket to further assignments.

WHEN TO BE AN "EQUAL" AND WHEN NOT TO BE

When you think about it, you're not expected to know as much about his or her respective field as the person you're interviewing. If you did, why do the interview? But does that make you "inferior" to your subject? I hope not. You certainly should not think that way before meeting them. Nor should you dare consider yourself superior to anyone you're about to interview. Because either way, inferior/superior, you're going to have an attitude. It's best to be as neutral as possible. And to put yourself into a frame of mind that you're about to have an interesting conversation on whatever equal playing field you can create between you.

My mind-set is that once the research is done, the questions are written, and I'm prepared, then I know this person pretty well, and I should be able to carry on a conversation with him or her. And by being prepared, I'm feeling confident. And by feeling confident, I'm believing I'm on the same level as the person I'm going to see. Sometimes this takes a strong suspension of disbelief, like when I'm going to talk to a Nobel Prize winner, a mathematician, a technician, or some other master of the universe. I could easily shy away from such people. But instead, I just smile to myself and think about the things I do know, and there are bound to be things I know that this person I'm going to see doesn't. So, we're even. Only, I'm in the driver's seat. I'm the one asking the questions, controlling the direction of our conversation. Am I really the equal of Richard Feynman, Joyce Carol Oates, John Huston, Saul Bellow, Linus Pauling, Henry Moore? Does that question need answering? But when I go to see people like them, I've got to believe that I can engage them in a dialogue that will make others want to stop what they're doing to read what we have to say. And the only way I feel comfortable and confident doing this is by knowing where I'm going with them.

That said, there are moments when you're talking to someone and he asks you if you have read a certain writer or understand a particular concept. It's only natural to try and fake your way into the next subject, because you don't want to appear intellectually challenged. But that's a tricky slope to maneuver. Sometimes you can get away with nodding your head and moving on. And sometimes you might be asked to explore something that's over your head.

Hemingway used to claim he had a very good bullshit detector. He could tell when writing was false, or when people were phony. Before I flew to Tahiti to see Marlon Brando, I made a pledge to myself to not say I knew something if I didn't know it, because I figured that Brando is America's great actor and he must have a very keen bullshit detector. He was also a games player. I knew that if he sensed I was trying to be knowledgeable about something I actually wasn't, he would begin to pick me apart. And sure enough, when we were together he asked me if I liked to play chess. I said I did, and I knew I had made a mistake—because while I do know how to play chess, I'm not very good at it. I don't think more than two moves ahead. But Brando got out his chess set and as soon as he saw that I was no match for him, he tried to figure out a way to make the game more interesting. He put a piece of cardboard in the middle of the board so that we couldn't see each other's pieces and said we should arrange our pieces any way we wanted. Then he removed the cardboard and looked at my positions. I had tried to be clever by placing my queen on the front line. He grabbed it with his rook on his third move, and it was retreat and defeat after that. We didn't play another game.

MAINTAIN CONTROL

In the spring of 1973 I traveled with photographer Victor Englebert to the Llanos and the Guajira Desert in Colombia on an assignment for the Spanish edition of *National Geographic*. It was, at times, grueling: We trekked through the desert, hiked around salt mountains, rode wild horses. Victor had two heavy camera bags that he carried; I had a pen and a pad. I offered to carry one of Victor's bags, but he refused. "I never let anyone help me with my equipment," he said. "That way, I can never blame anyone if something got lost or stolen."

Victor told me that when he went to live among different nomad tribes in Africa, he wouldn't put film in his camera for the first week; he'd just go around snapping empty pictures until the nomads got used to him and stopped posing.

Victor was always in control of his work. He had figured out what worked for him, and he produced great pictures that appeared in books and magazines all over the world.

The same applies to interviewing. It's very easy to lose control of an interview. But that's the challenge, isn't it? If you're lucky and get an iconoclastic politician, like former wrestler Jesse Ventura, then you might come up with some surprises. But if you're with a seasoned pro, as most politicians are, it's going to take some serious thinking about what you want to get out of him. Usually, it involves the equivalent of snapping a lot of pictures without film in the camera. Tape is cheap. It's time that is expensive. It's very tough to get a compelling and revealing interview with a politician or a movie star in a short period of time. But if you can do it, it's because you've maintained control over the interview.

At one point early in my interview with Robert Evans we were talking about all the business he got done at his house, and he mentioned how he, Warren Beatty, Jack Nicholson, Sue Mengers, and Robert Towne used to sit around casting pictures. "I'd like to show you a tape about myself that might help you, if I may put it on," he offered.

I knew that if I agreed, the interview would stop and I'd be watching some vanity project of his. I didn't want to lose control of the interview, so I said: "No, no, let's keep talking. I can see it later."

As we continued to talk, he mentioned that he wasn't a very good executive, and then he bragged that within six years at the helm of Paramount Studios they went from "being no one" to "the biggest studio in the industry."

Before I let him blow his own horn, I interjected: "Yet you rate yourself as a lousy executive."

He admitted that he was, and I kept control of the interview, focusing on the difficulties of being a studio head.

Later on Evans went off the record to tell me about a critical letter he wrote to Stanley Jaffe, who was then the chairman of the board at Paramount, regarding the film *Sliver*. It was a strong letter, and I would have liked to get it on the record. So I asked him if I could mention that he wrote the letter. By asking his permission, I was losing control of the interview, putting Evans in a position of determining what could and could not be used.

"You can say the passion I had brought me to write a letter on *Sliver*. That's OK."

It took another few questions and a change of topic for me to regain control, and I did so when I asked him a tough question that got him talking about his personal life: "By 1989 you were contemplating suicide, and you put yourself in an insane asylum. Why?"

HARRISON FORD is rarely going to give up control in an interview, so I tried to get him talking about politics (since he played a president in *Air Force One*), asking him about President Clinton. At the time, Clinton was having problems with Whitewater and with Paula Jones. Ford answered, "I have nothing to say."

"How come?" I asked.

"Because of the framework of the question, for one thing. The framework is all focused on negatives."

I tried to make my point, that it was the negatives that concerned us when investigating the president's moral and ethical fiber, but Ford wouldn't bite. That's why he isn't a very compelling interview subject.

Still, it's your job to get the most out of whoever it is you're interviewing. As Ted Koppel has noted, "There is no such thing as a boring subject." Koppel also understands the issue of control: "If you let the other person control the interview, then you've lost."

RELYING ON YOUR PERSONALITY

This falls under the heading Things That Can't Be Taught. If you've got a pleasant personality, if you can amuse people and be serious, if you can make them laugh and then make them cry, if you can show your sensitivity, your sympathy, your empathy . . . then people will talk to you and confide in you. If you're brash, obnoxious, egotistic, self-centered, and cannot stand the feeling of being invisible . . . then turn your writing talents inward, write novels and poetry and plays.

On the other hand, as Harrison Salisbury, a Pulitzer Prize–winning *New York Times* writer said: "I think that the interviewer is just an ear. He may guide the interview a little bit. He is not a personality in the conversation. He may create an atmosphere so that the person feels free and easy in talking, but I'm not one of those who puts his own personality into the interview. . . . Some interviewers say, 'Well, I believe such and such.' That's not my style. It may be entertaining but it isn't what I call interviewing."

So there you are: Express yourself. Don't express yourself. Be congenial. Be just an ear and a guide. There's plenty of room on the playing field. Do what feels right for you.

GETTING BEYOND THE PLUG: OK, YOU'VE LET THEM PROMOTE; NOW IT'S YOUR TURN

Most people have a reason they're doing an interview. Very often it's because they have something to sell: a book, a movie, an activity, an event, themselves. They may have an issue they feel strongly about, or they may be running for office, or they may find it beneficial for them to be quoted in print. Knowing that, you can decide to get whatever topic they're eager to discuss out of the way first, or wait until you've asked all your other questions before touching on what most interests them. I do it both ways, depending on the time I'm being given. If I know I have unlimited time, then I don't mind starting out with whatever it is they want to promote. But if I know that I've only got a short period of time, then I will hold off asking them about their main concern until my time is almost up . . . because if anything will get me more time with my subject, it's that they have something they *want* to talk about.

RECOGNIZING GOOD COPY WHEN YOU HEAR IT

You never know when a conversation will turn from decent to Really Good Copy, but if you're alert and listening you should begin to develop an ear for when to keep your subject talking about a particular topic.

When I interviewed Mel Gibson in 1995, I asked him about his mother's death, and he spoke about how she was the mortar and the bricks that held everything in the family together. Then I asked: "Do you believe in an afterlife, and that you'll see her there?"

Here's how that played out:

GIBSON: Absolutely. There's just no explanation. There has to be an afterlife. Otherwise where is the evening-out process? There has to be an afterlife because Hitler and I both walked the planet and I'm not going to the same place as Hitler. Or Pol Pot.

His answer led me to keep asking related questions, and as you can see, his opinions are certainly not ones you might expect to hear from a major public figure.

Q: Is there a hell?

GIBSON: Absolutely.

Q: What's your image of the devil?

GIBSON: The beast with eight tongues and four horns and fire and brimstone. Probably worse than anything we can imagine, as paradise is probably better than anything we can imagine.

Had Gibson not been so graphic and specific, I probably wouldn't have thought to ask him this next question, but his answer and what followed certainly spiked up this interview.

Q: Do you believe in Darwin's theory of evolution or that God created man in his image?

GIBSON: The latter.

Q: So you can't accept that we descended from monkeys and apes?

GIBSON: No, I think it's bullshit. If it isn't, why are they still around? How come apes aren't people yet? It's a nice theory, but I can't swallow it. There's a big credibility gap. The carbon-dating thing that tells you how long something's been around, how accurate is that, really? I've got one of Darwin's books at home and some of that stuff is pretty damn funny. Some of his stuff is true, like that the giraffe has a long neck so it can reach the leaves. But I just don't think you can swallow the whole piece.

Q: I take it that you're not particularly broad-minded when it comes to issues such as celibacy, abortion, birth control—

GIBSON: People always focus on stuff like that. Those aren't issues. Those are unquestionable. You don't even argue those points.

Q: You don't?

GIBSON: No.

For someone asking Mel Gibson these questions, let me tell you, my ears were burning with joy! I've talked to hundreds of movie stars, and not one of them had ever expressed such rigid beliefs on the record. "How come apes aren't people yet?" If this isn't manna for an interviewer, I don't know what is!

THE SAME FEELING of elation occurred in 1994 when I interviewed Anthony Hopkins—or Sir Anthony Hopkins, as he had recently been knighted in England. Hopkins was outrageous in another way: He dared to take on the Bard himself. Which, in some circles, might be as heretical as Gibson challenging evolution.

Hopkins is a cynical man who puts down his craft in an articulate manner. We had been talking about his going from doing a Shakespeare play to a TV miniseries, which I thought might be considered a backward step. "But," I asked, "you don't see the worth or virtue in either the Bard or yourself, do you?"

HOPKINS: I don't like virtue, and I don't like worthiness. I don't like valor. Why keep being so nice? It's something in me, I can't stand that. My father couldn't stand all that stuff. I don't say that I'm not a phony; I'm as phony as everyone else. We're all phony. We're all charlatans, we're all flawed, we're all liars, and nobody really carries the mantle totally in their lives. But there's a part of it I can't stomach. Who gives a damn about a theater that was built four hundred years ago? Who cares? Pave it! Who cares? It's dead stuff. It's like the bloody Bard. Whether this *Lear* is better than that *Lear* . . . who gives a damn? You're doing what fifteen thousand actors have done before you. How the hell do you find something new? It's a fucking nightmare.

Q: What about the truism that every actor should do *Hamlet?*

HOPKINS: Most actors want to do *Hamlet* when they're at their craziest. I was the same way. I think it's a death wish.

Q: So actors should forget Shakespeare?

HOPKINS: I suppose it's good to have done it. I've done quite a bit of it, but I don't find it enriching. I never know what the hell I'm doing. I don't like Shakespeare. I'd rather be in Malibu.

Now, those last two short sentences are certainly quote-worthy, and you would expect that they would get picked up in the gossip columns . . . but Hopkins was on a roll, and so I switched from Shakespeare to actors in general, to see what he might have to say about his peers. And Sir Anthony did not disappoint.

Q: You're harsh on your profession. Are you also cynical about people in your profession?

HOPKINS: What's so special about being an actor? Actors are nothing. Actors are of no consequence. Most actors are pretty simple-minded people who just think they're complicated. Films? Actors? What is it?

Hopkins went on, and I continued to press him, but you can see that when you get someone who is willing to talk freely and honestly, then you, as the interviewer, must hold up your side by continuing to probe and question until your subject is spent of his emotion and opinions. And when your subject is an Academy Award–winning actor like Anthony Hopkins, you mustn't let his callousness or cynicism stop you in your tracks—you must take advantage of the openings he gives you, like a good counterpuncher in a prizefight.

CHARLIE SHEEN IS NOT the award-winning actor that Hopkins is, but he's an equally good interview. Sheen is one of those characters who has led an adventurous life and doesn't hold back. He loves to talk and tell stories about himself. He gives you the kind of material one hopes to get when conducting an interview. Here's Sheen in 1990 revealing how he went from being a petty thief to attacking his high school English teacher to packing a gun and dealing with his girlfriend who got accidentally shot.

"I had a four-day crime spree before I got arrested," Sheen told me. "We got credit card receipts from the trash of the Beverly Hills Hotel. I told the manager I left a term paper in the lobby and he let me look through the trash. I got all these receipts and we'd call up stores in Westwood and ask if they took phone orders. Then we'd order things like televisions, Walkmans, jewelry, watches, and say, 'I'll send my son in to pick it up.' So we'd go in and collect the loot and have the option of having it gift wrapped. Very blue-collar crime, when you look somebody in the eye and they say, 'You want your shit gift wrapped?'"

When one of his best friends got caught at a photo store, Sheen was implicated. "I'm standing in front of my art class, second period, senior year, when two cops came walking down the hallway," he recalled. "They said, 'You are under arrest for credit card forgery.' I was seventeen. I had to find an angle. I got to the station and indicted my friend and gave them all the receipts and told them everything. It was totally despicable and highly illegal but hell, we gave it a shot."

He wasn't thrown out of school then, but he managed to screw up by failing English. "I needed a C-minus to pass the course and if I didn't get it I'd be off the baseball team. There was a lot of shit riding on this test. And because I didn't have a note from my parents because of my absence the day before, my teacher wouldn't let me take the test. So I pretty much melted down in front of the whole class. I took the test, which was pretty thick, rolled it up into a ball, and fired a strike in the middle of the teacher's forehead. It knocked her glasses off. She stood there staring at me and in the middle of my rage I said to her that she was lucky I hadn't killed her yet. Then I ran out of shit to say, it was really an embarrassing moment, so I just started walking out, and there was that infamous trash can. I grabbed it and threw it about thirty feet into the chalkboard and said, 'Here's your fucking trash!' That was my exit."

High school behind him, Sheen became a movie star, got involved with women . . . and guns.

"With [actress] Rebecca Schaeffer being murdered at her own door one night by a lunatic, with John Lennon, with the continual threat of crazy people towards celebrity, I've been carrying a weapon for quite some time because I felt that if shit ever went down I'd want to return some fire. And that even if I was taken out I would want to take the sonofabitch with me. So I used to carry a little .22 Mag and five-shot revolver. I had it in my back pocket where it lived for a number of years. I was downstairs in the bathroom one morning and my girlfriend, Kelly, was upstairs. She went to move my pants off the weighing scale and the gun fell out of the back pocket and hit the linoleum floor and discharged a round that, thank God, didn't hit her directly, but it hit the toilet that she was standing next to. She got hit with the porcelain shrapnel and lead from the bullet itself. I heard the shot and I've been around enough weapons to know that it wasn't the shampoo bottle falling in the shower. I knew immediately it was gunfire. I rushed upstairs and there was Kelly in her underwear, holding her wrist and bleeding from several places. I was panicked. I picked up the phone and didn't know whether to call 411 or 911. It was a terrifying moment. The paramedics came and the police had to come because it was a shooting incident. The police didn't haul me away for shooting her, but she was taken to the hospital and then released the same day with four stitches, two in her wrist and two in her calf. I felt that if it should have happened to anybody it should have happened to me. We were very fortunate that the bullet itself didn't hit her directly. I took that particular weapon, after claiming it from the police station where they held it for seventy-two hours, and I threw it in the ocean because it had a vibe about it that was not healthy.

"It was kind of a turning point in my philosophy of arming myself in the streets. I'm studying hand-to-hand now instead of carrying a weapon, learning how to disarm the assailant. It doesn't mean that I've removed the weapons from my house. In the times we live in and the profession we work in I feel it necessary to keep armed. If some lunatic wants to come and do some damage, he's going to walk into an arsenal and I'll have a bead on him."

WITH QUOTES LIKE THAT, it's no wonder magazine editors like to assign stories on Charlie Sheen. There are three dramatic moments in what Sheen revealed above: the crime spree, the attack on the teacher, and the gun incident. A good interview should have at least one or two dramatic moments, like when Indiana coach Bob Knight started confessing that the university ripped his heart out when they fired him or when Patty Hearst joked that she'd like to shoot me or when Halle Berry said that no matter how light her skin, or the fact that her mother was Caucasian, she could never pass for white. When those moments come, absorb them. If what's said hits an emotional chord with you, it most likely will do the same with your readers. Go with it. Keep asking questions until you've drained that emotion.

ZERO IN ON SPECIFICS

Too often people speak in generalities. They will say, "That was a difficult time for me," and leave it at that. It's your job to ask, "How difficult?" "Why was it difficult?" There's nothing as frustrating as returning from an interview, listening to the tape, and hearing broad statements that weren't challenged. You've got to focus like a laser when soliciting answers to your questions. You want specifics. Details. Examples. Don't let a politician twist you around with his fancy presentation of facts when what you're after is where he stands on issues and why. Don't let a businessman throw numbers and statistics at you when what you're looking for is the bottom line. Don't let a celebrity who's said something provocative in the past skirt around that statement when you bring it up. There's almost an art to avoiding answering questions. It's the art of bullshit. Don't let anyone get away with bullshitting you.

GOING WITH THE UNEXPECTED

This has to do with listening. If you're trying to just get your questions answered, you may not be hearing what someone is saying. And sometimes a person can go off on a tangent that is more interesting than the direction you were steering them in. This can make for excellent copy, too.

In my *Playboy* interview with Governor Jesse Ventura I asked him about drug crimes and prostitution. He believed they were consensual crimes. "People who commit consensual crimes shouldn't go to jail," he said. "We shouldn't even prosecute them. That's crime against yourself." So I asked him if he would legalize those activities. He went on about how much better it would be if prostitution was legal, as in Nevada. "If it's legal, then the girls could have health checks, unions, benefits, anything any other worker gets, and it would be far better."

"This isn't a very popular position in America, is it?" I asked.

And Ventura gave an unexpected answer that turned this interview into a cause célèbre when it appeared.

VENTURA: No, and it's because of religion. Organized religion is a sham and a crutch for weak-minded people who need strength in numbers. It tells people to go out and stick their noses in other people's business. I live by the golden rule: Treat others as you'd want them to treat you. The religious right wants to tell people how to live.

WHEN I NOTICED that Freddie Prinze Jr.'s bookshelves were devoid of books I asked him about it. His answer—"I don't really read that much, I read comic books, play video games"—was so unexpected, I took the conversation in a different direction. All of the following is a result of my being invited, in the winter of 2000, to do our interview in his bedroom and by chance seeing those empty bookshelves.

Q: What comics do you mostly read?

PRINZE: My favorite titles are *X-Men, Dead Pool,* and *Hell Boy.*

Q: Do you collect?

PRINZE: Yeah, I have a ton of them in my office.

Q: What are your most valuable comics?

PRINZE: I have 2 through 10 *X-Men,* number 16 *X-Men,* 20-30 *X-Men;* I have number 11 *Spiderman;* number 4 *Silver Surfer;* number 4 *Fantastic Four.* The most valuable is number 2 *X-Men,* probably worth a few grand.

Q: Did you ever meet Stan Lee?

PRINZE: Yeah, I just met him. He was like the nicest guy in the world. He made life good for me when I was a kid. I was really nervous and canceled the first meeting with him. Because I was— what people now call artistic and brilliant—when you're a kid they call weird and "you're gay, you're dumb." I never really fit in to any of my schools when I was a little kid and I started reading comics and really related to his characters: that somehow they embraced who they were and they became great heroes and changed or saved the world. They made me feel that everything could be OK . . . and now everything is OK. Everything's awesome. I'm really happy, I like where I am, I do cool things, and I know this sounds weird but I feel I owe Stan Lee a lot for that. Because when kids made fun of me I'd go home and read his comics and be in this other world where it was cool to be me.

Q: Why did kids make fun of you?

PRINZE: When I was younger I'd make-believe a lot. I still do. I was an only child, I didn't have a dad to play football or anything like that, so I made up friends. I made up this superhero world that I lived in. I fought alongside of the X-Men. We'd fight against Magneto and Apocalypse and I would really do it. I would really see them and I would dive away from Magneto, sending these huge iron pylons at me, and counter-attack. Kids would see me out there in the field jumping around and perceive me as weird. I did this all by myself, not with any friends because they didn't think that was cool. But that was what was fun for me. I didn't have any brothers or sisters, I grew up on a street with all girls and they wanted to play house and I didn't like house. So that's what I did for fun; my teachers thought I was sick, they sent me to a counselor. When you do things like that, kids make fun of you.

Q: Why did they call you gay?

PRINZE: Because they thought I was weird. I still did that when I was 12 years old. I'll be honest—I have all the sound here in my bedroom so I can turn it up loud and I have a lot of open space and I still play like that. Because that's what's fun for me. I live alone and when I get bored or lonely, those are the kinds of things I do: I make up scenarios in my head and I play 'em out. And it's always different every time, because it's your imagination. When kids see someone who's a little too old to do that, they think it's weird. And kids can be mean, so they say things like "you freak; stupid fag."

Q: Did you ever become enough of a superhero to fight back?

PRINZE: I got in fights, but I don't like fighting. It feels worse to know that you hurt someone than to hurt someone. I once hurt a kid really, really bad . . .

Q: How old were you?

PRINZE: Seventeen. He got his face busted up, a broken nose, and I hurt his back a little bit.

Q: How did it happen?

PRINZE: He was drunk. It was at one of the few parties I went to in high school. I didn't know anybody there and didn't know what to do, so I was pouring beer for everybody, wanting to fit in. He was mad because I was trying to fit in or maybe his girlfriend liked me or I was trying to be friends with one of his friends, I don't know why. But I walked out of the place and he pushed me in the back and I fell down and everybody started laughing. I got up and tried to walk away and he came at me again, so we got into a fight. When he fell on the ground I just kept hitting him . . . and when it was over I just didn't like what I did.

Q: As you were hitting him, were you even aware what you were doing?

PRINZE: I knew exactly what I was doing. Nobody tried to break it up because he was a bully.

Q: Sylvester Stallone got into a fight as a teenager and said after he hit this bigger guy it was the first time he realized his fists were "loaded." Did you feel that way?

PRINZE: I didn't feel the same as that. I knew exactly what was happening and what I did, I just kept hitting that kid until his face wasn't hard anymore. I knew that I didn't want to stop beating him until he cried.

We covered his career, his love life, the standard things one expects in an interview with an actor, but this bloody fight where Prinze "just kept hitting that kid until his face wasn't hard any more" was what gave this interview with a young and relatively unproven actor some force. And it never would have been revealed had I not asked him about comic books and Stan Lee.

BURYING ONESELF IN CHAUVINISM

In these politically correct times it's rare when a nationally known figure will say politically incorrect things, especially about race, religion, or gender. When someone is willing to rub women, gays, blacks, Muslims, Jews, or whomever the wrong way, it not only makes for good copy, but is insightful as well.

And if you can find someone willing to share these views, then your interview might get quoted in the gossip and media columns, which will make your editor happy because such exposure often increases sales of the publication in which such remarks appear.

When former prosecutor Vincent Bugliosi started talking about how his father was the boss of his home when he was growing up in the *Playboy* interview I did with him in 1997, I asked him if that was the way it is with him and his wife, Gail.

Bugliosi responded, "I'm in charge, yes."

Well, immediately I knew this would be fun to pursue, and I wanted to do it playfully. Bugliosi is a tough, opinionated character who doesn't like to show any weaknesses. The conversation I had with him covered a wide variety of subjects. He had fascinating things to say about Charlie Manson, O. J. Simpson, the John F. Kennedy assassination, and the war on drugs. But what kind of guy just out-and-out states that he's in charge of a marriage?

"Who makes the important decisions in your family?" I prodded.

BUGLIOSI: I do. We're getting into an area here where I'm sure to get attacked, but it seems to me that someone has to be the boss. It's childish for someone not to be the boss—like two kids in a sand pile saying, "I got my way this time, now it's your turn." Marriage, the family, it's an organization, a unit. And like any other unit, someone has to be in charge.

"Women are going to love reading this," I said, feeling I didn't need much more than this comment to keep him going.

BUGLIOSI: But this is not looking down upon a woman at all. If people don't agree that the man should be in charge then the question is, do they want the woman to be in charge? I'd like to see a feasible arrangement where you have two people and neither one's in charge. How do you succeed in anything in life if you have no one in charge and everyone is going off in different directions?

I was thinking about my own marriage at the time and how my wife would look at me as if I really was from Mars if I told her that I was the one in charge of our marriage. And I asked Bugliosi, "Do you believe in equality in a marriage?"

BUGLIOSI: I believe in complete equality between men and women in every area except marriage. In marriage the woman has to take the subordinate role not because man is superior but because every unit has to have a leader, and the man is the more natural leader.

I wasn't sure if we were talking about military units or relationships here, so I continued to tweak, because I suspected this was going to turn into that joke about how the man is in charge of the big questions—like who should go to war, what we should do about colonizing space, and whether the ozone layer was going to become a bigger problem over the next century or two—while the woman dealt with all the insignificant things in life, like what car to buy, what food to eat, what shows to watch, and how many kids one should have. "So," I asked, "you see a woman as having a specific role to play in a marriage?"

BUGLIOSI: Unless it's not economically possible. I believe a woman's role is in the home. I don't view that as a subordinate role, as feminists do. Someone has to stay at home, take care of the children, cook for the family, and it's far more natural for the woman to fill this role. I don't know why feminists think that working in the highly competitive and treacherous business world is somehow superior to being at home. But hey, if that's what they want and the husband doesn't mind, that's fine. I just don't think that in the last analysis they're doing themselves any favors.

It was time to play the lawyer with him, to show how much like the cliché joke he was actually sounding like.

Q: Do you do any cooking?

BUGLIOSI: No. Coffee is about all I can do. I can make toast.

Q: Does your wife like to go out more than you?

BUGLIOSI: Yes.

Q: Do you find yourself going out more because of that?

BUGLIOSI: Yes.

Q: When you go to a movie, who selects the film?

BUGLIOSI: Normally, I will defer to her because movies are more important to her than they are to me.

Q: If she wants to go out and you don't, then what?

BUGLIOSI: She goes out with her girlfriends.

Q: What about your environment—who has furnished and decorated your house?

BUGLIOSI: Oh, she has. There are people in and out of this house—I don't even know who they are. She takes care of all that stuff.

Q: Who pays the bills?

BUGLIOSI: She has the checkbook, and she pays all the bills. She takes care of everything.

If this was a court of law, I would say, "No further questions, Your Honor," and rest my case. But it was an interview, I had no case, just a subject who liked to take firm positions, and sometimes such questioning can be very revealing.

BUGLIOSI ISN'T ALONE when it comes to speaking his mind about women. Mel Gibson has never been afraid of sticking a foot in his mouth to broaden the smile on his face. I discovered this when I asked him if women should be allowed to become priests. When he answered, "No," I asked why not. He said, "I'll get kicked around for saying it, but men and women are just different. They're not equal." Then he added, "Nobody's equal. Women are just different. Their sensibilities are different." When I brought up how feminists might find what he had to say offensive (he had a *lot* more to say), he responded, "Feminists don't like me, and I don't like them."

THE BATTLE OF THE SEXES

With men speaking out like this, it's no wonder women often see them as pigs. And it can make for equally quotable copy. Halle Berry was very sensitive about her first marriage with baseball player David Justice. It ended badly, and she didn't like talking about it. Still, when interviewing her, it's hard not to ask about it. I did it this way:

Q: There are two comments David Justice made to *People* magazine that I want to bring up.

BERRY: They're all lies. If he said it, it's a lie. I'll tell you that right now. [*Laughs*]

Q: He said, "I always felt I was walking on eggshells with her." How do you interpret that?

BERRY: Bullshit.

Q: And, "She was always suspicious. I've never known a girl who could throw a tantrum like she does."

BERRY: If your husband cheated on you with prostitutes, strippers, every twinkie walking by him with a skirt, you'd feel the same way. End of story.

Berry's passion and emotion come through in her response. You're not going to get much out of her about her first marriage, but this seemed sufficient to get some idea of why that relationship didn't work out.

Actress Lesley Ann Warren told me how distressful it was growing up in her body, which developed early. "My own sexuality was very uncomfortable to me," she said. "I hated my breasts. I hated them! Being thirteen and having all this attention from boys, the attention limited only to my body."

I asked her if her first experience with sex at seventeen was memorable.

WARREN: It was horrible. There was no caring involved at all. I cared a lot. I thought I was in love, but he wasn't. He was about twenty-four and it was horrible. There was no tenderness and no gentleness. I remember it well. After, I went home to my parents' house and got into my baby girl's bedroom and just cried and cried.

Q: Did you talk to your parents about it?

WARREN: Yes, I talked to my mother and my father. My dad was disappointed, but he was loving. My mom was pissed off. She was mad, and that didn't help, it didn't help at all.

Q: How turned off to the act of sex were you after that?

WARREN: Well, I used to have nightmares about giant penises. I swear. I was real turned off.

Sex has always been a viable topic of interest, but a lot of people, understandably, prefer to keep it private. Sometimes it seems with the proliferation of men's magazines (and women's magazines like *Cosmopolitan*) that talk of first sex, early sex, good sex, horrible sex, a lot of sex, or a lack of sex turns the subject into something less glorious than it really is. Sex should be a private act between consenting adults. But it's obviously also a primary topic for a lot of different media. If you're uncomfortable broaching the subject, and if your editor is expecting you to bring it up, then just be honest about it. Express your discomfort, apologize for infringing on one's privacy, and see if the person you're interviewing is understanding and willing to give you something. If not, you've tried; move on and learn from it. If the subject matter is uncomfortable for you, then you should not aim for those markets where it's expected. There are plenty of markets out there, and not all of them expect you to get the kind of response Lesley Ann Warren gave about her nightmares.

Goldie Hawn started her career as a dancer, and for a while after high school she entered the world of go-go dancing, where she performed in seedy clubs, dancing on tables, "with men whipping out their hoo-ha's." It was a sordid world of drunks, truck drivers, and masturbators, and as she told her stories I had to ask if she had ever met anyone at that time that wasn't a sleaze. Her answer was a detailed story that I felt had to be left uncut because it so well illustrated what young women are often up against when they are trying to break into a profession. Here was a casting couch story from the mouth of one who didn't compromise and survived to tell it.

HAWN: I had an experience when I was brand new in New York. I was going for a modeling job when a man picked me up on the street, saying, "You have a very unusual face." If he had told me I was beautiful, I would have known he was full of shit and walked away. But he said the right thing and he gave me a whole line of bull. He said, "Al Capp, the cartoonist, is casting parts for the movie version of *Li'l Abner* and has a wonderful character called Tenderleif Ericsson, and you seem like the right girl for this. Have you ever acted before?" And I said, "Yes, I did *Romeo and Juliet*." So I got into his Cadillac, thinking, This is great! I'm driving down Amsterdam Avenue in a brand-new Cadillac convertible; my mother and father will never believe this! He said to me, "You have to be very nice to Mr. Capp, because he can do a lot of good for you." I was really excited.

Well, he primed me for this visit for about two weeks, telling me how I would earn all this money and become a big star. My initial thought was, God, I'll be able to put wall-to-wall carpeting in my mother's house. So I learned my lines and went to this apartment, very nervous. The butler came in and said, "Mr. Capp would like you to pour the tea. He always likes his ladies to pour the tea." I sat there waiting for Mr. Capp. And he thundered in with his wooden leg. He had great presence. Very deep voice. "Goldie, I heard so much about you. I understand that you are a very nice girl. You're going to have to work very, very hard to get this part." He was in his bathrobe. I said, "Mr. Capp, I'm a dancer and I know what it is to work hard." He said, "Good. Now, would you stand up and start reading." So I read very loud. He said, "Goldie, speak softly for the cameras, because they can hear you." I was sucked in. I believed this man really wanted to help me. Then he told me to go across the room and pretend his eyes were the camera and take the dangling orange beads that I had hanging from my neck and put them in my mouth and act like an imbecile. So, like a jackass, I took the beads and put them in my mouth and acted like an imbecile.

Then I started to get very nervous. I smelled something coming. He said, "Would you walk to the mirror and lift up your skirt, 'cause I think you can play Daisy Mae." I was very proud of my legs; it wasn't something I was shy of. So I lifted my skirt. He said, "Higher." I went up an inch. He said, "Higher." I went up another inch. It finally got to the point of no return and I said to myself, "That's it; it's not going up any higher." He said, "Come and sit next to me"—at which point he had completely exposed himself. And this *thing* was staring at me!

I looked at it and started to shake. Then I threw the script down and did what any nice Jewish girl who was going to grow up and marry a dentist would do. I said, "Mr. Capp, I would never get a job this way." He said, "Oh, I had *all* of them, all the movie stars. You'll never make it in this business. You don't have anything; you're nothing." He started to put me down and I cried, running out of his apartment.

Q: Nasty story. Was that the end?

HAWN: Almost. The next year, almost to the month, this young, nice-looking Jewish man met me on the street and said, "Excuse me, I just have to stop you. You know, you have a very special look, and there's a man by the name of Al Capp; do you know who he is?" I started to scream!

SEARCHING ONE'S PAST FOR CLUES

Joyce Carol Oates is among the most prolific and diversified writers who has ever practiced the profession. Her work often explores the dark side of life—girl gangs, teenage rape, serial killers, riots, racial strife. When I went to interview her at her home in Princeton, where she also teaches at the university, I was looking for some key to what made her think the way she thinks. She told me that she had a malformation of a heart valve that causes tachycardia, which made her heart speed up, her body hyperventilate, and, at times, she would black out. I began to understand her drive: She felt she might drop dead at any time, so she had no time to waste. But what about some of those sordid themes? I knew I had to dig even deeper into her past. I found a partial answer in her childhood.

When Oates was nine or ten, she told me, she was molested. "And I couldn't tell my mother because I was threatened not to," she said. "However, I never forgot being chased, being mauled. It was extremely important for me, retrospectively, to have these early experiences of being quite a helpless victim, because it allows me to sympathize—or compels me to sympathize—with victims. I know what it's like to be a victim. I was part of a world where almost everybody who was weak was victimized. This seems to be the human condition: to be picked on, to be a victim."

Yet, when it came to what happened to Desiree Washington, the teenager who was raped by Mike Tyson in 1991, Oates showed a surprising empathy . . . for the former champ. "I refuse to look at a boxer whose physical being is an insult to a great sport," she said. "That's why I was so shocked when Tyson came in out of condition with Buster Douglas. I couldn't believe that he would demean the heavyweight title. Intellectually I saw that he hadn't done training. Emotionally when he came in the ring I couldn't believe what a bad fight he was fighting. To me that's much more profoundly disturbing and bizarre than the things that he did in his private life, which I can understand. I don't condone raping a young woman but I can understand that a lot more than I can a heavyweight champion coming in at a young age and not being trained. That was very shocking to me."

So here you have an example that demonstrates the complexity of a person. How does one reconcile what happened to Joyce as a child with her being more profoundly disturbed by Mike Tyson's being overweight at a championship fight than by his behavior with a young beauty queen in a hotel room that sent him to prison? That's not a question for me to answer, but to put in the minds of readers who can then draw their own conclusions, and it blossoms beautifully in print.

THE PROBLEM WITH PARENTS

There is often powerful material to be mined in the relationship between your subject and his parents, but unlocking that material is never easy. What child hasn't been traumatized by his mother or father? What child hasn't rebelled against his parents? Gotten in trouble? Been punished?

When the person you're interviewing agrees to lift the lid, even slightly, of the Pandora's box of their family life, the quotes can be revealing. And revelation is a definite goal in an interview.

ALLEN GINSBERG AND HIS PARENTS

When the poet Allen Ginsberg spoke about his parents it was hard to keep one's jaw from dropping, he was so brutally honest and forthright.

Q: When "Howl" was published, how did your father react to your coming out so publicly about private things?

GINSBERG: That was very difficult. That was the big barrier, because when I wrote "Howl" I wasn't intending to publish it. I didn't write it as a poem, just as a piece of writing for my own pleasure. I wanted to write something where I could say what I really was thinking, rather than poetry. From that point of view I thought I couldn't publish this. I didn't want to shove my ass in my father's face: "Who got fucked in the ass by handsome sailors and screamed with joy." I didn't want him to read that, because given our relationship that would be quite embarrassing. We never talked about sex seriously and certainly there was some subliminal erotic thing going on between us, which I shouldn't touch on lightly. Very strongly so. Without him knowing it. So it really would have disturbed him a great deal.

Q: What about your mother, where was she when she first read "Howl"?

GINSBERG: My mother was really mad. She was in mental hospitals. She thought people were walking up and down the apartment lobby with poison gas to spray at her. Some people were hanging around the bus station across the street spying on her. And my grandmother was climbing up on the fire escape with old clothes on to spray poisons on her. It was really very difficult. I sent her "Howl" at Pilgrim State Hospital where she was in her last months before her stroke. She hadn't recognized me about a half year before when I visited. She thought I was a spy, actually. It was very disturbing—I wept. It seemed like the farthest limit of dehumanization and illness and madness, that she couldn't remember me.

Q: Would you say your childhood was cut short by your mother's mental illness?

GINSBERG: Yes, I think so. I didn't get mother love, and that's always been a kind of grief. It's been a dominant motif in whatever I've done. I had to take care of my mother basically, and so I got sick of taking care of women. It was just too much trouble, too horrifying a task at that time. Probably alienated me from women's bodies and smells and situations and blood.

Q: So it's really no mystery figuring out what you meant when you once wrote that between you and oblivion an unknown woman stands. You asked yourself then why you feared the one hole that repelled you.

GINSBERG: Well, I'm talking about my mother's vagina. Since I had to take care of her, as I said, it was a repellent situation.

Speaking of mothers, I asked Ginsberg to comment on his friend Jack Kerouac's relationship with his mother, which paid off with this exchange:

Q: As a student of Freud, you must have some interesting thoughts on Jack Kerouac's relationship with his mother.

GINSBERG: It was interesting. They would get drunk together and speak the foulest language I've ever heard between them. She didn't like any of his friends. She particularly didn't like bearded Jews, but she also didn't like [William] Burroughs, or Jack's wife or his girlfriends. Jack was close with a painter, a strong, good woman, and his mother once pulled him aside and said, "I don't trust her, she's a witch, I saw her sharpening knives against the candles." She didn't like it that I was gay. At one time Jack said his mother was absolutely crazy like mine, but he didn't want to throw her to the dogs of eternity as he said I had. So he put up with shocking things. I still remember it, great phrase: dogs of eternity. But he paid the price of his own life by staying with her.

ELLEN DEGENERES AND HER PARENTS

When I asked Ellen DeGeneres about her decision to come out of the closet, I also wanted to know how her family dealt with the revelation. Here's her answer.

DEGENERES: As a girl I didn't know I was gay. I was boy crazy. But I look back now and realize how much I liked girls and identified with crushing on girls. But I never experimented.

I was fortunate that my parents didn't throw me out of the house or disown me when they found out, because that happens to a lot of kids. Their fathers beat them up if they're boys, or they're thrown out on the street. It's horrible. My mother didn't understand it and was in shock. She went to a library and started reading about homosexuality and ended up writing books to help parents better understand and deal with it. My father didn't say anything. I don't remember what my brother felt.

But it got to a point where I realized that there is something wrong thinking that you're supposed to live your life in order to fit in to a whole group of people's consensus to how you're supposed to be. Most people live their lives like that. They dress a certain way because it's the acceptable way to dress; they act a certain way because they've been conditioned and domesticated, they've been taught by reward and punishment of what's going to be tolerable and intolerable. But I realized that this is my life, it's my obligation to be true to my soul, my being. So I had to clear a space from all the rules that society has set up as to what's acceptable and what's not. I had to listen to the inner voice that often guides us. And that was to just be who I am.

JOHN HUSTON AND HIS MOTHER

John Huston was an extremely complex man. When the sculptor Jan de Swart met him toward the end of his life, he said, "I've read your autobiography—you must be three hundred years old!" Indeed, Huston had lived a rich and varied life. He had been a semipro boxer, a more-than-decent painter, a short-story writer, a screenwriter, a director, an actor, a collector, a gambler, and a father. He had five wives, dozens of mistresses, lived as an expatriate in Ireland and Mexico. There was plenty to write about when I started thinking about doing a biography of him and his family, but it wasn't until he told me that his mother—an adventurer and character in her own right—made three attempts at a memoir, all of which he had put away to read when he felt ready, but had yet to feel ready even at the age of eighty, that I felt the secret to understanding the man was to dig into his relationship with his mother. He gave me her writings, saying, "You read them, and tell me whether I should." Over the nearly two years I spoke to him about his life before he died on August 28, 1987, we spent a lot of time talking about his mother. And eventually he told me things that I felt would help the reader understand how he treated women over his lifetime, and why no relationship lasted.

When I interviewed some of the women who had loved him, they inevitably referred to his mother as the key to unlocking Huston's psyche. "She was a central character," Olivia de Havilland told me in Paris. "I always felt that John was ridden by witches. He seemed to be pursued by something destructive. If it wasn't his mother, it was his idea of his mother."

When I first attempted to delve into their relationship, Huston said to me, "We're about to get into deeper water here. Let's save her for another time."

It took a long time. I had to read her manuscripts. I had to interview dozens and dozens of people who had opinions about her. But eventually, through persistence and an understanding between us that his mother had to be discussed, Huston came through. It was never easy. I asked him questions about her personality, her independence, her feelings about her failed marriage to Walter Huston, her nomadic behavior, her sense of discipline, her religious beliefs, her demonstration of love toward him, her expectations of him. And when I wrote *The Hustons,* I edited our numerous discussions about his mother down to eight paragraphs, which, I hoped, would demonstrate the submission, suffocation, and deceit he felt about her.

"I have very mixed feelings about my mother," Huston said. "Great favor in one way . . . and, in another way, I thought she was suffocating. Not because she followed me from place to place, but she would adhere too closely. . . . She was a mass of contradictions . . . She could lie to herself as well as to others. . . . At one time she had a hysterical paralysis. . . . She was very nervous, tending toward the neurotic. . . . Very chaste. . . . She would go to confession but not take communion. She pretended—or didn't, I don't know which—to subscribe to the myth of Christianity. . . . I made fun of it, which would make her cry. . . . I did a caricature one time of Jesus as an absurd dramatic figure, and she burst into tears looking at this. . . . She gave me a few beatings as a child. She used a strap. I remember her saying, 'Say "I'm sorry," that you'll never do it again.' And I would say it. Submitting. Then she would stop."

JAMES GARNER AND HIS STEPMOTHER

In 1994 I interviewed James Garner, who told me that when he was four his mother died and a year later his father remarried "a nasty bitch" who "used to beat the hell out of me."

I asked him if she was the one who made him wear a dress and called him Louise if he did anything wrong.

GARNER: Yeah, where did you find that out? It was out in the country and we'd be in some little store and I'd just go hide because it would embarrass me terribly. Then my brothers would tease me and call me Louise and a fight would break out.

Q: How often did that happen?

GARNER: Oh gosh, a lot. If I did anything wrong I'd have to go put on the dress.

Q: At what point did you fight back?

GARNER: At around thirteen. I decked her. I had her on the bed, choking her. My dad and my brother pulled me off of her. I can understand how kids can rebel to the point of murder. I don't agree with it, but I don't know what I'd have done—because she was tough. *Tough.* I'm sure I wouldn't have let go of her until she quit breathing because she'd have killed me if she got up. Then they held me down so she could whip me. But that's the night that broke up the marriage with my dad and her.

This is strong, revealing, unexpected talk. It isn't very often when talking to a television icon like Garner that you're going to get a paragraph as graphic and shocking as this. More often than not you're going to have to deal with someone like Ray Romano, who turned down doing a *Playboy* interview because he was worried what his young daughter might think, and because he felt he didn't have much to say.

CHRISTINA RICCI AND HER FATHER

Christina Ricci didn't want to talk about her father, and though I try to avoid yes-or-no answers, in this case you still get the sense of her hurt in the shortness of her responses.

Q: What's your relationship with your father today?

RICCI: I haven't talked with him in six years.

Q: Are you sorry about that?

RICCI: No.

Q: Does he ever try to contact you?

RICCI: No.

DREW BARRYMORE AND HER FATHER

Drew Barrymore, on the other hand, is willing to talk about her absent father. She isn't shy about her early life experiences, which is why it's a challenge to pull new things out of her. In the previous chapter she answered the question about how crazy and what kind of genius her father was. Here she responds to a reported incident that is hard to believe, so must be asked.

Q: Were you exaggerating at all when you told the story of how he stuck your hand into the flame of a candle to demonstrate pain?

BARRYMORE: He did it. He held my hand there for a few seconds. I was three or four. And he told me it was mind over matter, that you could overcome pain through your mind. He was very into Yogi–Buddhism–Eastern philosophy.

HALLE BERRY AND HER FATHER

The children of divorce or separation always struggle to deal with what went wrong between their parents. They are often forced to choose sides, and it's never easy for them. It's always nice to hear someone say that their parents were very loving and they had an ideal family life, but it makes for boring copy. Perhaps that's why we don't read so much about that. Here's Halle Berry talking about her dad.

Q: Your own parents separated when you were four. Did your mother ever talk bitterly against your father after he left?

BERRY: My father was very abusive to my mother. I saw him kick my mother's ass. She often had less than pleasant things to say about him. But she always let us know that while he was a shitty husband and beat her up, she tried to separate their relationship from ours. She encouraged us to have him in our lives as a father. I didn't see him from the time I was four until I was ten, when he came back. My mother said, "I'm going to give it a shot." Because she wanted us to have him in our lives. He lived with us for one year, in 1976, and it was the worst year of my life. The worst. He beat on my sister. Never me. But our dog—we had a toy Maltese and he threw our dog across the dining room at dinner, and the dog almost bit its tongue off. The blood and that image—when somebody mentions my father, that's the first thing I think about, that dog flying across the room. I remember crying, God, let him leave, so my life could get back to normal. I'd been praying for my father and when I got him I just wanted him to leave. My mother would cry, they would fight. It was very scary.

OLIVER STONE AND HIS FATHER

Oliver Stone gives a good interview because he doesn't hold back—he'll talk about his mom taking him to a nudist colony when he was nine, about his father buying him his first sexual experience with a prostitute when he was fifteen. But when I read somewhere that he had once spiked his father's drink with LSD, I wanted the details. And Stone obliged.

STONE: I was doing acid and a lot of marijuana, and I was talking like a black kid. That drove him nuts: "Man. Groovy. Wow." I'd been really influenced [in Vietnam] by the black troops, that's where I learned how to smoke dope. I've been smoking grass all my life. My father just loathed everything about my habits after I returned from the war. I didn't have much money, and I was living for a while at his house. Somewhere along the way we just clashed one too many times, and I just fucking had it. I put the goddamn acid in his Scotch. We were playing chess, and all of a sudden you could see his face change, and everything was being taken really intensely. [*Laughs*] We were at a strange dinner party in the Hamptons. . . . And he was standing out there in the garden holding on to a tree, the whole world was moving. . . . At the dinner we were thirteen people. He stopped in the middle of the dinner, there was a silent pause, you could hear the silverware clank, and he said, "Who's the Judas at the table?" He looked around, and I kept a straight fucking face. It was a strange night, and he was out of his mind. But he loved it.

ANTHONY KIEDIS AND HIS FATHER

Anthony Kiedis is the lead singer of the Red Hot Chili Peppers. His parents were divorced when he was young, and Kiedis went to live with his father in Los Angeles when he was eleven. His father, who had gone to film school and had acted in a few movies, was a permissive parent who believed that he shouldn't hide his vices from his son; instead, he shared them. Anthony grew up very fast.

Q: When did you smoke your first joint?

KIEDIS: I smoked pot with my father when I was eleven in 1973. When I came out to L.A., my impressions of my father were that he had it all going on. He's always been, from a distance, my hero figure, because he was traveling the world and was sending me T-shirts and beads and pieces of art from England and writing me letters from France and sending me pictures of girls from Hollywood and I was like, this is a much more colorful world than what I'm experiencing here in Michigan. So when I moved out there and saw that he was constantly smoking weed, the first time I had a chance I took it from him and I smoked it and I loved it. It took me straight to this dream world that I was happy to be in. He thought he was being a good father, like in his mind, it's something that he wished his father would have done for him. He thought he was giving me a mind-extending thing just like he used to give me Hemingway novels and Woody Allen films and take me out and show me the world. By twelve, I was taking Quaaludes, Tuinals. I was probably fourteen when I sniffed my first cocaine. I started consciously seeking out heroin and injecting it at eighteen, around the time I quit going to UCLA. I was definitely going to get my education in a different place altogether.

PARENTS AND THEIR CHILDREN

The flip side of talking to people about their parents is asking them about being a parent. For the most part you would expect a certain pride in one's offspring, and it's rare when a parent will say something negative about his child. But when they're willing to be honest, it can make for scintillating copy. Here are a few examples.

JERRY LEWIS AND HIS SON

Q: In a 1973 interview you spoke of your son Gary as being emotionally destroyed by the Vietnam War. "Better he would have been killed," you were quoted as saying. Did you actually say that?

LEWIS: Yeah, I said it, and I'm sure at the time I felt that way. I was terribly upset. I didn't think there was a chance for him, he came back a vegetable, and I know what we produced. I say that in the most egotistical terms, a lot of which was his fault, he was a pretty terrific guy.

HENRY FONDA AND HIS SON

One of the most surprising rises I got out of Henry Fonda in an interview I did with him around the time he won an Oscar for his role in *On Golden Pond* was when I brought up an incident his son Peter claimed happened to him.

Q: Your son Peter has said that when he was a teenager he was attacked by three hoods, who hung him on a fence in New York and drove nails through his hands. What do you remember about it?

FONDA: [*Angry.*] Fucking lie!

Q: Peter tells that story.

FONDA: He's got the goddamnedest imagination and he's a compulsive liar. Now, I shouldn't say that about my son, but it's not a true story! It's not possible. He was living at home and that I would see this boy every day and not know he'd been crucified with nails through his hands? There's no way!

After this interview appeared I received a note from Fonda regretting that he said what he did about Peter, but understanding my right to bring it up. I was impressed with his ability to distinguish between his privacy and my journalistic responsibility.

ANTHONY HOPKINS AND HIS DAUGHTER

Anthony Hopkins didn't want to talk about his daughter Abigail, who is now an actress, because of his irresponsible behavior as a father when she was growing up. "You're not going to get anything out of me," he warned when I broached the subject. "I'm keeping the personal parts of my life that would be painful to my ex-wife and daughter." But I knew that he had played a character in a film called *The Good Father* where he had to vent his rage against his wife. When I brought it up, he first said he "didn't know what the hell the film was about." Then he remembered a particular scene where he was showing his wife his child's bed and it brought back the guilt he felt when he walked out on Abigail. "As I did it, I just broke down, which I've never done before. I've always kept myself in charge of my emotions, but I just broke down. I felt ashamed and very angry with myself. It's the first time I acknowledged that anything had any ties on me, because I've always tried to deny emotion. It kind of shook me."

This admission led us back to his daughter. "We got close a few years ago," he told me. "She stayed with us. But she was doing her own numbers, trying to impress me or being manipulating, and I said forget it. I just withdrew. I always withdraw from people. I try not to let people absorb too much of my energy. Once people start latching onto me and try to draw things out of me and control me I wave them good-bye, sometimes forever and I won't go back. I don't like being controlled by anyone."

Not even his own daughter? I asked. Especially after all those years of separation?

"I was quite prepared to go into the wilderness without her," he said coldly. "I was prepared not to see her again. It doesn't matter to me, you see. We have to be tough and callous about it all, live our lives; it's a very selfish way of looking at it, but I don't have a conscience."

MONTEL WILLIAMS AND HIS CHILDREN

Q: When your son was born, you said it was the first time in your life you felt a sense of immortality.

WILLIAMS: I'm sorry if I offend anyone but I have testosterone flowing through my body; I'm a male. In this society when a woman gets married, the woman takes on the male's name, that's how you get a family name. Without a male child being born in my family, the Williams clan ends here. That immortality thought was based on the fact that the family name will at least proceed on for another generation. I'm proud of the fact that I have a son, it's like a little me.

Q: You wrote to your son: "I've invested your future with more meaning than I have your sisters." How does that make your daughters feel?

WILLIAMS: I talked to my oldest about it who said, "I'm the first, so why don't you feel that way about me?" And I said, "Ashley, I do." I think there is a different relationship between a father and son. I didn't say it's better, it's different. I'm old-school male pig I guess. I'll definitely talk to him about whacking off, about condoms, about sex. . . . I talk to my daughters about sex, too. There are just different things within the sexes that we cannot deny.

JEAN—CLAUDE VAN DAMME AND HIS SON

When I first met Jean-Claude Van Damme we flew to a comic book convention in San Diego. His seven-year-old son Kristofer was with him, and he had his shirt outside his pants. Van Damme insisted that the boy tuck in his shirt. On the plane, he also got angry that the boy left half a melon uneaten. Later, I asked him about disciplining his child.

Q: How strict a father are you?

VAN DAMME: I believe a father has to be strict. You are preparing them for the jungle. . . . But you have to be very careful with your kids; you can fuck them up badly. One word from a father or a mother can give them sequels for the rest of their lives.

Q: Have you ever laid a hand on your son?

VAN DAMME: Yes, once.

Q: On his behind?

VAN DAMME: In his face. I told him something, he didn't do it, and he kept on. I was so pissed. He insulted me. Today my son respects me like crazy.

Q: Why do you insist that he tuck in his shirt all the time? He's just a boy.

VAN DAMME: Because I don't like it.

Q: But children today are wearing baggy clothes, they keep their pants low around the waist, their underwear shows.

VAN DAMME: That's not a style, you look like a bum. And they are all fat and have flat feet. Go to the mall, all those kids are knock-kneed, they don't do any sport, they play computer games day and night.

Q: And they talk back to their parents and don't always do their homework.

VAN DAMME: That's America for you. That's not America for me.

Q: You also don't want to see a slice of melon go half-eaten.

VAN DAMME: That's because when I came to America I was unable to buy a Dannon yogurt. Taco Bell was my Sunday, I enjoyed that Taco Bell from the beginning to the end. Even if I've got millions, billions, trillions of dollars, my children are going to finish their melon. Because I paid for it, I worked for it.

Q: And if they protest that they are not hungry?

VAN DAMME: Then I send them to bed. I will yell. Are you my child or what? You talk to me like that, you're my blood. Are you crazy? I will put that melon in the fridge, and the next day when they wake up, there's the melon. They will eat nothing else until they finish that melon. We have this saying in Europe: Who stole an egg will steal a cow. If you answer me for a melon, what will you do later when you have a car? If your father's telling you something, it's your duty as his child to listen to him. You have to respect stuff in life. That melon's life.

Q: You're one tough daddy.

VAN DAMME: It's my duty.

NIGHTMARES: WHEN IT JUST ISN'T WORKING

Often, getting people to reveal themselves means asking the right questions, touching on subjects that touch them emotionally. It can be a past issue with a parent, or a more current one with a child. It can be their feelings about the opposite sex, the struggles to get a career started, an embarrassing moment, or pride in some achievement. But there are times when no matter what you ask, the answers aren't forthcoming; or they're dull, uninspired, lazy. Some people, like Robert De Niro or Harrison Ford, just don't like to talk; others, like Chris O'Donnell, James Franco, or Freddy Prinze Jr., don't have that much to say. (I once asked O'Donnell a philosophical question and he answered that his father would be better at answering it than he would.) Some, like John Updike, Steve Martin, or Meryl Streep, would rather save their energy to invest in their work, and not exhaust it through revealing interviews. And then there are those like Elliott Gould, who, as I illustrated before, will talk your ear off, but when you go to edit it on the page, it just leaps around like spilled mercury.

The first time I interviewed Steve Martin in 1979, when he was making *The Jerk,* his first movie, I couldn't get him to budge from behind his desk. He would sit and answer my questions in a monotone; there was none of the spark or energy of the comedian I had seen on stage or when the cameras were rolling on the set. Martin was a talented comic actor, a physical comedian, and would eventually prove to be a witty and entertaining writer, but he was not a very inspiring interview. And when your editor is expecting something funny, Martin's serious, quiet nature can turn what should have been a fun assignment into a horror. Because Steve had agreed to a cover shot of him in a diaper with two *Playboy* Bunnies, I knew the reader's expectations were going to be geared toward laughter, so I had to warn the reader up front that we were dealing with a comedian who wasn't about to turn on his juices. This is how it began.

Q: The cover shows you in character—a wild and crazy guy. Is this going to be an in-character interview?

MARTIN: It's hard for me to be funny for fourteen days or however long we're going to do this. I can't disguise my true self that long. But I'll be funny when there's a question I don't want to answer.

Q: I thought we'd start with your background and work our way up through your—

MARTIN: Nobody gives a shit about where I grew up and all that. That's boring. Even *I* don't give a shit. When I read an interview and it gets to the part where the person grew up, I turn the page.

Q: What, then, interests you?

MARTIN: The only thing of interest to me is the future.

Q: How do you see your future?

MARTIN: I have no idea. I don't even know what my plans are. So I can't talk about it.

Q: Let's get this straight: You're bored with your past and you can't talk about your future. The present is probably too fleeting, so that leaves us with what? Sex?

MARTIN: Well . . . as long as I don't get into: Did I go to bed with Linda Ronstadt? Actually, I'm reluctant to talk about sex or my girlfriends or ex-girlfriends, because that's *really* your private life and you're affecting people who never thought they would be affected.

Q: No past, no future, no sex. What about politics?

MARTIN: I'm not political, because I don't know what's going on. Get someone who knows politics to talk about it.

Q: What you're saying is you don't have much to say.

MARTIN: In theory, you do an interview because you have great things to say. If I had great things to say, I'd say them onstage or in a movie, or somewhere else. In my work, I *disguise* what I have to say. That's what art is.

Q: What do you mean?

MARTIN: You can't just say, "Life is not worth living." You have to write a novel that says life is not worth living. In an interview, you're talking directly; you're not an artist anymore.

Q: You're forgetting that there is an art to conversation.

MARTIN: That's true. I've turned down all other requests for interviews because I want this one to have meaning.

Q: Which will be quite a feat, since you've put so many restrictions on yourself.

MARTIN: The interviews I've done in the past are so redundant. Superficial. Either you give it all or you shouldn't give *any* of it.

Q: My feelings exactly. Should we stop now or continue?

MARTIN: Obviously, this is where I end up giving it all.

Q: Terrific. Now—

MARTIN: Although there are some things I'm determined not to talk about.

Q: Let's start over. You're a comedian. This is an interview. To hell with the restrictions. Now, who's the funniest person in America today?

And so we finally began, but the setup above became almost like a comedy routine, and it served the purpose of lowering the reader's expectations, and thus when we did start getting into his background and opinions, it was like getting a bonus. (Oh, yeah, the funniest person for Martin was Richard Pryor.)

In the end, Martin actually had a lot to say, it was just a matter of setting a tone for the kind of interview it turned out to be.

But with the young actor James Franco, I'm still not sure what he has to say, or whether he is capable of articulating it. I interviewed him after he had completed *City by the Sea,* in which he played Robert De Niro's troubled son, and *Sonny,* where he starred as a male prostitute in Nicolas Cage's debut as a director. He was about to leave for Australia to begin *The Great Raid,* based on a true story about the rescue of American soldiers held captive in the Philippines during World War II. His star was definitely rising. He won a Golden Globe for his 2001 re-creation of James Dean in a biopic for TNT and followed that with a part in the ensemble cast *Deuces Wild,* then the wildly successful *Spider-Man,* where he got to play Tobey Maguire's friend and the son of the archvillain Green Goblin, played by Willem Dafoe.

I knew very little about Franco from reading previous articles about him because he never revealed himself. He left his home in Palo Alto, where his father worked in Silicon Valley and his mother wrote children's books, when he was eighteen to attend UCLA, but that only lasted a year because he hadn't applied for the theater department. Instead he joined Robert Carnegie's Actor's Playhouse, took some art classes at Cal Arts in Valencia, studied with a few painters, and chose to pursue acting. ("Painting is wonderful because it's so private, you're not beholden to a director or a producer; but acting has been really saving to me. It's so expressive and free.") He landed a part in a TV miniseries *(To Serve and Protect)*, did an episode of *Profiler,* got cast in *Freaks and Geeks,* which got wonderful reviews but was canceled in less than a year, and then won the role of James Dean.

When we finished talking, I still knew very little about Franco, because he wasn't ready to fill in the blanks. "As an actor it's probably not to one's benefit to be overexposed," he told me. "If you want to play different parts, you don't want to reveal too much of your personal life. It's defining." He wasn't ready to be pinned to the wall just yet. If Franco learned anything from James Dean, it was not just to "keep it real," as Dean told Dennis Hopper, who passed the advice on to Franco, along with the second tidbit, to keep the details to himself. To keep it abstract, not specific. To not give in to the "favorite" game: Favorite books? Favorite actors? Favorite CDs? Comics? Foods?

"Nah, nah," he'd say and turn his face sideways, lifting his head from his neck as if he'd like it to become a balloon to float above the fray of questions, separating his mind from his body. Nah, don't ask. Nah, I don't know.

But, of course, he did know. It was all an act. His interview persona.

I asked him these questions: Do you have a favorite scene in *Spider-Man?* What's the role that's most challenged you? What films have you turned down? What Ivy League schools were you accepted to and why did you choose UCLA over them? What were your SAT scores? Who are your favorite writers? What books touched your heart? What movie lines do you find memorable? What films would you like to remake? Do you collect anything—first editions, paintings? What does money mean to you? If you could live inside a painting, which one would you choose?

Franco's answer to all of the above: "Nah."

"What about the most gut-wrenching scene you've had to play?"

"Nah. I don't want to point at, 'There's me at my deepest.'"

My response: "This is going to be some interview. One day somebody's going to be assigned to do a long interview with you, but it's not going to be me."

YOU WIN SOME, you lose some. But you've always got to hold up your end. If Freddie Prinze Jr. says he's never read a book but that he collects comics, then you have to ask him about those comics. If Bette Midler mistakes you for the deliveryman when she opens her door, then use it as a running routine throughout your time together. If Steve Martin doesn't want to talk about the past, present, or future, turn it into a bit that helps jump-start the rest of your interview. If Mae West looks in horror at your tape recorder, pull out a pad.

Always remember to bring a pad.

ASKING THE TOUGH QUESTIONS

The most difficult moments during an interview are when your questions make your subject uncomfortable. Asking tough questions is part of the job. But there are ways to go about it that may keep you from getting your nose broken, your eye blackened, your tape recorder smashed, or your subject calling it quits. It's called tact.

"Interviewing athletes about what makes them shine is an easy thing to do," says Roy Firestone. "When you have to ask questions that you know a person is uncomfortable with, vis-à-vis in my case, to ask ballplayers about their drug use or their paternity suits or children out of wedlock, it can be a very imposing line of questioning. But you have to find a way to do it. There was a time when not only was it indiscreet to ask about certain things, it wasn't even that important. Now, you have to. *Today*'s Matt Lauer interviewed Paul McCartney after his wife had just died of breast cancer. McCartney's very active in animal rights, and there are a lot of people who don't believe that animals should be used in research for medical purposes. Lauer asked, 'If you knew your wife's life could've been saved, would you have gone ahead with experiments on animals for breast cancer?' Very good question! But they stopped the interview when McCartney sternly said, 'The interview is over!' So you have to be really careful. Jim Murray of the *L.A. Times* once said that my questions are coated in chocolate, but the questions are asked. I like the way he put that. Let's say I had to ask Barry Bonds about hitting his wife. I might say, 'You know Barry, I think everybody has times in their relationships where they're not proud, or they wish they could do something over again. In view of what has been speculated about your marriage, do you have any regrets?' Not: 'Did you ever hit your wife?' I would carve out a way to give the person a little dignity, if you will, a comfort level. I was never known as an ambush interviewer. I could do it in a way that's discreet."

WHEN I WANTED to ask Saul Bellow about the fact that he may not write as well about women as he does men, I tried to phrase it in a way that would get a response. Putting him in the company of Faulkner and Melville certainly wasn't a negative. But I knew no matter how I asked it, he would not be pleased.

"Joyce Carol Oates said that she couldn't think of many of her male colleagues who've written compellingly about women," I began. "She cited you, Faulkner, and Melville as great writers who never created any female characters of great depth. What writers have best captured the way a woman thinks and feels?"

And Bellow responded: "It's a question you should address to a lady, since evidently I'm down here not as a misogynist but as somebody who's missed the boat on the other sex. Is this for your lady readers—a sort of sop to throw them another victim? Somebody else to hate? It's one thing to write about women in a time when women are happy to read about themselves. It's another thing in an ideological age when women read you in order to see whether you measure up ideologically to their standards."

I was definitely put in my place, but I had excellent copy.

I HAD HEARD Lucille Ball say on *The Tonight Show* that she'd "rather not live more than five years more." This was Lucy! Everyone loved Lucy! It seemed like a shocking remark. I obviously had to ask her about it when I interviewed her in 1976. I saved it for my last question, though, asking her simply if she had meant what she had said. Sometimes what seems like a tough question allows for a thoughtful, reflective response.

"It put the whole family in an uproar, and half the country," Ball answered. "I got a lot of letters and wires. I should stop saying it, I guess. Naturally I know what I have to be grateful for. I don't know. I suppose it's the loss of so many people around me that were with me. And the changing of what I liked. The children growing up. Nothing that I want to do particularly. I don't say I'm without ambition or plans—at the moment I have a lot going, more than I can handle. But . . . I don't know. They sent me, right after that show, to a doctor—because the doctor was incensed, he called. I said, all right, I'm sorry, I apologize. I should be grateful. But I really mean it. My mother's 84 and she's happy as a bug. My family's all right, my brother's all right and all of his kids, and everything's okay. If I had a lot to worry about I guess I wouldn't feel like that. But everything's okay, what do I need 20 more years? It came to me in my subconscious. I'm not unhappy. I'm embarrassed that I've got things so good. I don't know. I've got my house in order."

CHRISTIAN SLATER DIDN'T have his house anywhere near in order when in the summer of 1997 he and a date went to

Petra Brando's apartment in Los Angeles, consumed drugs and alcohol, and Slater literally went out of his mind. The cops were called and Slater wound up in the slammer. The next day he was told that he had attacked his date and punched her repeatedly in the face, turned on Petra's date, kicked a janitor named Castro in the stomach, and then when the cops arrived, he attacked one in the stairwell and tried to grab his gun. Slater remembered nothing but knew, if this was true, that he was headed for rehab once again (he had been in trouble twice for drunken driving in 1988 and 1989, the second time involving a West Hollywood car chase with the police where he wound up kicking a cop in the head as he attempted to scale a fence after driving down a dead-end alley).

As it turned out, what the press was reporting and how E! Entertainment reenacted it in its one-hour *True Hollywood Story* docudrama on Slater was not how it went down. At least not how Slater heard it from one of the principles at the apartment that night—the woman he allegedly attacked. But it didn't really matter—damage was done, Slater was out of control, and on December 9, 1997, he was sentenced to ninety days at the LaVerne city jail. I knew Christian had his side of the story to tell, but when I interviewed him for *Rolling Stone* I also knew I had to ask him questions based on what had appeared in the media.

I started out by asking him a variation of the question Jay Leno asked Hugh Grant to explain his getting caught with a hooker in his car. "What the hell happened?" I asked Christian. He replied, "I was born! The rest has all unfolded."

Part of the unfolding, he explained, was that there were a lot of lies reported. I used this as my way of bringing up what had appeared in the media, and even though these became yes or no type questions, it put the tough stuff on the table, and allowed us to go from there.

Q: What are the lies?

SLATER: The most painful one is that I beat this girl up.

Q: You didn't beat her up?

SLATER: No.

Q: You didn't get on top of her and scream, "You German bitch, you're going to kill us all," while you pummeled her, as E! Entertainment reenacted on TV?

SLATER: No.

Q: And you weren't lifted away by Petra Brando's boyfriend?

SLATER: No.

Q: And you didn't punch this janitor named Castro in the stomach?

SLATER: I don't know. I have no idea.

Q: When the police arrived, did you grab a cop's gun?

SLATER: I don't know. I blanked on the whole thing. Just to share openly about it, I went over to this place, consumed a lot of drugs and alcohol. The fight that happened was not between me and the girl at all, it was between me and this guy. After the fight I tried to kill myself by jumping off the balcony. They pulled me back in. I made a mad dash for the door. I was trying to get out of there. I found all that out the next day from the girl. The cops were telling me that I had beat this girl up, so my first course of action was to call the girl, to see if she was okay. Called her up, she told me what happened, that I couldn't remember, and I was so shocked and horrified at the information *she* was giving me—that the cops were incorrect, and that the fight hadn't been between me and her. Still, it was humiliating. I asked her if I could pick her up so we could talk some more; she said yeah. I went, took her back to my house, and she told me some stuff about this guy—she told me that he lied to the police so they wouldn't take him away.

Q: Do you remember actually trying to kill yourself?

SLATER: I remember going to that apartment, walking out on the balcony on the fourteenth floor, and having the thought go through my head. It scared me, and there was nobody there who I felt comfortable enough to talk about it with. I was already in an uncomfortable place. Then once I started to imbibe, I acted on it. Not thinking clearly—not thinking at all!—having chemicals affecting my brain, I just wanted to end it.

We talked about his arrest, his time in jail, what his parents thought, the letters he received from fans, and then I tried to put his behavior in a Hollywood context.

Q: Not very long ago you admired the outrageous behavior of Hollywood stars, from Jimmy Dean to Roman Polanski and Jack Nicholson. You almost felt compelled to carry the Hollywood Babylon torch: live fast, die young, leave a bright corpse. Pictures of Robert Mitchum mopping a jail floor back in 1948 didn't hurt his career. Is this stuff going through your mind while you're in jail? Thinking, perhaps, that you've accomplished that part of the legend?

SLATER: No, it's not very fulfilling. It was a gift, a miracle, it gave me some time to realize that I've been in my own self-created cell for twenty-nine years anyway. I was actually more free in prison than I've ever been. That's honestly how I felt. I needed some solitude. And God gave me what I needed.

Listen, I'm not proud of this. I'm not happy. I've got to learn these lessons however it is I'm supposed to learn them. Hopefully my experience can benefit somebody else. There have been many moments where it's been, like, enough! I've taken about all I can take. But I made it because I know I'm not alone, I know there are people who love me and who I love. That's as simple as it gets. And where I had to begin. Because I just hated myself. I felt phony, a fraud, a fake. I couldn't look people in the eye.

One of the most difficult subjects to broach is that of child molestation, especially when it involves famous people. Harvey Keitel has never been known as an easy interview, and when I went to see him in 1995, there had been reports that he was in a custody battle with his former wife, Lorraine Bracco, over their daughter. The reason? Keitel had found out that Bracco's then husband, the actor Edward James Olmos, had settled with a young girl's family, paying a large amount for them to drop charges of molestation against Olmos. Olmos was never convicted of anything, but Keitel was concerned enough to want his daughter out of that house. It was a very delicate issue, and one had to be careful about how the questions were asked. My margin comments show you what I was thinking, and the subtext of my questions.

Q: You're now dealing with pain in a custody battle with Lorraine Bracco over your daughter Stella. Lorraine is married to Edward James Olmos, who in 1992 was accused of molesting a 14-year-old girl. The case never went to court, so it remains only an accusation, but the press has covered it, and the name-calling has gotten pretty nasty. Obviously, it's not an easy subject to talk about, but would you be willing to say what you can about what's going on?

KEITEL: I will not stifle you in your work, so go ahead and ask what you need to.

> **COMMENT**
>
> *This is an example of a question mostly written after the interview. I didn't need to repeat facts about Bracco and Olmos to Keitel, who already knew them. But for the reader, who may not know anything about this, it's important to provide the information, as concisely as possible, and also in a way that doesn't accuse Olmos (the magazine's lawyers will never let an allegation appear as a fact). What I did ask Keitel was the last sentence of the question.*

> **COMMENT**
>
> *Note the "possible." Important to make sure the person under discussion doesn't have grounds for a lawsuit.*

Q: Do you believe that your daughter lives with a possible child molester?

KEITEL: He has been accused of that, but he denies it.

Q: In the July 25, 1994, issue of *New York* magazine, Olmos is quoted as having called you "vicious and disturbed" and "out of control. He doesn't want Stella. He's using the whole situation to hurt Lorraine and myself."

KEITEL: He knows that statement is a lie. There is evidence in court that he paid $150,000 to the alleged victim's family, and of a secret agreement that he entered into with the parents of this child who made the allegation of molestation.

Q: Are you trying to get full custody of your daughter?

KEITEL: We are involved in a custody suit now, yes.

Q: Did you sign over custody to Lorraine when you split up?

KEITEL: Yes. My suit for custody was not brought until I found out about the money Olmos paid.

Q: What did you do after you found out about it?

KEITEL: First I called the parents of the child. They wouldn't speak to me. I was stunned because I knew these people. Then I called Lorraine. She wouldn't speak to me.

Q: Did you ever talk with the girl who made the accusation against him?

KEITEL: Yes.

Q: Olmos claims he was trying to protect his teenage son, who broke this girl's heart.

KEITEL: His son was never accused of anything.

Q: Did you question your daughter about any suspicions you had concerning Olmos?

KEITEL: I'm not going to go into that, except to say that I ensured the safety of my daughter as best I could, given that I do not have custody.

Q: How did you do that?

KEITEL: As of this moment, there is a court order that prohibits him from being alone with my daughter without adult supervision. That order originally went into effect on October 20, 1993, and was modified slightly after the 14-year-old's testimony in January 1994 concerning the custody aspect of the case. Since that date Olmos and his son Bodie have given testimony and the court order remains in place.

Q: In that *New York* article Lorraine says that you are "motivated by jealousy and hate." And in an August 8 letter to *New York* she wrote: "Keitel is both a destructive and a self-destructive person. His jealousy and hatred at my happiness in my new marriage have reached a new low."

COMMENT

Here's an example of asking a really tough question of someone, but cushioned by quoting from something that had appeared in print.

KEITEL: I'm not going to comment on my daughter's mother.

COMMENT

Oh well, I tried.

Q: After Michael Jackson's reported big payoff to the family of the child who accused him of something similar, does it seem to you that there are inequities in the justice system?

KEITEL: It's a subject that needs exposure. This is an issue that all parents should be discussing, to protect their children. It's a very difficult area. That's why Linda

COMMENT

We have broadened the discussion here, but we really should get back to the specifics of his situation.

Fairstein of the Manhattan district attorney's office formed a sex crimes division. She was the first in the country, I believe, to give children a place to come and discuss their abuse. Children need our protection.

Q: Have you talked with her?

KEITEL: She was the one person who was good enough to give me information. She told me about the allegation of molestation and Olmos' money settlement. I didn't know about those things for about a year. And that's when my lawyers got involved.

Q: Did you confront Olmos about any of this?

KEITEL: He wouldn't talk to me.

Q: But you tried?

KEITEL: Yes.

Q: Was he afraid to talk to you?

KEITEL: That doesn't matter. The time for him to talk to me was before he paid the money and entered into this secret agreement to hide these allegations from me.

Q: Before this problem arose, you said in *Interview* magazine, "I am dying to see my child navigate the waters between the womb and death on her own terms, without her mother and me burdening her with our sins." Do you think that's still possible?

KEITEL: No.

Q: Do you see it as sad?

KEITEL: Very.

Q: Is she aware of what's going on?

KEITEL: Yes.

Q: Will she be in the position of having to choose between parents?

KEITEL: I have an obligation to protect my daughter, and I'm going to live up to that.

Jazz great Miles Davis also felt an obligation when he was interviewed, and that was to speak the truth. I went to his Malibu home to interview him for *Playboy* cable TV in 1985. The subject of the very first *Playboy* interview, Davis was a proud man who wasn't afraid to speak out about the problem of racism in America. "I can't walk into a restaurant without looking for the way out," he told me. "I don't like that feeling. And I don't like people who make it possible for me to feel bad. I don't think it's fair because I make so many people feel good with my music." It wasn't hard to get Miles going on the subject, but there was one thing I had come across in my research that I felt compelled to ask him about. I wasn't sure how he was going to respond.

"You once said," I began, "that if you had only an hour to live, you'd like to spend it strangling a white person . . . slowly. Did you mean it?"

And Davis replied: "No, I found out I need more time. About a week. It'd be a big bonus."

And then Miles Davis did something you rarely see in photographs of the man. He smiled.

AVOIDING CONFRONTATIONS UNTIL THE END

Oriana Fallaci claims to have begun her interviews by confronting her subjects. Hers are "moral rules." As she says, "It is to have the guts to put in the very beginning the very difficult questions, because journalists are cowards very often."

It's a matter of tact. If you can get away with confrontation in the beginning, it can become your style. Fallaci says in Jack Huber and Dean Diggins's *Interviewing America's Top Interviewers* that she began her interview with the Ayatollah Khomeini by saying: "We all know that you are a tyrant, that you are the new king of Iran, that you have taken the place of the shah. You are the new shah of Iran. Given this fact, I wish to ask you . . ."

I, on the other hand, would be more cautious. I might have asked him to tell me the difference between being a shah and an ayatollah. I might have suggested that certain rulers consider him a tyrant and wondered if he thought the same of them. I might have then looked at tyrants of history and asked his opinion. I don't think I would have been as brash as Fallaci. But an interviewer never knows until he or she is faced with the subject. It's best to be open to any situation and circumstance. If you can make your subject respect you, you have a better chance of obtaining a good interview.

The last time I interviewed Angelina Jolie, in the summer of 2003, I was told that she didn't want to talk about her father (Jon Voight) or ex-husband Billy Bob Thornton. But how could I not ask about them, since in her previous interviews, they were *all* she talked about? I adapted a wait-and-see attitude, since our interview was going to be done via videoconferencing, with her in London (where she was completing *Tomb Raider 2*) and me in L.A. I knew if I asked her the wrong questions she could very easily disconnect.

We only had ninety minutes, and somewhere after the first hour I asked her the following questions.

Q: What do you think about what happened to your *Girl, Interrupted* costar, Winona Ryder? Was she treated fairly in the press during her trial for shoplifting? Did you ever talk to her about what happened?

JOLIE: I haven't talked to her but I heard from friends she's doing well. I think you feel for anybody who is so in the public eye. If she's going through something or if something is wrong with her, it certainly doesn't make things any easier to be so public. I don't think anyone is going to forget it anytime soon and focus on her work, so it's going to be hard for her to come out of it when such a circus has been made; it makes it very difficult to move on. I hope

she can. I hope she takes care of herself in whatever ways she
can.

Here was my opening, and I took it.

Q: A circus was also made of your last marriage and divorce. I know
you don't want to be asked about Billy Bob or about your father,
but is there anything at all you'd be willing to talk about at this
time?

JOLIE: I really just have nothing to say. Especially about my father.
I've moved on and I'm trying to stay in a very strong and healthy place
so I can do good things with my life and so I can be a really good
parent. I need to have only things that are good for me around me.

Q: Is it that you have nothing more to do with your dad or that
you're angry with him?

JOLIE: There's a long history and like most families we all have
very complicated relationships with different people in our family
that go very deep. There are reasons why we are not friends.

Q: Regarding Billy Bob, the last time we spoke, half our
conversation was about him. Do you have any regrets about being
so publicly in love?

JOLIE: I know every time I said something nice about him it made
him very happy, so at the time that was just really worth it. And I
don't believe in regret. You learn and you move on. If you decide to
share things in your life with the public then you share with them.
Certainly I've shared the darkest side of myself when I was upset or
down or questioning myself at times and I can share now. What
people might have identified with me then they can see now what
I've discovered, and maybe that will help one girl somewhere. I'm a
public person. I know there was a time in my life when I thought I had
found my best friend and we both had similar darkness in our lives
and we both had found a friend we could laugh with and that's a
beautiful thing. That was the best thing about our relationship,

that we made each other smile, because we're both pretty heavy people in many ways. And that friendship will be missed.

Q: Is there no contact at all?

JOLIE: Not at the moment.

Q: Are you bitter?

JOLIE: No.

Q: What have you learned about fathers and husbands—is there anything you can say?

JOLIE: No, because I just had my husbands and my father and I assume everybody is different. I know that [my son] Maddox doesn't have certain male figures in his life and I'm aware of that, but I will find a way to balance that. He does have men in his life, there are men that I work with and men around in Cambodia, there are different people working on schools and different programs, fathers of other children, there are certainly men around, none though that are involved with his mother.

Q: You had Billy Bob's name removed from your arm. Is removing a tattoo as painful as getting one?

JOLIE: Depends on how much you want to remove it.

DEALING WITH SUBJECTS WHO TREAT YOU BADLY

When I was a teenager I had a summer job working for a pharmaceutical company, selling items to individual drug stores on Long Island. I traveled to every suburban township, wore a jacket and tie, had a car trunk full of free samples and a catalog of products to present. Most pharmacists were decent and would see me when I walked into their store, but a few were bastards. They'd make me wait, sometimes for no apparent reason. And after keeping me waiting for as long as an hour, they'd skim through the catalog and ask how many free samples I was willing to give them if they gave me an order. Then it was my turn. I never cared about the samples, since they didn't come out of my wages, but I didn't like giving these greedy, thoughtless pharmacists something for nothing when they had wasted so much of my time.

My feelings haven't changed when dealing with people I've come to interview. Most of them are decent, and they often go out of their way to be polite and friendly because they're hoping for good press. But some can keep you waiting, or have a chip on their shoulder about the media, and this can be very frustrating.

Barbra Streisand had a reputation of always being late. For the first two or three sessions of our marathon interview she was on time, and I told her that if our interview showed nothing else, it would disprove the bad rap she had regarding keeping people waiting. Over the following months, she was never on time again. Apparently, she didn't mind being known for her tardy arrivals.

Robert De Niro also didn't seem to care about being punctual. As I mentioned previously, for one of our sessions he was to come to my hotel room at 9 A.M. I didn't have a phone number to reach him, so I just had to wait for his arrival. By noon I was feeling frustrated. By three, I was angry. And when he showed up around five, I wasn't in a very good mood. Is it any wonder that he wasn't happy with the interview when it appeared?

With Meryl Streep, I still don't know what to think. In 1992 I had an hour with her on the set of *Death Becomes Her,* and she told me to call her assistant to arrange a time to return the next day. But no one ever answered my calls, and I didn't see her again. I still wrote the piece, but I felt manipulated.

I remember once interviewing E. Joseph Cossman, an iconoclastic entrepreneur who made fortunes in mail order. We were talking in his Jacuzzi in Palm Springs and he was telling how he found writers to work for him cheaply. I said that since he often sold schlock, like rubber shrunken heads or a hundred toy soldiers for a dollar, he was just not used to paying someone what they were worth. And he said, "No offense, Larry, but to me, writers are a dime a dozen." He wasn't being insulting, just matter-of-fact. All I could say to him was that you get what you pay for.

Though it doesn't happen frequently, there have been occasions when a subject has his own agenda or can't control his temper or just doesn't like journalists. As far as I'm concerned, it's not how one treats you, it's how they treat themselves that counts. It's what they have to say. If they're angry or have a grudge against journalists or they had a fight with their partner or kid or they heard from their agent that they didn't get a job they wanted just before you walked through their door, that's their problem, not yours. You're there to feel them out, to sense the atmosphere in the room, and to play good cop or bad cop with them, depending on what gets them to respond.

Just remember that as a journalist you will always have the last word.

NOBEL PRIZE WINNERS

When you're interviewing someone who has won a major prize, you obviously are going to ask about it. What you're looking for in the answer is something insightful, interesting, and hopefully not said a dozen times before. That's a tough one, because anyone who has won a Nobel Prize or an Oscar is going to have been asked how he or she felt about it every time someone comes to interview that person. In such a situation, it's best left for a time after you've established some communication with the person, so when you do bring it up, perhaps they'll be willing to confide in you. I've talked with three Nobel laureates, with some interesting results.

The first one I interviewed actually had won two Nobel's—one for chemistry, the other for peace. Linus Pauling wasn't shy about either of them. In fact, what made it memorable for me was how he quickly pointed out that he was the only person to have won both of them without having to share either. "I am pleased to have received two *complete* Nobel Prizes," he told me in 1975. "In the Guinness *Book of Records* it says I have the championship."

The second such Prize winner was also a scientist; Dr. Richard Feynman won his for quantum electrodynamics in 1965. He told me in 1986 he wished he had never gotten it. "It's one of the miseries of my life," he said. "It's very annoying to have everybody ask you for an opinion, and you're supposed to be wise all of a sudden, and I know I'm not wise all of a sudden. I used to be able to go to any old high school and answer questions at the physics clubs. But now, they won't even ask me. They're afraid. They wouldn't ask a Nobel Prize winner just to come to talk to a physics club. And if some student finally gets up enough nerve to do it, what happens is, I say OK. And when I go there, it's not just the physics club but the whole damn school is there. The principal finds out or the physics teacher finds out what the kid in the physics club has done, and they say, 'Oh, he's such an important man; everybody should be interested in this guy.' It's kind of out of proportion. I'm not up to it. I wouldn't say that my physics wasn't up to the prize, but I'm not up to it on a human side, being a Prize Winner and an Important scientist. I'm not, that's all. I was a kid fooling around. I was in my pajamas working on the floor with paper and pencil and I cooked something up, OK? Does that make me a great wise *schmaltz* that everybody should see? It's a distortion. I'm looked at differently. It's a pain in the ass!"

The third Nobel laureate I spoke with was Saul Bellow, who won his for literature in 1976. Bellow has an acerbic wit and he put it to good use when it came to this topic. I got into it by saying that Truman Capote didn't think he deserved it.

BELLOW: Maybe I didn't deserve the Nobel Prize, but it's a cinch he didn't even deserve the Pulitzer. I can't see what Truman deserved at all, except a kick in the ass.

That delightful insult led to a discussion about Capote, whom Bellow felt hated him. After he had a chance to take a few more shots at Capote, I returned to his Nobel Prize, asking if it meant a great deal to him.

BELLOW: I didn't give a hoot about it one way or the other. I don't exist for that sort of thing and I was very careful to see that it didn't affect my life too much.

Q: How can it not?

BELLOW: It's just a prize, like any other. Proust didn't get it, or Tolstoy, Joyce. So it isn't as though you were in the royal line and you went to Stockholm for the coronation.

Q: Is there a downside to having won the prize?

BELLOW: Yes, people feel that you are a public functionary, that you have to produce a certain amount of cultural shrubbery on God's little acre.

Q: You said once that it's better to write a marvelous book than to get the Nobel Prize. Don't you have to write at least one marvelous book to get the prize?

BELLOW: I can think of writers who didn't write marvelous books and got the prize. But don't push me because I don't want to make more enemies than I already have.

Q: Norman Mailer's been campaigning for it for years; think he should get it?

BELLOW: Well, I'd give it to him . . . if he had anything to trade.

And then Saul Bellow laughed. He was pleased with himself, with his remark, and he knew it would reverberate throughout the literary world—which it did when the interview was published and that comment made a few syndicated columns.

So, you never know where a topic may lead, but if your subject has won a Nobel or an Oscar, an Emmy, a Pulitzer, or a MacArthur Grant, don't shy away from the subject. Let their egos flow!

DON'T OVERLOOK ASIDES

I once asked Nicole Kidman if she played the piano because she had long fingers, and she told me that Barbra Streisand had the most beautiful hands she'd ever seen.

You never know where interesting observations will come from, but very often it happens when someone goes off the topic and tosses out what may seem like a throwaway line. Governor Jesse Ventura did it with his remark about religion being a crutch for weak-minded people. Jimmy Carter did it when he admitted that he lusted in his heart. Truman Capote did it when he told me that I lost one point of my IQ for every year I stayed in California. All of these asides make for excellent copy in the finished interviews.

KNOWING WHEN ENOUGH'S ENOUGH

When Streisand was being difficult, I said that I wouldn't turn in our interview until we both agreed we were done talking. With most people, that would mean a few hours . . . but with Streisand it stretched on for months. And when she was finally ready to call it quits, I said to her I just had a few more questions. And she said, "With you, it's never going to be enough."

She was right. As long as they're willing to talk, I'm willing to listen. I spent close to two years talking to John Huston and everyone who knew him and would probably have spent another two years interviewing him had Huston not died. Once he was gone, I started writing my book.

On the other hand, after five hours interviewing Billy Bob Thornton in the fall of 2003 for *Rolling Stone,* after he had finished making *Bad Santa* and *The Alamo,* I knew I had more than enough material and surprised him when I wrapped it up. "I've got to go," I said. "No one's ever said that before," he laughed. "I'm usually the one who says it's over."

Knowing when you've got enough is an instinctual thing. Most movie directors prefer to shoot scenes from different angles, and over many takes, just to make sure they will get the perfect shot. But certain mavericks—like John Huston, for example—could shoot a scene in one or two takes and feel secure enough to move on to the next shot. The same holds true with interviewing. You can talk to someone for four hours and wind up using ten minutes' worth of conversation, or you can talk for a half hour and get the same amount of usable information. It depends on how much time your subject is willing to give you, how much time you're going to spend talking yourself, and how quickly you can get down to business and get your subject warmed up. Once again, there are no set rules. It's always better to have too much material than too little. It's always good to know you've got your beginning and your ending. And it's just as important to have the good conversation in between as well. Knowing when enough's enough comes with experience. Until you feel you can "see" the interview inside your head, keep asking questions. Even when your subject's mind starts wandering, as long as she doesn't ask you to leave, take all that you can get. Learn to cover the angles.

4. I DON'T WANT TO TALK ABOUT THAT!

WHAT TO DO WHEN YOUR SUBJECT CLAMS UP

> The reason I won't do a long-form interview is because it's just too personal. Don't need it. I'm not John Huston or Truman Capote, I'm just a simple guy who doesn't have that much to say and is not that interested in hearing it back.
>
> —HARRISON FORD

Entertainment Weekly's Benjamin Svetkey: Okay, here's something you probably hate about being famous: personal questions about your relationship with your dear friend Lara Flynn Boyle . . .

JACK NICHOLSON: I don't talk about that. I never have.

EW: Well, there were all those reports in the press earlier this year about how the breakup with Boyle—

NICHOLSON: Not by me. I didn't say anything to the press.

EW: No, but your friends supposedly said that they were worried about you after the breakup, that you were losing weight and looking haggard.

NICHOLSON: It's the one area of my life where none of my friends think I know what I'm doing. They think I'm goofy, a fool for love. And I guess I am sort of naïve in the area of romance. Some relationships certainly shattered me for longer than the average person. But the thing about friends is that whenever they attempt to counsel you on these matters, it's always more about them than about you. They always end up talking about themselves. It's grueling. It's like, God, what about *me?*

EW: It's hard to imagine you needing advice about women. You and Warren Beatty marched through Hollywood like the Sherman and Grant of the sexual revolution.

NICHOLSON: You know, I can tell you exactly when the sexual revolution ended: when *Time* magazine put herpes on the cover [in 1982].

—Entertainment Weekly, *January 3, 2003*

In [Confessions of a Dangerous Mind, Chuck] Barris made the astonishing claim that while he was being "crucified" by critics for "polluting the airwaves with mind-numbing puerile entertainment," he was simultaneously receiving presidential citations for his work as an undercover CIA assassin. . . . When he is asked how much of Confessions *is fantasy, he says, "I'll never answer that question. . . . Believe what you want. I wrote the book and that's how I felt when I wrote it."*

—Los Angeles Times, *December 30, 2002*

Back in the seventies, Lou Reed and David Bowie and Iggy Pop were regarded as an unholy triumvirate. They broke down all kinds of barriers—between pop and performance art, male and female, lyricism and cacophony. "I don't know what you mean," Reed says. Again, he stares me out. "I haven't a clue what you're talking about."

Reed makes me feel like an amoeba. I want to cry. Look, I was a huge fan of yours, I say. "Was?" he sneers. I still am, I say, but I'm less sure by the second.

—Simon Hattenstone, *Globe and Mail, June 11, 2003*

So, what's an interviewer to do? A guy writes a book and claims he killed thirty-three people for the CIA, and when you ask him about it, he clams up. When David Letterman tried to get it out of him, Barris said he'd go to his grave with the answer. Of course, Barris was promoting a movie based on his book, and by remaining mysterious he became more intriguing. If he said he didn't do it, that he made it all up, then why bother to go to the movie, the guy's a liar, it's a bogus movie. If he said he did it, then what kind of a creep is this guy? But if you're a journalist doing a story on Barris, how can you not ask him about what he himself wrote? How can you not ask Jack Nicholson about his relationship with the young and beautiful Lara Flynn Boyle? Or Lou Reed about his and Bowie and Pop's influence on the music of the seventies? People who read about these guys want to know. Did Boyle leave the great Jack Nicholson? Or did he dump her? Did Reed break down musical barriers? Did Barris stick the barrel of a gun into some bad guy's mouth and blow his brains out in Germany while chaperoning the winners of *The Dating Game?* C'mon Chucky baby, tell us. Lighten up, Lou! Fess up Jack, you da man!

Notice, in the Nicholson exchange above, how neatly our hero sidesteps the issue. First, he says he doesn't talk about his love life. Then the intrepid interviewer tries again, mentioning that it's been reported in the press, but Nicholson doesn't fall for it. Then another tack is tried: Your friends were reportedly worried about you. Jack responds . . . not about him and Boyle, but about "some relationships" and about friends. He trumps the reporter here, subtly changing the subject. But the reporter isn't quite finished; he gives up on getting anything on Boyle but still tries for the women question. He ties in friends and women with Warren Beatty, and Nicholson shows why he's a pro at this: He moves the subject from his and Beatty's womanizing days to *Time* magazine killing the sexual revolution. Checkmate. Time to move on.

BUT HOW DO YOU get someone like Nicholson or Barris to open up? Obviously, it's not easy. And it's not going to happen in a controlled situation where the clock is running and you have a lot of territory you want to cover. Because intimate questions take time to ask, and more time to go back to, and even more time to get answered.

BEFORE I AGREED to write that biography of the Huston family in 1987 I had lunch with Anjelica Huston, at her father's request, to discuss the scope of the project. I told her that the only way I wanted to attempt her family's story was to cast a wide net and to dig as deeply as I could. She was hesitant. "Every family has a lot of twists and turns," she said, "and in my family there are probably more than in others and I'm not sure I'd like to see all the layers peeled." I didn't, at that time, know the nature of the twists and turns that weighed on her psyche, but I said that I saw my job as attempting to unpeel as many of those layers as I could. Because her father trusted me, she agreed to cooperate, but it wasn't easy for her.

Nor was it easy for me. During the course of my research I interviewed hundreds of people who knew members of the Huston family personally and professionally. The most crushing blow to Anjelica and her brother Tony's lives came when they were teenagers and their mother, Ricki, was killed in a car accident. Different people told me about this incident and it soon got back to Anjelica that I had found out, perhaps, too much. Just the fact that I was investigating her mother's death and the reaction to it among her friends and family was upsetting to her. On the set of *The Dead,* which her brother had adapted from the Joyce short story and her father was directing from a wheelchair, Anjelica told her father that my presence affected her concentration because when she saw me, she thought of her mother. John Huston knew that it was important for me to be there, so I could observe him at work firsthand, but he couldn't have his leading lady emotionally distraught for the wrong reasons. When he came to speak to me about his dilemma, I understood and disappeared. "I promise you that Anjelica will talk to you," Huston said. "She'll give you all the time you need."

Eventually, Anjelica and I spent a few days together, but it wasn't at all easy for her. There was a lot of family history that she found uncomfortable to discuss, and it was especially hard when it came to her mother's death. But by asking the right questions, I was able to get Anjelica to open up to me.

"How did it hit me?" she said when I asked. "It *hit* me. My whole world collapsed. It changed my life. It changed my entire consciousness. I don't believe that I can ever really be shocked again. Barring the loss of a child, to be told that your very young parent is overnight dead almost takes you beyond the realms of sanity. It almost makes you crazy."

Her parents were already separated by then and I wanted to know what she and her father talked about at the funeral. John had returned to London from Rome, where he had been working on *The Kremlin Letter*. "He was devastated," Anjelica told me. "I thought he was going to die. I don't remember sitting down and having any long talks. It seemed unnecessary. It's like if an atom bomb goes off, there's not a whole lot to talk about, and that's how it felt."

After the memorial service, Anjelica went back to the house she'd shared with her mother and brother. "It was as if everything had died," she said. "The entire house was lost, gone, finished. It is hard to describe what it is like when actual objects lose their lives. I went into her closet . . . all her beautiful Balenciagas I used to crave; it was as if they had gone limp. They didn't even smell like her anymore."

Dylan McDermott also lost his mother too early and was uncomfortable talking about it. The best one can hope for on such sensitive issues is to get some response, and allow the person the opportunity to open up if they want to. McDermott was only five when his twenty-year-old mother was killed in a gun accident involving her live-in boyfriend. I wasn't sure how I was going to bring the subject up, knowing from reading clips about him that he didn't like talking about it. I found my opening when he responded to a question I asked about studying with acting teacher Sanford Meisner. "He made you go to a very deep place," McDermott said. Rather than pursue that, I used it to transition to the more delicate subject:

"I'd guess that the deepest you could go was returning to five when you lost your mother in a shooting accident."

McDermott looked at me—he's somewhat of a reluctant interview, and I wasn't sure if he was going to answer or just keep silent. "That's certainly the most painful," he said. "That's a well you keep tapping. Whatever pain I have as a person I try to tap into if it's called for in my work. I've used it to better me rather than to kill me, because it could have easily killed me."

That's just the tip of the iceberg, obviously, and that's all I was able to get . . . but at least it was something. And something is always better than nothing.

As I mentioned in Chapter 2, when I was going to interview Jodie Foster in 1991, her publicist said that I could not even bring up her sexuality or John Hinckley, the guy who shot President Reagan in his attempt to garner Foster's attention. I said I'd like to at least ask her why she wouldn't talk about those subjects and was told even that was off-limits, take it or leave it. So in order to still get at those issues, I approached Foster with questions that skirted them, but eventually led me close to where I wanted to go with her. For instance, though I didn't mention Hinckley directly I did talk to her about guns and violence, legitimate subjects since she did win an Oscar for her performance as FBI agent Clarice Starling in *Silence of the Lambs*.

Q: To get into the role, how much did you learn about cannibalism, sexual psychosis, and ritual dismemberment?

FOSTER: I know everything that every character I play knows. But I don't want to get into the curiosity factor of violence, because that's obviously a dangerous topic. But I'm absolutely fascinated with violence in our culture.

Now that answer just begs for a follow-up. She doesn't want to get into it, but she's fascinated by it. So I asked her if she was fascinated with serial killers.

FOSTER: With the fact of violence as an established piece of American culture. It isn't just serial killers, it's about child abuse, subtle abuse. Those things that make the hero the hero and the villain the villain.

I asked her about what she learned from spending time with an FBI specialist in serial killers, and if she worried much about the glorification of violence. She answered both questions, and then I asked if she was for or against gun control.

FOSTER: I don't discuss it.

We had hit her wall. She knew where this might be going and she wanted no part of it. But I simply said, "It's pretty straightforward."

FOSTER: Am I for or against it? Absolutely for it. Guns are not information. It's an entirely different issue.

After talking about other things, I again tried to get her to open up about Hinckley without breaching my agreement not to bring his name up.

Q: How difficult was it having to have security guards while going to college?

FOSTER: I've spoken on the topic, so it's not like I ever have to talk about it again. But it is hard being a public figure. And there are times when you are more public than others. Thank God that's not always like that.

Not much of an answer, and other questions were just waiting in the wings. So, I made my attempt, by carefully phrasing the next question, and quoting something she had already said.

Q: I know we're skirting around an issue you plainly don't want to discuss, but in *Vanity Fair* you said you felt at that time it was your "God-given responsibility to endure this martyrdom." What did you mean?

FOSTER: I don't know. The writer was talking about my psychological makeup. And I said, "I'm here for you to stick darts in me, go ahead. You can have any conclusion you want, but you're not going to get it out of my mouth."

And neither was I. As for her sexuality, what I went for was to bring up the fact that she played rape victims in *The Hotel New Hampshire, Five Corners,* and *The Accused,* and I asked her to talk about that. Then I brought up something she had once said.

Q: Why do you believe that men start out liking themselves but women have to learn to like themselves?

FOSTER: That's always a quote that ends up haunting me, because taken out of context it sounds sexist when in fact it is a very feminist commentary about how men in our society are dubbed "human" immediately. The human experience is the male experience, and the aberrant experience is the female experience. Within the forming of the male psyche, men are given direct messages about who they are supposed to be. And women are continually given confusing and mixed messages, things that don't make sense. Like, "Yes, you should grow up and be a business person; no, you shouldn't work and have children because you won't be a fulfilled person if you don't [have children]." These messages get even more confusing as the years go on. It builds in you a way of coping with being disappointed that I don't think men are as equipped with.

We're getting some of her views here, and I think they're interesting, but how personal can we go without stepping over the line of our agreement?

Q: In 1987 you told *Interview:* "Girls from single-parent homes really want to get married. I do. I really believe in marriage." Still?

Jodie answered this, and my next question about her desire to have children (this was before she had two), but we never touched on her own sexuality, just as we never talked about her missing father—another taboo subject, I discovered.

Q: Your mother has said that your strength maybe came from being raised without a father. Would you agree?

FOSTER: I don't know. For a lot of people that's been a disaster in their lives. I don't talk about him. It's something that doesn't exist in my life, so I choose not to talk about it.

Q: I'll drop the subject.

FOSTER: No, no, that's your job to ask. And it's my job not to answer.

When a subject has made up his or her mind not to talk, you have to accept that you may not get anywhere trying to get them to change their minds.

Family problems are often subjects that people would rather avoid talking about. When I once asked Harrison Ford about his grandfather, who had been a blackface comedian in vaudeville, he told me: "It was a rough life, and my father is very unwilling to talk about it. He had a rough time when he was growing up. My grandfather was an alcoholic. When he died, he left my father a virtual orphan. His mother was unable to care for them, so he and his brother were raised by nuns in an orphanage."

It was an area worth exploring, but not for Ford, who said all he wanted to about that.

Over the course of sixteen years, between 1981 and 1997, I interviewed James A. Michener for a book that would eventually be published as *Talking with Michener.* There was nothing

Michener wouldn't talk about, but there were some things he just couldn't talk about—not in any satisfactory way. It wasn't that he was stubborn or that he asked for the subject not to be brought up—he just never was able to go into any kind of deep analysis about his first two marriages, or about giving back the children he and his second wife adopted. In the more than one hundred hours I spent talking to Michener, I was never able to penetrate this subject with him. This is the best I could do.

Q: You're obviously no stranger to marriage . . .

MICHENER: I've had three, been divorced twice. Any person who has been divorced is a monument to failure.

Q: What went wrong the first time?

MICHENER: We were separated for four years during the war. She was in the Army in Europe, and I was in the Navy in the South Pacific. She came back and we were together for maybe three weeks, and it was primarily her decision to split up. I was very unhappy about it, but we were so changed that any reconciliation was just impossible.

Q: And the second one?

MICHENER: I was away in Asia, in Korea, most of the time, and she didn't come with me. I put my work first and that relationship just faded away.

Q: Did you ever try to have children?

MICHENER: I had always thought that my not having children was my deficiency: I had a savage case of mumps when I was a boy, and that often produces sterility. My second wife and I had adopted two children, but when we separated she made the decision to turn them back to the orphanage. At the divorce the courts gave the children to the mother and the adoption was voided. I pleaded with the court not to do it, but that's the way they wanted it.

Q: Did you ever find out what happened to them?

MICHENER: When [his third wife] Mari and I decided to get married, we talked about readopting them, but there was some concern that my ex-wife would make it unpleasant and we didn't want to hurt the children, so we decided not to reopen a potential can of worms.

Q: Still, you must have had some regrets.

MICHENER: We had regrets, but we didn't belabor them. We usually had children living with us, and we assumed the responsibil— ity for the education of a few kids, so we'd been in touch with children all along.

Honestly? I feel that I failed at getting anything more out of Michener than this. God knows I tried, but there are times when you have to be thankful, I guess, for getting what the person is able to give. That's what happened when I did a cable TV interview with Norman Mailer in 1983 and brought up a subject that was never very comfortable for him. He may not have answered in depth, but his responses were such that you can still feel the tension in our exchange, and that's what makes it work.

Q: In 1942 you worked for a while in a state mental institution in Boston. Some years later, after you stabbed your second wife, you wound up in a mental institution in Bellevue for a while. Did you feel in any way that you came full circle from that experience?

MAILER: No. I mean, I thought of it. One could not help think of the fact that one worked in a mental hospital earlier on the other side, as an attendant. That may have been of some help for me to get out of that place after seventeen days.

Q: Because?

MAILER: When I worked as an attendant, I learned one thing: don't make the guards pay attention to you. The less attention the guards pay to you, the better your chances of getting out are.

Q: Were you crazy at that time?

MAILER: Let's say I was highly strung and let it go at that.

Q: I don't think you're going to answer me, but why did you stab your wife?

MAILER: You made your try. Why do you want to get into something that personal?

Q: It's a subject that you really haven't discussed, except in a poem you wrote, where you said, "So long as you use the knife . . ."

MAILER: *A* knife.

Q: ". . . a knife, there's some love left."

MAILER: The poem was written after the fact.

Q: I know it was.

MAILER: It's not a lively topic of conversation for me.

Q: The doctor who treated your wife, Adele, said you were having an acute paranoid breakdown with delusional thinking and that you were both homicidal and suicidal.

MAILER: Well, since I didn't kill anybody after that and I didn't commit suicide nor have a mental breakdown, my guess is that he wasn't too accurate.

Q: But you later wrote that had you not done that act you might have been dead in a few years yourself.

MAILER: Yes.

Q: Have you ever contemplated suicide?

MAILER: No, I never have.

Q: When a movie is made of your life, whom would you like to play you?

MAILER: Larry Grobel.

Q: You're getting angry with me now.

MAILER: No. Edgy.

Q: Okay. You blamed early success as the reason for the breakup of your first marriage . . .

MAILER: I'm not getting angry, I'm getting offended. You want to discuss my life. I'm not going to give away my life. My life is my material. I would give you my life no more than I would give you my mate. That belongs to me, not to an interviewer.

In 1997 Saul Bellow came back at me when I brought up a remark by John Gardner, in which he called Bellow a male chauvinist pig. "Why should I defend myself against charges by John Gardner or anybody else?" Bellow asked. "Why do interviewers ask people questions that they wouldn't ask their neighbor for fear of being punched in the nose? Like, 'Why are your bowel movements such a strange color?' Or, 'Why do you piss through your ears?' Some of these things, it's 'Let's you and him fight.' 'So-and-so said about you the following, and what have you got to say?' I'm not responsible for what so-and-so said about me. I don't mind obliging you, I just don't like being put through the shredder."

Bellow is obviously aware of the nature of interviewing, and how one method in an interviewer's bag of tricks is to bring up something someone said to get a rise out of the person being interviewed. It's not necessarily to get "you and him" fighting, though it can often lead to memorable, and quotable, remarks. When I once asked Al Pacino about some negative remark critic Pauline Kael said about him (in her review of *Serpico,* she wrote that as he grew his beard, she couldn't distinguish him from Dustin Hoffman), he responded, "Is that after she had the shot glass removed from her throat?" That one line has had a life of its own over the years.

When I interviewed Truman Capote in 1984 and brought up the feud between him and Gore Vidal, Capote replied, "Gore has an obsession about me." And when I asked if he thought that perhaps Vidal might be jealous of Capote's work, Truman said: "Of course he's jealous. Gore has never written anything that anybody will remember . . . talk about fifty years from today, they won't remember it ten years from its last paperback edition. See, Gore has literally never written a masterpiece. He has not written an unforgettable book or a book that was the turning point in either his or anybody else's life. Without that, it doesn't matter how much he does or what he does. . . ."

Vidal seems to have gotten under a lot of people's skin, and even when his name isn't in a question, he pops up in an answer. With Oliver Stone in 1997, I brought up a remark actor Joe Pesci made about him, that he was a terrific director but a "piece of shit" as a person. Pesci had given a memorable performance as the bewigged David Ferrie in Stone's controversial *JFK* and I asked the director if Pesci ever called him to deny what he had said.

STONE: No, he wrote me a note of apology for saying it publicly. But the sentiments he felt the same. He's known to have a temper. Joe's a strange guy. In his own way, he probably felt threatened, but I didn't pick up on it. How many actors get called a "piece of shit"? You know who else did that to me recently, out of the blue? Gore Vidal was all over the goddamn newspapers saying he hated my work and that he had blown me off when I tried to get him to do *Alexander the Great* for me. Which was bullshit. I was shocked to see that because we were at a party, so somebody leaked it. It might have been Gore. He said I had no talent at all and that he didn't want to work with me. It was an embarrassing, violent, angry, aggressive quote. I've very rarely seen that degree of hostility. I've known Gore Vidal for years, off and on. In fact, when he offered to write *Alexander the Great* for me in 1990 at his villa in Ravello, Italy, I turned his ultra-homoerotic suggestions down. He's bitten by a temper. It's festered for years. People react to me without my knowing it. Artists are very jealous, angry people. They're the most envious people in the world.

Oliver Stone's remarks, Pacino's response to Kael, and Capote's take on Vidal are all answers to Bellow's question about why interviewers ask people questions that they wouldn't ask their neighbor for fear of being punched in the nose.

Still, Mailer's remark about his life being his own and his not wanting to give it up to an interviewer is something every journalist has to contend with. Mailer's sentiment echoed something Marlon Brando said to me back when I interviewed him on his island in Tahiti for *Playboy* in 1978. This interview, which I've mentioned before, would prove to be one of the most laborious but fascinating of my career. "I'm not going to lay myself at the feet of the American public and invite them into my soul," he told me. "My soul is a private place. I just don't believe in washing my dirty underwear for all to see. What people are willing to do in front of a public is puzzling. I don't understand why they do it."

In a phone call prior to our meeting, Brando had told me that he only wanted to talk about the Indians. I said that we could cover the subject extensively, but not exclusively. He then asked to see my questions, which I refused to show him. Without my realizing it, we were in a negotiation. He made certain demands; I didn't want to give in to any of them. I wanted the interview to be freewheeling, wide ranging, and spontaneous. I didn't want him knowing what I was going to ask so that he would be prepped to answer. What kind of journalism would that be?

But I also knew that if I didn't come up with a solution that would pacify him he would tell me that he wouldn't meet with me and that would be that. So I suggested that instead of sending him my questions, which I hadn't yet written, could I send the topics that I hoped to explore with him? He agreed. And I sent him a very short list that included the following: The Indians. Civil Rights. Social Injustice. Politics. Men. Women. Entertainment. The Arts. The World.

I was testing his sense of humor. Because my list eliminated nothing, and included everything. Either he would shake his head, laugh, and say come to Tahiti, or he would say I'm nuts, what kind of stupid list is that, and tell me to forget it. He told me to come.

What he really wanted to focus on was the plight of the American Indian and so I read every book I could get my hands on about the subject—*The Indian and the White Man,* Stan Steiner's *The New Indians,* Earl Shorris's *The Death of the Great Spirit,* Dee Brown's *Bury My Heart at Wounded Knee,* Vine DeLoria Jr.'s *Custer Died for Your Sins,* James Welch's *Winter in the Blood.* I read old editions of the *Congressional Record,* I watched cowboy and Indian movies, I spoke with Indians who claimed the government sterilized their women. I wrote four hundred questions dealing with the Indians, from our early history with them in the sixteenth century to the present. My strategy was to out-Indian Marlon Brando, to subject him to so many questions that his head would begin to throb and he would welcome the relief of a personal question or two; he might even offer up a movie example that could lead to my asking him about how he dealt with social injustice in *On the Waterfront* or *Viva Zapata!* or *The Godfather.*

In other words, I wasn't going to allow the interview to be limited to one subject. We would go in depth on what he wanted to talk about, so in depth, in fact, that he would feel as if we were in a submarine. But we would also come up for air. And that was where the gold would be.

For the first three days on his island in Tetiaroa we talked neither about the Indians nor about the movies. He wouldn't let me turn on the tape recorder, so we wound up talking about . . . my life. Every once in a while he would tell me something interesting about his life and I would say, "Can we save that for when we start taping?" And he would wave his hand and say, "I'll remember it." But I knew that he wouldn't tell me the same story in the same way with my tape on if he already knew that I had heard the story. So I told him about the time the cops once thought I was a cat burglar when I was sixteen, and how I once had three girlfriends on three different continents, and what it was like to witness a fetish priestess coming-out ceremony in Larteh, Ghana. My plan was to out-Indian him, but first I had to bore him to tears with my life stories before he finally agreed to let me start recording. On the fourth day, as we sat on the sand, our backs against his thatched hut, he told me about hearing a muezzin's call in Morocco and sleeping with an airline stewardess, while the tapes ran.

My "plan" worked. We taped three long days about the Indians. I asked him how he first became conscious of the issue, what was most shocking about their treatment, what was it the Indians wanted from the government, what was the biggest mistake the Indians made, were the Indians more discriminated against than blacks, would he have been a militant had he been born an Indian, and what did he think of Hollywood's treatment of the Indians? Once in a while I'd change the subject. For instance, I brought up a comedy he did with David Niven, *Bedtime Story*. Brando said that he couldn't do comedy, and I used that negative to transition to a question about how he worked as an actor, thus moving away from our previous topic—Indians.

Q: Another "can't do" associated with you is your inability or your refusal to memorize lines. Do you have a bad memory, or is it that you feel remembering lines affects the spontaneity of your performance?

He seemed to welcome the chance to stop thinking about the Indians and began to answer.

BRANDO: If you know what you're going to say, if you watch somebody's face when they're talking, they don't know what kind of expression is going to be on their face. You can see people search for words, for ideas, reaching for a concept, a feeling, whatever. If the words are there in the actor's mind. . . . OH, YOU GOT ME! [*he exclaimed, laughing*]. YOU GOT ME RIGHT IN THE BUSH. I'm talking about acting, aren't I?

His outburst caught me by surprise.

Q: For a man who likes to talk, it's a pity that you brake yourself.

This was obviously not one of my prepared questions. I was just being in the moment with him, as I always try to do when interviewing someone. I wanted Brando to talk about acting; as fascinating as he could be about the Indians, had he never appeared in the films that made him a star, I wouldn't be there interviewing him.

BRANDO: I'm fascinated about anything. I'll talk for seven hours about splinters. What kind of splinters, how you get them out, what's the best technique, why you can get an infection. I'm interested in any fucking thing.

Q: But will you talk for seven hours about your career?

BRANDO: Of course not. Not two seconds about it.

And there was the challenge. He didn't want to talk about what so many of us wanted him to talk about. And my job was to get him to change his mind. I thought to myself, I may not get seven hours out of him, but surely I could get more than two seconds. And, over the course of the ten days I spent with him on his island and another day a few month's later at my house, I did anything and everything possible to unlock the mystery that is Marlon Brando.

Q: Does being labeled a method actor mean anything to you?

BRANDO: No.

Q: Does it bother you?

BRANDO: B-o-r-e. Bore.

Q: Is that what a method actor does—to bore through to the core of an actor's being?

BRANDO: It bores through and goes beyond the frontiers of endurable anguish of interviews.

We're playing here—I'm trying to pull him out, he's resisting; I'm commenting on his resistance, he's commenting on my comments. But we're not through.

Q: Well, this painful interview is almost over.

BRANDO: Oh, listen, it hasn't been painful at all. It's been delightful. Although I feel like I got in a rummage sale: would you want this dress? No, that *schmatte*. How about this corset? Well, we could take the rubber out and make a slingshot out of it. I'm dizzy. We've gone from the temples of Karnak to the halls of William O. Douglas.

I couldn't resist: his mentioning temples triggered my next question:

Q: Speaking of temples, do you believe in God?

And that led to our continuing discussion about God, order in the universe, life on this planet, aging, death . . . which got him to quote Shakespeare, which led me to ask if he remembered more of Shakespeare than any other author, which got him to say why that was so, which led to the rumor that he was going to do *King Lear* on Broadway . . . and so it went, back and forth, moving from topic to topic like the rummage sale he thought it was. And in the end we had a chance to rummage around Marlon Brando's mind. It wasn't easy, but getting this complex and reclusive man to speak out was definitely worth the effort.

WHILE BRANDO WAS TOUGH, he was also playful. One of his favorite books was Stephen Potter's *The Theory and Practice of Gamesmanship.* Thus, his tactics come as no surprise: You try to catch him, he tries to avoid being caught.

With Robert De Niro, however, it was different. He wasn't much of a player. He was as interested in being interviewed as he probably is in visiting the dentist or a cardiologist. Though one may read about his dislike of talking publicly, a journalist doesn't fully know what to expect until he comes face-to-face with his subject.

De Niro is an interviewer's nightmare. He is a very private man who doesn't like to talk to the press—and when he does talk, he doesn't have very much to say. He isn't book smart, his head isn't filled with arcane bits of knowledge like Brando's, and he doesn't see an interview as any kind of gamesmanship. When I first met him it was at the Chateau Marmont in West Hollywood. He seemed nervous, on edge, and he couldn't sit still. He spoke in half sentences, contradicted himself constantly, and made me wonder why in the world he had agreed to talk in the first place. The reason was that the movie studio put pressure on him to do some publicity for the film he had coming out. With the cost of movies skyrocketing, studios feel more and more that the actors they are paying millions of dollars to should at least do something to help get the word out. Whether De Niro helps his own movies by answering (or avoiding) questions, I can't say. But for his own personal comfort level, the man should just be left to act and not be made to endure the slings and arrows of frustrated journalists.

It took me seven sessions on the West and East Coasts to finish my interview with De Niro in 1988, because De Niro refused to sit still for more than an hour or ninety minutes. Every time we started to actually get comfortable, he would look at his watch and say, "I've gotta go." I wondered where he was always going, and finally I asked him. "I'm meeting friends," he said.

"You're Robert De Niro," I said, "your friends can wait." But he didn't want to keep his friends waiting, so our interview was suffering.

What set De Niro off were simple things, like bringing up his childhood. When we were in New York there were sirens outside the hotel window, and I observed that the sounds of Manhattan were very different than the sounds of L.A. And then I asked him what it was like growing up in the city.

De Niro jumped up from the couch where he was sitting and started yelling at me: "You see why I can't do this? You see? I just don't want to do this."

I hadn't asked him about his mother, his father, his friends . . . just a general question about the city itself. When he calmed down, I tried again.

Q: Didn't you once belong to a street gang?

DE NIRO: That's a whole other thing to talk about, not here. No big deal.

If not here, where? I thought. But I tried another angle.

Q: Wasn't your nickname Bobby Milk?

DE NIRO: That was one of a few I had.

Q: What were the others?

DE NIRO: I don't want to get into that.

Q: Why Milk?

DE NIRO: Maybe because I drank milk. I don't want to go too much into that.

Q: We don't have to go too much, but maybe just enough to get some idea of where you came from . . .

DE NIRO: Listen . . . [*Reaches over, turns off the tape recorders, talks about the pressures on actors to do interviews.*]

At this point I realized that an "in-depth" interview with Robert De Niro was going to be out of the question. But I just couldn't let him get off that easily, so I asked him this.

Q: What kind of kid were you—introverted, extroverted, shy, loud?

DE NIRO: It's hard to talk about yourself, about what kind of kid you were, and so on. So I don't feel that disposed to it.

I didn't believe him, so I just asked another question.

Q: Why is it hard?

DE NIRO: It just is. That's why I don't do interviews. I think it's self-evident. I know people who don't want to talk about things in their life. It's a personal thing and it's really nobody's business.

What De Niro considered nobody's business was really the stuff that makes interviews interesting. I tried to get him to understand this, but his mind was set, and his body language was visibly uncomfortable. I brought up his past, but that was off-limits. I tried the present, but he didn't like talking about what he was doing. I asked about future plans, and he told me that he didn't want to speak about that because he might "jinx" any projects in the works. I tried to make light of his being so closed off but, he didn't see any humor in anything I said. He would just pace the floor, wanting to be anywhere but in the room with me and my tape recorders.

"Well, Bob," I finally said in exasperation, "where do we go from here? You don't want to talk about your past; you don't want to jinx your future; and you're not real nuts about discussing the present."

His response was to lean forward for the fourth time and

turn off the tape recorders before asking me if he could see a transcript of our conversation. I told him no, that wouldn't be possible. He then gave me his reasons why he thought I should make it available, violating the common sense of good journalism.

DE NIRO: I know it's a form of censorship and that's not good, and I know it takes away from what you're doing—I know all that. But, on the other hand, if I could look at it, see if anything that I said I would feel very uncomfortable about, you know, then . . . Now I have to edit my own thoughts. There's a lot of things I'd like to say, but I don't feel I am very clear in my thinking right now, so it comes out wishy-washy. "I don't think this, I don't think that"—it's boring; who cares? And why come off that way? I think, in time, down the line, maybe when I'm old, looking back, it will all make sense; I'll be able to say something.

And there it was, spoken in choppy dialogue: De Niro's fear of being interviewed. He didn't feel that he could articulate his thoughts, he didn't want to come across as dull or boring, he was insecure about his opinions. "Maybe when I'm old . . . it will all make sense." What can one say to convince the man that whatever he had to say would be devoured by tens of thousands of readers who admired him for the brilliance of his acting? The only thing we were able to agree on was that he was one tough nut to crack. So I stopped trying to get him to talk about anything personal and steered the conversation to his films. There were certainly plenty of those to discuss, and unlike Brando, De Niro was willing to talk about playing the young Don Corleone, the angry Travis Bickle from *Taxi Driver,* the raging bull, Jake La Motta, the Russian roulette–playing soldier from *The Deer Hunter,* the brash Rupert Pupkin from *King of Comedy.*

There was plenty more I wanted to discuss after we covered his career, but he wasn't going to hang his laundry out to dry in public. I knew it. He knew it. I also knew that a good part of our interview would include De Niro's reluctance to talk, his turning off the recorders, his wanting to leave. This was what it was like interviewing Bobby De Niro: you brought up subjects, he deflected them; you tried again, he turned away; you tried a third time, he looked at his watch. And that is the portrait that was drawn of the man. De Niro was the incarnation of Lewis Carroll's White Rabbit, always late for a very important date. And that date was never going to be talking intimately or revealingly to an interviewer.

With De Niro and Brando, I had the chance to capture two great actors who rarely spoke to the press, and were both reluctant to reveal themselves. One wrote me a letter in which he was initially annoyed that our interview didn't totally concentrate on the plight of the American Indian, but then he thanked me for making him "more articulate than I remember being." The other called me a "Judas" when I saw him at Al Pacino's fiftieth birthday party, angry that I made him look, to his mind, bad.

Twelve years later, I was with Pacino at the 2003 Tribeca Film Festival, where De Niro introduced Pacino's film *Chinese Coffee*. Afterward, about a dozen people went to eat at Zitoune in the Village. De Niro sat opposite me and said, "I don't know if I'm supposed to like you or hate you."

"Oh, you like me, Bob," I said with a smile. "Though the last time I saw you, you were shaking my wife's hand, saying, 'Nice to meet you, I hate your husband.'"

"Yeah," De Niro laughed, "I probably said that."

"But you were smiling," I added. And though more than a dozen years had passed, that interview we did wasn't forgotten by either of us. The problem, in De Niro's eyes, was that I should have been more sensitive to his indecision and discomfort. "It works both ways," I said to him. "How do you think I felt, expecting you to show up at my hotel at nine in the morning and you didn't come until five in the afternoon?"

"That's unlike me to do that," De Niro said. "Usually if I'm going to be late, I have someone call and let the person know."

"I guess that time it slipped through the cracks," I said.

"Oh, now I get it, it was revenge!" he said.

"Maybe we should try it again some time."

"Yeah, maybe we should. I'll talk to you, you'll print how I didn't want to talk, and I'll go, 'He did it again!'"

We both laughed.

I don't know how he feels, but I'm certainly willing to give De Niro another crack at an interview, to see if he's changed.

5. STRUCTURE

WHEN THE TALK STOPS

> I compare myself to a gold prospector . . . I start asking questions and up comes all this ore, dirt, everything. Now you gotta find the gold dust. I start editing, cutting. Now you've got to find a form. Then it's not just gold dust; it becomes a ring, a watch, a necklace, a tiara.

—STUDS TERKEL

I've often wondered how much behind-the-scenes work television journalists who have become stars actually do. Is Diane Sawyer or Barbara Walters sitting in an editing bay late at night telling an editor she wants a close-up over a two-shot, or a shortened version of a forty-second sound bite? According to Walters, the answer is yes. "It's important to be able to do your own editing, and not to just turn it over to somebody else," Walters says. Though she's talking about television, it holds true for all kinds of editing. Walters admits to

being compulsive. "I will not only agonize over questions; I will agonize over editing."

Agonize is the appropriate word. Here's an example of a structural "adventure."

Al Pacino presented one of my greatest challenges. I didn't know, when I first went to see him in 1979, that I would wind up talking to him over a period of months, and that the transcription of that extended conversation would run to over two thousand pages! Once I had that towering manuscript in front of me I felt overwhelmed. How was I going to reduce that to eighty pages? (Nowadays, it would have to be reduced to thirty pages!) There was just too much material, covering too many topics.

The first thing I did was read it from start to finish, high-lighting phrases, sentences, and sections I liked. Then I wrote down in the margins what each of the highlighted areas was about. Then I indexed these notations, indicating the page numbers where the topic was discussed, so that it read some-thing like this.

ACTING: 14–8, 26–35, 94–7, 141–2, 189–93, 267, 303–14, 479, 722–50, 1266–71, 1480–8, 1735–44, 1907

REHEARSAL/PREPARATION: 1391–5, 1652

CHILDHOOD: 57, 68–9, 107–8, 264, 269, 312–5, 570, 1400–14, 1836

MOTHER: 107, 267–9, 314, 1836–41

FATHER: 110, 175–7, 780–3, 891–2

EARLY JOBS: 86–9, 212–15, 901, 1560

WOMEN/WOMANIZER: 417–9, 1020–4, 1674

SHAKESPEARE: 325, 333–6, 1920–5

LEE STRASBERG: 124, 255, 877, 1483

THE GODFATHER: 30–2, 45, 68, 246, 310–3, 450, 980, 1212, 1520–28

FILMS TURNED DOWN: 447, 503–5

DRINKING: 27, 40, 128, 395, 889, 1742

FAME/ANONYMITY: 31–4, 228–32, 1991–3

INJURIES: 68–75, 283–87

[THIS INDEX CONTINUED ON FOR PAGES.]

Once I had this index, I was able to better control the mate-rial. If we were talking about *The Godfather*, I could look at the index, go to the pages referring to that film, and work with just those pages. I would take a sentence or two from page 30, another from page 68, a paragraph from page 310, a question from page 450, and put it together to make it seem flawless. I never put words in Pacino's mouth; I just condensed all the words he said into succinct responses. I did this with every topic in the index. And that became my first draft.

Next, I read through that draft, highlighting anew what I thought worked best. Like a sculptor, I continued to carve away at the material until I felt I had captured my subject. I knew I had to include Pacino's comments about the major roles he had played, but I also knew I had to include material about his growing up, his early struggles, the women in his life, and his perception of some of the people he worked with. Once I had all of that, I wanted something more—I wanted to try and capture his personality, his quirkiness. I wanted to be able to give the reader a sense of being in his apartment, of seeing him as he lived. So I looked for instances that could capture something new about him, something one might not expect when thinking of this man who played such steely characters as Frank Serpico, Bobby Deerfield, and Michael Corleone.

To flesh out the portrait I tried to create a few memorable scenes.

When we were talking about acting, Pacino quoted his favorite line from *Richard III:* " 'Nay, for a need.' For the need! The need is everything! That is what it is about. Appetite and need."

As he spoke, he took a cookie and dipped it into his Perrier water. I noted this in a parenthetical aside and then asked: "Do you know what you just did?"

Pacino looked down and answered: "Now I'm dipping my cookies in water. Next thing you know, I'll be sitting on the windowsill."

This little cookie scene allowed me to take our conversation in an offbeat but charming direction, a brief interlude before getting back to more serious matters.

Q: There's a box of cookies on top of your refrigerator, the majority of which are half-eaten. Is it that you don't expect many visitors or you don't care if you offer them half-eaten cookies?

[Pacino gets up, goes into the kitchen, discovers the box of half-eaten cookies.]

Q: OK, tough question: What's your favorite cookie?

PACINO: My favorite cookie? Lavagetto. Cookie Lavagetto played third base for Brooklyn in 1940. I once knew a bartender I used to call Cookie. "Hey, Cookie, let me have a couple of beers."

I liked this comment because it demonstrates how playful and quick Pacino is. It shows that his love of baseball is real. And it also hints at the drinking problem he had, which he talked about in other parts of the interview. He didn't ask for a beer, but a couple of beers, something a person who had a drinking problem would do. And this all came out of the innocuous question about a favorite cookie.

ANOTHER SIDEWAYS GLIMPSE into Pacino's droll character occurred during an exchange we had regarding Jack Nicholson's winning the Oscar for his performance in *One Flew over the Cuckoo's Nest* the same year Pacino was nominated for *Dog Day Afternoon*. This aside started with a simple question and turned into a kind of Abbott-and-Costello comedy routine.

Q: You and Nicholson were involved in a Best Actor race for the Oscar that many people felt was extremely close. Did you think you'd get it?

PACINO: No, I never thought I'd get it.

Q: You thought Nicholson would?

PACINO: Yeah.

Q: Do you feel he deserved it?

PACINO: Yeah, he did. He'd been out there a while, he's made a lot of different films, he's been great.

Q: Would you have turned the role down?

PACINO: Yes, I would have turned that down.

Q: Because of *Dog Day?*

PACINO: No, because I thought *Cuckoo's Nest* was a kind of trap. It's one of those built parts: I don't think it has much depth. Commercially, it's very good, but as far as being a really terrific role, I don't think it is.

Q: You still don't?

PACINO: Yeah, I just don't see much depth in the role.

Q: But you said that you thought Nicholson deserved the Oscar for it.

PACINO: Who said that?

Q: You did.

PACINO: When did I say that?

Q: A little while ago.

PACINO: I'll bet you $5,000 I didn't say it.

Q: Five thousand dollars? You *said* it. Would you really bet?

PACINO: I'd bet ya $5,000. Yeah.

Q: You would?

PACINO: Yeah.

Q: OK. So if you didn't think he did, do you think *you* did?

PACINO: [*Smiling.*] You really want to corner me, don't you?

Q: You've been sitting on it too long. It's got to come out.

PACINO: You're asking: Do I think I deserved the Academy Award for *Dog Day Afternoon?* Not any less than he did. For that.

Q: Do you think you deserved it *more* than he did?

PACINO: *What do you think?* WHAT DO YOU THINK?

Q: Now we're cooking. Did you think *Cuckoo's Nest* deserved to win for Best Picture?

PACINO: Did it win?

Q: Yes.

PACINO: It won? Well, I didn't think so. If you asked me, Did I like *Cuckoo's Nest?* I have to tell you I didn't. Did you?

Q: Yes.

PACINO: Finally, we disagree on something. Finally.

Q: What the hell.

PACINO: Get out of my house, then. [*Laughs.*]

So, instead of the kind of falsely modest response you would expect if you were watching James Lipton interviewing someone like Pacino on *Inside the Actor's Studio* ("No, I never thought I'd get it." "Yeah, I think [Nicholson deserved it.] . . . He's been great") a more in-depth interview gives you far more insight into Pacino's true feelings ("I would have turned *[Cuckoo's Nest]* down. . . . As far as being a really terrific role, I don't think it is."). And then, after another playful exchange (the bet) we go even deeper: "Did I like *Cuckoo's Nest?* I have to tell you I didn't."

What I was attempting in this interview was to show how much of a battle it could be, how truly like a cat-and-mouse thing it was. After all, my job was to try and strip Pacino's defenses, and he worked hard not to allow that to happen. In the process, there were these revealing moments, and at the end, when I asked him for any last words, he shouted out the George C. Scott line from *The Hustler:* "YOU OWE ME MONEY!"

It was one of the few times I've ended an interview with my own comment, and not the subject's. I concluded: "Not after you read this."

SO, HOW DOES ONE pick and choose what material to use and what to discard after you complete an interview? How do you know when enough's enough about a particular subject or when you need more? Experience, of course, is the obvious answer. Learning to edit is similar to learning how to play a musical instrument or how to play ball or how to memorize dialogue.

With editing, you have blocks of material to carve and arrange. If you're talking to someone about something specific—a book just written, a topic in the news in which she is knowledgeable, a particular performance—then you know it must be included in the final draft, and the chances are good that you might want to begin the piece with the current project. If the person you are interviewing has a large body of work worthy of inquiry, then that's got to be figured in. If the person is known for his outrageous or witty or humorous remarks, then you're going to be looking for those in the transcript. Once you have your "givens," you begin to look for things the person said, or exchanges you had, that can liven up the piece. After all, you want the interview to be entertaining. You want it to move and you want the reader to keep turning the page, to call out to a friend, "Listen to this." You want to stimulate.

Before the 2000 presidential election, Governor Jesse Ventura was encouraged by some of his followers to run as a third-party candidate. He never took it too seriously, but he did say at one point that he thought Colin Powell should run for the presidency. When I interviewed Ventura, I asked him about that and followed with some other questions. This is the longer version, followed by what I eventually chose to use.

Q: You're a big supporter of Colin Powell, saying if he ran for president you'd run for vice president with him. What's so great about Powell?

VENTURA: General Powell and I are alike. We have differences: he supports Affirmative Action, I don't. But he's fiscally conservative and socially liberal. I find him to be a very powerful leader. One doesn't get to be the head of the Joint Chiefs of Staff not knowing how to be a leader. It would be very hard for me to accept orders from anyone today, and yet I could accept orders from him. I judge him that way. I've only met him once, but I'm pretty good on first impressions.

Q: So of all the people in the U.S. the one you most endorse is Powell for president?

VENTURA: I've given him as much of an endorsement as I can give anyone else, otherwise I'd have to endorse my best friend, Jerry.

Q: Could your best friend be president?

VENTURA: I'd pick him over any of the others because I know what he stands for. He's a pattern maker. We grew up together. I know he'll never lie to me. With him I'm not the governor or Jesse the Body. I would recommend him to be president.

Q: So how do we get to know who a politician really is? Including you?

VENTURA: You don't.

Q: While the public Jesse denies any presidential ambitions, could the private Jesse be thinking he can deny himself right into that Oval Office one day?

VENTURA: The more I say no the more they keep pushing me. Like I jokingly said, What happens if you win and you don't run? Do you have to do it? [*Laughs*]

Q: Though you deny wanting the office, you actually believe you could get elected president if you ran, don't you?

VENTURA: Right. Everyone says I can't, but I believe sure I could. This is America. And I proved it here. If you look at California's poll, I have an 80% recognition rate already, so I don't have to buy name recognition.

Q: Have we entered the Age of Jesse Ventura?

VENTURA: It's a possibility, if I wanted to exploit that.

Q: Let's exploit it here for a moment. If you decided to run for president, what would be your game plan?

VENTURA: My plan would be to stay out of it until next July. I would let these two [Gore and Bush] hang each other with all the rope they're gonna have, to where the public can't stand them. Their disapproval rating will skyrocket. Then you enter the race three months before and take the whole thing.

What I wound up using was just the first and last Q&As, eliminating all the material in between. Why? Well, I liked the part about his friend Jerry, it seemed so absurd and so like the governor to say something like that—and if a former pro wrestler was now sitting as the governor of Minnesota, why shouldn't a pattern maker run for president? But since I knew we had a lot of territory to cover in this interview, I couldn't allow space for Jerry; and since Ventura was still a potential third-party threat to Gore and Bush, the focus had to remain on him. In spite of his denials, he did have a plan in mind, and he said it here—so why have that lost among all the other talk? Better to go from the possibility of him running for vice president under Powell to how he would campaign if he went for the presidency himself. It's more concise, more focused, and more potentially newsworthy to edit the above 450 words to these 200 words:

Q: You're a big supporter of Colin Powell, saying if he ran for president you'd run for vice president with him. What's so great about Powell?

VENTURA: General Powell and I are alike. We have differences: he supports Affirmative Action, I don't. But he's fiscally conservative and socially liberal. I find him to be a very powerful leader. One doesn't get to be the head of the Joint Chiefs of Staff not knowing how to be a leader. It would be very hard for me to accept orders from anyone today, and yet I could accept orders from him. I judge him that way. I've only met him once, but I'm pretty good on first impressions.

Q: Since Powell is not going to run, and there's still open speculation about you—if you decided to run for president, what would be your game plan?

VENTURA: My plan would be to stay out of it until next July. I would let these two [Gore and Bush] hang each other with all the rope they're gonna have, to where the public can't stand them. Their disapproval rating will skyrocket. Then you enter the race three months before and take the whole thing.

BEGINNINGS

What you soon discover after conducting a number of interviews is that they each have their own internal structure. That structure should reflect the personality of the person being interviewed. A comedian might prefer to be serious, just as a dramatic actor might want to try out some of his favorite jokes, but one must throw the reader into the equation when molding an interview, and the reader has certain expectations. If you pick up a magazine to read an interview with Jennifer Aniston, you expect to read something about what she thinks of the actors she worked with on *Friends* as well as something about what it's like being married to Brad Pitt. An interview that doesn't touch on either of these subjects might be notable for their exclusion, but she would have to say some pretty startling and exceptional things to satisfy most readers. If you're interviewing Robin Williams, you expect insight, commentary, and high antics. If it's Anthony Kiedis, it's got to include sex, drugs, and rock 'n' roll. If it's Bill Gates, you've got to touch on his wealth, his social conscience, and his vision of the future.

But no matter who it is you are interviewing, it is important to make it interesting from the beginning, because if you don't, you're going to lose a lot of newsstand browsers who are going to make up their minds whether to buy the magazine on your opening lines. It's the same, really, as choosing books to take with you on a vacation. If you're not familiar with the writers, you may pick up a half dozen novels and read the first page or two to see what grabs you.

My wife is a weaver, and she once taught me how to make a basket. When you start, you need to make it very tight or else there will be a hole at the bottom. When you begin an article or an interview, you also need to make it strong, to capture the reader, to propel him to read on. If you are lax in your beginning, if it has any holes in it, then no matter how good the interview may get, you may not keep your reader.

That's why I find *Interview* magazine curious—because the majority of interviews it publishes start poorly, aren't very substantive, and when you finish reading them you often feel like you'd like to get back the time spent. But then, it isn't exactly journalism *Interview* is doing—it gets one actor to talk to another, or a musician or an artist to talk to another musician or artist. It isn't very critical; it's more of a lovefest, a lot of fawning over how terrific the subject is. In October 2003, I went to see Billy Bob Thornton, and he told me about his experience with *Interview* and what he learned from it.

"Interviewing people is hard," Thornton said. "It's a real skill.

I know that because Julia Roberts once asked me to interview her for *Interview* magazine. I thought it would be a piece of cake. Hang out with Julia for a while, ask her a bunch of questions. . . . What I told myself was: I'm not going to ask her the usual shit. Because we're both actors. I'm going to be edgy and real and give her the things that she wants. So I got there and it was like, what the fuck do I ask her? 'So Julia, what was it like growing up in South Carolina? Or Georgia? And being in the movies?' I was a total moron! If I'd just been sitting and bull-shitting with her as a friend we could have done it. But because that was the setting, it became . . . like, did I really just ask her that? That's the shit that I don't want to be asked! I found myself mumbling and looking at the floor. It was hard. I gained a real respect for people who do it well. It was an eye-opening experience for me. To be on the other side."

At least they were in the same room together when they spoke. Many of *Interview*'s conversations are done over the telephone. The June 2003 issue had Renee Zellweger "interviewed" by rock star Pete Yorn, Harrison Ford by his "roommate" Calista Flockhart, documentarian Andrew Jarecki by actress Sandra Bernhard, Stephan Jenkins by author and rock lyricist JT LeRoy, and the various members of Fleetwood Mac by Matt Diehl. Here's how each of those interviews began:

PETE YORN: Say your name for the record.

RENEE ZELLWEGER: No! [*both laugh*]

PY: State your name! [*both laugh*]

RZ: That's mean!

PY: All right. Now, I'm going to be bouncing all over the place here. Ready?

Five sentences into this and I'm ready all right—ready to stop reading and move on to see how Flockhart talks to her boyfriend.

CALISTA FLOCKHART: [*to her dog*] Hey, Webster! Come here! [*to Ford*] So, your new movie, *Hollywood Homicide,* is really terrific. You're very funny, very slick. Congratulations. Can you tell us a little bit about the story and your character Joe—what's his last name?

You've got to be kidding, right? She begins with her dog, which has no meaning whatsoever to the piece, then she congratulates Ford on his "really terrific" new movie, which is not really terrific at all, and then she shamelessly asks him to just plug away, though she hasn't done enough research (did she even see the movie?) to know the character's name. Ford's answer is so straightforward and dull, there's just no way one can stay interested in this little tête-à-tête between lovers. Let's see how another actress, Sandra Bernhard, began her talk with Andrew Jarecki, director of the documentary *Capturing the Friedmans.*

SANDRA BERNHARD: Hi, Andrew. How are you?

ANDREW JARECKI: Hi. Very well. Can you hear me okay? The Roman telephone system goes back to the days of Julius Caesar.

SB: I know. It's pretty rickety.

So nice to know that the magazine won't spare any expense to talk to these people; they'll settle for phoners, and then have them complain about the connection. On to Third Eye Blind lead singer Stephan Jenkins.

JT LEROY: Um, hi.

STEPHAN JENKINS: Huh-huh. Huh-huh. [*imitating a Beavis and Butt-head laugh*]

JTL: What time is it there?

SJ: It's 9:40 A.M. San Francisco time, but I just got into New York.

Is this any way to start an interview? With beginnings like these, you have no expectations. Does the interview with Fleetwood Mac singer Stevie Nicks begin any better?

MATT DIEHL: Stevie?

STEVIE NICKS: How are you?

MD: I'm awesome.

SN: Great! [laughs]

MD: I don't mean to sound like an obsequious sycophant, but I really love this new record.

SN: You do? It's heavy, isn't it?

And there you are! The interviewer is telling us he's awesome! And he's defining what it is to be an interviewer for *Interview* magazine: an obsequious sycophant.

COMPARE THESE OPENINGS with the way Italian journalist Oriana Fallaci began some of her interviews. Fallaci told Jack Huber and Dean Diggins in 1991 that she sees interviews as "*pieces de theatre,* because they are written by a writer . . . I'm not a journalist. . . . So my approach is that of a novelist, of a playwright. And when I go to do an interview, I really see it as a playwright. Something happens which tells me, by instinct, where the play must go."

Her interviews set a high standard for journalists. Here's how she started her conversation with Sean Connery in 1965:

"As far as I can gather, this meeting of ours is truly exceptional, Mr. Connery. I don't believe that any actor today is as difficult to approach as you are. There are certainly none who defend themselves from the curiosity of others with such ferocity, such desperation."

She's letting you know, right from the start, that she's ready to do battle. She takes him to task for being so hard to get, then adds the word "desperation" to alert you that she's not going to let him get away with any games-playing, because she sees through that.

When Fallaci went to interview the leader of SNCC (Student Nonviolent Coordinating Committee), H. Rap Brown, in 1967, during the civil rights movement, she opened: "Mr. Brown, it has been said that the blacks are organizing trained guerrilla outfits in various American cities, and that your movement has something to do with this. Is it true?"

Blunt, direct, to the point.

In Saigon, during the Vietnam War, Fallaci went to interview Nguyen Cao Ky, commander of the air force and vice president of the Republic of South Vietnam, and began by throwing a quote of his back at him: "General Ky, many disconcerting things are said about you, but the most disconcerting I have heard is what you said about yourself a few days ago: 'I know that someone is trying to kill me. But this someone will not be a Communist.'"

Let the conversation begin!

TO PLAYBOY'S HUGH HEFNER, who prides himself on never having to leave his mansion because all of his fantasies were fulfilled within its walls, Fallaci asked: "A year without leaving the House, without seeing the sun, the snow, the rain, the trees, the sea, without breathing the air, do you not go crazy? Don't you die with unhappiness?"

Hugh Hefner, playboy of the Western world, unhappy? Nice twist.

To Sammy Davis Jr. Fallaci approached with: "On my way to your house, Mr. Davis, I had a very disturbing thought. You have absolutely everything to make you hated by the multitudes of mean-minded and stupid people: you're a Negro, a Jew, married to a beautiful blond . . . Truly there's no other internationally famous person who contrives to combine so many 'sins' into one. And I concluded: goodness, this man must positively enjoy doing battle with the world, irritating people, provoking them, defying them. . . . But do you really enjoy it, Mr. Davis, or does it make you unhappy?"

There she goes with that unhappy question again, but Fallaci's being provocative, she's making an effort to draw her subject out right from the start.

She began her 1972 interview with King Hussein of Jordan by challenging him: "Majesty, but who is in command in Jordan? At the check points people are stopped by the fedayeen, at the borders the fedayeen attack, in the villages it's the fedayeen who decide. It's no longer paradoxical to say they've set up a state within your state."

She said to India's Indira Gandhi: "Mrs. Gandhi, I have so many questions to ask you, both personal and political. The personal ones, however, I'll leave for later—once I've understood why many people are afraid of you and call you cold, indeed icy, hard . . ."

Fallaci's tack is not what you'll read in *Interview* magazine. She has definitely chosen the road less traveled; she is putting herself on the line, daring her subjects to react . . . and to possibly end the conversation before it even begins.

Here are a few other examples.

Eric Norden spent close to a year putting his Albert Speer (Hitler's architect) interview together for *Playboy* in 1971. And he used the technique of quoting others to hit him hard in the beginning: "Critical acclaim for *Inside the Third Reich* has not been universal. Rebecca West brands you a 'repulsive criminal,' and historian Gudrun Tempel writes that 'Speer may easily have been as brutal, as ruthlessly ambitious and almost as sick as Hitler . . . one puts his book away with a greater fear of men like him than of any Hitler.' How would you respond to such critics?"

Claudia Dreifus was playful but effective in getting CBS anchor Dan Rather to open up in her 1995 interview with this beginning: "David Letterman did a Top Ten list the other night about the CBS–Westinghouse merger. Among his predictions: the current CBS brass would be replaced by a 'whole new batch of weasels,' and your next coanchor would be a coffeepot. Can you work with a coffeepot?"

When I was thinking about how to start my interview with Marlon Brando, I wanted to give the reader a sense of place, since we were doing it on his private island in Tahiti, which up until then he had kept out of the media glare. So I started this way: "This island you own is certainly a perfect place to talk— no phones, no unexpected visitors, no interruptions." And after he responded to that, I could follow up with this: "As a kid growing up in Nebraska, did you ever imagine you'd end up as the caretaker of a South Sea island?"

COMPARING AND CONTRASTING the way someone was to the way that person is now can be a useful method to help begin a conversation. When you're talking to an elected official or a president of a company or an accomplished artist, remember that person wasn't always in that position. So ask: "Before you got to where you are, you were_____," and fill in the blank: a schoolteacher, a secretary, a short-order cook, an amateur musician. And then you can ask: "Can you reflect upon your life then and compare it to your life today?" Or, "Did you have big dreams or ambitions then? Did you ever think you'd wind up where you are now?" Or, "With the pressures you have now, do you ever long for those days when life wasn't as complicated?" This is one way of breaking the ice with someone you're first meeting. Because no matter who it is, that person had to work his way up to where he is. And that journey is often a good way to begin a conversation, even if, in the end, you don't use it (that will depend on how interesting his answers are!).

HERE'S AN EXAMPLE of how I started an interview with someone not everyone would immediately recognize—by being as provocative as I could. Before she laid down her boxing gloves in 1999 to take care of her dying father and to appear in the movie *Rollerball,* boxer Lucia Rijker held two world titles: the WIBF and the WIBO super lightweight/junior welterweight belts. She won all fourteen bouts she fought between 1996 and 1999. Before boxing, Lucia Rijker spent eleven years as a four-time international champion kickboxer, knocking out twenty-five of her thirty-six opponents. But the only fight that would have truly determined her greatness was with Christy Martin, a fighter controlled by Don King. Martin had brought women's boxing to a wider public when one of her bouts was televised as the undercard of a Mike Tyson fight. Martin's bloody victory landed her on the cover of *Sports Illustrated.* She and Rijker were the same age and in the same weight class (135–140 pounds) and there was bad blood between them. Martin had become Rijker's nemesis, and she returned to the ring solely to draw Christy Martin out and settle, once and for all, who was the better female fighter. When I interviewed Rijker for *Penthouse* my editor wanted the title of the story to be "Why Is Lucia Rijker Mad as Hell?" I wasn't about to begin with "Hi, how are you?"

Q: I want to talk about what pisses you off, and at the top of the list it would have to be Christy Martin and her apparent reluctance to fight you. True?

RIJKER: I've tried for three years to get that fight. I sat down with her promoter, Don King, a couple of years ago, he couldn't guarantee me the fight. He said, "She doesn't want to fight you." But now, in the media, she says that she's preparing for us to fight, and I think she is because she's fighting tougher opponents. She knows she needs to fight me to go out on top. Could she retire without it? If I'm still in the ring, she couldn't.

Q: And you're back in the ring. Didn't she accuse you of taking performance-enhancing drugs?

RIJKER: I've heard her say the weirdest things. Out of fear. If I needed steroids to be great, that would be the time to stop. I've been an athlete my whole life. I've done weight training since fifteen, three times a week with heavy weights, because I needed my strength, because I had these skinny legs. And my body developed into the body of an athlete. Christy saw that and got scared, because her body doesn't look like mine. I've had a kickbox career, those workouts are severe. So what's the next thing she's going to say to avoid the confrontation?

Q: What is it about Christy Martin that so pisses you off?

RIJKER: I just don't like her as a person, that's why I want to fight her. I don't think she's a role model for woman's boxing. She's at the top, being protected by Don King. I have so much emotion about it, it's become personal.

NORMAN MAILER HAS LED a controversial life, and any interview with him has to deal with a number of issues. So I stuck a few of them up front, to let the reader know we were about to enter some deep waters with Mailer: "Whenever there's a brief introduction about you, what's usually included is that you ran for mayor of New York twice, stabbed your wife, and won two Pulitzer Prizes."

Mailer responded to the negative of the three, and didn't disappoint in the hour and a half we had together.

I TRY NOT TO ask long, involved questions, but sometimes in the beginning you almost can present an outline of what the rest of the interview will be, and when I went to see priest and novelist Andrew Greeley in Tucson in 1993, that's what I did.

"You seem to be your own best—or worst—critic: one chapter in your autobiography lists the most common complaints about you: one, that you write too much and have never had an unpublished thought; two, that you're the richest priest in America; three, that you have serious psychosexual problems; four, that you write pornographic trash; five, that your novels are puerile potboilers that sell because of the novelty of a priest writing about sex; six, that you're brokenhearted that you were not made a bishop."

"Yeah," Greeley answered, "that's a pretty good list."

"So where do you want to begin?"

I USED A MUCH shorter opening gambit with Neil Simon: "You're considered to be the most successful playwright in history. Is that a blessing or a burden?"

CRIME WRITER JAMES ELLROY has been known to toot his own horn loudly and often, so when I interviewed him, I started by asking: "You've been known to say you want to be the Tolstoy of American crime. The greatest crime writer who ever lived. Did you learn from Mailer and Muhammad Ali how to draw attention to yourself?"

I BORROWED FROM MAILER again when I began a 1985 interview with poet Allen Ginsberg: "Norman Mailer once wrote an ode to you saying, in part: 'I sometimes think/that little Jew bastard/that queer ugly kike/is the bravest man in America.' What did you think when you read that?"

IT'S RARE WHEN an interview in print begins with the first question actually asked, and for good reason. It takes a few questions and answers for the interviewer and subject to warm up. There's enough strain going into an interview with someone you've never met before, armed with intimate, detailed questions about that person's life, that you don't have to add to that pressure by expecting charming, quotable material to come forth immediately. It takes work. It takes a mixture of small talk and incisive talk; it takes adjusting to the person you're talking with. You may not even recognize your beginning until you're through with the interview and reviewing the transcript. What you hope to find is something timely that is also revealing, perhaps humorous, perhaps serious. Something that draws the reader in and makes him want to continue. What you're looking for in the beginning is something that allows the conversation to *begin;* it can't stand on its own as a comment. There has to be a follow-up, a next question, another answer, until your verbal portrait begins to unfold.

IN 1985 I INTERVIEWED Alex Haley, who besides writing *Roots* and *The Autobiography of Malcolm X* did the first *Playboy* interview (with Miles Davis) and six others after that. I wanted to know which of his interviews he was most proud of.

Haley responded:

"In a clinical sense I would say the one with the Nazi leader, George Lincoln Rockwell. Because I learned most about how an interviewer needs to be detached from the subject and even be hospitable to what the subject may say and feel, because your job is to communicate to the reader what that person feels. The magazine was looking for controversial and exciting people to interview. They told me they would like to interview the head of the Ku Klux Klan and the head of the American Nazi Party. I selected the Nazi party leader because he had more education. It wasn't that the other man didn't have any, but he didn't have anything like the background of Rockwell, who was a graduate of Brown University. He had become a lieutenant commander in the Navy. He'd been a jet pilot and commanding officer of a pursuit squad. No matter what you thought, you couldn't be stupid if you'd done those things. I was living in upstate New York at the time and he was in Alexandria, Virginia. He wasn't sure he wanted to do this interview but felt he could use the exposure. He called to ask me a personal question: 'Are you a Jew?' I quickly said, 'No, sir.' Well, when I turned up there was a very shocked set of Nazi people! *[Laughs.]* It just never occurred to them that I was black. They were so upset. There were six gentlemen standing on the porch with swastikas, belts and side arms. He was not there. They put me in a station wagon, two in the front, two behind me, I was in the middle seat, and drove me down the highway into the woods. There was a clearing with a white farmhouse and a big pole with swastikas flying. They frisked me before I entered the house. As I went up the steps I felt very, very uncertain about the whole thing. He came to the door—a darkly handsome, angry man. Very angry. Had on a white shirt with dark trousers. He flung his fingers right in my face, almost on my nose, his face mottled with anger. 'I'm going to tell you right now,' he said, 'we call your kind niggers and we think you should all be shipped to Africa.' Somehow a calm descended on me, right at that moment, and I said to him, 'I've been called nigger before and this time I'm being paid very well for it, so now you go ahead and tell me whatever you've got against us.' And that was how the interview began."

The first question Haley asked? "Before we begin, Commander, I wonder if you'd mind telling me why you're keeping that pistol at your elbow, and this armed bodyguard between us."

Tell me you're not going to read on!

AS YOU CAN SEE, beginnings are important. Unfortunately, many interviews in magazines today are tied to a promotion—an author is selling his book, an actor her film, a businessman his product, a politician his agenda—and so opening questions are often about that, which immediately dates the interview and makes it old news a month later. But when a journalist considers himself a writer first, the beginnings are more thoughtful and can be powerful. And so are the endings.

ENDINGS

Endings, like beginnings, are extremely important to interviews.

Endings must be just that: an end. You must feel that you've taken a journey through the life and mind of the person you've been talking with and that you've reached some destination, a sense of closure. You want to go out as strongly as you came in. And, if possible, you want to leave the reader smiling, or shocked, or pumped. You want to leave the reader satisfied.

Sometimes when I'm talking with someone something they will say sticks in my mind, almost like a little bell going off. I'll think, "That's a good ending," and jot a note to myself while still continuing the interview. That may happen two or three times during the course of our conversation, and I'll be satisfied, because I know that one of those remarks will work to sum up our talk, or to end it on a humorous or solemn note. If that little bell doesn't go off, then I know that I'm going to have to search for my ending. Hopefully it's in there somewhere, but I won't know until I start editing the transcript. If you're being careful with transitions, so that one topic flows seamlessly into another, then you will know by the time you are nearing the end that you have certain topics that haven't been included, and you can start aligning them in such a way that the last few pages fall into place and the last words sound like a good place to go out. It's not always easy: when I get back sixteen student interviews with the same person I often find sixteen different endings. Some of them work, most of them don't. I'll read aloud the ones I think work and try to show why. The ones that don't just sort of peter out; they don't leave you with a sense of fulfillment or with any type of emotion. The ones that work sound right; you know it when you hear it. You might want to read the last few questions and answers out loud, the way you might read the ending of a book out loud. If it sounds right, it probably is.

I remember getting back the galleys to the first interview I had done for *Playboy*. It was with Henry Winkler, who as the Fonz on *Happy Days* in the mid-1970s was the biggest star on television. It was the first time a magazine had sent me galleys to review, to make sure whatever editing changes they made met with my approval. I read it carefully, and when I got to the end, I saw that there wasn't one. At least, there wasn't the end that I had included, the one I thought was absolutely necessary. Winkler had taken a walk-on role and turned it into an iconic one. The show was often written around his character. His mannerisms, his leather jacket, his DA haircut had entered the seventies culture. I was aware of Winkler before any of this had happened to him. My friend was his roommate when they were both at Yale, so I knew stories. I saw how the interview should be, like a three-act play, taking Winkler through the various stages of his life, his highs and lows, culminating in his being crowned King of Mardi Gras in New Orleans. That was the image I wanted to go out on, the man who would be king, the man who *was* king of sitcom television. The symbol I was using was a pop culture bacchanalian event for a pop culture god.

But when I read the galleys, the story of his crowning moment was gone. The ending just sort of petered out. I didn't understand.

I called my editor, with whom I was working for the first time, to ask about this egregious cut. He said that it had to do with space. The interview was running long, they had to cut something, so they just lopped off that last paragraph.

"That was the wrong paragraph to lop," I protested, explaining how I saw the interview, how I had carefully tried to structure it so that it climaxed with that Mardi Gras scene. How it didn't make as much sense without it.

"Gee," my editor said, "I never saw it that way; let me look at it again." He did, but my ending wasn't restored. Instead, I got to put it at the end of the introduction. A quarter of a century later, I still think about that bad ending.

SOMETIMES AN EDITOR will recognize a better place to end an interview than the one you've chosen. This can happen because you may be too close to the material and you may be trying to include more than is necessary. If an editor suggests cutting out the last few questions and answers, or moving some Q&A from the middle to the end, don't be offended right away. Give yourself some time to digest the new ending, to see what the editor has seen. If it doesn't sit well with you after you've slept on it, then bring up your objections with your editor and see who is more convincing.

Though I was upset about the way the Winkler interview

ended, I've had editors make good and thoughtful suggestions about endings—ones that worked better than the endings I had chosen. When that happens, thank your editor and show what a good team player you can be.

Just keep in mind that endings are the last words, the final impression. It doesn't have to be a summing up, or a punch line, but it should veer away from cliché and strive toward leaving the reader with something memorable, something one can nod at and say, with some satisfaction, well done, you didn't waste my time or disappoint.

Here are some examples of provocative, smart ending questions (and some answers), garnered by skilled interviewers.

WHEN ORIANA FALLACI finished with Secretary of State Henry Kissinger, she threw one last right hook at him: "I've never interviewed anyone who evaded questions and precise definitions like you, anyone who defended himself like you from any attempt by others to penetrate to his personality. Are you shy, Dr. Kissinger?"

TO CONCLUDE HER 1969 interview with General Giap of the North Vietnamese Army, Fallaci asked: "How long will the war go on? How long will this poor people be asked to sacrifice itself, to suffer, and die?"

FALLACI ENDED HER INTERVIEW with H. Rap Brown on this note: "It's one thing to talk, and another to act. Are you quite ready to kill?"

FALLACI DIDN'T LIKE director Alfred Hitchcock after she met him, and let him know it. When she asked if he had ever been involved in a dramatic situation in his life, Hitchcock said, "No. Never. Only in movies. I never get involved in dramatic situations. You're the one who's in a dramatic situation."

"Why, Mr. Hitchcock?" Fallaci asked.

"Because you have to write an article about me. And you don't know anything about me."

To which the writer had the last word: "That's what you say, Mr. Hitchcock. But I do, Mr. Hitchcock. With all your cordial humor, your nice round face, your nice innocent paunch, you are the most wicked, cruel man I have ever met."

C. ROBERT JENNINGS ended his *Playboy* interview with Tennessee Williams by asking him about sex: "Do you believe that, in the final analysis, a man follows his phallus?" To which the distinguished and forthright playwright responded, "I hope not, baby. I hope he follows his heart, his frightened heart."

BEFORE I LEFT Saul Bellow's office at Boston University I asked him this question, which wound up being the ending I used: "In 1995 Nigerian writer Ken Saro-Wiwa was executed. Salman Rushdie observed that 'all over the world, writers are being thrown in jail. They mysteriously die in police custody. It is open season on writers and it must stop.' In America will it ever be dangerous to be a writer?"

"No," Bellow responded. "They may knock us to the ropes once in a while and give us a rabbit punch to the kidneys, but nobody takes us seriously enough to kill us."

I liked this because Bellow had taken himself seriously throughout the interview. He had poked fun at other writers, defended himself from charges of chauvinism and being a "Jewish" writer, and had opinions about politics and politicians, marriage and therapy, meeting with Jack Nicholson, and winning the Nobel Prize. And he ended with "nobody takes us seriously enough to kill us." The juxtaposition was perfect.

WHEN WRITER ERICA JONG told Gretchen McNeese that fame is not one of the things that really matter, McNeese got her ending by asking, simply, "What is?"

JONG: Well, in the cosmic scheme of things, how hot you are today, or whether your picture is on the cover of a magazine, or how much money you get for the movie rights to your novel, matters *not at all*. It's nicer to have fame, success, than not to have it, just as it's nicer to be comfortably fixed than poor, but the things that truly matter, and I think will always matter, are: Can you write a poem that will last, like one of Emily Dickinson's poems? Not will they put your picture on the cover of a magazine but can you write something that people will still be reading to each other 100 years from now? Can you really love people, care about people and give yourself to them? Those are the things that matter. And all the rest is total delusion.

Martin Luther King Jr. gave a long and eloquent answer to close his interview with Alex Haley in 1965. Haley's final question to him was "You are now the universally acknowledged leader of the American civil rights movement, and chief spokesman for the nation's 20,000,000 Negroes. Are there ever moments when you feel awed by this burden of responsibility, or inadequate to its demands?"

After talking about his time in a Birmingham jail, a call from President Kennedy to his wife, Coretta, and the seven-year-old black girl who told a white cop she wanted "fee-dom," King summed up: "I welcome the opportunity to be a part of this great drama, for it is a drama that will determine America's destiny. If the problem is not solved, America will be on the road to its self-destruction. But if it is solved, America will just as surely be on the high road to the fulfillment of the founding fathers' dream, when they wrote: 'We hold these truths to be self-evident . . .'"

I KNEW I HAD my ending when I asked Sharon Stone if people were envious of her. "Sure, come on," she said. "I got to be tall and blond and a movie star. That's a lot to get in life."

FOR MARLON BRANDO, I thought that I should come full circle and end where I began, on his island in Tahiti. The setting was unusual enough, and the fact that this man felt the need to find some kind of peace halfway around the world from where he achieved his fame was noteworthy. I had teased him earlier, trying to get him to talk about Marilyn Monroe when he preferred to keep the conversation on a somewhat higher plane, so when he made a reference to a Robert Frost poem, I couldn't help myself, it was an opening to tweak him once again. And in keeping with his playful and sarcastic nature, Brando rose to the occasion and took us out with a smile.

Q: Do you find it impossible to leave this place once you're here?

BRANDO: It's very hard. But . . . "miles to go before I sleep, and miles to go before I sleep."

Q: Didn't Marilyn Monroe write that?

BRANDO: I think Marilyn did, yeah. It was either her or Fatty Arbuckle, I can't remember.

BECAUSE THAT PARTICULAR interview was a continual battle of one-upmanship, that ending worked because Brando was thrown a curve and hit it out of the park with his Fatty Arbuckle reference. Most interviews aren't as engaging as this one was, the struggles of the interviewer don't often play so prominent a part of the interview itself. And when it comes to a conclusion, a sense of one's mortality might be a way of summing up.

When an interview attempts to be far-reaching, it's not uncommon to end it with a question about the Great Beyond: what thoughts your subject may have about it, how he or she would like to be remembered, what would they like to come back as, what words would they like carved on their headstone. The question can be put directly, or with a sense of grace and style. This was how Sam Merrill closed his interview with Joseph Heller, the author of *Catch-22*.

"Snowden's secret, which Yossarian learned when the young

gunner's guts slithered out through a flak wound over Avignon, was that 'the spirit gone, man is garbage . . . Ripeness was all.' Can you bring yourself to contemplate that inevitable transition from spirit to garbage?"

"I've come to look upon death the same way I look upon root-canal work," Heller replied. "Everyone else seems to get through it all right, so it couldn't be too difficult for me."

ORIANA FALLACI FINISHED her conversation with Israeli prime minister Golda Meir asking, "How do you look on death?"

MEIR: I can tell you right away: my only fear is to live too long. You know, old age is not a sin and not a joy—there are plenty of disagreeable things about old age. Not to be able to run up and down the stairs, not to be able to jump. . . . And yet you get used to some things without difficulty. It's just a matter of physical troubles, and physical troubles aren't degrading. What is degrading is to lose your mental lucidity, to become senile. Senility . . . I've known people who died too soon, and that hurt me. I've known people who died too late, and that hurt me just as much. Listen, for me, to witness the decay of a fine intelligence is an insult. I don't want that insult to happen to me. I want to die with my mind clear. Yes, my only fear is to live too long.

AFTER NEIL SIMON said he didn't want to live to ninety-two when I asked if he thought about death much, I mentioned that George Bernard Shaw lived into his nineties.

SIMON: Yeah, but he ate vegetables and I hate them.

Q: Have you thought of an epitaph?

SIMON: Ssshh, he's writing.

GOVERNOR JESSE VENTURA came through with a quotable ending to my question, "What would you like to come back as?"

"If I could be reincarnated as a fabric, I would like to come back as a 38 double-D bra,"Ventura responded.

WHEN I ASKED Andrew Greeley how he envisioned his own death, he said he'd like to die with a smile.

Q: And still with the epitaph: Nothing but a loud-mouthed Irish priest?

GREELEY: It wouldn't be a bad epitaph.

MY LAST QUESTION to Anthony Hopkins was "Do you have any fears about your own death?"

HOPKINS: I don't. I know that in the end there's a peace, a real peace, and maybe darkness and nothing. I don't have morbid thoughts about it, I'm in a state of grace, I suppose. Maybe it's Zen. My epitaph, if I ever have one, will be, "What was that all about?"

TRUMAN CAPOTE KNEW what it was all about, and had an answer to just about any question anyone ever asked him. He had once said he'd like to be a sea turtle in another life, so I brought that up to him when I was looking for my ending. "I said that before," he told me, "that's because they live to an old, old age and become very wise."

"What would you like to come back as?" I asked, sensing that he no longer believed he'd live to that old, old age.

"A buzzard," Capote said.

"Why a buzzard?"

"Because buzzards are nice and free. Nobody likes them. Nobody cares what they do. You don't have to worry about your friends or your enemies. You're just out there, flapping away, having a good time, looking for something to eat."

DOLLY PARTON HAS ALWAYS been fun to talk to, and you can count on her to give good quote. She can be outrageous, endearing, funny, subtle, and sincere. When she brought up that she expected to go down in history as "good and solid," I suggested that as a possible line for her tombstone. And she said, "I don't want a tombstone. I want to live forever. They say a dreamer lives forever . . . I want to be more than just an ordinary star. I want to be a famous writer, a famous singer, a famous entertainer; I want to be a movie writer; I want to do music movies, do children's stories; I want to be somebody important in time; I want to be somebody that left somethin' good behind for somebody else to enjoy.

"Everybody wants to be successful at whatever their inner dream is. I'm not near with what I want to do, with what I want to accomplish. When I feel like I have accomplished the things that I want to accomplish, then maybe I will personally think of myself as a superstar. I want to be somebody that extremely shines. A star shines, of course, but I want to be really radiant."

Where do you go from there, except out the door and to your computer to see how it looks in print!

THE MEAT BETWEEN THE BEGINNING AND THE END

Between the opening and closing questions and answers, there is the meat. This is where all your research pays off. You have studied your subject, you know what he or she has said in the past, and you have an idea of what your editor is expecting: There are areas that must be covered, and it wouldn't be a bad idea to make a list of them. Then, when you're going through the transcript, you can highlight the best remarks about these subjects and try to work them into the final draft of the interview. You also want to look for those quirky and offbeat moments that can reveal your subject's personality in a way that hasn't been shown in previous pieces written. Your aim is to present a fresh and insightful interview. In this way, you will hold the reader's attention, because you won't be giving them a rehashing of something they might have read before.

Contrary to Pete Yorn's warning to Renee Zellweger—"I'm

going to be bouncing all over the place here"—at the beginning of their *Interview* magazine conversation, each question should appear to follow the previous answer, so that the interview reads like a coherent conversation. Thus, transitions are important. Every interview is different, and yet if they are carefully and thoughtfully edited, they have certain similarities. They don't read like a transcript, they don't read like a casual conversation, they don't bounce all over the place (though they can still be broad and wide-reaching); the opinions are more weighted on the side of the subject, the probing on the side of the interviewer. And when they work, there is an art to them. Good interviews have an arc, a drama; they take you on a ride, they make you think, and hopefully they display the subject you're reading about in a new and different light.

I've given examples of opening gambits that I thought worked, and of endings that I've liked, but to give a sense of how an interview can be structured I have selected one I did with former Indiana basketball coach Bob Knight a month after he was fired in the fall of 2000 (see Appendix 2), along with commentary in the margins to indicate what was going on in my mind as I edited this emotional and at times scary interview.

6. EDITORS ON EDITING AND EXPECTATIONS

I've regretted most interviews. Because they don't write what you say or they'll get you out of context or they'll juxtapose it in such a way that it's not reflective of what you've said. And then you can say something in a certain spirit, with a smile, but when it appears in print there's no smile.

—MARLON BRANDO

I once returned from Europe, where I had interviewed the sculptor Henry Moore at his summer home in Forte dei Marmi, Italy, and stopped in New York to pitch the story to Robert Shnayerson, the editor of a magazine called *Quest*. He had the October 1977 issue of *Playboy* with Barbra Streisand on the cover on his desk, which I thought was prescient, since I had done that interview. I told him about my visit with Moore, the things he had said, how I thought it would work for his magazine. He agreed that Moore was of interest, and if I was willing to submit the piece "on spec" (i.e., *speculation,* meaning no assignment, no contract, no guarantee of any payment, no financial risk on his part) he would be happy to take a look at it.

As I had been freelancing for seven years, I didn't think it was fair of him to expect me to do this on spec. After all, I had already been to see Moore, the interview was done, and the expenses were out of my pocket.

"I really am not familiar with your work," Shnayerson said to me.

"It's sitting right there on your desk," I said, pointing to the *Playboy.* "That Streisand interview is mine. I no longer work on spec."

"Well, you don't have to get persnickety about it," he said.

"If you can't make it an assignment," I said, "I'll try to sell it elsewhere." I stood up and walked out. I never wrote for *Quest* magazine. Some months later they put Henry Moore on their cover. And a year or two after that they folded.

Had I not been dealing with editors for years by then this one experience might have soured me about the profession. It's such a delicate thing, one's relationship with an editor. My first real experience with an editor was at *Newsday*'s *LI* magazine, which was their Sunday supplement. They were just getting off the ground when I returned from my three years in the Peace Corps. I talked my way into a meeting with the editor by saying that I had won a *Newsday* American history essay contest when I was still in high school, so when we met he asked me two questions: Did I know anything about aviation? And did I like to do research? I answered truthfully: No, I didn't know anything about aviation, but I could learn; and no, I didn't *like* to do research, but I could do it.

"We want to do a piece on the history of aviation on Long Island. Interested?"

"Sure," I said. Over the next three weeks I immersed myself in the subject and learned quite a bit, mainly that a great deal of the history of aviation, outside of the Wright brothers, occurred on Long Island. While researching, I also discovered that there were people who were building their own planes, going up in gliders, jumping with parachutes, and learning to fly on Long Island, and I suggested sidebar stories on each of them. The editor was game, and I was soon following a woman learning to fly; chuckling over stories of people who built planes in their homes and had to knock out walls to get them out; getting nauseous catching thermals in sailplanes; and jumping solo out of a plane at the narrow end of Suffolk County. My history story turned into four other articles; and instead of sidebars, these human interest stories were featured as individual cover stories. All of them required my asking a lot of questions about subjects I knew very little about.

My experience with editors has generally been positive, which is probably why I'm still writing for magazines thirty-three years after I began writing professionally. Editors are the bottom line, the final arbiter of what Brando once called the "salade Niçoise" of our endeavor. If your editor doesn't like your work, it ain't gonna be published. Simple as that. So while most beginning writers think they are out there trying to please a reading audience, the truth is much narrower and more focused: You're trying to please your editor. The majority of editors want writers to succeed. When they give you an assignment, they give you a contract, and in that contract there is what is called a kill fee. If the assigned piece is rejected, you will get paid, but usually only 20 percent of what the agreed-upon fee was. So if you were to get $1,000 for your piece, you'd be sent $200, and you probably would have a tough time getting another assignment with that editor. This isn't to say that editors are always right if they reject you. They are opinionated, like anyone else. Sometimes something just rubs them the wrong way, and no matter what you do to rectify it or suggest changes, they just aren't interested. It's happened to me over the years with one book publisher and a few magazine editors.

To be a writer, especially a freelance writer, one must develop a thick skin, because you're going to have to learn to deal with rejections. With me, it started with poetry. I used to write a lot of poems when I was a teenager, and instead of sending them to the smaller reviews and university anthologies, I went directly to *Harper's, Atlantic Monthly,* and *The New Yorker.* I began to build up a considerable pile of rejection slips—form letters that told me my work wasn't suitable for their publications. I pinned each of these rejections to my wall, and by my fourteenth birthday I had enough to consider them wallpaper. But then I got one that lifted my spirits. It was from *Esquire,* a mere three-by-three inches square, and underneath the logo was a handwritten "Sorry, no," signed with the letter "N." The reason for my elation? All the other rejections weren't even signed; there was no indication that anyone had even read my poems. This *Esquire* editor read what I sent and thought enough of them to actually write to me! I stuck that note in the very center of my rejection wall.

Esquire has figured into my freelance life as well. I had heard about a man living in Harlem named Hubert Fauntleroy Julian, who was once known as the Black Eagle. During World War II he was a pilot in a black unit, and afterward he went to Ethiopia to develop Emperor Haile Selassie's air force. Julian also claimed to have come very close to assassinating Mussolini. An editor I knew at *Esquire* gave me the assignment to profile Julian, and I did. What I discovered was that Julian lived in a world of fantasy. "Feel my skin," he said to me after we had talked for a few hours. "Is that the skin of a seventy-year-old man? Of course it isn't. And you want to know why? Because every ten years I go to the planet Krypton for a blood transfusion. It's kept me feeling and looking young." Julian thought he was Superman!

I wrote the story, but when I turned it in I found out that my editor had been called up by the National Guard and his replacement had no interest whatsoever in the life of the Black Eagle. I was given a kill fee and sulked for a week before *Playboy* came through with my first article assignment. I had pitched them on E. Joseph Cossman, an iconoclastic entrepreneur who made millions in the mail-order business and then wrote a book about it. I flew out to Palm Springs and spent three weeks interviewing Cossman, returned to New York, and worked on the story for a month. After I turned it in, I heard back from my editor: he was so sorry, he said, but he had assigned five different stories on con-type men, figuring three of them would come through. It was the first time in his experience that he liked all five articles, and since I was the newest writer, I was the low man on his totem pole. "I could hold on to it," he said, "but since I would have to space out these stories we wouldn't get around to publishing yours for two-and-a-half years. You'd be better off taking it back and selling it elsewhere."

I wanted to say, "Keep it! I'll wait!" but instead I tried to act professionally and accepted another kill fee. *Esquire* and *Playboy,* two of the magazines I most wanted to write for, neither of which was going to print what I had written for them. I felt wounded. I even cried. I was twenty-five, I wanted to be a freelance writer, I didn't want kill fees. But what could I do?

Instead of folding my tent and looking for a real job, I just became more determined. Just as I wanted to show those editors who had rejected my poetry that they had made mistakes, I wanted to prove to myself that I could write for national magazines. I was inspired by Jack London's character Martin Eden, whose stories kept getting rejected until he finally broke through, and then all those rejected stories began to get published. I did my best to ignore Eden's eventual suicide.

Once I broke through with *Playboy,* the interviews came regularly. After Henry Winkler and Barbra Streisand came Dolly Parton, Brando, Pacino, Steve Martin, George C. Scott, James A. Michener, Henry Fonda, Patty Hearst, and Luciano Pavarotti, all of which I've mentioned throughout this book. I was on a roll. And then came Truman Capote. I interviewed him for the cable TV show, and when we finished I asked if we could continue talking for the magazine. My editor, Barry Golson, was all for it. And after spending a long afternoon with Capote I met Golson and Christie Hefner for dinner in Manhattan, where I told them, "This will be the most quoted interview of the year." I was so confident, so elated with Capote's outrageous remarks. Golson agreed with me when he read what I gave him, but Don Gold, the managing editor at the time, did not, and neither did Arthur Kretchmer, the editorial director. Golson even showed me Gold's three word response to the interview: "I hate it."

He may have hated it, but I loved it . . . and believed in it. Capote may have sounded too bitchy for their tastes, but he was too original to dismiss, and so I asked to buy the material back—something I'd never advise any writer to do. But, in this case, I felt that Capote was marketable, and that it was worth owning. Soon after I got back the rights in 1984, Capote died at the age of fifty-nine. His death was totally unexpected. Two weeks later I sold the material I had to New American Library, and within six months it published *Conversations with Capote* in hardcover. James Michener wrote an introduction and it made numerous bestseller lists, including topping the list at the *Village Voice* and one of the San Francisco newspapers. The book was then published in England, Japan, Germany, France, Spain, Austria, Czechoslovakia, and Poland. I still receive royalties.

BEING REJECTED ISN'T the only thing one must have to deal with when working with editors. There's also the little matter of being believed. When you're interviewing or profiling people, you are dealing with their words, and sometimes the subject cries foul. "I never said that" are the words that make the hairs on the back of an editor's neck bristle. And he probably hears them often. So one has to be prepared to back up the stories one submits with the tapes and transcripts that provide the necessary proof that the words you are quoting were actually spoken.

THERE ARE TIMES when an editor may change his mind about an assignment, and you can get stuck between that rock and the hard place. You're out there trying to land the subject, and when you finally do, the story gets pulled out from under you. Then what? It happened to me with Saul Bellow. I had wanted to interview him ever since I read his work as a teenager, but *Playboy* never went for it—too intellectual, perhaps; too smart; too small an audience; not appealing enough for nineteen-year-old boys; whatever. But I never gave up. I suggested Bellow every two years, and finally, after nearly a decade of getting turned down, I got the go-ahead. So I called the university where he taught and spoke to his assistant. Bellow wasn't well and couldn't do a strenuous interview. Was that a final no, I asked, or could I try again in six months? Try if you like, I was told, and six months later I did. Again, he was still recovering, and he was also working on a novel. So I waited another six months, and this time I got a yes. Saul Bellow would talk to me. I immediately called my editor with the good news and he said, "Let me get back to you about him."

Get back to me? Why?

Because, I would soon find out, *Playboy* didn't think it would sell many magazines featuring a Saul Bellow interview, and it would just as soon pass. Pass? It was an assignment! I had spent a year trying to convince Bellow to do this. How could I salvage this one?

I did it this way. I told my editor that I couldn't tell Saul Bellow we weren't interested in him. I just couldn't do that. Since the top editor was the guy who nixed it, I decided to write him a note saying that Bellow should be rejected with an explanation, out of common courtesy, from on high, not from me. A few days later my editor called and said to go ahead and do the interview. Apparently, his boss also couldn't tell Saul Bellow he wasn't a good enough subject for *Playboy*.

And, as a fitting end to this little story, that interview was the first one ever submitted by *Playboy* for the national magazine awards in the category of nonfiction.

Then there are times when an editor can't make up his mind whether he'd like to go with a Q&A or with a profile. When I was working on boxer Lucia Rijker for *Penthouse,* I told my editor some of the things she was saying and he thought we should go with a Q&A. After I gave it to him, he liked the way the introduction read, and asked if I would just put the rest of it in prose form. I rewrote it. But he changed his mind again and, apologizing, thought that perhaps it should be a Q&A after all. Soon after this, he lost his job, and the piece came out as a profile.

MOST OF THE TIME editors do not get involved with the people you're interviewing. They're there to bounce ideas off before you meet your subject, and sometimes they have specific things they'd like you to cover. When an editor has a suggestion, listen to what he has to say. He is, after all, the person who will be editing your piece. He is your first, and toughest, reader. When an editor tells me to make sure I ask Kiefer Sutherland about the bands he's discovered or Robin Williams about his bicycle collection, I take notes while we talk, and find it useful later. Editors are often more attuned to the social and political barometer than I am. Had I not sat next to the editorial director of *Playboy* at a luncheon in the spring of 2003, I would have still been going after John Updike and Tom Wolfe, both of whom turned down previous interview requests. Both are writers worthy of being *Playboy* interviews like the ones I've done with Bellow, Joyce Carol Oates, and James A. Michener. But the editorial director set me straight: He preferred having these brilliant writers' bylines in the magazine, rather than appearing as interview subjects. The same held true for Don DeLillo, Philip Roth, David Foster Wallace, and T. C. Boyle. He said he also felt the same way about TV anchors like Peter Jennings, Dan Rather, and Tom Brokaw. They reported the news, they didn't make it. I did not agree with him about this, but it was certainly good to know what he was thinking. When he was relieved of his position a year later, I was relieved that the Wolfes and the Woodwards were once again fair game.

Sometimes editors assign you stories for personal reasons and, as a pen for hire, you have to go through the proper motions. *Newsday*'s Sunday magazine editor once asked me to write a story about people who owned aquariums. I wondered why he was interested, and he said that his son had got some tropical fish and a tank and he became curious about it. I spent a few weeks interviewing aquarists, as they are known, and found out that outside of photography it was the largest hobby in the United States. I spoke with people who were as passionate about their Black Mollies and Peppered Corydoras Catfish as book collectors are about their signed Cormac McCarthys and Stephen Kings. When I turned in the article my editor looked at its length and said, "Three thousand words! Who wants to read three thousand words about fish?"

"What happened to your son's fish?" I asked.

"They died."

WHEN I WAS interviewing Barbra Streisand, she said she'd like to look at the transcript of our interview after we were done, to make sure she didn't say anything that might hurt her mother. This wasn't possible, because I knew that if she got her hands on the transcript it would be more than her mother she would want to check on. Streisand thought her request was reasonable. She only wanted to look at the transcript, she wasn't insisting on making changes. I stood firm about this. So she tried a different tactic: "What if your editor agreed?" I brightened. My editor would never agree. No editor would. So I said, "If he agreed, then you can do what you want. I'll ask him."

"Let's call him now," she said.

"Now? We're still doing the interview, Barbra, let's not get sidetracked."

"What's his number?"

I called and, unfortunately, he was there to answer. "Barry, I'm sitting here with Barbra—," I began, but before I finished, Streisand took the phone.

"Barry, this is Barbra," she said in her seductive movie-star diva voice. I was smiling, so confident that my editor would blow her off that it never occurred to me that he could get flustered, that having a star of the magnitude of Streisand calling him would melt him just by the sound of her voice. But that's what happened. Barbra said she was concerned about offending her mother and how could I be so heartless as to not let her have a peek at what she said, it wasn't going to mean changing anything really, it would just put her at peace. She nodded her head twice, smiled triumphantly, and handed me the phone.

"I think I just blew it for you," Barry said morosely.

It was another lesson learned. Editors are not the people on the front lines. They are in their offices and they deal with people mostly by phone, or with writers over lunch. They're no different than the average person when it comes to going one-on-one with someone famous. They get tongue-tied. They say yes too quickly. They want to be liked.

A VARIATION OF THIS happened again two years later after I finished interviewing Al Pacino. I was working on the piece at home in Los Angeles when I got a call from my editor, who said, "I'm sitting here with Al Pacino."

"No way," I said. "Pacino's not going to go to your office."

"Hi, Larry," came Pacino's unmistakable voice.

"All right, what's going on?" I asked.

"Al came here because he was concerned about something he told you about the draft," my editor said in our three-way conversation.

Shocked, I replied, "Don't tell me, Al, that you're worried that what you said will get you in trouble with the Army. You're too old to get drafted now."

"These things are very strange," Pacino said. "I don't care about anything else I said, but, you know, maybe it would be better if we just let that stuff slide."

I actually started to laugh. Of all the things that Pacino had said in our sessions, he was losing sleep over his comments on the draft. As ludicrous as it was, I understood his concern, because I had spent agonizing years trying to beat the draft myself.

"So why are you calling me?" I asked.

"Because," my editor said, remembering the Streisand incident, "I didn't want to agree to anything without calling you first."

"Yeah, sure, take it out," I said.

It wasn't that big a deal to me. And it taught me something: that these big stars take what they say seriously enough to pop in unexpectedly, using their fame as leverage, and the element of surprise to keep you off balance. But I *was* able to rely on my editor to let me make the call, in this case.

It was this same editor who had let me know after I had returned from Brando's island in Tahiti that he only wanted the interview to include 10 percent about the Indians. I balked at this when he told me because 90 percent of our conversations were about that subject, but the editor knew how much the readers would tolerate and stood firm. That became one hell of an editing job!

EDITORS—THEY AREN'T EASY to please. Rick Barry, at the 2003 UCLA/*Los Angeles Times* Festival of Books, called them "the enemy; they're evil; they're scum." But without them none of us, including Barry, get published. Love 'em or hate 'em, you've got to deal with editors. There's no getting around that, unless you publish your own magazine or website and pay yourself to do interviews. So what do editors think about this whole subject, of dealing with writers and publicists, of choosing subjects, of editing interviews? I asked eight experienced magazine editors if they'd be willing to answer some questions, and though all complained that they were overworked and didn't have the time, they all made some time. What follows are questions I thought most writers would like to have answered, followed by these editors' responses in a roundtable format. Take what they have to say to heart, because they are the final word.

THE EDITORS

Stephen Randall (Executive Editor, *Playboy*), **Peter Bloch** (Editor, *Penthouse*), **Andrew Essex** (Executive Editor, *Details,* formerly writer/editor at *The New Yorker, Entertainment Weekly,* and *Salon.com*), **Heidi Parker** (currently West Coast Editor, *Playboy,* but when this was done she was still the editor of *Movieline),* **Barry Golson** (formerly at *Playboy, TV Guide,* and *Yahoo),* **Bill Newcott** (Features Editor, *AARP the Magazine,* formerly *Modern Maturity),* **Janice Min** (Editor, *Us*), and **Will Dana** (Assistant Managing Editor, *Rolling Stone*).

1. Why do you think there has been such a proliferation of interviews in magazines?

STEPHEN RANDALL *(PLAYBOY):* Q&As are more easily digestible by the reader, unlike profiles—especially longer profiles—which require more time and effort to read. As magazines cater to younger readers and compete with TV and the Web, shorter, easy-to-read stories start to push out more demanding articles. It's not a dumbing down—many Q&As are smarter and better than many profiles.

ANDREW ESSEX *(DETAILS):* Because our world is completely devoted to celebrity culture, it's the lingua franca. It's the coin of the realm. It is, without exception, the unifying subject of this country, for better or for worse.

WILL DANA *(ROLLING STONE):* Interviews have been staples of magazines for as long as I have worked in the field, about fifteen years. But there are certainly more magazines than ever these days, and certainly more of an interest in celebrities than ever before. But the main reason for what seems like this proliferation of interviews is that with so much demand for a celebrity's time, publications are simply not able to get as much time with a subject as they once did. The interview form is probably the most efficient way to maximize what is often minimal face time.

BILL NEWCOTT *(AARP)*: Along with in-depth investigative pieces, thoughtful, lengthy interviews are one of the few things that magazines can uniquely provide to readers. An interviewer prepares at length, a subject gives serious consideration to the questions he or she might be asked, and they come together in a venue that requires no sound bites, no from-the-hip rejoinders, no fear of uneasy silences as the subject formulates a substantive answer. The closest thing electronic media can provide is, perhaps, the work of Charlie Rose—but even his body of work ultimately takes on a churned-out, let's-see-what-my-researchers-have-come-up-with-this-time aura.

JANICE MIN *(US)*: Interviews are fascinating to readers. In an age of celebrity—whether celebrity is defined in the classic Hollywood sense or just as people of note—it is always intriguing to hear the voice of someone who has been so lionized in the press.

PETER BLOCH *(PENTHOUSE)*: I think more magazines and newspapers are publishing interviews because the public's attention span has grown shorter and interviews are easy to cut down into tiny bite-size snippets, easy for the readers to digest. Plus they are much easier to edit than longer pieces and they're certainly easier to "write."

HEIDI PARKER *(MOVIELINE / HOLLYWOOD LIFE)*: Our society is becoming increasingly interested in people and their personal experiences. With the Internet, blackberries, cell phones, and e-mail, people are getting more closed off from each other because the communication is not being done in person and therefore it lacks depth. How often does anyone ever sit with their friend and open up over a cup of coffee? The compensation comes in the form of reading about strangers' very intimate experiences.

BARRY GOLSON *(PLAYBOY, TV GUIDE, YAHOO)*: Because (a) readers like them and (b) journalists perceive that they're easier to produce than profiles. They can be, unless they're good, in which case they're not easier at all, and can require more effort, not less.

2. What is the difference between a profile and an interview and which do you prefer?

BLOCH *(PENTHOUSE)*: As a reader, I certainly prefer a good profile to an interview, but as an editor, interviews are easier to present to the reader and much easier to fit whatever space requirements are necessary.

PARKER *(MOVIELINE/HOLLYWOOD LIFE)*: With a profile a writer is examining someone's career and summing them up in their own words. With an interview (we call it a Q&A), questions are asked and someone answers them, it's very straightforward and you're getting the information from the horse's mouth: it's not being reworded by a writer. I prefer the interview because there is less editorializing.

GOLSON *(YAHOO)*: The difference is self-evident. I like profiles when the people who are part of the subject's life, whether pro or con, are essential to understanding him. And where the setting can be as interesting as the people. I like interviews when it's the subject's own words and ideas that are the attraction.

NEWCOTT *(AARP)*: I really like the Q&A format when the subject is well known to the reader. You don't have to paint a word picture of Henry Kissinger lording behind his desk, or of Susan Sarandon gesticulating every word. And if there is verbal byplay between the questioner and the subject, even better.

Profiles work best when you are introducing the character, and, frankly, doing a bit of a sales job on just why we'd want to read about him or her. You paint them into their environment—home or office or representative setting—and occasionally interrupt the stream of quotes to bring up biographical informa—tion. Inevitably, the writer becomes more of a focus in a profile, and not always in a good way—unless, of course, you've nabbed some truly great writer whose asides and observations are as irresistible as the subject, or even more so.

DANA (*ROLLING STONE*): As an editor you always prefer a good profile. But to get a good profile, you need a lot of unrestricted access to your subject. And, of course, you also need a very talented writer. Sometimes a Q&A is simply the most efficient way to get at your subject.

RANDALL (*PLAYBOY*): A Q&A relies on the subject and interviewer. A profile can bring in all sorts of third parties and other information to make points. Also, the writer's point of view and powers of description play a giant role in a profile—describing a celebrity's house, for instance, can tell a reader more about that star than all the great questions in the world.

I think, as a general rule, Q&As have more energy, more immediacy. They give you that sense of you-are-there-ness. That's one of the reasons they're so popular with younger readers and are seen as a natural competitor to TV and the Web. (This is true of well-done interviews—frankly, I'm not sure which is worse: a boring profile or a boring Q&A. They're both painful.)

As a magazine editor, I prefer Q&As—they seem right for *Playboy* and the current state of the world. As a reader, it's a toss-up. I like them both. Though, to be honest, when I'm thumbing through a magazine, I'll stop and glance at a Q&A every time. That's not necessarily the case with profiles. With profiles, I need to have an interest in that particular person. Q&As are easy to sample—and then you get hooked, even if you didn't care about the subject. Profiles are less accessible and require a commitment, but I still read them.

ESSEX (*DETAILS*): There's a huge difference. In a perfect world, the profile is much more about the craft of the writer and an active disinterest in what the celebrity has to say. The Q&A form is much easier, it requires transcription, so it's more expedient and, in some cases, there is probably a cynicism about the profile form being exhausted.

MIN (*US*): We've found at *Us* magazine that profiles written as so-called write-arounds—without a full cooperation interview from the subject—can be very informative, especially when there is news that may be controversial surrounding the subject. If there is controversy or news about the person, there are often limitless numbers of other people who know the subject who want to talk about them, offer opinions, offer information, and it helps to be able to put the person in context. Oftentimes, the best stories— the most revealing stories—are ones done without the subject's full cooperation. You can get a better-rounded, more informative piece that way and not feel obligated to or tied down by some of the mental constraints a writer may feel—deliberately or not— when the subject gives cooperation. Other profiles, where the subject cooperates, while at the same time also opening up sources—Mom, a friend, a sibling, a coworker—can equally be revealing. Interviews per se, when run, say, as a Q&A, are most successful when the subject is someone who people just love to hear from, period. Hugh Grant is unbelievably witty, George Clooney is charming. It helps to have people in the Q&A format who have the star power, or intrigue, to make the audience want to hear their words, and their words alone. Also, straight interviews are useful when you don't want to get lost in that writerly mumbo jumbo that so often accompanies stories on celebrities—those stories that always start out with the writer meeting the subject at a restaurant and commenting on how surprised he∕she is by how the subject looks in person, what he∕she eats (typically in quantity), et cetera. . . . Q&As cut to the chase.

3. What makes a good interview?

RANDALL *(PLAYBOY)*: I don't think there's one rule. I like to be surprised (that is, finding out that someone I admired is really insane or vice versa). I like to be entertained. I like to laugh. I like controversy. I like information. I like to be introduced to new and different worlds. I like to feel as if I've met the person from the comfort of my home. Lots of different interviews have pleased me on lots of different levels. The worst sin: the boring interview and∕or the one with obvious questions that you've heard before. It rarely matters who the subject is. I can read an interview with anyone, even if I have no interest in that person (e.g., a NASCAR driver) and if it's a good interview, I'm happy. On the other hand, even if I'm fascinated by the person (e.g., David Letterman), a badly done interview is not worth the effort. That's my view as a reader. As an editor, sometimes I find myself publishing bad interviews with good people because it helps the magazine.

BLOCH *(PENTHOUSE)*: The best interviews make readers feel as if they're having a conversation with the subject.

ESSEX *(DETAILS)*: There are two important factors: one is that the person being interviewed is touched by metaphysics, is articulate, or has some sense of humor. The other is the ability of the interviewer to extract interesting information.

PARKER *(MOVIELINE / HOLLYWOOD LIFE)*: When someone is candid and shares good stories about themselves that explain who they are. Heart. Soul. Humor.

GOLSON *(YAHOO)*: A prepared interviewer who is a skillful questioner and is willing to toss the prepared questions to pursue a real conversation; and an interview subject who is articulate—not eloquent necessarily, but articulate.

MIN *(US)*: A good interview is one in which the subject (or the subject's publicist) sets no ground rules as to what is and what isn't off limits. Also, it helps to have the subject be open, unguarded, relaxed. Also, time constraints are killers. At *Us,* we've had time constraints as small as fifteen minutes with celebrities. Rarely do those interviews work, and oftentimes, they never run.

NEWCOTT *(AARP)*: If the subject shares just one truly personal moment in a manner you've never heard before, you're on your way to a very good interview. When Henry Kissinger confessed to us that he first supported the Vietnam war because "I didn't understand it well enough," or when Harry Belafonte said, in remembering Paul Robeson, "I loved him," or when Maya Angelou offhandedly mentioned that she thinks of her body as one big ear . . . you can pretty much hang the whole piece on that. People, especially people who talk about themselves for a living, are notoriously nonrevelatory. We had a very good writer spend an entire day with one of the top TV news anchors, and the newscaster spent the entire day deflecting questions about himself.

DANA *(ROLLING STONE)*: The first thing you need to get a good interview is an interesting subject. Someone who is not articulate or voluble, and who isn't interested in really providing answers to all your questions, will provide a great obstacle to getting a good interview. The next most important thing is preparation. I always think you should overprepare. This is not necessarily so that you can ask your subject a lot of obscure questions. If you are prepared, you will generally put your subject at ease. He or she will feel that you have done your homework. If it's a friendly interview, this might get them to lean back and tell you some great stories. If your approach is more investigatory, your subject will know that he or she cannot safely evade your questions.

The other thing is that it's a part of human nature that people like having attention paid to them. If the person who comes to interview is well prepared and well versed in your life and your achievements, you will most likely be flattered. And when people are flattered, they tend to be more generous. So, I think it's also a good trick, early in an interview, to ask a question that makes it clear you know a lot about this person.

4. Is there a structure you look for in an interview?

PARKER *(MOVIELINE/HOLLYWOOD LIFE)*: I like interviews that have unusual structures. There's nothing worse than predictable three-act interviews.

BLOCH *(PENTHOUSE)*: I don't look for any particular structure— that's easy enough to accomplish in the editing process.

MIN *(US)*: There is no structure per se that I look for in an interview. Rather, I want the interview to be as revelatory as possible. Especially with celebrities, you can see a canned quote, a canned response a mile away. Just as interviewers go in with a certain agenda—they want to get the subject to cover topics X, Y, and Z—subjects, too, have their own agendas. They need to promote their project, address something in the news, dodge difficult questions. It is the job of the interviewer to find ways, small openings during the interview, to get the person to say something off-the-cuff and unscripted that adds warmth and intimacy to the story.

DANA *(ROLLING STONE)*: I don't necessarily think about a structure beforehand.

RANDALL *(PLAYBOY)*: I'm certainly looking for structure—a beginning, a middle, and an end—but I'm not looking for a particular structure. Basically it works best if current, newsworthy stuff is near the beginning and childhood, personal history, et cetera, are toward the end, but I'm sure there are exceptions to that.

ESSEX *(DETAILS)*: Ideally, no. There should be some kind of internal structure and architecture, but that would imply that there's a full-blown formula—and though there are many formulas, you don't want to impose it from the get-go.

NEWCOTT *(AARP)*: The one liberty we take with our Q&As is to lend shape to them after the fact. We link pertinent segments that may have actually occurred an hour or so apart. This is fine with the subjects. So I'd prefer an interview, in its raw state, to resemble a casual conversation, even rambling. There's plenty of time to impose order on it later.

5. What balance do you like to see between substance and irreverence in an interview?

ESSEX *(DETAILS)*: I never think of it in those simple equations. I want to see it be interesting. I can't stand fawning and I can't stand hagiography. Sometimes you have to suffer some of that, but what I want is an entertaining read.

MIN *(US)*: That depends, really, on the person being interviewed. But humor is always key. Depending on the subject, readers often just want to be entertained. And hearing people be funny is always irresistible. And for some reason, it's always a surprising trait in people, whether that person is a Hollywood celebrity or Alan Greenspan. Just as humor is engaging and puts people at ease in person, it does also in print.

DANA *(ROLLING STONE)*: Again, I think this entirely depends upon the person being interviewed. Mainly, I think you have to decide for yourself what role the irreverence is playing. Is the subject evading your questions by making jokes. Or is something being revealed.

NEWCOTT *(AARP)*: Irreverence on the part of the interviewer almost always looks forced and fake, like this writer is somehow best pals with the subject. We're interviewing this person because we think he or she has something of substance to say—even if they're a performer. If the subject is funny and irreverent, that's great—but if there's no substance the piece probably won't run.

GOLSON *(YAHOO)*: Well, I'm not sure irreverence is opposed to substance—most good substance upsets subjects of reverence. It depends on the subject. If it's a comedian, I want no reverence whatever. But most serious interviews could use some light turns, and often it's up to the interviewer to set up the subject for a good line—for the sake of the reader.

RANDALL *(PLAYBOY)*: Depends on the subject. If you're interviewing Howard Stern, you want lots of irreverence. If it's Dick Cheney, you'd go for substance. For people in between, you'd want a mix—but that balance would depend on the subject.

PARKER *(MOVIELINE/HOLLYWOOD LIFE)*: Ninety percent substance, ten percent irreverence.

BLOCH *(PENTHOUSE)*: I always like irreverence in an interview—especially with an "important" subject. This humanizes the subject and makes the final interview more entertaining to read. But some serious people are never irreverent.

6. What makes a good interviewer?

MIN (US): A good interviewer is someone who can put people at ease, who knows how to warm up his or her subject, who knows how to ask questions that can solicit the best answers. A good interviewer is someone who never confuses his/her own status with that of the story subject. Some of the most annoying interviews these days are the ones done by writers who constantly interject themselves into the piece, or who, in a Q&A format, craft questions that show that they are "funny" or "clever." Oftentimes, those questions only get back one- or two-word answers from the subject. How is that good for the reader? It's funny for the writer, but probably not that many more people.

DANA (ROLLING STONE): A good interviewer is (a) not afraid to ask stupid questions and (b) not afraid of silences. Remember that the answer is always more important than the question. When you are interviewing someone, you have, as much as you can, to suppress your need to impress your subject. You want to be as much of a blank screen as possible. The subject of the interview should be trying to impress you—and, by extension, the reader. A good interviewer, I think, has to train himself not to try to fill in the blank spaces between questions and answers. When you are having a conversation with someone, a blank spot in the back-and-forth is something that produces a little prick of anxiety. When you are interviewing someone, that blank spot is your friend—as long as you don't rush to fill it. It's not your job to make your subject feel comfortable. In fact, it's probably best to create little moments where he or she might feel uncomfortable—that's when you will get them saying things that are interesting. As long, of course, as you don't go too far.

BLOCH *(PENTHOUSE)*: The best interviewers are well prepared in advance and can easily jump from topic to topic with the subject. They are friendly but can, if necessary, be con—frontational enough to bring out responses that are unexpected—but without actually fighting with the subject, of course.

RANDALL *(PLAYBOY)*: Fearlessness, curiosity, a sense of humor, intelligence, charm, combativeness, timing, diligence—and the sense to know when and how to use them.

ESSEX *(DETAILS)*: Craft, familiarity with the subject matter, and the ability to deploy that in a way that extracts interesting answers. A kind of playfulness and peripatetic intelligence.

GOLSON *(YAHOO)*: Good preparation, curiosity, willingness to ask often obvious questions (as well as repetitive, what-do-you-mean-by-that questions), tenacity, stamina, and—almost always—a gift for drilling down toward the most rewarding (for the reader) areas of interest.

PARKER *(MOVIELINE⁄HOLLYWOOD LIFE)*: Someone who knows the other person's life well and is not afraid to ask the hard questions.

NEWCOTT *(AARP)*: Our best interviewers prepare extensively before going out, of course. And they persist in steering the subject away from ". . . and then I wrote . . ." answers. If subjects sense that the interviewer is intimately familiar with their biography, they won't insist on wasting time on it. Good interviewers know when to challenge the subject, and when to nurture a relationship. And they also know when to just let 'em riff.

7. Are interviewers different from other writers?

NEWCOTT *(AARP)*: Yes, they often insist on getting paid up front.

RANDALL *(PLAYBOY)*: Not really.

MIN *(US)*: Yes. Interviewing is a skill. I've known some great writers who I would never, ever send out on an interview. Interviewers need to possess a certain confidence, a charm, an ability to connect with people right away. It's a seductive quality in certain ways— you need to be able to be a person whom someone wants to spend time with, not someone they have to spend time with. Not everyone can make that connection right away. They also need to convey a certain authority and doggedness, depending on the interview. It takes skill to try to get people to tell you things they might not have planned to tell you. Sometimes it requires asking the same question in different ways. One has to be clever and relaxed enough to know to listen well, to jump in with questions where you might not have thought there were questions to ask. Some of the best material comes from these sort of unplanned, unscripted moments in interviews. It's also important to let the subject talk. Don't be afraid of dead spaces. When given the opportunity to talk, and go on, a subject can be incredibly revelatory. Also, an interviewer needs to make sure to get examples and anecdotes that can make the story come alive. If the person says, for example, that she can't believe how lucky she is to be famous, an interviewer should ask, Why? How? Specific examples of how that person's life has changed. It is very clear when you read the transcript of an interview if the interviewer connected or not. Sometimes it's not the interviewer's fault, but it helps to increase the odds by sending out the person with the best chances.

BLOCH *(PENTHOUSE)*: Some interviewers are no different from "other writers" because they are writers themselves. But some others are almost illiterate, but can get a good hour or two on tape, which is fine—that's why I have copyeditors.

DANA *(ROLLING STONE)*: Not necessarily, but I guess in some instances it's true.

GOLSON *(YAHOO)*: Yeah, they're better listeners and better editors, I think. Like playwrights and script writers, they focus more on speech—it's the dialogue that counts. Expository prose is less important.

PARKER *(MOVIELINE/HOLLYWOOD LIFE)*: Yes, they don't inject their own opinion as often and they rarely have an agenda.

ESSEX *(DETAILS)*: Yes, definitely. There are certain people who are very good at it, it's a craft unto itself. In fact, sometimes you might want to hire a good novelist, but he will be terrible at that job.

8. How do you assign writers? Do you try to match subject with writer? Or do writers come to you with the subject?

GOLSON *(YAHOO)*: All of the above.

RANDALL *(PLAYBOY)*: All. Certain interviewers have certain strengths and you try to use them. Some writers, for instance, do well with comics while others do not. Some can work very quickly. Some know a lot about sports or technology or whatever. Many can't interview actors to save their lives—interviewing actors is one of the toughest challenges.

Sometimes, people just have great ideas. Or great access. And you go with it.

ESSEX *(DETAILS)*: They never come to us with a subject. In the golden age of the publicity mechanism there's no reason for a writer to pitch something as you're completely aware of it either through a publicist or through your own open eyes. In other words, there are no surprises, someone can't come up to me and say, "How about a profile on George Clooney?" That's kind of a no-brainer.

The honest answer is that I know in a perfect world a dozen people who are experts at the art form. In an ideal world, I would go to them. And in that context, there are certain people whose personalities lend themselves to certain types of subjects, so you might want the kind of urbane, dapper expert to work with the sexy, voluble ingenue; and you might want the charming and shrewd expert to work with the shy and self-important actor. We're talking in the context of celebrity. If it's someone who's an obscure carpenter in South Dakota, that's a different story.

DANA *(ROLLING STONE)*: You are always trying to find a good match between writer and subject—regardless of whether the writer comes to you or you to him or her. Just because a writer comes to you with a subject does not necessarily mean he or she is the best person to write that article.

NEWCOTT *(AARP)*: I'm more interested in the personality mix. If your subject is some larger-than-life political figure, you want someone who's going to burst through the door ready to rumble. A showbiz character needs a wolf in sheep's clothing—someone who at first glance is a garden-variety weekend style section hack, but inside whom beats the heart of an archaeologist.

PARKER *(MOVIELINE/HOLLYWOOD LIFE)*: I figure out who the subjects are going to be then I match them with the writer. I rarely take pitches because they seldom fit our style.

BLOCH *(PENTHOUSE)*: If the subject is a "celebrity" or someone difficult to get, I usually pick a writer who has a connection that seems promising. For other subjects, I select a writer who has experience and background that is appropriate. Of course, if a writer approaches us with an idea for an interview, we will never assign it to another writer. . . . we will work with the original writer if necessary to give him the proper background information and suggested questions.

MIN *(US)*: At *Us,* we typically make assignments to people in the office already on staff. And yes, we do try to match the appropriate person to the subject.

9. How do you decide who you want to interview?

DANA *(ROLLING STONE)*: Pretty much the same way we decide to assign any story: Is it timely, is it interesting, and do we have a good angle?

ESSEX *(DETAILS)*: There are certain people who are so good at it that they have a voice or an approach that you can categorize, and you want that X flavor. If that lines up in a felicitous way with the subject, that's the ideal choice. When I know that I'm doing a cover on, say, Matt Damon, who is a kind of cipher who isn't known for his wit or colorful personality, it's very difficult to find someone who can bring something to that that will make for an interesting read. It's an equation—you fill in the blanks, see who you're dealing with, and what that would require.

BLOCH *(PENTHOUSE)*: In this era of celebrity journalism, we're always looking for "name" subjects of interest to our readers that will boost newsstand circulation. In addition, we seek people who have something vital and interesting to say—and, in keeping with the magazine's profile, we would like this to be outspoken, provocative, and controversial.

RANDALL *(PLAYBOY)*: Oh God, that depends on many factors. Post 9/11 we were looking for one type of interview because the mood of the country was so dark. During the Clinton era, it was party time, and the interview reflected that.

We try to have a mix from one month to the next. We need to play off other things in the magazine. Sometimes we feel the need to make a certain type of statement. And other times, I'm just trying to make my boss happy.

MIN *(US)*: It's easy to decide who we want to interview. It's always the people who are most fascinating, newsworthy, interesting at the moment. Sometimes it's because they have a big movie coming out, or they've made news with a marriage, a child, or something controversial. Whatever the case, the determining factor is "Is this someone who our readers want to know about now?"

PARKER *(MOVIELINE/HOLLYWOOD LIFE):* I look at who has upcoming projects (if they don't have a product to push they'll never talk to anyone) and I choose people who have rich personal lives and aren't afraid to say what they think. Perfect example: Angelina Jolie.

NEWCOTT *(AARP):* As one of the few thriving genuine general interest magazines, we enjoy the luxury of seeking out anyone we think is interesting in any number of ways. Yes, we tend to focus on subjects who are within our demographic, but not exclusively.

10. How have publicists changed the way you work and what you can or cannot print?

PARKER *(MOVIELINE/HOLLYWOOD LIFE):* They tell their clients to not open up, to deliver pat answers and to be politically correct. But often the publicists are just trying to keep their client out of danger, which I can respect. The real problem is that the celebrities themselves have become less interesting. They're younger, safer, and they often lack character.

NEWCOTT *(AARP):* Not in any way I'm aware of. Once someone has agreed to be interviewed, we're pretty much on our own.

DANA *(ROLLING STONE):* Not necessarily. I mean, there might be some discussion beforehand about what can or cannot be asked. And, by the same token, we might say to the subject, sure, we are interested in talking to your client, but if we can't bring up a certain subject, then we'll pass, thanks.

Of course, the main power that publicists have is in restricting access. It's one thing to have lunch with a celebrity in some nice restaurant in West L.A. It's another when you can just follow that person around for a while and see them in action. In terms of time, I think it's usually best to break up your interview session into a few segments. After about ninety minutes, usually the interviewer and the subject have run out of things to say. It's best if you can do a few sessions over a course of a few days. It's even better if you can catch the person in a variety of settings: If people are on the move, they are often more forthcoming, I think.

MIN *(US)*: Publicists can be very useful, and sometimes detrimental to the process. It depends on the personalities involved. Their interests lie in protecting their clients; ours lies in informing the reader. In the end, though, when publicists need you, they come to you. It can be mutually beneficial. But we've found that making concessions to publicists backfires: The story invariably isn't as good, and it creates problems with future stories—more and more ground rules that limit the story are set. We prefer not to get involved in this kind of deal making.

RANDALL *(PLAYBOY)*: Right now, the biggest problem is access. A celebrity's time, apparently, is like gold—much too valuable to be frittered away on journalists. Limited time affects the interview adversely. And yet sometimes you need those big celebrity names, so you make compromises, agreeing to less time than you'd want.

I haven't had other types of interference from publicists. But the access issue drives me crazy enough.

ESSEX *(DETAILS)*: They increasingly control the situation. They have consolidated their power to the degree that one has to be careful of saying something extremely negative, because there are ramifications. In other words, "If you say something bad about my client X, I will never let client Y appear in your magazine." So that's something one thinks about. You try not to let it dictate everything, but you have to be politic about that stuff. Then again, because that industry is increasingly consolidated and powerful, you're fighting, they have more power, they have the ability to take away the subject because they're going to another publication—there are more publications, less stars, and more publicists, so they have become more and more an impediment to interesting interviews and to diversity. They don't want anything provocative or anything other than softballs because they want their stars to be stars.

GOLSON *(YAHOO)*: With showbiz celebs, the answer is yes, to a frightening extent. With other kinds of prominence, you can still conduct a flack-free interview. But that's becoming rarer.

BLOCH *(PENTHOUSE)*: Unfortunately, publicists and other celebrity handlers have made compelling celebrity interviews almost impossible. And because *Penthouse* is so controversial, they almost always veto us as a venue.

11. Do you ever make deals with the subject or with the publicist setting parameters before an interview begins?

MIN *(US)*: Never.

ESSEX *(DETAILS)*: Constantly. An agreement that certain subjects are off-limits. An agreement that a certain type of writer will be used. There are compromises made constantly. We try to avoid them but sometimes you're not in a position of power. It depends on who the star is. If you're dealing with one of the biggest stars in the world, they have the most leverage and generate the most compromises; whereas someone who is grateful to be in a magazine will not be in a position to dictate.

PARKER *(MOVIELINE / HOLLYWOOD LIFE)*: It hardly ever comes up except when the celebrity is dating another celebrity and they don't want to talk about the relationship because they don't want it to seem like they're cashing in on their mate's fame. I can understand that but I appreciate it when they offer a few bits of information so the reader can understand the star a little better.

DANA *(ROLLING STONE)*: It goes both ways. A good interviewer also can approach forbidden subjects through the back door and get the person talking. Because, if you think about it, usually the thing that the publicist puts off-limits is going to be something that is on the subject's mind a lot. All you have to do is get them relaxed enough that they will bring it up.

And, as I said before, the publicist's greatest weapon is in restricting time. It's only when you have time that you can wear down these defenses.

BLOCH *(PENTHOUSE)*: The only deal I recall making with a publicist is to try to arrange the timing of the interview to coincide with a subject's new venture.

NEWCOTT *(AARP)*: Only insofar as we will often agree to touch on the specific subject the person is trying to advance: a branch of medical research, a movie, a political cause, a social condition. This, to be honest, is often what is making the person worth interviewing in the first place. We never cede the overall thrust of a piece to anyone but the editors.

RANDALL *(PLAYBOY)*: Not yet. Harrison Ford made it clear he wasn't going to discuss his newly single life. We asked anyway, and he swatted the question away like a pesky fly and gave us nothing usable.

12. How many assigned interviews get killed—and what are the reasons for not running them?

NEWCOTT *(AARP)*: I don't really have a percentage—but it happens with some regularity. Almost always, an interview gets killed because we simply did not get anything interesting. And it's almost never the fault of the writer. The subject, in most cases, just didn't come prepared to talk.

BLOCH *(PENTHOUSE)*: A small percentage of assigned interviews get killed (maybe twenty-five percent) usually because the subject backs out.

RANDALL *(PLAYBOY)*: Two reasons. Sometimes the subject turns cold, culturally speaking. Other times, an interview is just too dull to run. We're more likely to kill an interview because we've lost interest in the subject. A boring interview with a hot subject can usually be fixed, at least enough to run.

It's pretty rare. Most interviews run.

DANA *(ROLLING STONE)*: It's hard to say exactly how many interviews get killed. And there are so many reasons why they get killed. Either the interview isn't interesting. Or, there's just not enough space. Magazines tend to overassign.

MIN *(US)*: Almost none, unless the subject didn't cover ground we had thought he/she would cover, or time constraints led to a truncated interview.

PARKER *(MOVIELINE/HOLLYWOOD LIFE)*: I've never killed an interview. I have chopped several down to very short pieces, but I never kill. There's always something to say about someone.

ESSEX *(DETAILS)*: Over here I would say very few, maybe two percent. The reasons would be, in order of prominence, a disastrous photo shoot; a movie getting held indefinitely; a person who turns out to be so uninteresting that there's nothing to salvage; a piece so poorly written that it's also unsalvageable. There was one particularly difficult person who stormed out after ten minutes, so there was just ten minutes of conversation on the tape—in this case you have to turn that into a meta-story, where those quotes are just a fraction of the piece. But we never actually shit-canned a piece because there's just nothing there—it's not viable commercially speaking, because these things take money to set up.

13. As an editor, how often do you work with the writer before he/she does the interview?

PARKER *(MOVIELINE/HOLLYWOOD LIFE)*: I always talk to the writer for about twenty to thirty minutes before they go into an interview so I can make sure we're on the same page.

NEWCOTT *(AARP)*: I'll have two or three phone conversations, depending on how confident I am that the interviewer knows what we're going for. And recently I've taken to writing up letters of assignment, outlining the areas we hope the interview will cover.

RANDALL *(PLAYBOY)*: It depends. Guys who have been doing *Playboy* interviews long before I came on the scene don't much need me. A new writer—or a weaker writer—gets a ton of my attention. Sometimes I work on questions; often I just try to set goals—like making sure the finished Q&A has breadth and doesn't focus on too few subjects. I'm more inclined to attempt to reorient a writer's way of thinking (getting them to think outside the box) than to hammer away at individual questions.

ESSEX *(DETAILS)*: Always. You have to discuss what's interesting about the person, and some general sense of angle, without dictating the piece so it becomes predictable. You have to have a conversation to establish why you're doing this, especially in this age where everyone's been profiled a hundred times.

DANA *(ROLLING STONE)*: Depends. If it's an established writer, you will give him or her a good assignment, even though you may have never worked with that person. Then again, if you are bringing a young writer along, you will give him or her a bunch of smaller assignments before the plum interview.

BLOCH *(PENTHOUSE)*: If an interviewer is skilled and experienced, I usually do not do much work ahead of time, other than discussing the general parameters of the interview. Otherwise, I will gather research and suggest questions.

GOLSON *(YAHOO)*: Always.

MIN *(US)*: Very often. As an editor, I'll try to go over a list of questions and topics for the interviewer to discuss. The expectation is that the interviewer has already done a full clip search and done background research on the subject. A subject can get easily insulted and turned off if the interviewer seems less than educated on the materials he/she is covering.

14. How much editing is done on your end?

BLOCH *(PENTHOUSE)*: The amount of editing I do usually involves the experience of the interviewer. Good interviewers don't need much editing—usually cutting for space is the most I need do. But with others, rewriting questions and restructuring is often necessary.

RANDALL *(PLAYBOY)*: It depends. A bad interview takes days of work. A good one can sail right through. Of course, even the good interviews tend to run too long. Since the magazine has such limited space, I'm almost always cutting things down.

PARKER *(MOVIELINE/HOLLYWOOD LIFE)*: Depends on the writer. Some writers require no editing at all while others have to have eighty percent of their stories rewritten. This makes editors very unhappy. But if the content is good, editors don't mind spending a lot of time on a piece.

MIN *(US)*: Tons. Oftentimes, if the interview was incredibly all-encompassing, it's the editors' job to focus the story, to give it a point of view. It's always a pleasure to work with too much material that's good and winnow it down.

ESSEX *(DETAILS)*: It depends on the writer. I would say quite a bit.

NEWCOTT *(AARP)*: Lots. Especially in the Q&A format, I pretty much consider the writer's version to be raw material. His or her considerable expertise is in drawing interesting, provocative, thrilling words from a subject—mine is in shaping those words into a compelling read. I'll rearrange the order, find hidden themes—even mine the full interview transcript for buried treasures. Certainly, the writer has a major voice in the final draft, but by that time it often bears little resemblance to the original version.

GOLSON *(YAHOO)*: Honestly, it depends. Some interviews (and interviewers) require wholesale editing, just to achieve clarity. Others, relatively little, other than for space.

DANA *(ROLLING STONE)*: A lot. Remember, a good interview is not necessarily a transcript of a conversation.

15. What kind of expenses do you allow for a hard-to-get interview?

RANDALL *(PLAYBOY)*: Often, that's a decision made on a corporate level. When a company has limited funds (or prefers to spend its cash elsewhere), it changes things. Some years are better than others. This past year has been tough.

One of the reasons I wanted to work at *Playboy* was a story I'd heard. I'm not even sure if it's true. I was once told that *Playboy* sent Marcia Seligson to India to land an interview with Mother Teresa. Seligson spent a month trying to convince Mother Teresa to cooperate, spending thousands of dollars in the process. Anyone with an ounce of common sense would have known that MT would never agree, and, indeed, she came back empty-handed. But I was impressed that *Playboy* had tried. I was working at a magazine that thought small and I wanted to think big.

Today, of course, we'd never spend money on a fool's errand like that. I have budgets now—I never used to. I need a hard-and-fast guarantee before I okay unusual expenditures. I'm not sending anyone to Israel because he or she *might* get Ariel Sharon.

ESSEX *(DETAILS)*: For Matt Damon we sent someone to Prague, then to Vegas, then to London. We're willing to do within reason what's necessary to make a good piece. Everyone is budget conscious in these difficult times. But you dread an hour in a restaurant or a hotel room; you want to have, ideally, more than one setting, more than one meeting. You want as much color as possible to make a good piece.

NEWCOTT *(AARP)*: We pay our interviewers well, but we're not in the business of throwing around cash just to get a particular subject.

MIN *(US)*: We never pay for interviews. However, we will pay all necessary travel expenses if we feel the reader wants to know about this person.

DANA *(ROLLING STONE)*: Again, depends. Sometimes the writer might have to wait around for a week before the subject starts talking. So, these decisions are made on a case-by-case basis.

PARKER *(MOVIELINE/HOLLYWOOD LIFE)*: None.

16. What are some of the memorable interviews you've worked on, and what made them so?

NEWCOTT *(AARP)*: We did a truly funny Q&A with Bob Carroll Junior and Madelyn Pugh, the original writers for *I Love Lucy*. They interrupt each other, finish each other's sentences. The reader comes away feeling like it's a transcript—yet in reality it's a seamless edit, given shape and context after the fact.

DANA *(ROLLING STONE)*: The most fun interview I ever did was with Barney Frank, who was on the House Judiciary Committee during the Clinton impeachment hearings. We did the interview in our office, right after the hearings were over. He just ranted for about an hour and a half.

ESSEX *(DETAILS)*: As a writer, I really enjoyed doing U2's Bono, seeing him perform before seventy thousand people, and being in a helicopter with him just as his father had died, so sometimes you have those circumstances. Or driving around Hollywood in a Mercedes with Jim Carrey, getting lost, which created an unexpected dynamic. As an editor, we had a piece with Puffy Combs—he was the man who stormed out after ten minutes. It was fun to turn that lemon into lemonade. I worked with the novelist Rick Moody on Ethan Hawke. I thought Hawke would be very uninteresting—so getting a novelist to deal with what they think is the lowly form of the profile and trying to somehow subvert that. Again, getting a novelist like Thom Jones to work with Mike Tyson, having to go up on his roof and look at his pigeons, then go to Vegas to watch him train. Some of that can be very fun.

BLOCH *(PENTHOUSE)*: There have been very many memorable interviews over the years—these are just some that stick in my mind because they were vivid and compelling and who jumped off the written pages into the reader's consciousness: Muhammad Ali, Joe Pesci, Roseanne, Jerry Brown, Jesse Jackson, Howard Stern, Don King, Gore Vidal, Jack Henry Abbott, Loretta Lynn, Oliver Stone, Pete Rose, Bill Phillips, Anthony Kiedis, Ted Turner, Jerry Lewis, David Lee Roth, Al Sharpton, James Carville. As you see, there aren't too many "establishment" types here—*Penthouse* is just too controversial for them!

RANDALL *(PLAYBOY)*: Jesse Ventura: the single biggest newsmaker of my career and watching the uproar was the most fun I've ever had.

Frank Zappa: because he was a personal idol and we got his last interview. That meant something to me.

Betty Friedan: because (in my grandiose way) I thought it broadened what *Playboy* magazine was.

Bobby Knight: because I couldn't believe my good fortune that he went crazy in front of you.

Spike Lee and Darryl Gates: They ran back to back soon after the Rodney King incident and they were my first really controversial, newsmaking interviews.

Bill Gates: because it's just a really good interview.

Robert Downey Jr.: because it was so revealing.

Mike Tyson: ditto.

Robert Maxwell: He's faded into obscurity now, but he was larger than life at the time and the whole Maxwell experience was just a trip.

Saul Bellow: a personal favorite because it reminded me why I had wanted to be a writer.

17. *Do you ever allow a subject to see an interview before it's published? How do you deal with those who ask to see it?*

MIN *(US)*: Never, never, never.

GOLSON *(YAHOO)*: It's a far, far better thing to say no than to open up this can of worms. The experience of a lifetime is that it's better to lose an occasional interview than wade into the inch-that-takes-a-mile negotiation over final cut.

RANDALL *(PLAYBOY)*: That's just a form of self-torture. I would always say no, but frankly, I can't recall anyone asking.

BLOCH *(PENTHOUSE)*: If subjects ask, I have no problem allowing them to review the interview transcript. I do not consider an interview to be reporting—which I would never allow a subject to review. Furthermore, since we do not pay for interviews, and since subjects often spend hours with interviewers, I consider this the same courtesy I would allow to a writer to be able to review the galleys of an article. I do not allow subjects to review the introduction or edited interview, however.

ESSEX *(DETAILS)*: Never. We dig our feet in the earth. We will agree to avoid certain subjects, but they can't see unpublished material, that's a slippery slope that ends up in the gutter.

PARKER *(MOVIELINE/HOLLYWOOD LIFE)*: No, and when people ask to see it I say no way. Too much trouble.

NEWCOTT *(AARP)*: We just don't let it happen.

DANA *(ROLLING STONE)*: No, I have never been involved in a situation like this. In some cases, I think it's appropriate. I believe that the *Paris Review* allows subjects to see the interview before it's published. If you are going to do this, though, I think pretty clear ground rules need to be established ahead of time. You don't want to cede to the writer control of the finished product.

18. *Joyce Carol Oates has written: "If the Interview as an art form emerges as a predominant prose genre in the twenty-first century, it will be the result of interviewers who manage to be both invisible and yet subtly dominating." Do you agree that the interview can be an art form? Do you think it will emerge as a predominant prose genre this century?*

ESSEX *(DETAILS)*: I absolutely agree with the first part of that. When she says "predominant prose genre" I assume she's talking about something that's more interesting than the short story or the reported piece of journalism. I would hate to think that, because it wouldn't say much about us as a country, but I think it's probably already happened.

NEWCOTT *(AARP)*: Yes, it is an art form—but a collaborative one, like moviemaking. The interviewer is the maestro, but the interviewee must be similarly engaged in creating something worthwhile. And the editor, if I do say so myself, gives the whole thing context both before and after the actual interview.

BLOCH *(PENTHOUSE)*: I don't think published interviews are an art form (unless you consider anything an art form—are photo captions? are music reviews?). As I've said, a good interview can be very compelling—and this is almost always the result of having a compelling subject. I've seen interviews that bring out interesting information, but I don't think an interview is the best way to do that. But given the fact that writing (and reading!) seem to be vanishing from magazines, as magazines like *Lucky, InStyle, Maxim,* et cetera, are being more like catalogs than magazines, it's entirely possible that before this century is out, interviews might be the predominant prose genre of our time. I won't be sorry to miss that.

RANDALL *(PLAYBOY)*: An art form? That seems a tad grand. I'm much too cynical to think like that. The century is still very young, so I'd be reluctant to make any predictions. Certainly, I see Q&As being an increasingly important way to tell stories in magazines.

But if they're overused by too many magazines, there might be a backlash.

DANA *(ROLLING STONE):* I am not sure it is an art form. I'd say it's more of a craft—and an extremely effective way of conveying information about either a personality or a subject. I think interviews are especially good ways to get people to explain dense or complicated ideas in an accessible form.

PARKER *(MOVIELINE/HOLLYWOOD LIFE):* Yes, I think it can definitely be an art form, but I don't think it will emerge as a predominant prose genre of this century because subjects are not consistently compelling. Much more often than not writers write better than interviewees speak.

GOLSON *(YAHOO):* Not usually. I see it as a craft, and cannot frankly think of an example that rises to that sort of Joycean, yea, even Oatsian, level. As a predominant prose genre this century: Let's just see it get better. Because it's not very good, in my opinion. For reasons noted above (publicists, lack of space) I believe interviews of the last century were better than what I see today.

19. How does a young interviewer break into your magazine?

ESSEX *(DETAILS):* Can't be done. Categorically. That young writer would have to write something other than an interview piece. The only plausible way that can happen is if they have some unexpected and unique relationship with this person—they worked with them before, or they wrote the script for the movie that that person is going to be in. Someone who's on staff at my magazine who has proven himself through other things might be given that opportunity. A lot of it has to do with the experience and knowledge that the person you've hired has done this before and will give you something interesting. Then there's another practical matter, which is given the power of publicists, they will say no to someone as our choice for a writer, so it's a complicated equation.

BLOCH *(PENTHOUSE)*: Young interviewers can break into the magazine by having access to someone we want to interview. This has happened several times. It is important for the potential interviewer, however, to have a reasonable expectation that the subject will talk to him or her. This means at least one call to the subject (or agent or publicist) saying, "Would you be willing to be interviewed in *Penthouse?*" The way to ensure that you will *not* break into the magazine is to propose interviewing impossible subjects that you've just read about in the day's newspapers (this happens many more times than you might imagine). As I said elsewhere, we will happily work with inexperienced interviewers if they have the potential to talk to someone we are interested in getting into the magazine.

PARKER *(MOVIELINE/HOLLYWOOD LIFE)*: They have to have excellent writing skills.

MIN *(US)*: A new writer can get his or her foot in the door of our magazine by knowing what makes the magazine work inside and out and being able to articulate it. Obviously, we know why, but we want to make sure people who work for us get it. If they don't, they won't be able to accurately understand what it takes to produce one of our stories. Then, of course, on top of that, they just have to be good. We have to love their writing, their tone, their ability to structure a story smartly.

NEWCOTT *(AARP)*: Show through your work at other publications that you can do thoughtful, probing work—and, at least at the start, bring us a subject whom you'd (a) like to interview, (b) have a compelling reason to interview, and (c) have reasonable expectation of getting to sit down with you.

RANDALL *(PLAYBOY)*: Bringing along younger interviewers has been a failing of mine for two reasons: (1) if a big-name says yes to a *Playboy* interview, I don't like to gamble on newcomers and risk having something unusable, and (2) the regular stable of interviewers creates enough work to fill the year and I have no pressing need to find outsiders.

That said, my advice would be the same for any writer. Have good clips—*Playboy* is not a magazine for entry-level writers. Start small—suggest shorter, low-risk, middle-of-the-book interviews or "20 Questions." Or write good stories. I'm much more likely to entrust a big interview to someone I've worked with successfully or whose work for other magazines has impressed me.

DANA *(ROLLING STONE):* By having lots of ideas, a lot of energy, and a lot of talent. And, of course, by having the good fortune of getting the attention of one of our very busy editors.

7. OTHER VOICES/OTHER WRITERS

> The whole process is one of seduction.

—MARIE BRENNER

So far, other than the previous chapter, this book has been my take on interviewing, the dos and dont's, the personal anecdotes, complaints, horror stories, frustrations, successes. But no two writers work exactly alike; each brings to his or her work a unique and individual perspective. So I asked eight talented interviewers if they would answer some questions about the subject. I promised them that if they participated, I would list their credits right up front and not in an appendix. And, as you can see below, this is a pretty distinguished group.

KEVIN COOK

Writer and talker Kevin Cook has interviewed celebrities from Johnny Depp, Michael Jordan, Jay Leno, Barry Bonds, and Quentin Tarantino to Adam Sandler, Pamela Anderson, and k. d. lang. A former senior editor at *Sports Illustrated,* Cook has written for *SI, Playboy, GQ, Details, Men's Journal, Vogue,* and other magazines. He also hosted a daily talk show on Internet radio, *The Skybox,* that became a cult favorite of dozens of listeners. He lives in New York City.

CLAUDIA DREIFUS

Claudia Dreifus, a prize-winning journalist, is considered to be one of the best political and scientific interviewers working in English. Her Q&As appear in national magazines and regularly in the *New York Times,* where she is a contributing writer. Dan Rather has said of Dreifus, "Being interviewed by Claudia Dreifus is like playing tennis with Steffi Graf; you do your best and you learn a lot; anything less and she'll pave the court with you." During the 1980s, she was one of several *Playboy* interviewers—and had extensive conversations with Gabriel Garcia Márquez, Arthur Schlesinger Jr., William Safire, Susan Sarandon, the Sandinista junta, Donald Sutherland, and others during her time there. Two of her five books, *Scientific Conversations* (Times Books) and *Interview* (Seven Stories), are about interviewing and are still in print.

In addition to her interviewing, Dreifus currently teaches at Columbia University's School of International and Public Policy and is a senior fellow at the World Policy Institute of the New School University. Her current project involves catching up with women politicians globally as part of a book on women heads of state. Dreifus lives in New York City with her partner, Andrew Hacker, the author and political scientist.

MICHAEL FLEMING

Michael Fleming has been a columnist and reporter at *Daily Variety* for thirteen years, where he writes the "Dish" column. He has written for such magazines as *Playboy, Movieline, Details, Fade In,* and *TV Guide.* He wrote *The Three Stooges: From Amalgamated Morons to American Icons,* which was the basis for an ABC telepic produced by Storyline and Mel Gibson's Icon Productions. He has interviewed celebrities such as Gibson, Harrison Ford, Denzel Washington, Kevin Spacey, Robert Downey Jr., Will Smith, Jennifer Lopez, Drew Barrymore, and George Clooney, as well as directors such as James Cameron, Peter Jackson, Martin Scorsese, John Woo, Ridley Scott, and Curtis Hanson.

KRISTINE MCKENNA

Kristine McKenna is a widely published critic and journalist who wrote for the *Los Angeles Times* from 1977 through 1998. She was music editor for *Wet* magazine from 1979 through 1984, and wrote regularly for *Rolling Stone, Musician, New York Rocker,* and *Slash* during those years. She was West Coast editor for the British music weekly *New Musical Express* from 1979 through 1982, and during the mid-1980s hosted a weekly radio show for Santa Monica public radio station KCRW that combined music and interviews with artists such as Leonard Cohen, Joe Strummer, and Don Van Vliet. In 1987 she shifted the focus of her writing to film and visual art and published pieces in *American Film, Artnews, Premiere, Playboy,* the *L.A. Weekly, Arthur, Another Room, Numero, Mojo,* and *Artforum.* In 1991 she received a Critics Fellowship from the National Gallery in Washington, D.C., and in 1994 guest edited an issue of the literary quarterly *Grand Street.* In 1999 she co-curated *Forming: The Early Days of L.A. Punk,* a historical survey presented at the Track 16 Gallery in Santa Monica, California, and in 2001 Fantagraphics Books published a collection of her interviews titled *Book of Changes.* Fantagraphics will publish a second volume of interviews in 2003. She is presently working on a biography of artist Wallace Berman, and is co-curating *Semina Culture: Wallace Berman and His Circle,* a traveling exhibition that opened at the Santa Monica Museum of Art in 2004. She edited the catalog that accompanied the exhibition, as well as a book on photography by Wallace Berman, which will be published by Twin Palms Twelvetrees Press.

STEVE POND

Steve Pond has been writing about music, film, and popular culture since 1975. He has served as assistant editor, associate editor, and West Coast music editor for *Rolling Stone,* has been a contributing writer for *Premiere* magazine since the magazine's debut issue in 1987, and for ten years wrote a weekly film column in the *Washington Post*. He has also written regularly for publications ranging from the *Los Angeles Times* and the *New York Times* to *Playboy, GQ, Movieline,* and *TV Guide*. He is the author of *Elvis in Hollywood* (New American Library, 1990).

DAVID RENSIN

David Rensin is the coauthor of several *New York Times* bestsellers, including Tim Allen's number one hit, *Don't Stand Too Close to a Naked Man* (Hyperion). His latest books are *The Mailroom: Hollywood History from the Bottom Up* (Ballantine), an oral history of what it's like to start at the bottom in a talent agency mailroom, dreaming of the top; *David at my Heels: A World War II Hero's Epic Saga of Torment, Survival, and Forgiveness* with Louis Zamperini (William Morrow), and *Yanni in Words* (Miramax), cowritten with the world-reknowned composer/ performer. Rensin also cowrote *Where Did I Go Right?* (Little Brown) the widely lauded memoir of show business legend Bernie Brillstein. His next book, also with Brillstein, is *The Little Stuff Matters Most: Fifty Rules from Fifty Years of Trying to Make a Living* (Gotham), pithy advice for those who want to chart a unique path to success. Rensin is also working on an oral biography of rebel surf legend Miki Dora. He is a longtime contributing editor at *Playboy*, where he specializes in Q&As.

DIANE K. SHAH

Diane K. Shah has been a general editor for *Newsweek* and a West Coast editor for *GQ*. She has written for the *New York Times* and *Los Angeles Times* Sunday magazines, *Esquire, Playboy,* the *Columbia Journalism Review, Los Angeles* magazine, and *New York*. She has published four mystery novels and cowrote (with Daryl Gates) *Chief: My Life in the LAPD,* a *New York Times* bestseller. She has written on sports, first for *Newsweek,* then as a columnist for the *Los Angeles Herald-Examiner* (the first woman in the United States to have a sports column for a big-city daily), and now as a contributing writer for *ESPN* magazine.

DAVID SHEFF

David Sheff's articles and interviews have appeared in *Playboy,* where he works as a contributing editor, the *New York Times Magazine, Rolling Stone, Wired, Outside,* and *Fortune; Esquire* and *Observer* magazine in England, *Foreign Literature* in Russia, and *Playboy (Shueisha)* in Japan. His books include *China Dawn* (HarperCollins), *Game Over* (Random House), and *All We Are Saying* (St. Martin's), based on his 1980 *Playboy* interview with John Lennon and Yoko Ono. Other interviews, including those with Ansel Adams, nuclear physicist Ted Taylor, Gore Vidal, Steve Jobs, Tom Hanks, Sting, M. Scott Peck, Betty Friedan, and Keith Haring, received wide recognition, as did his "Portrait of a Generation" in *Rolling Stone.* His radio documentaries for National Public Radio on John Steinbeck's *The Grapes of Wrath* and Harper Lee's *To Kill a Mockingbird* won several awards. He also wrote and edited *Heart Play: Unfinished Dialogue,* which won a Grammy Award nomination for Best Spoken Word Recording of 1984.

Sheff, formerly an editor of *Men's Life, New West,* and *California* magazines, attended the University of California at Berkeley, where he received a degree in Death and Human Consciousness. He lives in the San Francisco Bay area.

1. Do you prepare differently when you are doing a Q&A or a profile?

KRISTINE MCKENNA: Not really. Obviously, when I know my questions are going to appear in print I try to phrase them as elegantly and concisely as possible, and I always try to avoid asking questions that have been asked before. But basically, my preparation for any encounter is the same: I try to know as much about the subject as possible.

DAVID SHEFF: I read and take notes on volumes of research material—whatever I can dig up—and speak to tertiary sources for both. I then take an extra step for a Q&A. Based on the research, I prepare a detailed outline that includes everything I want to be sure to cover in the interview. The outline doesn't necessarily include specific questions, though it may include some. The outline is a road map to follow during the course of the interview. The interview may well veer from it, but I always return to it. I want to be sure I cover every critical subject—ask every critical question.

MICHAEL FLEMING: Doing the Q&A is a bit easier, because you don't have to worry as much about noticing the setting you are in and what is going on around you. I am relatively new to the interviews, compared to you [Grobel] or David Sheff, or a guy like Steve Rebello at *Movieline's Hollywood Life.* You all seem adept at working background in, but it distracts me from concentrating on my core questions and follow-ups based on the answers given by a subject. You know that dream every kid has about having aced a test, sitting there wondering why everyone is scribbling away and realizing too late that you've forgotten to turn over the paper and do the other half? My adult version of that is going through an entire interview and forgetting to notice where I was or the color of what the subject was wearing. The journalist I most envy for an uncanny ability to capture setting and color, and be at ease doing it is Lynn Hirschberg.

DAVID RENSIN: Yes. To me, profiles are more visual than Q&As, and require more observational hang-out time compared to the broad range of questions in a Q&A, where "coverage"—in movie terms—is most important. I need to have lots of material to get the best result, which is something some subjects (or publicists) don't understand (or don't legitimately have time for). Time spent is not just good for me, but for them.

DIANE SHAH: I prepare much differently for a Q&A than I do for a profile, even a lengthy one. For a Q&A, I try to read everything I can about the subject and I'll write out thirty or forty specific questions. Since the *Playboy* interview is open-ended, I want to tackle as many areas as possible because you never know ahead of time which angles the subject will best respond to. With a feature, I usually have an angle so my scope is more limited. This is true today more than ever because the length of feature articles continues to shrink. I used to routinely write articles of six thousand words. Now most editors are looking for two thousand to three thousand—at most. Often they are twelve hundred to fifteen hundred words. Secondly, in a profile you can set the scene and use a lot of descriptive reporting, which often conveys more than a subject's answers. I usually go into these situations with some specific questions written down, which I use as jumping-off points.

STEVE POND: I don't think I prepare differently—the amount of research and the type of research I do remain the same. But I conduct the interview differently, because the form has different requirements. In a profile, it's much easier to finesse an incomplete or evasive answer, to supply your own context and to write around gaps. In a Q&A, if they don't say it, you're out of luck. So I'm certainly aware that I need fuller answers if I'm doing a Q&A, and in many cases that affects the number and type of follow-up questions.

CLAUDIA DREIFUS: Well, yes, when I'm doing a profile—I try to get more time for "action scenes," I'm looking to get some dramatic scenes that I can retell and that can give real instructive information of my subject's life. With an interview, it's the interview time that counts above everything. I do far more headwork, intellectual work—because what the interview will really be about is ideas, ideas above everything.

2. What do you think accounts for the proliferation of Q&As in print?

KEVIN COOK: They're easier to execute and harder to screw up than profiles. People like to hear celebs' own voices.

MCKENNA: I don't think there is a proliferation of Q&As in print. I think it's an underused and generally undervalued form. In fact, I once had an editor—who will remain nameless—tell me I should be paid less than the standard rate by his publication, "because Q&A's aren't writing." I don't consider all the little ten-question sound bite pieces that do proliferate to be Q&As. A real Q&A demands length, because that's the only way you can illuminate the subtleties of a person's thinking and personality. And at their best, that's what Q&As do.

RENSIN: I'd say the paradigm of "20 Questions" is responsible for the abundance of short-form interviews, many designed with the wrong-headed assumption that kids these days just don't read. These are not about brevity, but about clever and unusual questions and responses.

Longer-form Q&As are more prevalent because, as Tina Brown once said, "I couldn't take any more of the kind of celebrity journalism that begins, 'I'm sitting in a restaurant with Tom Cruise.' We need less mediation." She cites the late *Talk* magazine's oral histories and Q&As, and their place in the *Playboy* interview lineage, as a place to find a "true voice" and not "what journalists think." It's all about the voice, baby, and always has been.

SHAH: The proliferation of Q&As is the result of two trends: one, people don't want to spend as much time reading and Q&As move faster. Second, with the media explosion, famous people (even not-so-famous people) are reported to death. How many stories can you write about Julia Roberts? So it's often more interesting to simply get some quick, presumably telling or controversial responses. Also, well-known people often won't give print journalists the time needed to do a well-rounded profile—or *Playboy* interview—when two minutes on TV reaches a far bigger audience. This is especially true in sports. A couple of years ago then Jets coach Bill Parcells turned me down for *Playboy*. Aside from his agent's demand for payment, Parcells, he said, could not afford even three hours. I was also turned down by Mark McGuire, Sammy Sosa, Mike Piazza, and, most recently, Jason Kidd.

POND: A couple of reasons. I think that with the glut of magazines covering entertainment, the standard celebrity profile was trotted out so frequently that it became a real cliché. Readers and especially editors were desperate for something other than that standard Revealing Anecdote/Why He's Important/Meeting over Lunch/What the Costars Have to Say/What He Has to Say/Another Revealing Anecdote boilerplate. But at the same time, those self-conscious anti-profiles that many magazines started running tended to be awfully self-indulgent and not very satisfying. So the Q&A format looks like an attractive alternative, a way to limit profile-ese. Also, it makes it easy for an editor to look at the transcript and screw around with the story. Plus, if you buy into the idea that readers have shortened attention spans and the days of long, thoughtful pieces are numbered, a Q&A is a quick and easy way to establish the subject's voice, get a few good quotes, and get out.

DREIFUS: I believe many editors think of them as stories on the cheap. They also live under the illusion that anyone can do them—including sometimes themselves. Well, it's an art, and not everyone can.

SHEFF: One often learns more about the writer than the subject of profiles. Given that and particularly in a world of televised sound bytes, Q&As allow the subject to speak in depth and in his or her own words. They retain the voice of the subject. There's more. Good Q&As ask the questions that readers would want to ask and in addition the ones that most readers would never think of. It's a very satisfying dynamic when it's done well. Readers respond both "I'm glad she/he asked that" and "I can't believe she/he had the guts to ask that." On the other hand, when I read a Q&A in which the interviewer fails to ask an important question or crucial follow-up, it's maddening. Q&As are satisfying in another way. After reading a good Q&A, we feel as if we participated in an engaging conversation—entertaining, instructive, or both.

FLEMING: I think it makes the celebrity more comfortable because they feel some confidence that the magazine will print something close to what they said. When you do a profile, you have no idea what you're getting into. You might just be a foil for a writer's exercise in style, or that person's attempt to solve a person in a single meeting or two. I like them because I'm no good at being passive aggressive. If I'm going to take somebody to the woodshed, which I have done particularly in my work at *Daily Variety,* it somehow feels more honorable if they know what's coming. I once broke a story about how the director of a Disney movie called *Powder* had a pedophile past which the studio was trying to keep secret. Now, the idea of finding out a Disney director was convicted of such a thing is like finding out that the fire chief is an arsonist. But I told the director's agent exactly what I was going to write. It got international headlines, and his agent relayed thanks from his client for handling it with as much respect as could reasonably be mustered.

3. How different are you when you have the luxury of time versus a time limit with a subject?

SHAH: Time means everything. If limited, you can get all of your questions asked, but you will not get a true sense of the person you are interviewing. For that, you need fool-around time; time to shoot the breeze, jump in the car, get a bite to eat, exchange stories, and allow your subject to become comfortable with you. It is, after all, like dating. First date, everyone is on good behavior and looking their best. It's too bad if you only get that one chance. I used to find that I would be a sponge, absorbing everything, and coming away fairly impressed at the first meeting; during the second, I began to harbor suspicions; finally, after a third meeting I would feel I had a fairly good sense of what the person *was really like.*

SHEFF: If I have a time limit there's an urgency to get through the outline—that is, to cover the range of subjects that need to be covered. It requires a different, necessarily faster pace. I am less willing to indulge a subject's digressions unless they are germane or otherwise add to the interview. I make less small talk. An interview conducted under a time crunch may have a particular energy to it, but I much prefer the luxury of more time. Most subjects respond better to a slower pace. There is time to cover everything and to explore the unexpected twists and turns. I can afford to follow areas of conversation that may not pan out and yet sometimes lead to important revelations. I can leave an important subject because I know that I can return to it later. Follow-up questions—the "yeah, but" questions—can make or break an interview. Under a time crunch it isn't always possible to do the important follow-up.

DREIFUS: This is the key to all interviewing. A time limit means that the subject has control throughout the process. There's less likely to be openness; there's no flow—just formality; there's no "getting to know you." If someone gives me too little time, I just say, "Thank you very much, but no."

POND: The difference is enormous. If you have time you have the luxury to let the conversation flow more naturally, and to follow the subject on tangents that might lead to unexpected areas. You also have time to ease into the interview, to spend awhile in a more informal conversation that can establish common ground and, with luck, build up trust. Putting a time limit on the interview completely changes the dynamic. I find myself constantly checking my internal list of priorities to determine how many crucial areas we have yet to cover, and how soon I need to move the conversation on to something else. It just takes a situation that's already artificial and makes it even more unnatural, and as an interviewer you wind up changing the subject not because you've gotten everything you can out of a topic, but because you're running out of time and you have three more areas you have to cover. Some people are well suited to short interviews, but many aren't—much of the time, you need to put up with a lot of rambling before you get to the best stuff.

MCKENNA: I'm somewhat different when the meter isn't running, because I feel less pressure to cut to the chase and ask the hard questions. I would add, however, that having the luxury of extensive time with a subject is becoming a thing of the past. When I first started doing Q&As in the late seventies—the first big one I did was the *Rolling Stone* interview with Sting—I met with him repeatedly and spent several hours every time. Those days are done, perhaps because there are so many more outlets these days, that people approach the promotion of their work much differently. And let's face it, promotion of their work is what it's about for most people who do interviews. Taking pleasure in the art of conversation is not on their agenda.

FLEMING: There is nothing like having all the time you need. If you asked a movie star a question at the beginning of the interview, or within the first hour, you are going to get a different answer than if you asked it five hours into the interview. If you've got the time, you can actually reapproach questions and topics just by asking a bit differently. Usually one answer is more colorful than the other. I'd say unlimited time improves the interview by fifteen percent or more. Trouble is, the ones who sell magazines are the ones too busy to give you ten hours.

RENSIN: Time limits equal pressure; there is a less of a chance to ask enough to make certain I'm getting it right. Q&A is an art form that like film needs lots of little pieces with which to construct the final product that conveys ideas followed through and the sense that a real conversation took place. Actual conversational transcriptions—à la *Interview* magazine—suck. Time also helps develop the relationship between subject and interviewer.

COOK: I try harder to lead the interview when there's a time limit—interrupt, move things along in order to cover enough ground.

4. Do you do anything to help put your subject at ease in the beginning?

DREIFUS: Oh sure. I think really hard about what my first question will be. It's the most important one. Will it be hard, soft, funny, intellectual? Like a chess player, I will wonder where I can move with it.

I try to interview my subjects at their house (or if they are coming to New York from out of town at my house)—so that they are in a relaxed environment. No offices, if I can help it. Certainly no restaurants. I might bring a gift—if it feels right. I might bring one of my books.

FLEMING: Depends on the situation. When I interviewed Denzel Washington and Jennifer Lopez for *Playboy,* there was chitchat time while they got photographed, a process which takes fifteen minutes if the photographer is good. That's a good time to feel each other out. Just like any physical activity, a warm-up is advisable.

SHEFF: I most often begin interviews on safe territory. The goal is to build a relationship and sense of trust. Subjects reveal themselves when they are comfortable and feel safe. If the interview subject is an artist, writer, musician, actor, or the like, I generally start by asking about their new work. It's the freshest on their mind. There's normally an excitement about the new. Or we may begin by talking about something everyday—the day's news or something personal. If waiting for an interview to begin I am in a hallway with family photos, I may ask about one. It's a way to open up a dialogue rather than a more stilted and adversarial exchange. The interview by its nature may be a controversial one that will include some sparring, but I'm much more likely to get candid and thoughtful responses if I begin with lighter fare. I save the most pointed and challenging question until the end.

COOK: I usually praise something they've done, and always remind them what magazine the interview is for, and when it will come out.

MCKENNA: Yes. I do what I can to communicate to them that I'm on their side—and more often than not, I am. I don't tend to go after interviews with people I don't admire. I prefer to celebrate all that is worth celebrating, and leave the muckraking and shocking exposés to others.

POND: All kinds of things—and again, how much you can do often depends on how much time you have. If there's time to go to lunch and talk about favorite movies or Elvis records or the Lakers, that's great. If there's not, you hope to have enough time to at least establish a little common ground—reminding them of previous encounters, or friends of theirs I might know, or anything to suggest that I'm something other than another junketeer with a list of questions and a stopwatch. And if I don't even have time for that, I tend to start with stuff you think the subject likes to talk about, and to try to use those early questions to somehow suggest to the subject that I deserve more than the stock answers. Whatever the time limit, you're looking for some sort of comfort level where you can engage the subject in at least a slightly fuller and more meaningful way than the interviews they're used to giving.

RENSIN: Just be my charming self. I know it sounds self-serving, but part of being able to do a good Q&A—and profile, et cetera— is the natural ability to be inquisitive, empathetic, responsive, and to listen. You need to have the personality for it. Maybe there's something in my posture and face and tone of voice that radiates intelligence, curiosity, humanity, and humor. Hoo-haa! It's just me.

5. Do you write questions, or use notes on general topics?

MCKENNA: I write questions, and arrange them in the order that I intend to ask them.

POND: Generally, while I'm doing research I start keeping lists of the subject areas I want to explore. Then I sit down with the notes and plot out the general way in which the interview might proceed, writing more specific questions. Then, usually just before I go to do the interview, I transfer these notes into a reporter's notebook, usually jotting down topics rather than specific questions. Then I put the notebook in my pocket, and I usually keep it there. Occasionally I'll pull the notebook out and consult it during the interview, but normally I remember the areas I want to cover, and I'll only look at my notes if there's a break in the interview.

RENSIN: I used to write specific questions under the general topic heading, but more and more I don't like to write them and just want to go in with less. My fantasy is to be able to have it all in my head: the questions, the various permutations of follow-ups (or to be prepared for any possible response thread), and just have a little notebook to remember ideas.

COOK: Write the first several questions (not verbatim), and then topics after that. But I'm willing to ditch the list of topics if the conversation goes elsewhere in interesting ways.

SHEFF: I write a detailed outline that includes some must-ask questions.

FLEMING: I like to have thirty to fifty questions at the ready, though the preordained order never works out. I cross them off as I go.

DREIFUS: I write questions and place them on color-coded file cards.

6. How closely do you work with an editor before going to interview your subject?

COOK: Not very. Most of my interviews are on celebs, many in sports, which is my particular turf. In sports I'm well versed enough to conduct an interview with little or no input; with other celebs, they're so well known that the task is just to get a memorable interview.

MCKENNA: Not very closely. I make a point of finding out what the editor wants the interview to be, and make sure they understand and are in accordance with how I envision it. I find out if there are specific questions they want me to ask, but beyond that, I don't want their input.

DREIFUS: I try to work as closely as possible. I'm a tailor. I want to present a suit that fits.

FLEMING: I rely a great deal on editors. I'd say I learned everything from Steve Randall and former *Movieline* editor Virginia Campbell. I like them to see the questions before I go out on the job.

RENSIN: Depends. Usually not much, though in the case of "20 Questions" I so enjoy the creative process of coming up with the snappy questions that I consult my editor every time. I make up a lot of the questions myself, often on the spot, but the editor I work with is an artist in this regard and I love watching him at work.

SHEFF: This depends on the editor and subject. In general I'm on my own. There are exceptions. Editors may have specific interest or knowledge in the subject. Sometimes an editor has specific needs. For example, *Forbes* sent me to interview Richard Branson. Since the interview was for a special issue about travel, the editor provided a list of key points that would be raised in the issue. Though I discussed many subjects with Branson, I was careful to focus the conversation.

POND: It depends on the editor, the magazine, and the subject. In most cases, it's probably no more than a general preliminary conversation about why the magazine is covering this person, and what the editor thinks is most important. Then I go from there and do the rest myself. Sometimes editors will want a follow-up conversation before the interview takes place, and on rare occasions they'll ask for a list of questions. But this is extremely rare, thank God.

SHAH: I try to get a sense of what the editor wants, especially if he or she comes to me with the assignment. When an editor says, "Oh, I know you'll come up with great stuff," I know I'm in trouble. These are the editors who are never happy with what you turn in. The editors who have a good grasp of the subject and know how to explain what they're looking for are a pleasure.

I'll give you an example. A couple of years ago, an editor I didn't know, for a publication I'd never written for, called and wanted a cover story on Paul Newman. I suppose the idea was hatched because Newman had a picture coming out and his publicist got on the horn. But what, exactly, did this editor want?

"Get him to talk about his marriage, and what movies were his favorites and his car racing." Subjects, in other words, that Newman had talked about endlessly in the past. "Just hang out with him," the editor said. "We want a piece like you did with Cary Grant."

Yeah, right. The piece he was referring to had been six or seven thousand words long and I had spent the better part of a year talking to Grant off and on. This editor wanted two thousand words in less than three months and I seriously doubted that Newman, who rarely gave interviews any more and was about to turn seventy-five, wanted to *hang out* with a reporter.

Worse, once I turned the story in, the editor seemed OK with it, though not thrilled. Then the editor in chief, who I had never spoken to, weighed in at that late date with what he wanted. I finally had my way, but I don't think any of us ended up happy. It was only when *Esquire* ran a Newman piece shortly after mine, that my editor told me he thought I had gotten Newman to open up more.

7. Can you tell when you've hit "gold"? When you know that something said is going to work well when printed?

MCKENNA: Absolutely.

RENSIN: Yes. Of course. You see it on the page, in your mind. Your inner alarm goes off. In some cases this is when it's good to keep a poker face.

DREIFUS: Yup. I can see what it will look like on paper, as it is being spoken. Mostly, I'm right in that instinct, but I have been surprised on a few occasions—for better and for worse. I think a lot of it is experience. Once you've done enough of them, you can tell what works and what doesn't.

FLEMING: Sometimes, but not always. I usually know when I've nailed it as far as a whole interview is concerned.

POND: Most of the time, yes. It's pretty common for me to be in the middle of an interview, hear something, and think, "Well, there's my lead." If I walk out of the interview knowing my lead and my conclusion, I know I'm in pretty good shape. Other times I won't be sure if something works until I see it transcribed, and realize that it was better than I thought. And then there's the scary flip side, where the subject is skilled enough to make you think that you're getting good stuff, and then you look at the transcript and realize that they didn't say much at all. That's when you know you've been worked by a pro.

SHAH: Sure, I know when someone has said great stuff. (Though occasionally, my editors are less enthused.) I mean, isn't that what we're trained for?

SHEFF: I usually know when I hear something that will work well in the interview—a humorous or poignant line, an important or even newsworthy revelation, or something surprising or moving. I make a note to myself. I may have found a moving place to begin the interview or a poignant place to end it.

COOK: Anything both new and sexual jumps out. Another hot button is intra-Hollywood sniping—getting a celeb to rip another celeb can often make news.

8. How severely do editors edit your work?

DREIFUS: Not too much.

MCKENNA: It depends on the editor. If an editor tampers with my work to the extent that I feel that my voice has been erased, I don't work with that editor again.

RENSIN: I wouldn't use the word *severe.* But everyone needs editing.

SHAH: I'm told I'm not edited much. But that doesn't mean I'm happy. In a feature story or profile, as opposed to a Q&A, the writer's voice is important. The best editors are careful when making changes to keep the writer's voice; the worst substitute their voice and this annoys me no end.

POND: It depends on the editor and the magazine. In general, not very severely. I suppose it's pretty common that an editor will take out something I like or make annoying little changes because I've written too much and they need to fit the space. But there have only been a handful of times where I felt as if the story was seriously hurt by editing.

SHEFF: Generally the majority of editing is for space—interviews are trimmed to fit.

FLEMING: There's always a meeting of the minds. My job is to meet my editor's needs while my obligation is to maintain the substance and integrity of what the interview subject has told me. I've never had someone complain that I'd misquoted them.

9. Do you ever have to explain to an editor why something they deleted should be included?

MCKENNA: Yes. Editors are certainly capable of editing mistakes into pieces and making stupid, illogical cuts. Don't get me started.

FLEMING: That kind of give and take is always necessary. You should fight for your stories, but you should always be painfully aware of the needs of the magazine for which you did the interview.

RENSIN: Sure. They weren't there. They occasionally ignore structure and how one quote depends on another. They sometimes want less of the person and personality. I think showing humanity is very important and sets up the context in which other answers appear. Sometimes they'd sacrifice that for space or for a more newsworthy moment. I like the complete picture.

POND: Sure. That doesn't mean I always win the arguments, but I try. I also find that I'll frequently delete something on my own, and then the editor will want to put it back in and I'll end up explaining why I thought it was expendable.

DREIFUS: Sure. Like most writers, there are times when I have to fight, gently, for my material.

SHAH: My most memorable example of this occurred after I turned in a Sean Connery cover story to *GQ*. I had gone to see him at his home in Nassau. We were sitting at either end of a sofa in his living room. Never once, in that first two-hour session, did he meet my eyes. Instead, he stared straight ahead. But he worked harder at producing thoughtful answers than anyone I had ever interviewed. At one point I said, "You are known for your physicality. How do you create characters by the way you move?"

Without a word, Connery stood and left the room. A moment later, he came back, slouching as he walked. He went out. Came back in moving jauntily. He did this four times, then sat down on an ottoman, faced me, and gave me a fascinating lesson in how simple movements can be used to convey personality. I was mesmerized. I wrote out this scene in my story. Then I got a call from Editor in Chief Art Cooper. He liked the piece a lot, but had several suggestions. The part where Connery gives his little drama lesson was too technical. It would be good to shorten it, if not get rid of it altogether.

Oh, and by the way, Cooper said, did I ask Connery if it were true that his first wife ran around on him?

I was mortified. I began to wonder if I were a good reporter after all, if what interested me was of no interest to anyone else. Also, Connery had been divorced from wife number one for twenty-five years! It never would have occurred to me even to ask that question.

In the end, the drama lesson stayed in, though somewhat shortened. I never went back to Connery with the adultery question.

10. What do you think of publicists in general, and has dealing with them changed over the years?

POND: It's changed a lot. I started writing profiles and doing interviews in the late seventies, and back then you rarely dealt with independent publicists. You called the record company or the film studio, dealt with them, and that was it. But gradually more and more layers were added to the equation. It certainly doesn't make my job easier, but I guess that's the whole point, isn't it? And the rare actors who don't have publicists can be even more difficult to get to than the ones who do, so there's obviously a useful service being performed. I just object when it seems to me that the publicist's power is being used arbitrarily, to demonstrate that the power exists rather than to help the client.

RENSIN: I have rarely had a problem, except with Julia Roberts's publicist after an interview came out and she ragged me because she hated the intro—which I had written but which had also been extensively rewritten by the editor to include all her lovers' names, which I had purposely left out.

DREIFUS: Depends on what kinds of publicists. Movie star publicists are one thing. Book publicists are very nice, they're always civil. But when I come representing the *New York Times,* I find that even the hardest of movie people become businesslike. They know that the *Times* doesn't make deals and they are straightforward. That changes the minute I call representing a magazine.

SHAH: Hollywood publicists have to be the worst species ever put on this earth and are a large part of the reason I rarely interview film stars anymore. The games you have to play before the interview is finally set can be nauseating. At times I walked into an interview so fed up that I wanted to scream at the celeb, "Why are you doing this?"

In sports, it gets even worse. We used to set up interviews with the team PR guy, who generally was helpful. Now, with the biggest stars, you have to go through their agents. Half the time, the agents won't even return your calls.

That said, there are still times when publicists really do make a writer's life easier. I was assigned a big story on *Law & Order* creator Dick Wolf. I had met him casually several times and decided to drop off a note at his apartment building in New York. No response. When I called his office, his overly protective assistant told me to go through Dick's publicist. The publicist said Wolf didn't do profiles. But we kept talking, kept working on approaches and the publicist finally did persuade Dick to see me. In the end, I am told, I had more access to him and his operation than any reporter ever had. But these stories are rare.

FLEMING: Publicists get a bad rap for suppressing real journalism. But let's face it, magazines sell issues based on getting certain cover subjects, so some attempts at bargaining are inevitable. Publicist leverage has increased somewhat. You can work with them, but I don't think they have any right to tell you what's off-limits in terms of a person's life. An interviewer has the right to ask any question and a publicist's job is to brace their client. The only area where I'm pliable is children. I have three of my own, and if a celebrity wants to maintain privacy for their kids for safety or other reasons, I find it laudable and will honor it.

COOK: Some are actually people, while others are awful. They're no worse than most folks, but are more powerful now and have a lot more say in who does an interview and what gets said. I think it's imperative to keep the publicist from sitting in on an interview, though I have done a couple that way. Magazines haven't done enough to resist the rise of publicist power.

SHEFF: A few publicists are great advocates for their clients, who tell the truth. Many aren't and don't. Over the years I learned who I could and couldn't rely on. The publicists for the biggest stars are far more controlling than they used to be.

MCKENNA: I think publicists have really horrible jobs, and generally I empathize with them. Basically, they're forced to babysit the most spoiled babies in the world—movie stars and assorted famous people—and they get endless grief on both ends, from the press and from their clients. Publicists are like any slice of humanity— some of them I like very much, and others are horrible.

11. What horror stories do you have concerning publicists?

POND: The usual, I suppose. I was once one of what I was told were sixteen writers rejected by Tom Cruise's publicist as unworthy of writing a *Rolling Stone* cover on the *Days of Thunder*-era Cruise. I was yelled at by one publicist and told I'd never again speak to any of her clients—until about a year later, when she needed to flex her muscles with an editor and so told a magazine that they could only get a Dennis Quaid interview if I did the story. And I was subject to a full-frontal assault from Arnold Schwarzenegger's then publicist, who flipped out when he admitted in our interview that he'd smoked marijuana. On that story, my editor had decided that one of the only ways to get Arnold out of his preprogrammed salesman mode would be to ask him a series of deliberately silly questions, which I did at the end of the interview. It led to some of the best stuff in the interview—who but Arnold could turn his inability to answer the question "Who's your favorite Beatle?" into an impromptu homily on the importance of teamwork?—but it also caused him to nonchalantly admit that he had, in fact, inhaled. As soon as we finished the interview, Arnold's publicist asked me to take the comment off the record, insisting that the silly questions had not been a real part of the interview. I told her that the admission wasn't a big deal, and that my editors would see the transcript and I didn't think they'd be willing to cut it, so she embarked on a two-week campaign to badger everyone at the magazine, from my editor to the editor in chief. It didn't work, the comment ran, and Arnold survived.

DREIFUS: Typical story, and not the worst, a Hollywood publicist representing a B-level television star almost killed a *TV Guide* story on her client because she unrealistically insisted on a cover story. I got to the actress through the producer of the TV movie, instead. I don't think the actors really know how often their publicists have undone publicity for them.

SHEFF: I have no horror stories, though I think publicists who insist on sitting in on interviews are doing their clients a disservice in the guise of protecting them. If a client needs a babysitter, they shouldn't be doing the interview in the first place.

MCKENNA: I don't have horror stories because as a rule, I don't interview the megastars that have the ultra-aggressive publicists. Moreover, journalists should make a point of remembering that publicists don't work for them. They work for the people who hire them to protect them from the media, and control the press that goes out about them.

RENSIN: None really. I want more time; they want to give less time. I figure when I see my subject I will get what I want from him or her. At least one extra session when they see they have nothing to be afraid of.

FLEMING: I've had one or two people ask to see an interview before it is published. If there was a particularly sensitive issue and the subject wanted to review how they said something, I'd consider it depending on the circumstance and if my editor said it was okay.

12. What makes an interview stand out in print?

RENSIN: Great answers and a sense of the person and their voice. Smart questions that show the interviewer is listening. A whole that is greater than the sum of the parts. A feeling that you are there when it's happening. Interesting interplay between subject and interviewer. Depth. Humor.

FLEMING: Answers that veer from the path of what a star has said to everybody else while promoting a certain film. Spontaneity that comes from the way you view a particular part of that person's life.

DREIFUS: The sense the reader gets that they are reading a two-person play where both interviewer and subject have been absolutely honest.

SHAH: What I try to convey to the subject is this: "Think of our story as a business deal the two of us are doing together. If you work really hard at it, and I do, we're going to have a great story." I mean this. The interviewer can't alone make the piece stand out. I think the trick here is to engage the subject by showing that you are prepared, listening very very well, and bringing a sense of fun to the proceeding. When the subject is engaged, you're almost always going to pull off a good piece.

SHEFF: An interview stands out when the subject, famous or not, is candid and able to articulate something unique or interesting about their work or field of expertise. The best interviews say something important about the world—something more than the subject at hand.

POND: Many things. Often it stands out if you get more from the person than you were expecting, though sometimes just getting what you expected from someone you admire is good enough. An interview also stands out if I leave the room admiring somebody I hadn't cared about going in—or vice versa, in which case it stands out in the wrong way. Mostly, I feel successful if I think I've gotten beyond the stock answers into more interesting and revealing territory.

MCKENNA: A subject who understands that it's possible to speak from the heart without telling secrets and betraying confidences.

13. What goals do you set for yourself as an interviewer?

SHEFF: To try to make each interview compelling, revealing, and honest.

MCKENNA: To win the subjects' trust, and discover the part of them that warrants exploration and is worthy of the public's interest.

POND: As I said before, to go beyond the stock answers. To walk away knowing I won't have to use any of the anecdotes I've read in other interviews with the subject. To figure out, in some small way, what drives the person.

COOK: I want to give the reader a memorable look at a celeb. I want to make my editor look good. I want to get paid.

FLEMING: Hopefully to get a glimpse of a person beneath the surface, maybe even break some news once in a while.

RENSIN: To get it right.

DREIFUS: Each interview is different.

14. Have you ever gotten really comfortable with a subject where you almost forgot it was an interview?

COOK: Often. The goal is to make it a conversation that touches on all or most of the stuff readers are curious about, and to get at least a few quotes that will look good in boldface type.

MCKENNA: No.

RENSIN: Comfortable, yes. Forgot my purpose—never.

FLEMING: Not really, because you are concentrating so hard the entire time. If you get too comfortable you lose track and that is when you break rhythm and both of you feel uncomfortable.

DREIFUS: No. I know why I'm there. It's to get the story, not to make new friends. These people aren't my friends and they aren't going to be.

SHEFF: I always remember it's an interview, but there have been times when it didn't feel so much like work—an eager and engaging interview subject. It's dangerous when interviewers forget they are a journalist on assignment.

POND: For a moment, perhaps. But when you're sitting there with a tape recorder on the table between the two of you, there's an artificiality to the conversation that you can never really forget for long. There are certainly moments in good interviews, especially if you have a lot of time, where you'll go off into areas that clearly are not going to be part of the story, and in those moments things might change from an interview to a conversation. But it's hard to ever really forget that both of you came to the table with an agenda.

SHAH: I almost always get comfortable with the person I am writing about. That is my job. Actually, my job is to make *them* feel comfortable and talk freely. But I can't ever recall that I "forgot" I was on assignment. I am always listening for the revealing quote, or looking for the telltale action. In fact, I tend to be so focused that it is only *after* the story is done that I may think, "Hey, I liked that guy. We coulda been friends!"

15. Have you had any awkward or embarrassing moments during an interview?

FLEMING: Not really in recent interviews. When I began my career in journalism, I worked on a showbiz column at *New York Newsday.* I was assigned to interview Brian De Palma for *The Untouchables,* it was my first big profile. I'd liked De Palma's movies, and I liked *The*

Untouchables. I walk in, he looks up and says, "Oh, they're sending interns now to do these things." I must have been twenty-five or so, probably looked younger, but that set the tone for an awful interview. He was an insufferable, pompous jerk through the entire interview and I have never enjoyed another one of his movies since. The difference between then and now is, I have enough confidence in myself to realize that he's got the problem, not me.

SHEFF: While interviewing George Lucas, the tape recorder malfunctioned and I had to confess that an hour's conversation was lost. We started over. (Since then I use two tape recorders.)

POND: There are small, awkward moments during every interview. I think I've blocked most of them out of my mind. Malfunctioning tape recorders, I suppose, account for most of them—realizing you have to go back over territory you already covered, because the tape wasn't running. I once had to search Michael J. Fox's trailer top to bottom because I thought I'd left one of the interview tapes there, and he was accommodating enough to offer to do the entire interview over again if I couldn't find the tape. But I later found it back at my hotel, so I was spared that particular embarrassment.

RENSIN: When River Phoenix freaked out and thought I was trying to sneak questions about homosexuality and how he prepared for his role in *My Own Private Idaho.* I wasn't. But he got up and called an end to the interview in such an erratic and paranoid way that to save the interview I told him he was scaring me. He immediately sought to reassure me and continued our talk. He also asked me not to reveal that he was a smoker. Didn't want to disillusion the fans.

16. *Do you ever worry about asking a stupid question?*

RENSIN: Like this one? (Sorry, couldn't resist. Kidding. Really.) Nope.

MCKENNA: No, I'm all for stupid, simple questions along the lines of: What are you afraid of? What's the first thing you do when you get up in the morning? Questions like this tend to catch people off guard, and they often garner surprisingly candid responses.

FLEMING: Not really. When I stumble in an interview, I always figure I have become Chris Farley in those great *Saturday Night Live* skits where he interviews the likes of Martin Scorsese. He asks, "You remember that time in *Taxi Driver* where he said, you talking to me, you talking to me? That was awesome." But I find that if you are too polished an interviewer, you're going to get polished answers. If you're a blue-collar guy doing the best he can, sometimes they want to help you.

DREIFUS: Sorry. Nope. I don't think of myself as stupid. I some times ask off-the-wall sort of questions because I'm seeking off-the-wall sort of responses. Even when I asked Sir Martin Rees, the Astronomer Royal of Great Britain, what his astrological sign was, I did that deliberately: to see if he knew. (He's a Taurus.) Recently, I asked military historian Tom Pakenham, who is an expert on trees, a Barbara Walters-type question, "If you were a tree, which would you be?" But it was done with a knowing smile.

POND: Sometimes stupid questions prompt good answers. I'd rather not ask any stupid questions, but sometimes they come out, and you just laugh and move on. If you get self-conscious about that ahead of time, you'll end up verbally constipated during the interview.

SHEFF: I ask stupid questions all the time. Sometimes they get the best answers.

SHAH: There's a difference between a basic, kindergarten kind of question and a stupid question. It took me a long time before I understood it was okay to ask the former. This would be like "Sorry. The difference between a slider and split-finger fastball . . . I get them confused." I think people don't mind "helping." A stupid question, one that reveals you didn't do your homework, would be "Um, are you a right-hander or a left-hander?" Which is insulting.

17. How much of an interview is acting?

FLEMING: None of it. At least on my end.

MCKENNA: I wouldn't describe it as acting. It's more of a mutual seduction.

POND: It's acting in the sense that many of the people I talk to are people whose work I don't find completely fascinating. So you're acting like you're interested in them, when in all likelihood you're not. It's acting when somebody goes into a long story or a detailed explanation or a rant about something you know will never make it into the story, and you have to stay focused and interested.

SHAH: If I were good at acting, I would have headed for Hollywood. I've never found it necessary to mislead people. Nor do I lie. If a subject asks me if I'm writing a puff piece, I tell the truth. I say I try to be like a photographer snapping a picture. I'm going to do my best to capture them as they are. So far, nobody's sent me away.

SHEFF: I don't act. I am always interested in the people I'm interviewing. That may not be completely true. What's true is that I am always able to find something that is interesting as long as the subject is honest.

DREIFUS: I think that what you are bringing into the room is *who you are,* and that is what people respond to. You don't want to be anyone else.

RENSIN: Depends on who is playing the other part.

18. What interviews have you read—or conducted—that show you what the form is capable of?

DREIFUS: A lot of the *Playboy* interviews.

RENSIN: My *Playboy* interview with Garry Shandling was less of a typical one, in the classic sense, than this weird interplay of insult and ingenuity. It was about the wholly temporary personal relationship of the interview. He went at me in his passive-aggressive way and I gave it back—always showing the proper respect, but not so much that I wouldn't take a shot. He liked that I was not a pushover. He invited challenge.

MCKENNA: The interviews conducted by Jonathan Cott for *Rolling Stone* during the seventies were a real inspiration to me because he managed to communicate the mystery and magic of people. The interviews I've done with Leonard Cohen were also a high point for me, largely because Leonard is able to speak so poetically off the top of his head, he's extremely funny, and he's an extraordinarily empathetic person.

SHEFF: There are many great interviews, some known and some unknown. Alex Haley's *Playboy* interview with Miles Davis set a high bar at the magazine. Jann Wenner's John Lennon interview in *Rolling Stone* was a model when, a decade after Wenner, I had the opportunity to meet up with Lennon for *Playboy*. I remember great interviews with the greatest actors—Grobel's with Brando and Pacino, to name two—and some of Rensin's interviews with comedians. I recall how some of the quirkiest interviews reveal an enormous amount about their subjects. Ted Turner and Ted Kennedy come to mind.

POND: Jann Wenner's *Rolling Stone* interview with John Lennon right after the Beatles broke up is high on the list. Robert Palmer's *RS* interview with Sam Phillips, the guy who first recorded Elvis. A fair number of *Playboy* interviews, I suppose, dating back to Miles Davis and Bob Dylan in the sixties.

19. *How do you get a reluctant subject to open up?*

POND: A variety of things, but I guess they all boil down to gentle persistence. Doing whatever I can to convince him that I am more understanding or more thoughtful or more deserving than the other interviewers whose similar attempts he may have resisted.

DREIFUS: I try to get eons of time and I try to figure out what really moves that person, what they care about, what can get them off their dime. I spend two weeks trying to figure out what my lead question will be.

COOK: I think almost everyone will talk about his childhood.

FLEMING: No set way. Prayer doesn't hurt. Some people are frosty, and that's just the way it is. Some stars don't have much to say, which doesn't mean they are bad people. They just don't have much to say, or they're shy.

RENSIN: Be empathetic. Ask why he can't talk about something. Tell him he can call me to discuss anything afterward, in which case there's a small negotiation and we both walk away with a win.

SHAH: Some people aren't going to open up no matter what. Example: Barry Diller. His answers are short; his manner cold. But then, I'm not talking about an extended interview with Diller; in fact, I doubt he gives them.

Perhaps the worst person I can recall interviewing was Harrison Ford. He had recently made an Indiana Jones picture in which Sean Connery was playing his father. This was when I was doing the *GQ* profile of Connery and I was collecting anecdotes. Ford, famously media-shy, agreed to be questioned on the phone. His publicist kept making me promise that I would use some of his quotes. But of course! But talking to Ford was like pulling teeth. He couldn't think of any stories to tell about Connery; yes, he had been fine to work with, et cetera. Finally, I ended the interview to put both of us out of our misery. In the end, I had nothing of Ford's I could use.

Normally, though, I try to begin an interview with a subject I think the person will enjoy talking about. More often than not, I am the one who ends the interview when I have what I need; not them. People love talking about themselves.

MCKENNA: I find that reluctant subjects generally don't open up, regardless of what you do. The Coen brothers and Linda Ronstadt come to mind here. Basically they hate being interviewed, and I truly don't know why they ever agree to do it, because it's extremely unpleasant for both parties. I really resent it when public figures behave that way to the press.

SHEFF: I try to start on safe and easy territory. Sometimes it takes time. Only once did I have to chastise a subject. One subject was in a grouchy mood, reluctantly offering yes and no answers. After a long and discouraging session, I said, "If you didn't want to do this, why are you here? Why waste my time or yours?" He apologized and transformed. It was a very good and very funny interview.

20. How do you deal with off-the-record if the subject prefaces it? Or, the subject asks for something he's already said to be deleted?

RENSIN: It's off the record then. But I always preface an interview by saying that I'm going to feel free to ask about absolutely anything. If they don't want to answer, fine. If I disagree, I'll make my case. If they still don't want to answer, fine. That way they're not afraid of seeing it in print, and once they talk about a subject, once the words are in their mouths instead of just rumbling around anxiously in their heads, there is less fear.

A subject can call me anytime to ask for a deletion. They don't always get it. But I try to have enough material that the interview never hangs on one quote.

DREIFUS: If someone says "this is off the record," it is off the record.

SHAH: The off-the-record issue is always troublesome. If the subject begins to answer a question by saying, "This is off the record, OK?" I will sometimes tell them forget it. If I can't use it, I don't want to know. Occasionally that ploy will work and they will go ahead and tell me on the record. Other times I will agree to keep it off. Then at the end of the interview I will ask if I can use it. Or maybe I tell them that if I decide I want to use the quote, would it be all right if I phone them and read what I've written? Sometimes that will work.

If, however, they tell me something's off the record after they've said it, it's tricky as hell. If it's something really important, and I say I'm using it anyway, it could end the interview, though I can't remember that ever happening. If I'm writing a profile, sometimes I can work the information into the story without attributing it to the person. But the best thing to do is to begin the interview by making it clear: "Hey, we're totally on the record here!"

FLEMING: If it's prefaced, I honor it. If they ask later, I weigh it, with the help of the editor. Sometimes it's worth being flexible because it will get you something else. Often, you can talk somebody into going along, it's part of the give-and-take.

SHEFF: If a subject wants to speak off the record, I'll consider the specific circumstances. I may agree to go off the record with the proviso that I can revisit the subject. I may afterward ask to put all or some of the information on the record. I may say, "Now, I want to discuss the same subject, but on the record." I won't allow a subject to delete something after the fact unless there are extenuating circumstances. I agreed to omit a story that compromised a child's privacy, for example.

MCKENNA: If I were a political reporter or a hard-news reporter, I'm sure my answer would be different here, because in cases like that there's often a lot more at stake in regards to published information. With entertainment figures, off-the-record often adds up to nothing more than a crack about an ex-husband. So, generally, I honor off-the-record requests. There have been cases where I've been asked to delete things after the fact, and in those cases, if I feel it's important, I negotiate.

COOK: I tell them that if it's off the record, there's no point in saying it. They'll often go ahead and say at least part of what they were going to say—on the record.

There's no way to put something already said "off the record." I think celebs know that; it's inexperienced interviewees who think they can make off-the-record retroactive. But if the subject has second thoughts, and is a decent person, I'll consider a different version of the quote. If I can spare somebody's feelings without shortchanging the reader, I think that's OK.

POND: If the subject prefaces a comment by asking for it to be off the record, I will generally agree. I'd rather hear him say it, and then go back later and try to persuade him to put it on the record. If he says something and then later asks for it to be deleted, it's different. If it's something that is merely embarrassing or won't make sense to use in the story, I'll agree. If it's something I really want to use, I'll usually hem and haw and fall back on what I told Schwarzenegger's publicist: that the editor will see the entire transcript and may insist on using the comment. When in doubt, blame the editor.

21. Will you lie to a subject in order to get him/her to open up?

DREIFUS: No.

SHEFF: No. I won't lie.

POND: Is it a lie to convince someone whose work you don't care for that you are terribly interested in them? If so, then I guess I've lied. But other than that, I don't think so. Except that I think I've probably given subjects the impression that I've seen movies of theirs I haven't, or that I'm familiar with work of theirs that I'm not.

COOK: I'll flatter subjects but not lie to them. They're famous for a reason—Dennis Rodman may be a jerk but he was a great, fierce rebounder. I told him I admired his rebounding, his fierce energy on the court, and we talked about that. I would soon admire his tolerance for alcohol, too.

FLEMING: Never. If I make a promise, I have to keep it. My reputation is all I have.

MCKENNA: Yes. I won't say I was born in Tahiti (I wasn't), but I will tell them I loved their mediocre movie.

RENSIN: Nope. You'll get caught, and reputation is all anyone has as a calling card.

22. Have you ever allowed a subject to view the transcript before submitting it to your editor?

DREIFUS: Rarely—but with the proviso that they could only make changes for language, grammar—never content.

FLEMING: I'd sooner submit to a proctological exam with rusty salad tongs.

RENSIN: Nope. Shirley MacLaine did get to see an edited version of one session, and I forget why. The editor cleared it at her request.

SHAH: Yes, one time I let a subject see a story ahead of time. I was a brand-new reporter and I had spent several days with Jane Fonda and no sooner had I finished writing the story than she phoned. Would I read it to her, please? Not knowing any better, I did. It was a long story and she quibbled over everything. She went beserk when I referred to her as an actress. She was in her antiwar phase and wanted to be identified as such. I don't think I changed much to appease her. But oh, did I learn my lesson.

SHEFF: No. One time a magazine made an agreement that allowed a subject to do an "accuracy check" of a transcript, the opportunity to correct factual mistakes. That's an editor's call, not mine.

POND: No. Many years ago I had an editor who made a deal with the subject's publicist to let them see the piece before it ran, but I was completely unaware of the deal. And around the same time, in the mid-1980s, I also wrote a Jackson Browne cover story for *Rolling Stone*, and after the interview Browne called Jann Wenner because he was worried about some things he'd said about his young son, and about the divorce he was going through at the time. Wenner let Browne review those particular parts of the story prior to publication, though again I knew nothing about it until later. (Ironically, the story wound up far more negative than the piece I turned in, due to some heavy-handed editing and a general anti-Browne sentiment in the *Rolling Stone* offices in those days. So looking at the piece ahead of time didn't do him any good.)

23. Who are some of the disappointing people you've interviewed?

COOK: Tom Green wasn't funny. Farrah Fawcett made me wait three hours, then gave me an insincere kiss (her flunkies buzzed around, whispering, "Farrah's Evian isn't the right temperature!"). Pamela Anderson got mad because I had "made her sound promiscuous" in a previous story about her. Jay Leno left a passive-aggressive message on my phone machine, saying he "kind of liked" the *Playboy* interview we'd done, but wished it had mentioned his new book, which was the reason he'd done the interview. I felt bad about that, but neither he nor his publicist had mentioned the book.

MCKENNA: Steve Martin, Jeff Daniels, Jeff Goldblum, Peter Weller, Treat Williams—there are plenty of assholes in Hollywood. The Coen brothers were especially difficult. They seemed to be completely unaware of the fact that I was simply a journalist trying to earn a living and help them promote their movie. It was clear that they found having lunch with me a tremendous imposition.

RENSIN: River Phoenix. Jeff Lynne of Electric Light Orchestra. All years and a lifetime ago.

POND: The two members of Steely Dan were openly contemptuous of the interview process and more interested in wisecracking to each other than in dealing with me. Tom Waits, whose work I admire enormously, was sunk so deeply into playing his colorful barfly character that getting anything the slightest bit personal or revealing proved to be impossible. Robert Culp was arrogant and dismissive long after his career gave him any reason to be. The director Ralph Bakshi was also arrogant and uncooperative; after he told me something (I've long since forgotten exactly what it was) he announced that he'd sue me if I used it in the story. I put it in the story along with his threat—and while I didn't hear from Bakshi, I did get a call from his publicist thanking me for exposing his client's tactic. Tom Cruise was ferociously bland.

FLEMING: I'd rather not say, I'm sure they feel they tried. It would be like revealing someone was a bad kisser.

DREIFUS: One: Mel Brooks—he was so solemn, also he was jiving me. I mean really, he kept saying there were no Jewish themes to his work! I was pressing him on the roots of his humor.

Two: Tipper Gore—she was so dull that the piece never ran. I hate when that happens.

Three: President Aristide of Haiti. He had absolutely nothing interesting to say, which was a shame because Haiti is such an interesting society, and he blew a wonderful opportunity to make his case to the wider world. This one also didn't run.

Four: Issac Bashevis Singer—not at all lovable, not funny, not kind—he was the opposite of his work. This piece did run, though.

Five: Carl Sagan—who was anything but that genial, open person that played on TV.

Six: Stephen Jay Gould.

24. Is there anyone you'd like to go back to try again?

SHEFF: Many. Some great subjects have gone on to do important or otherwise significant work. I'd love to go back and talk to them. Other people were interesting enough to want to revisit regardless of what they have been up to. Some who I would like to go back to: Gore Vidal, Tom Hanks, Steve Jobs, Billy Joel, Shintaro Ishihara, David Hockney, Lucas, nuclear physicist Ted Taylor.

POND: I'd like to try Waits again, because I think a good portion of the failure of that interview was due to my reluctance to shift gears, go along with his role-playing and see where it led. And I'd love to try my hand at Bob Dylan, who I only spoke to for about fifteen minutes after a concert many years ago. In that short conversation, he completely eluded every question and struck me as the slipperiest person I'd ever spoken to (with the exception of then California governor Jerry Brown, and politicians don't count). I suspect Dylan would be an impossible interview, but it'd be a kick to try.

FLEMING: I'd interview Robert Downey Junior on a weekly basis if I could.

DREIFUS: Mel Brooks.

MCKENNA: I'd like to interview Leonard Cohen every week—he always has something inspiring to say. I'd also love to interview the photographer Robert Frank again, simply because I didn't get enough time with him.

RENSIN: No. I need to keep moving forward. I have done repeats, though, and although there is familiarity and trust, it's often never as edgy and real in the outcome.

25. Has anyone ever asked you to leave?

MCKENNA: No.

SHEFF: No, though I left Puff Daddy after being strung along for days. I was unable to ask one question.

DREIFUS: Yes. Henry Kissinger. He threw me out of his house. He did apologize to me later, and as my boyfriend said to me, at that time, "I think you're the only person in the world that Henry Kissinger's ever apologized to."

FLEMING: Part of you dreams that would happen, that you'd have a Mike Wallace moment, where you're chasing the subject down the street with your microphone. All my interviews have ended amicably.

RENSIN: River Phoenix.

SHAH: No one has ever asked me to leave. Once, I was doing a cover story on Denzel Washington for *GQ* and I was flying with him from L.A. to London. Ten hours, right? We'd met several times before and after takeoff he came over and sat beside me. Things were going well until I asked if he still felt it was harder for him to get the roles he wanted because he was black. He had complained about this in several of the interviews I had read. But this time he got very angry and accused me of being a racist. He got up and stormed back to his seat. *Oh—oh.* But several hours later, he returned, sat down, and answered the question.

POND: No, though Waits and I came to an agreement that the interview wasn't working and we should end it. Back in his *Rain Man* days, Tom Cruise briefly and abruptly left the room a couple of times during our interview, apparently because he felt I wasn't showing him the proper respect. But he came back and finished the interview, and I had no idea why he'd left the room until much later.

26. Has any question you've asked ended an interview prematurely?

RENSIN: Not quite.

MCKENNA: No.

SHEFF: No, though Matt Drudge kept threatening to walk out, but he didn't.

POND: No, but certain questions certainly make an interview difficult for a while. Generally, the worst that happens is that the subject becomes uncomfortable and begins to offer short, curt answers. But I find that if you steer the conversation to a topic area they're more eager to talk about, you can get them to relax again. And then maybe later you can sneak back to the problem area and try again. . . .

DREIFUS: Yes, I got thrown out by the late Elia Kazan, when I asked him the bingo question, something like "You've said that the one thing in your life you're most ambivalent about is your testimony before the House Un-American Committee. What exactly did that ambivalence involve?"

27. Who are some of the more articulate—as opposed to merely verbal—people you've interviewed?

FLEMING: Kevin Spacey, director Curtis Hanson, James Cameron, Ridley Scott. Martin Scorsese was quite good, though he seems not to understand why he's held in such reverence.

DREIFUS: The late Israeli general Harkabi, who was the only interview I ever did that didn't have to be edited. Sir Martin Rees, Sir Roger Penrose, Jane Goodall, the Dalai Lama, Aung San Suu Kyi, Isabel Allende, Thomas Pakenham, Cher, John Maeda, Gloria Steinem, Colin Powell, Abba Eban, Hanan Ashwari, Christopher Reeve, Sir Arthur Clarke, Cesar Chavez, General John Shaliskasvili, more. I mean, "articulate" is what you're looking for when you're trawling for interview subjects.

POND: Rosanne Cash, Peter Gabriel, Patrick Stewart, David Duchovny, Wynton Marsalis, Randy Newman, Pete Townshend.

SHEFF: John Lennon, Gore Vidal.

MCKENNA: Joni Mitchell, Lou Reed, Atom Egoyan, Madonna, Gena Rowlands, Jessica Lange, Pauline Kael, and Brian Eno all come to mind.

28. Are you ever nervous or on edge before an interview?

RENSIN: Always. No matter how long I do this I get butterflies. I've often toyed with the fantasy of standing up in the middle of an interview and announcing, "Sorry. Don't take this personally. It has nothing to do with you, but I'm retiring right now!" It almost happened once.

MCKENNA: Always.

DREIFUS: Definitely.

POND: I'm edgy before an interview only when I'm going to be speaking to somebody who's notorious for being a tough interview. The level of fame has nothing to do with it, but if I'm anticipating difficulties, I will occasionally get nervous.

SHEFF: I'm often a little nervous before we start, but the feeling quickly disappears.

SHAH: I am almost *always* nervous before an interview. I worry about every possible thing. Getting lost, arriving too late, the subject not showing up, the subject not giving me interesting stuff, not enough time . . . everything! And, oh yes, the most realistic worry of all: my damn tape recorder screwing up.

COOK: There's always low-level dread, like the feeling of having a big test coming up in school. But it's a terrific feeling when you bag a good interview, shake hands, and head for the airport.

FLEMING: I once got my black belt in karate. That sickening flow of prefight adrenaline is always there before an interview, I suppose it is what ensures you will do a good job. That's another reason why I could never feel relaxed during an interview.

29. How often was a person not like what you expected?

SHAH: Almost always people are not quite what I had expected. Usually I get on with them better than I had anticipated. Usually they are nicer than I had imagined. Which doesn't mean I don't keep the antennae up for lies or their attempts to spin me.

The most memorable example of someone not being what I had expected was former L.A. police chief Daryl Gates. I went to do a *Playboy* interview with him. I knew absolutely nothing about police work and was convinced, based on the reporting in the *Los Angeles Times*, that he was a racist. To my astonishment, I found him patient with me, never, ever condescending, amazingly smart, and, it would turn out, one of the least prejudiced people I had met in L.A.

POND: Fairly often. And usually for the better. When I'm surprised, more often than not it's because a subject who was reputed to be difficult turns out to be a much more willing and open subject than I was expecting. Sometimes it'll be the other way around, but the surprises tend to be pleasant ones.

COOK: Depp is the only one I clicked with on anything much more than a superficial level. We have similar quirky interests, like insects. I gave him a killer bee in amber; he gave me the address of his favorite curio shop in Paris.

MCKENNA: Not very often.

RENSIN: Always. I go in with an open mind and always find something surprising.

SHEFF: Many people are different than I expect them to be. It's one of the great joys of the job.

FLEMING: My surprises were Harrison Ford, who was more fun than I'd imagined, Drew Barrymore, who is trippy but just adorable and so in the moment. Sam Jackson, I expected gruff and found he would be atop the list of celebrities you'd invite over to watch football and have a beer with.

DREIFUS: It happens a lot. I can't quantify the numbers. But I think that's a hazard of interviewing the famous—they are often miles from their public persona.

30. Have you had any moments of self-revelation while interviewing someone?

SHEFF: Often. These are another joy of the job. I often learn insights about myself, my life, my family.

DREIFUS: Of course. Just like one hopes that the source will learn from you, you will learn from them. I mean jeez, this is an exploration.

MCKENNA: Absolutely. That's why I do this work. It allows me to ask accomplished people the questions I'm wrestling with in my own life.

POND: Nothing major, but minor moments pop up from time to time. Generally prompted by realizing certain similarities between myself and the person I'm interviewing.

FLEMING: I always go in nervous, thinking it will be a train wreck. So far, it has never been that, so the revelation partway through is, I can do this.

RENSIN: Always. I choose my subjects mostly and that has to be based on what I'm going through in life to a certain extent. I ask about what interests me, as well as questions that reflect whatever brief I believe I'm carrying for the magazine. In books, this is even more pronounced.

31. Do you have a favorite question which you ask all the people you interview?

POND: No. I've always been a little wary of the one-question-fits-all approach. For the most part, I think you need to tailor every interview for the person and the time—and while certain questions may pop up frequently, I've never found anything that feels right to ask every person.

SHAH: I don't have a favorite question I like to ask everyone per se. But since most of the people I write about are very successful, I find myself trying to understand what drives them. What kind of childhood and how they go about doing what they do, their work habits, etc.

DREIFUS: Nope. Every interview is custom-made. I do go through phases though, which are highly dependent on what my interests are at a given moment, what I've been reading or seeing.

FLEMING: "If you were a tree . . ." No, actually, I don't have a favorite question.

SHEFF: I enjoy talking to people about their teenage years, since adolescence is so unkind to so many people. It's not appropriate in every interview, but I fit it in when I can.

RENSIN: Can we meet just one more time?

MCKENNA: Yes. Why does love die?

32. How does an interviewer maintain his/her own identity?

MCKENNA: Through the people one chooses to interview and the questions one asks.

DREIFUS: By being as centered as possible on the work, by knowing why you are there, and not having any illusions about it. Psychotherapists have the same problem.

RENSIN: A better question is how do they lose it? Not possible beyond the natural tendency of some interviewers to be like chameleons and take on the coloring of their surroundings temporarily in order to lull the subject into feeling safe. But once at the computer, you are you again—which accounts for some people who act nice in person and kill you later.

SHAH: I have never had an interview situation where I felt I was losing my identity.

POND: I suppose one way would be to ask the same questions of every subject, but that leaves me out. It's not all that hard, even with a Q&A, unless you ask nothing but the kind of stock junket questions a subject answers in every *Entertainment Tonight* bit and Electronic Press Kit interview. As long as you get beyond that, your identity will come across. But I'm also wary of interviewers trying too hard to establish their identities. I know that the readers are far more interested in the interview subject than they are in me, and that it's far more important to accurately capture the subject's identity than to figuratively wave my hands around in an attempt to show off mine.

FLEMING: The way I got into these interviews was through my position as a reporter and columnist at *Daily Variety*. I am a big fan of the process of making movies. I grew up wanting to be a sportswriter, but I love being a dad and noticed the high divorce and drinking rates of newspaper reporters who are always on the road. I cover the film biz like I would sports. It's the behind-the-scenes anecdotes, changes that are made in the making of movies, creative decisions, et cetera. A lot of the stars and directors I interview read my *Variety* stories. They know what I'm about. I'm this schlub who covers Hollywood from his house on Long Island, who is just passionate about the entire process. It disarms them because they quickly realize I'm more interested in what they do for a living than in most other areas of their lives they are uncomfortable talking about. They talk about those things, sometimes I think they want to make that part of themselves sound interesting to me.

SHEFF: I enjoy the separation I have from the interview subjects. I may respect them, but I don't want to be them. I'm always happy to return to my world and my life after a visit into theirs.

33. Finally, what are some of your favorite moments during interviews you've done?

POND: Shopping at the Wal-Mart in Branson, Missouri, with Johnny Cash ranks right up there for a wonderful blend of cool and surreal. Sitting in an empty arena watching Bruce Springsteen's soundchecks. Sitting in a tiny rehearsal space in London watching the Who rehearse for a tour. Hanging out with Roy Orbison just a few weeks before his death. Listening to Trey Parker and Matt

Stone cheerfully trash the entire entertainment industry was a great kick, because I knew how well it would work in print.

COOK: Two long sessions with a very slyly funny, thoughtful Johnny Depp. I was the only bald guy in a polo shirt in the Viper Room. He actually called after the first long session and said we should meet again—he thought he could improve on his answers. When my father died in a car accident, Depp sent flowers.

Shaking hands with Michael Jordan and Shaq (on separate interviews), and finding that Jordan's hand is bigger. Interviewing Shaq as he stuffed himself into my rented Taurus, with his knees almost touching the ceiling; he held the tape recorder while I drove, chasing his agent through traffic on the 405 in L.A. I was to deliver Shaq to dinner with Quincy Jones, and we were hurrying, changing lanes; at one point Shaq's eyes get big as we skid in front of an oncoming semitrailer. I could see the next day's headline: SHAQ BRUISES THUMB; ANONYMOUS MAN KILLED.

During an all-night *Playboy* interview in Vegas, Dennis Rodman tried to buy me a lap dance. When I said no thanks, he shouted, "Your wife can't see through walls!" Little did he know.

Playing golf with the notoriously prickly Barry Bonds, I saw his charming side. Like a kid, he *needs* you to see his best shots, and he thought it was hilarious when I hit a ball out of bounds. He can be funny, and I think he is a lot smarter than most ballplayers; it irks him to be asked the same questions day after day by swarms of newspaper guys. I also saw him sign a bunch of autographs for fans, but when he finally said he had to leave, one fan tried to poke Bonds in the eye with a souvenir program.

I watched blaxploitation flicks with an antic, giggling Quentin Tarantino; had James Brown show me a dance step; and had k. d. lang sing a song just for me, with nobody else within earshot.

SHEFF: There are numerous examples. Dozens come from my interview with John Lennon and Yoko Ono. I knocked on the kitchen door of the Lennon's Dakota apartment one day. John opened it singing, to the tune of "Eleanor Rigby," "Here's David Sheff, come to ask questions with answers that no one will hear." Another time I was in the studio between interview sessions. John, holding a guitar, sat nearby. He began playing and singing a haunting version of "Help." There were many moments during the conversation with Lennon when I felt enormously moved or inspired by what he said. It was a remarkable experience even if it hadn't been punctuated by tragedy.

Each evening throughout the Ansel Adams interview, the old master photographer (and dissident and philosopher) stopped the interview. He insisted that everyone around gather by the picture window. Sipping martinis made by his wife Virginia (Adams's was watered down; he wasn't supposed to drink), we watched for the "green flash," the phenomenon caused by the sun as it appears to disappear into the Pacific Ocean. At first I couldn't see it, but by the end of the interview Adams had taught me to see the elusive flash.

One evening I was asking Adams about politics. In a particularly fiery mood he told me that he would like to drown Ronald Reagan and his interior secretary, James Watt, who were systematically dismantling environmental protections that had been in place for decades, in his martini. Adams caught himself. Speaking into his martini olive as if it were a surveillance device, he said, "It's just a figure of speech. I don't really want to do physical harm to the interior secretary." To me, he said, "That's for the FBI in case they're listening in."

Mid-sentence, Robert Maxwell cut off the conversation taking place on his yacht moored near the River Club in Manhattan and told me to meet him at the airport in London. Just like that. I flew to London and met him at Heathrow, where I was escorted to his jet. On board, we continued the interview en route to Jerusalem, where he was met by the prime minister and president.

Frank Zappa was in enormous pain throughout our interview. (His cancer—incurable—was advancing. He only had months to live.) When his pain seemed unbearable, I asked if Zappa wanted to take a break. No, he said, he wanted to keep going. We spoke for eight consecutive hours like that. Though sometimes the pain worsened, he opted to continue. He had much to say and he said it with the urgency of a man who knew that his time was limited. It was a remarkable conversation about politics and art and Zappa's humanistic definition of family values.

DREIFUS: Seeing the toys in Sir Roger Penrose's office.

Bringing chocolates to Gabriel Garcia Márquez.

Walking in Golden Gate Park with the late Luis Baptista as he explained the various accents and life histories of the local songbirds.

Hanging out with Sue Savage-Rumbaugh and her signing bonobos [great apes] and watching Pambanisha ask for mineral water.

Hanging with Christopher Reeve—and seeing what real courage looks like.

The Dalai Lama telling me about his dreams.

FLEMING: I was concerned that Harrison Ford would be standoffish. He cooked me a killer breakfast of eggs, bacon, and toast and we had a good interview. He was quite funny in a dry manner. I fondly recall Samuel L. Jackson sitting there poolside at a hotel, reminiscing on how he once could stick a match up one nostril and pull it down the other, because he'd dissolved the cartilage through excessive cocaine usage. Sam, who was easily the coolest and most likable guy I have interviewed, was so at ease with himself that he had no desire to hide the rough spots in his life. Hanging out with Mel Gibson on the set of *The Patriot* was great fun, but perhaps the favorite interview moments would be those spent with Robert Downey Junior. I had the good luck of interviewing him twice, and he is very much the way you see him on-screen. His creativity knows no bounds. Like Sam, he is very honest and unflinching as he describes the dark spots of his life.

MCKENNA: I suppose my favorite moments are when I've interviewed someone I had a great deal of respect for prior to our meeting, and they lived up to my expectations. Krysztof Kieslowski, Jim Jarmusch, Ricki Lee Jones, and Johnny Rotten would be examples of that. And, of course, I treasure the meetings that led to friendships—with Brian Eno, Leonard Cohen, David Lynch, and Artie Shaw.

RENSIN: Every interview has a great moment. That is one big reason I do this. It's tough to recall them all, of course. One, however, was while driving through Texas with Larry Hagman in his Mercedes. He revealed that while he was "flying" around on TV as Major Nelson on *I Dream of Jeannie,* he was flying around in private on LSD.

I also remember Bill Gates slamming a Plexiglas ruler into his hand repeatedly, in sort of a nervous gesture, whenever he heard a question he didn't like or wasn't of the sort he'd heard before. And he did it while rocking back and forth in his chair. He also gave me a raspberry (the noise one makes) at one question, and I had to return the favor a couple questions later at one of his answers. When we flew to Portland, he flew coach and sat next to me with a blanket over his head, sleeping.

When Garry Shandling told me that he'd love to find a woman like me, who came to the house, talked only about him. He went further and said I was the woman in our relationship. That's when I asked him if this was the moment he took his shirt off.

Dennis Miller, who was feuding with Jay Leno during the talk-show booking wars, called him to apologize after I asked him in the interview how long he was going to hold a grudge against someone who had been a close friend.

When Marty Scorsese gave me ten hours instead of the agreed-to four.

When Jack La Lanne took me into his gym and I failed the pull-up test.

When I told Kenny Rogers, during an emergency follow-up session, that his previous answers had all the weight of his movie *Six Pack,* and that to get the interview into the magazine he had to come up with something more emotional and real. He did.

Cindy Crawford's legs in shorts.

Eating cereal with Jerry Seinfeld.

Going to a double feature with Shirley MacLaine during our seventeen-hour marathon, and not speaking a word to each other.

Bryant Gumbel looking out the window of his Rockefeller Center office and pointing out blondes as if he were calling aircraft positions.

Eddie Murphy asking me if there was such a thing as "the right woman" because he was afraid any love commitment would fall apart and the woman would take half his money. Beating Eddie at Ping-Pong.

Larry King soliciting love advice.

Whoopi Goldberg telling me her mother loved her interview.

Patti D'Arbanville jumping into my arms because she liked her interview.

Richard Gere and I talking about the gerbils.

Telling Tom Cruise he wasn't so good-looking in person—and him laughing.

Driving behind Roseanne and Tom during a wild ride to the boonies in Iowa.

Diane Lane, at nineteen, asking me what I was doing that evening. Calling my wife, I said.

Asking Geena Davis if I could interview her again, as soon as we finished, because it had been so much fun.

Talking with Chris Farley about clown paintings.

When Jackie Mason asked if it was okay if his rabbi and girlfriend joined us for the interview.

Ron Howard telling me he wanted to direct Penny Marshall in a nude scene.

Martin Mull telling me that a man of culture doesn't lick the sink in public restrooms.

William Shatner denying he wore a hairpiece.

Gene Simmons showing me his collection of nude photos of his four thousand sexual partners.

Lena Olin offering me a cigarette.

Sean Penn giving me his phone number so we could go surfing.

Spending five hours with Michelle Pfeiffer and talking about her dreams.

Being able to interview Alex Trebek because everything was in the form of a question.

Eating bratwurst at Brewer Stadium with Bob Uecker.

Watching Sigourney Weaver peel a banana.

Cooking dinner for Sissy Spacek and her husband, Jack Fiske.

Spending a lonely Valentine's Day night with David Caruso.

Interviewing Lucy Lawless in a limo, cruising Mulholland Drive, drinking wine.

The moment I know that a subject has gone beyond giving all the answers he's given before and is now an active partner in making sure the interview turns out well. I typically preface sessions (after the first) by saying that I've reviewed the tape and we're doing great. I make my subject partners in the process.

8. THE INTERVIEWER INTERVIEWED

> Look, you're going to be the arbiter of what is important and what you think the particular salade Niçoise ingredients of this interview ought to be—it's going to have a little shtick, a little charm, a little of Marlon's eccentricities, we're going to lift the lid here and pull the hem of the gown up there, then we're gonna talk about Indians.

—MARLON BRANDO

After I finished interviewing James A. Michener for my book *Talking with Michener,* I asked if he would consider interviewing himself as the final chapter, to cover things on his mind that I might not have touched upon. He was reluctant, but then he read an interview that Isaac Bashevis Singer did with himself. When he later ran into Singer he asked him how that interview worked out. Singer answered, "Fabulously. I covered all the untouched spots. And I could be sure that my answers were reported correctly, because I was doing the reporting." Michener figured if Singer was comfortable doing it, he'd give it a shot.

This is my shot.

Whatever I might not have covered in this book so far, I hope to touch on here. I never knew when my *Newsday* editor called me in 1974 to ask me to interview "household names" that I'd still be doing it thirty years later, but I'm not complaining. It's been an educational life. I'm still learning, and I have more questions than I do answers.

Q: Can an interview really be called an art? What's next: *The Art of Window Washing? The Art of Penmanship?*

A: I think a case can be made, but it just depends on how cynical and elitist you want to be about it. After Truman Capote wrote *The Muses Are Heard,* about the American *Porgy and Bess* troupe that went to Russia, he challenged himself to see if he could turn something truly plebeian into art, and he chose a celebrity interview because it was, according to him, "the most banal thing in journalism." He wanted to do it in one day, and chose Marlon Brando as his subject. Brando—who, by the way, doesn't believe that movies are an art form, nor are actors or singers artists— was in Japan making *Sayonara,* and Capote went there for *The New Yorker,* spent an evening with him, and then spent a year working on it. "It had to be perfection," he said, "because my part was to take this banal thing and turn it into a work of art."

Joyce Carol Oates, in one of her introductions to someone else's book, speculated on the interview as an art form that might emerge as a predominant prose genre in the twenty-first century.

So, is the interview, when done right, more than good craftsmanship? Is there an art to it? I wouldn't put it in the class of high art, but I do think there's more than clever editing going on when it's in the hands of a writer and when it's not being cut to fit a certain space. I'll grant you that it's a stretch to call the genre an art form, but that's because there are so many mediocre interviews published today. If you weed out the bad and the boring and the space-fillers, there's some art there. Whether it might emerge as a predominant prose genre of this century only speaks to the dumbing down of what passes for our culture, perhaps.

Q: Maybe Oates was just pulling your chain when she wrote that. And why be so circumspect? She wrote that in her introduction to your first collection of interviews.

A: That was just modesty, not circumspection.

Q: Funny that you're making a claim toward modesty when the majority of the anecdotes in this book are about you.

A: No, they are not; they're about the people I've interviewed over the last thirty years. And what's wrong with that?

Q: What do you think of J. P. Donleavy's conclusion in his foreword to this book, that interviewers have become as or more famous than their subjects?

A: You've got to remember that Donleavy lives in Ireland, so he has probably been spared the parade of youth who have achieved greater fame than those in the past who have earned it. Certain TV interviewers like Barbara Walters or Larry King have achieved a measure of fame, but even they don't hold a candle to Britney Spears or that Paris Hilton girl or the vampire Michael Jackson, who keeps coming back from the dead to knock wars, assassina—tions, and presidential visits to Baghdad off the front pages. But Donleavy has a definite take on our times, and if he draws this conclusion, just keep in mind that he has always written with his tongue pressed firmly into his cheek.

Q: Wasn't it Brando who asked you how on earth you could spend a career interviewing other people, especially actors?

A: OK, look, here's the way I see it. My ambition was to be a novelist. I started writing nonfiction as a way of gathering experience—I'd jump from planes, study martial arts, practice Transcendental Meditation, learn archery, drive demolition derby cars, all to get a perspective and insight into aspects of our culture that I wouldn't normally know about. Then, in 1974, I moved to Los Angeles and was asked by *Newsday* to interview Mae West. Who knew that would become a life-altering experience? Not that she was so mind-blowing—she wasn't, just an old woman who had a ton of life experience behind her—but that led to other interviews, and after a few years of doing these three-thousand-word pieces I began to wonder what it might be like to really delve deeply into someone's psyche. I had glimpses with Lucille Ball, who told me she no longer wanted to live because most of her friends had died and her children weren't calling; with Warren Beatty, whose phone never stopped ringing; with Henry Moore, who compared himself favorably with Rembrandt and Michelangelo; with J. P. Donleavy, who happened to mention that director George Roy Hill was one of the prototypes for his Ginger Man, Sebastian Dangerfield. If I had more time, if I had more space, how much could I get someone to reveal? Once I started thinking this way, I looked for a publication that would allow me to find out, and in the mid-1970s, that was *Playboy*. So I focused on convincing the editors there that I was capable of doing a *Playboy* interview. And once I began doing those, I saw the difference between a two-hour, three-thousand-word interview with someone and a nine-month, fifty-thousand-word interview (as the one with Barbra Streisand turned out to be). And so I learned the "art" of the interview. I learned how to shape questions, how to go with the mood of the subject, and how to index and edit transcripts. But I still wasn't satisfied—I wondered about taking the form to the next, final, stage: a full-length book. Could one truly write a biography of someone as an interview? The subject I chose was Truman Capote, and every six months I would fly to New York and see him in Sagaponack, Long Island. But Capote died before we finished, and the book that resulted was, to me, not the book I had hoped for. It was playful, gossipy, at times malicious, often very funny, but my vision for it was much broader. Then I was asked by an English publisher if they could make a book out of my interview with Marlon Brando, so I agreed to that, reworking it, adding material that wasn't in *Playboy*, writing about my time with him on his island, and about what happened to him and his family afterward. But, again, it wasn't a full-fledged biography. My third interview book, with James A. Michener, was. At least, it was the kind of book I had envisioned doing. Michener allowed me to interview him over the seventeen years I knew him. We taped well over a hundred hours; I visited him in Florida, Maine, Texas, New York, and California. We had talks that went into the late hours of the night, and I was able to devote individual chapters to the various aspects of his life. The book was quietly published by the University of Mississippi Press in 1999. Michener had told me from the start that he may have been the wrong subject for such a project, since he wasn't as sexy as Brando or as outrageous as Capote. I think he was right, but at least I achieved my goal. And maybe, who knows, future generations might discover the book.

Q: Has all this been a pitch to draw people to your books or to make a case for an art that may or may not exist?

A: Is this your attempt at provocation? Are you expecting me to throw you out of my house?

Q: That would be a neat trick.

A: Let's not get sidetracked.

Q: The 1970s seemed to be the golden age of interviewing— subjects took interviews seriously, they got more coverage. Jimmy Carter said in an interview that he lusted in his heart and may have won over enough young voters to get elected president. Streisand called her *Playboy* interview "the bible." Pacino read and reread your interview with Brando and agreed to talk to you because of it. What happened to that time?

A: The interview became mainstream, other magazines began doing them, and then the publicists came along and began making demands to protect their clients. If a dozen publications wanted their clients, then the publicists could pick and choose. They could insist that the interviews be shorter, that certain tough questions not be asked. And then along came *InStyle* magazine, which promised cover puff pieces; and *Maxim*, which reduced stories to boxes and irreverence, and often irrelevance. And when these two magazines succeeded, others took notice. So those wonderful, long, in-depth interviews that appeared in *Playboy* in the seventies and eighties were cut by half in the nineties, and cut again for the new millennium. Add to that the Internet, and search engines, where you can type in any celebrity's name and get a website, or a quickie interview, and you begin to see that there's just too much out there, and it's broad, not deep.

Q: So is the interview as you've conducted it dead?

A: Not dead, just sick. Anemic. Compromised.

Q: And is there any hope, or is your so-called *Art of the Interview* a Dying Art of the Interview?

A: I can't answer that question. I believe there's a pendulum effect—it swings one way, where it went deep and insightful, and then it's gone the other way, where it's often shallow and insignificant. But pendulums go both ways. Eventually people are going to tire of the insipid blather that appears in *InStyle*. It's really an advertising question. The magazines that published the in-depth interviews have gotten thinner because their ads are down; if their ads pick up, there will be more editorial pages to print longer interviews, and that's when the pendulum will swing back. On the other hand, we may experience an era of special-interest magazines, Internet "chats," and TV "magazines" in which the total number of words spoken in any particular interview would barely fill four typed pages.

Q: What about those *Inside the Actors Studio* programs? Those *E! True Hollywood* shows? The A&E biographies? The two-hour prime-time interviews with Michael Jackson? The *Up Close* sports interviews on ESPN? Larry King's talk show on CNN? E's *Revealed?*

A: Yes, what about them?

Q: Aren't they in-depth enough for you?

A: No.

Q: Why not?

A: Because they are, for the most part, shows that have given in to the demands of the people they are interviewing. Many of them are shows about a person and so they are interviewing people who aren't about to bad-mouth the person whom the show is about. I know, I've appeared on some of them. I wasn't going to say what I actually knew about the person being profiled. Not on

TV. And those Actors Studio shows, come on, that's like Larry King's show, they aren't going to hit a nerve with the person who has willingly come to their studio to be praised and applauded. They can be entertaining, sure. I watch them. But they aren't truly revealing. They can't be. It's television. There's a camera crew there, there are lights, microphones, time-outs for tapes that have to be changed: it's a show. It's not like going off to an island to spend two weeks talking to someone one-on-one. It's just not.

Q: In Chapter 1 of this book you touch on some of the TV interviewers, but you seemed to shy away from giving your real opinion about most of them.

A: What do you want to know?

Q: Well, Larry King, for example. You just brought him up. He's from Bensonhurst, in Brooklyn, just like you. Why do you think he doesn't get his guests to reveal themselves?

A: He does, at times. But Larry King prides himself on never being prepared. It's such a strange thing to be proud of. He's lasted a long time and keeps getting big-name guests because he doesn't go for the jugular. He'd rather be kissed by Marlon Brando and go out singing a song then press the actor on his girth, his cynicism, or his failures as a father. King doesn't come across as someone who graduated with honors from any class, but rather a guy who won't put his job in jeopardy by taking risks or asking troubling questions. Listen to the people who call in to the Larry King show; most of them say hello to "Larry" before they ask a question of his guest. Viewers are familiar with King; they're comfortable with him. And to be a really good interviewer, there should be an edge to the person asking the questions.

Q: Have you ever been on his show?

A: No—when my Huston book came out I thought I had a shot, but was told that he doesn't like to talk to biographers of people who are still alive. John Huston was dead by then, but his children weren't. If Anjelica wanted to come on, he'd take her.

Q: So, sour grapes then?

A: You can call it that. I see it differently.

Q: OK, you were once on Charlie Rose's show for that book, what's your problem with him?

A: No problem, I'm glad he's doing what he does, because he brings timely guests on to discuss timely issues. Rose does his research, he can be passionate about subjects, but he often talks too much and doesn't let his guests respond to his first question—they sometimes wait until his third and fourth questions get asked in the same breath and then try to choose among the questions to answer. But considering that Rose is doing an hour show five nights a week, and that he often has three different guests each show, one has to tip one's hat to him: He's not about fluff, nor about getting someone to cry; he's looking for answers, tackling current events, and if he gets flustered trying to ask a question at times, it shows he's human. He's trying.

Q: Do you feel the same way about Ted Koppel?

A: Yes, Koppel is the John Updike of television. You can always count on him to be intelligent, prepared, and confident. Koppel has a calm, assured presence; he's comfortable on camera, and he has a droll sense of humor that rarely shows on *Nightline* but is always on display when he's a guest on Leno or Letterman.

Q: Speaking of which, which of those two annoys you more?

A: The most annoying "interviewer" on TV is probably Jay Leno, because of the way he prefaces each and every question with "Let me ask you this question." I'm sure he doesn't even know he's doing it. But Leno isn't a journalist, he's a comedian, as is David Letterman, and their jobs are to entertain, to create witty banter. There's really no spontaneity going on with those "conversations." Their guests are there to promote their latest projects; Leno and Letterman are there to keep the audience awake so that they may buy some of the products pitched during the commercials.

Q: Still, you can't dismiss those guys; they do occasionally get to show a different side of a celebrity.

A: You mean like when Drew Barrymore stood on Letterman's desk and bared her breasts? Sure, but we didn't get to see them—he did! Of course, every once in a while Leno or Letterman hit it out of the park, as Leno did with Hugh Grant after Grant got caught with his hand up some cookie's jar in Hollywood. "What the hell were you thinking?" Leno asked, and people laughed, Grant looked uncomfortably humble, and we all nodded: That's right, what was he thinking? Or when Letterman started taking abuse from Madonna; no matter what he tried to say to her, she snapped at him, and it made for great television, it worked.

Q: What about Baba Wawa, as Gilda Radner used to portray Ms. Walters? She often makes great television.

A: If kissing Julianne Moore on the lips is great TV for you. Me, I prefer Madonna and Britney Spears. Barbara Walters has become a caricature of herself. She asks Pacino to dance the tango with her on camera and seems more enthralled when he dips her than in getting any really solid answers out of him. She's better with politicians than she is with movie stars. At least when she's talking to a queen or female prime minister she's not asking them to kiss her on the lips. And she's not doing the tango with Colin Powell or Yasir Arafat.

Q: She did a good job with her jailhouse interview with Robert Blake, though. When Blake denied killing his wife and started to scream at her for being unfeeling and unkind, you could see Walters's heart start to break, that she saw what we all saw— this gaunt man with a foot in the grave, screaming his innocence to an audience who could only look at him with pity, aware that he did not have much of a chance of ever being acquitted.

A: Yeah, that's true. But that's your observation, not a question. You're going out of character here.

Q: OK, let's bring this back to your own expertise and not go where you're on more shaky ground.

A: I beg your pardon.

Q: A lot of the anecdotes and examples in this book deal with celebrities, but most people who might be curious about interviewing won't be interviewing celebrities. Why didn't you devote a chapter to how to talk to farmers, pharmacists, salesmen, teachers, and others who might make interesting stories for local newspapers and such?

A: Because there's no difference: You prepare for a papermaker or a geologist or a restaurateur the same as you do a movie star. It really doesn't matter who you interview, the process is the same: You do all the research you can, you look for areas of interest, you aim for originality, you write down questions or topics, you try to keep your questions concise and to the point, and you listen. And always remember that you're in charge. If you lead, your subject will follow.

Q: What's the difference between a conversation and an interview?

A: A conversation is something people do when they open their mouths and talk to each other. An interview is a conversation that is edited, structured, put together like a jigsaw puzzle, and focused more on one person than the other. Andy Warhol's *Interview* magazine is ironic, because what he published were mostly conversations. . . . you sat in on a lunch and heard what they ordered, you listened in on petty gossip. Capote turned such scenes into art when he was writing *Answered Prayers,* but in the raw, they're mostly boring, as most conversations tend to be.

Interviews, hopefully, are conversations with the boring parts edited out. An interview is not a true dialogue, but a prompted monologue. Someone is asking someone else questions and eliciting answers.

Q: Like what we're doing here?

A: Exactly.

Q: Let me ask you this: in Chapter 6 of this book you interviewed eight editors—did anything they say surprise you?

A: Yes, what Bill Newcott of *AARP The Magazine* said about editing the copy he's given. He said he considers the writer's version to be raw material. He feels the writer's job is to get the subject to talk, and his job is to shape those words into a compelling read. That surprised me, because what I've tried to show in this book is that an interview is a highly polished piece of work. I can understand raw transcripts being looked at as raw material, because that's what they are. But a writer should never give an editor the transcripts. Newcott, obviously, has a different take, and though I disagree with him, he's the feature editor of that magazine and that's how he works. My stomach got a little twisted when he said, "Certainly, the writer has a major voice in the final draft, but by that time it often bears little resemblance to the original version."

Q: Have you had that experience with him?

A: No, I haven't done anything for that magazine in a long time.

Q: Is Newcott the only editor you're going to take issue with?

A: Janice Min talks about interviews as if there are many in *US,* but the format of the magazine hardly has any in-depth pieces. The magazine has changed considerably—just as *Movieline* has. What can I say? We're going through tough times for writers. Editors seem convinced that people don't want to read magazines, that they want to look at them instead; they are more eye candy than food for the brain. *US* looks like it's taken the short pieces usually reserved for the front of the book and turned that into the magazine. And *Movieline* has added *Hollywood Life* to its name, which looks more like *InStyle* than the razor-edged magazine it once was. If this is what the public wants, then so be it. I just hope the *Atlantic, Harper's,* and *The New Yorker* don't follow suit.

Q: Moving on, I'm not going to ask you who were your favorite subjects—

A: Thank you.

Q: Many people get asked the same questions over and over. How do you make an interview seem unique?

A: Precisely because I'm aware of the repetition of questions. What I strive to do is go a little further, dig a bit deeper. And the only way to do that is to know what's been asked before, so you have to do your research. The goal is always to present fresh material.

Q: What type of environment should you set?

A: That's not always up to me. If I'm meeting the person at their home or a restaurant, the environment is already there. If the person is coming to my house—and I've done quite a few interviews in my living room or office—then I can affect the environment. I can make sure my dog's been walked, so she doesn't bother us. I can have fruits and vegetables cut up, water in the kettle ready to be boiled. I can make sure my answering machine is on to cut off any calls. And if my wife is in a good mood, she might prepare some food, which always warms people up.

Q: Is there any way to interview someone you don't know much about?

A: Sure, as long as you have a curious nature and are up to date with current events. If you need help, there are dozens of books out there that list questions you can ask—you can check those out, see what questions stir your interest, make a list. Or you can just think about what's going on in the world—if you look at a newspaper, there are sections about your hometown, about the country, the world, about books, sports, obituaries. Surely you can come up with questions to ask someone to find out what they are interested in.

Q: How do you overcome the jitters before an interview?

A: I find that the more prepared I am the calmer I feel. I'm most nervous when I'm least prepared . . . and I don't like that feeling, so I always try to be prepared. Nonetheless, jitters are healthy, it shows you care, draw from it; let your adrenaline put intensity behind your questions; let your subject know you want to do a good job. If you're too jittery, then try to meditate before you ring the doorbell. Take some deep breaths. And keep in mind that the person you're about to see is probably feeling the same way you are.

Q: What was your first published interview, who was it with, and what do you remember asking?

A: That would have been with the West African sculptor Vincent Kofi, which I did for *African Arts* magazine back in 1970. He was a fascinating artist who had trained in England with Constantin Brancusi, and he gave me one of the best answers to my question: What is the truth in art? "Truth," he said, "is like the color turquoise. Under natural light, it's one color, under artificial light, another." We all have our own truths, and it's based on how we see things. My first celebrity interview was the one I mentioned with Mae West. She told me the secret to her longevity and good health was that she had taken an enema twice a day since the early thirties, when she had to wear a corset onstage and didn't have enough time to take it off to go to the bathroom between acts.

Q: How do you interview someone famous without being intimidated by their celebrity?

A: That takes practice. I don't know what it is about celebrities, but people do go gaga when they see one. Just remember that celebrities are often as nervous as you are about being inter—viewed. They don't want to be exposed, to give up their mystique. And believe it or not, there are very few happy celebrities. If you're in a good relationship and have friends you often laugh with, they probably envy you.

Q: When Diane Keaton came to your class, she said that she wouldn't talk about her relationships with Woody Allen, Warren Beatty, or Al Pacino. Is it OK to let a subject limit the interview so severely?

A: It's not a matter of it being OK or not OK—if someone sets a parameter you either accept it or challenge it. If Diane didn't want to talk about past relationships, what choice was there, other than to ask her why she felt that way? And with someone as multitalented as she is, you shouldn't feel limited because she didn't want to talk about Woody, Warren, or Al—she's a director, an actor, a fashion trendsetter, a mother, a dog lover, a writer, a photographer, a collector; she's published books dealing with advertising, salesmen, clowns . . . there's plenty to talk with her about besides failed relationships.

Q: In your class you read a passage written by Norman Mailer about Muhammad Ali concerning ego. Some students felt that Mailer was writing more about himself than about Ali. As a reporter∕biographer how do you keep your own personality from clouding that of your subject? Is transparency always desirable?

A: If you're Norman Mailer, you've learned how to make yourself as interesting as your subject. I like to read some of Mailer's work aloud because a lot of students aren't as familiar with him as they should be. Mailer may insert himself into his work, especially his essays, but he writes with a novelist's eye, he's perceptive, his metaphors are often dazzling. It takes guts to put yourself into a story about Ali or Madonna and I wouldn't advise it, but Mailer can get away with it. In general, yes, transparency is desirable—the journalist shouldn't intrude in the story. But there are times when your personality can make the piece more personal and enjoyable, and in those cases, jump in!

Q: Does talking about yourself, even if you're not going to use what you say in the final copy, make the interviewing process smoother?

A: Only if you have interesting things to say. Some people love to hear stories; others prefer the sound of their own voice. It's not hard to figure that out once you get going. If the person you're interviewing gets a blank, glazed look when you start talking about yourself, stop your story and get back to why you're there.

Q: Do you ever make something up about yourself to get an interviewee talking on a certain subject? For example, when interviewing Sharon Stone you said, "I always thought if I got incurably sick I would drop acid."

A: I didn't make that up, I meant it. I never tried acid but I know a lot of people who have. I've always been afraid what it might do to my brain. But if I knew I was going to meet my maker and all I had left was watching TV, waiting to exhale, hell, introduce me to Lucy in the Sky with Diamonds. But that doesn't really answer your question: which is, have I ever lied to get someone talking? Probably. I've been married a long time, but I've been known to bring up sexual dalliances in my past that I might make sound as if they happened just the other day, if I'm trying to get my subject to share some intimate stories about his or her life.

Q: Do you laugh at a subject's attempts at humor even if you don't think it's funny?

A: It's hard to fake laughter, but I try. Why offend someone by not laughing at his joke?

Q: Since your interviews cover such a wide range of topics, do you ever have to pretend you know more about something than you really do?

A: All the time. But when I'm with someone who might call me on it, as I felt Marlon Brando would do, I am careful not to fake it.

Q: What is the best technique to draw out a subject who is unwilling to speak about himself?

A: There is no best technique. Interviewing is the art of capturing and shaping smoke; it's holding up a mirror and hoping you'll get a true image and not discover you're talking to a vampire who shows no reflection. Sometimes I find myself talking about other people, waiting for the subject to interject—you know, "Hey, what about me pal?" Other times I just tell the truth: If the subject is being reluctant, I say that. It's like being the clown with the electric prod, touching the rump of people passing, hoping to create a stir. Truman Capote brought a bottle of vodka when he went to interview Marlon Brando in Japan. They shared the bottle, and Capote told him about his rotten childhood. Brando reciprocated with stories of his childhood, and Capote wrote a memorable interview.

Q: How would you rectify a slow, boring interview that is not going anywhere?

A: By cutting it short. Saying, "Thank you for your time, but I don't think this is going anywhere." Hopefully the person will say, "Well, where did you want it to go?" And then tell him.

Q: When you interview someone you don't like, can you show it?

A: I wouldn't, but then, I like my teeth.

Q: How can you get someone to open up after you screw up and close them up?

A: That happened to me with Bob Knight. He literally wanted to throw me out of his car. What I had to do was apologize for pissing him off and try to restart. You have to be prepared to sit in silence for a while . . . and that can be agonizing. Brando thinks the best interviews happen in silence. I wouldn't know.

Q: How do you deal with someone who is bullshitting you?

A: If you recognize the bullshit, call the person on it.

Q: Should you interrupt to shut them up?

A: Depends on your time. If you have a set period of time, you absolutely must be prepared to interrupt. If you have unlimited time, let them talk, eventually you'll get what you need.

Q: How does an interviewer go about establishing intimacy and trust?

A: By demonstrating that you can be trusted. Intimacy is established by the nature of your questions.

Q: How do you adapt to all the different personalities, or is your approach the same every time?

A: No, my approach is never the same because people are different. An interviewer is a chameleon. If you can't adapt, do something that brings interviewers to you.

Q: Why do you often focus on bests, worsts, and favorites?

A: My brother-in-law accuses me of this. I don't focus on it, but I do find that people are often interested in someone's favorite movie, book, CD, video, and so on. If you like the person you're reading about, you're interested in what they like . . . and you'll probably check out what they recommend.

Q: How do you know when to draw the line? How far can you push?

A: You try not to draw lines, just go as deep as your subject will allow you to dig.

Q: If there is a certain energy or connection during the interview, how do you transfer this to print?

A: Study magazines that publish interviews. Read collections of interviews, focus on how they move from topic to topic, how they change from light to dark and back again. Read plays—Williams, O'Neill, Shakespeare, Albee, Miller. Study drama. See the way these writers get their characters to talk and keep you interested as a reader. There are dynamics between people that occur on the page in all of literature; they can happen in real life as well, and especially in interviews.

Q: How much can you change your question when you're writing the piece?

A: As long as you're not taking things out of context, you can change your questions for clarity, to make the transition smoother, or because the answer you're using had no original question attached to it.

Q: How much can you change a subject's response when you're editing?

A: This is much trickier. You can't put words in your subject's mouth. You can take something said on one day and something said on another day and combine them if it makes more sense.

Q: Are there questions that you always open with, close with, ask in general?

A: No, that would get boring. You want to keep these things fresh, you want to challenge yourself each time out to do something different.

Q: Do you always have an angle before you write your stories?

A: I try not to, but a lot of people I talk to complain that many journalists come with an agenda. If that is the case, then the subject will often end up feeling cheated and even duped. Of course, if your subject has just gotten out of jail, as Christian Slater had when I saw him, then you have to talk about what happened to him that landed him there, but that's not an angle. If you're out to show that actors often fuck up and use him as an example and don't give him a chance to present his side of things, that's an angle.

Q: How often does that angle change after the interview?

A: If you're open-minded and fair, and you should be, then of course it can change during the course of your conversation. However, if your editor has given you a specific agenda to match a theme for his issue, that can be a problem.

Q: Transcribing tapes is a bitch—do you have a better way?

A: There is no better way, unfortunately. When I began I transcribed all my interviews, and it took hours and hours. When I work for *Playboy*, they cover transcription expenses—for years I'd give the tapes out and get back huge manuscripts that I had to wade through, highlight, and reduce. I hate to admit this but I've stopped using transcribers and have returned to doing it myself, because even though it takes forever to do, I edit as I go along, so that when I finish with the transcription I pretty much have my first edited draft.

Q: What happens when your subject asks to see the transcription? Or your final draft before you submit it to your editor?

A: I say no.

Q: Because . . . ?

A: Because it will turn into a nightmare if you do that. Trust me on this. I went through it with Streisand. Streisand went around me and got to my editor. She didn't make any major changes, though she managed to add her own ending—but dealing with it is just too great a hassle.

Q: Is there a conflict in becoming friends with the people you interview?

A: Absolutely. And you have to be up front with your editors about that. It doesn't happen often, but once in a while you will click with someone, and then you will find yourself wondering what you can or cannot write about. It's agony.

Q: When writing a biography like *The Hustons,* how do you know what to leave in and what to cut out?

A: I was criticized in a *New York Times* review for leaving nothing out in that book, which wasn't true. I wrote twenty-two hundred pages in manuscript and had to reduce it by eight hundred pages before it was published. I tend to write long, to make sure I've covered all bases, quoted everyone involved, and then I put it away and go back to it with, hopefully, a fresh and critical eye. You begin to sense what quotes are important and what aren't. Editing is tough. They say that there is no such thing as writing, it's all rewriting. The more people you interview, the more dialogue you work with, the more you develop an ear for these things. If you have a tin ear, you'll find that out when your editor starts marking up your copy.

Q: Have you interviewed everybody you wanted to?

A: No, that would mean there were no more interesting people left on the planet. As long as there are people writing books, making movies, making breakthrough medical and scientific discoveries, leading countries, breaking athletic records, then one has something to look forward to as an interviewer.

Q: Who do you regret not having talked to?

A: I regret not doing dictators like former Uganda president Idi Amin and Iraq's Saddam Hussein. I would have liked to interview artists like Picasso, Matisse, Andy Warhol. Writers like Philip Roth, John Updike, Toni Morrison, Don DeLillo, and Tom Wolfe. I'd like to interview the American president, the English prime minister, the Israeli head of state. I wouldn't mind going back to talk to Marlon Brando.

Q: Back to Brando? He's an old man now, why would you want to return to someone like him?

A: Because Brando has a particular take on things that borders on brilliance and paranoia. I like talking to accomplished people in their eighties or nineties because they have a different perspective than they did when they were younger. That's why I enjoyed going to see Henry Moore, Henry Fonda, John Huston, James Michener, and the artist Jan de Swart. They gained a certain wisdom with age. Editors rarely call me to interview octogenarians; they prefer hearing what the current hot generation has to say. That's just the way it is. But do you have any doubt that an interview with Brando today would be far more interesting to read than one with Keanu Reeves or Brendan Fraser?

Q: Gee, I don't know . . . Reeves has those three *Matrix* movies. He is "The One."

A: You know something, you're beginning to bore me. I think we can end this now.

Q: But I've got so many more questions to ask you.

A: Save it for another time.

Q: What other time? This is the end of the book.

A: Fine, you want the last word, you've got it.

Q: What if I say, "YOU OWE ME MONEY!"

A: Like hell I do.

DREW BARRYMORE QUESTIONS

In Chapter 2 I covered how I prepared to interview Drew Barrymore, reading articles about her in magazines and on the Internet, hearing what others had to say about her, seeing her films. I thought it might be appropriate here, in an appendix, to show you the questions I wrote before I saw her. I tried to imagine an order to our conversation, starting with some small talk about the Beatles, then touching on her current projects, and then, once we've warmed up, her personal life. After we began talking in her trailer on the Sony lot in Culver City, where she was producing and shooting the sequel to *Charlie's Angels,* the questions weren't asked in the order they appear here—they never are. But it's always best to have questions like these ready to go, and then when the interview begins, you can go with what feels right, and have the questions as a backup.

THE BEATLES

1. A friend heard you on the radio talking about the Beatles and he told me just from what you said, you gained a lot of points in his mind. What is it about the Beatles?

2. Why has their song "Things We Said Today" resonated with you?

RECENT FILMS (2003)

Confessions of a Dangerous Mind

3. Did you spend any time with Chuck Barris?

4. What's your take on him?

5. Did you ask him whether he really killed anyone?

6. What do you think?

7. Do you remember *The Gong Show?*

8. If you were to go on a talent show like that one, what act would you bring?

9. How was George Clooney as a director?

10. What does an actor bring to directing?

11. What do you think of Sam Rockwell's performance?

12. Were you surprised that Julia Roberts agreed to play a small role?

13. Steven Soderbergh was the executive producer, was he around much? Did you have any dealings with him?

Duplex

14. So what happens when you and Ben Stiller want a house that an old woman still lives in?

15. How funny is Ben Stiller?

16. Is he as amazing as Adam Sandler, whom you've called the most amazing person in the world?

17. What's so amazing about these people?

18. Are you prone to hyperbole when you get excited about something?

19. Are you producing *Duplex?*

20. Was it a stretch at all for you?

UPCOMING FILMS

21. Where are you with *Barbarella?*

22. Jane Fonda, who appeared in the original, gave you her blessing. Has a friendship evolved?

23. You also got to know Anjelica Huston when you worked together in *EverAfter.* When you, Fonda, or Huston meet, is the talk about families?

24. Other Upcoming Films: *So Love Returns. A Confederacy of Dunces. Fifty First Dates.*

PRODUCING

25. You got into producing as a way of surviving this business, didn't you?

26. Did you ever imagine you'd be as successful as you are?

27. What have you learned from producing that you didn't know from acting?

28. What do you look for in a script?

29. Are you looking first for stories you can be in, or are you just as happy to put the pieces together and remain off screen?

30. Were you satisfied with the way *Donnie Darko* was received?

31. What have you learned about producing from Harvey Weinstein, whom you've called your mentor?

32. Have you found a project you'd like to direct yet?

33. When your partner Nan wrote you a letter, it made you cry. Why?

FAMILY

34. You have an older half brother and two half sisters: how well do you know them?

35. John is 21 years older, Blyth is 13 years older, not sure about Jessica: but do they ever try and get in touch with you?

36. What's your relationship like now with your mother?

37. Is she someone you feel you can call for advice? Or to trade stories?

38. Can she count on you when she gets in trouble, like when she was arrested in NY for possessing a handgun?

39. You don't blame your mother for robbing you of your childhood, do you?

40. Have you gotten over being embarrassed by her as well?

41. You said in *Marie Claire* that when you were in school, someone knocked you to the ground and you wound up needing stitches. Were you also scarred?

42. And were you surprised when your mother came to your defense?

43. Is she still planning on writing a book about you and her?

44. After the mental institution you lived with David Crosby and his wife Jane for a year. How did that come about?

45. You were around 15 then, what did they bring to your life?

46. Then, a year later you moved in with film director Tamra Davis and her husband. How long did you stay there?

47. Were you feeling like Little Girl Lost, moving from family to family, hoping to find your place in the world?

48. Dolly Parton told me she learned about sex in the barn with her older cousins. Where did you learn about it?

49. Why do you believe that you're the reincarnation of your grandfather?

50. You've said that you're crazy because of him. Why do you think that?

51. You've been very open about your disappointment with your father, calling him crazy, a genius and a nomad from hell. How crazy?

52. And what kind of genius?

53. Was Steven Spielberg the dad you never had?

54. Colin Farrell called Spielberg "the coolest nerd you'll ever meet." Fair description?

55. Spielberg recalled a time when you were six telling him you had a better way of doing a scene in *E.T.* Do you remember that?

56. Was the 20th anniversary re-release of *E.T.* emotional for you?

57. The story of your time in a mental institution has been told, but I just wanted to ask you about the comment you made that the experience changed your life. How?

58. When you worked at Music Plus you often recommended videos to customers: what are your top ten favorite videos, ones that you can watch over and over?

PAST (AND FUTURE) FILMS

Charlie's Angels

59. It's been noted that you're the first actress-producer since the '70s to have made a ton of money by starring in and shaping movies to your own tastes. How does that make you feel?

60. The first one had 17 writers on it and still had problems: was it a case of too many cooks in the kitchen?

61. You fought to get McG his first feature: with such a big-budget film, how did you have such confidence in someone who had only directed music videos before?

62. Was it also your decision that the Angels should not carry guns?

63. Will there be Angels shooting in the next one?

64. The disparity between contracts for the first one was glaring: you got $8 million, Cameron Diaz got $12 million-or-10% of the gross, and Lucy Liu got $1 million. Is there still a wide gap in pay between the three of you for the sequel?

65. How much fun is it playing a badass?

66. How much training was involved learning how to kick ass?

67. Was your introduction to kung fu through your father?

68. Were you exaggerating at all when you told the story of how he stuck your hand into the flame of a candle to demonstrate pain?

69. Did you, Lucy, and Cameron get along as well the second time around?

70. Are the three of you in better shape emotionally and physically now than you were when you were making the first one?

71. What are some of the dirty jokes you tell each other?

72. Did you really grab Lucy's boob in front of Prince Charles?

Riding in Cars with Boys

73. Some felt you deserved a nomination for your performance—was it the most draining thing you've done to date?

74. Why do you feel it's your destiny not to win any awards?

75. You've said that you opened up a serious box inside yourself to play Beverly D'Onofrio. How serious was it, and how deep did you dig?

Poison Ivy

76. How eerie was it when you read this script and saw that the girl in it had a tattoo on her leg of a cross with rose vines?

77. Did you think that the writer knew of your tattoo and wrote it in?

78. How many tattoos do you have, and what do they each mean to you?

ACTORS

79. You've said that that the most profound moment of your life was telling your mother you wanted to be an actress when you were three. Were you aware of your family's history at that age?

80. Who are the actors you most enjoy watching?

81. You, Jodie Foster, and Kurt Russell managed to bridge the gap between child and adult actors. Do you know them? Do you talk about such things?

82. *Bad Girls* director Jonathan Kaplan said that you reminded him of Jodie Foster. In *Talk* magazine they wrote that you were the anti-Jodie. Different people, different perceptions. Who knows you better?

83. What do you think of Reese Witherspoon? Claire Danes? Gwyneth Paltrow? Christina Ricci? Natalie Portman? Halle Berry?

84. What's your take on what happened with Winona Ryder?

85. Does she need rehab more than punishment?

86. Why are so many actors troubled—Robert Downey Jr., Ryder, Slater, Chris Farley, Belushi, etc. . . . .

RELATIONSHIPS

87. By my researched count, you've had 10 men in your life: would that be accurate?

88. On: James Walters, Phedon Papamichael, Jeremy Thomas, Val Kilmer, Eric Erlandson, Luke Wilson, Jeremy Davis, Tom Green, Alec Pure, Joel Shearer.

89. Your first marriage to Jeremy Thomas: in retrospect, was it a mistake?

90. Do you still feel you are secluded in your world, that you don't get out enough to meet guys outside show business?

91. Why are so many Hollywood relationships doomed?

92. Why don't you think you're capable of being loved?

93. What do you look for in a man?

94. You thought you found it all in Tom: "He's funny, extremely understanding, loves to go on adventures, he's kind and a good communicator and inspires me to do good things in life and be a good person." What was missing?

95. Your second marriage was played out in public: you and Tom seemed so in love and in-your-face, so carefree and wild. Can you talk about what went wrong?

96. How hard was it for you when you had to be on the set of *Charlie's Angels* when Tom went in for his operation?

97. On *The Tonight Show* you admitted to being controlling at times in the marriage. Was that a problem for Tom?

98. In *Marie Claire* you said that your attraction to "bad boys" was that they validated the fact that you were a bad girl—is that accurate?

99. You also said that what would eventually drive them away is that you'd get in their faces all the time—did that make your bad boys claustrophobic?

100. Did you try to change Tom?

101. Do you have a problem trying to change people?

102. Tom believed in permanence, you didn't. Did your breakup just reconfirm that nothing lasts?

103. How did you decide who got what when you split up?

104. Where are you in your head now about having children?

SELF-ASSESSMENT

105. How secure are you today? ["I've been through way too much fucking shit to be insecure."]

106. What are your limitations?

107. Do you still feel crazy inside your head?

108. You told YM that you treat everyone "with a lack of judgment." Why is your judgment so poor?

109. Your godmother is Anna Strasberg, a proponent of method acting, yet you are not a method actor—have you ever studied the Method?

110. Do you feel it's necessary to bring a lot of yourself to each part you play?

111. You've spoken about making promises you couldn't keep—what kind of promises? And do you feel guilty about broken promises?

112. Has your life changed in any way since 9/11?

FIRE

113. You told *Movieline* that the recent fire that destroyed your house happened for a spiritual reason. Have you figured out what that reason was?

114. You were hurt by the *Saturday Night Live* send-up of that fire, weren't you?

FEMINISM

115. In an *LA Times* book review for the book *Women Who Run the Show*, Lynda Obst wrote about the changes in the way young women view feminism: "I first noticed the sea change when I read Drew Barrymore—a woman I know to be smart and ambitious—deny with horror that she was a feminist. The word suddenly had

an icky old-fashioned quality that she took for granted. It stunned me." Were you aware that you've stunned producers like Obst?

116. What does feminism mean to you? [Nicole Kidman an avowed feminist]

117. It's been said that yours is a post-feminist sensibility. What does that mean?

118–20. Obst called it a backlash, which is "anti-mentor, anti-superwoman, pro-girly girl. It is—as we know by watching Christina Aguilera—OK to be a slut. It is not OK to break into a sweat out of the gym."

—Are you anti-mentor, anti-superwoman, pro-girly girl?

—Is it okay to be a slut?

—Do you ever break into a sweat outside of the gym?

121. Why do you try to make your breasts look smaller?

122. Do you still have your first gray hair? Where do you keep it?

123. What other things do you save?

124. How many years have you been in therapy, and what have you gotten from it?

BOOKS

125. What's on your night table?

126. How many books do you read at one time?

127. How important was the book *Conversations with God* to you?

128. Did you ever meet one of your favorites, Charles Bukowski?

129. What poems of T. S. Eliot can you recite?

130. Are you familiar with *Four Quartets?*

COMEDY

131. Is your drug of choice still comedy?

132. Who gets you high? [Jim Carrey, Steve Martin, John Hughes, Peter Sellers]

133. Are there any shows on TV that you won't miss?

MISC

134. Gary Busey once called you "The Badger." How'd he come up with that, and how affectionate a nickname is it? [short, fast, close to ground]

135. How often do you go to the Silent Movie Theatre on Fairfax?

136. Who are your favorite silent film stars?

137. What is this thing you have for David Letterman?

138. Does he know you swore that you would one day marry him?

139. How can you top what you did on some future show of his?

140. Did you ever think that flashing your breasts would be one of the things you would forever be remembered for?

141. Are you still afraid of hygiene and food?

142. Have you given up being a vegetarian?

143. Did you really once spit into someone's coffee when you worked as a waitress?

144. What have you learned about sending food back when eating out?

145. Why don't you like chocolate?

146. Why have you been afraid of the ocean?

147. To prepare for *Charlie's Angels* you sought life-changing experiences: skydiving, scuba diving, diving off cliffs & waterfalls: what's been the most liberating adventure you've had?

148. What are you still afraid to try?

149. What has yoga taught you?

150. How many new friends have you made in the last few years?

151. Are you happy these days?

152. With the new year coming, will you make any resolutions?

153. Do you still have a hard time believing you will have a future?

154. How many dogs do you have?

155. What have your dogs taught you?

156. Where are your favorite places to shop in LA and NY?

157. Who are you living with now?

158. What is the sexiest profession for a man? (musician: Jagger, Plant, Bowie—)

ON THE ROAD WITH THE ANGRIEST MAN IN AMERICA

"Why are you writing about Bobby Knight again? He tried to kill you," my wife wondered as I prepared for the sixteenth sports radio talk show to call since my interview with the former Indiana coach appeared in the March 2001 *Playboy*.

"He didn't try to kill me," I said. "I was on assignment."

"He attacked you."

"True. He was just being Bob Knight."

"You were pretty upset when you called me about it. I'll never forget that call."

"I was just relieved I'd survived the car ride. I had to talk to someone and at two in the morning, who else would listen to me?"

"Who told you to drive with him for twelve hours? That was pretty crazy."

"He invited me."

"And then he tried to throw you out of the car, not once but twice!"

"Threatened. Yeah, that was pretty crazy."

"So how come you keep thinking about him? He's a jerk!"

Excuse my wife. She's not media savvy. She didn't see the story Bill Conlin of the *Philadelphia Daily News* wrote in a funny column that began, "You are Lawrence Grobel and you are certifiably insane." My insanity, according to Conlin, was that I agreed to go from Bloomington, Indiana, to Akron, Ohio, and back in a car with "America's angriest man." What was I thinking?

He and my wife were not the only ones to question my sanity. For a full month after that interview appeared, my phone didn't stop ringing with requests from sports talk radio producers and hosts to describe in graphic detail what has now been dubbed "the ride from hell." They called from Seattle, Portland, Chicago, St. Louis, and Jacksonville, Florida; from Atlanta, Cleveland, Los Angeles, Indianapolis, and Fargo, North Dakota. And they all asked the same two things: What happened in the car that so ticked Knight off, and should Knight be allowed to coach again?

The ride I could, of course, describe—I was there. Knight's move to Texas to coach at Texas Tech was testament to Leo Durocher's famous quip about nice guys finishing last. Knight is no nice guy, though Duke's coach Mike Krzyzewski said Knight's return was "great for the game." (On February 5, 2003, Tech beat Nebraska, 74–49, giving Knight his eight hundredth career win, only the fourth Division I men's coach to reach that mark. Knight spoke to the crowd after the game and when he was finished his team circled around and hugged him as the hometown fans chanted his name.)

I WENT TO SEE Knight less than two months after the president of the University of Indiana fired him for violating the "zero-tolerance" policy they had imposed on him. Knight had become something of an embarrassment to the university over the years as his temper kept drawing attention to him and not the athletic programs. During the twenty-nine years he served as coach of the basketball team he made national news for throwing a chair across the gym floor in a game, for taking his team off the floor for the second half of a game against the Russians, for firing a starter's pistol at a reporter, for slam dunking a drunken fan into a garbage can, for headbutting his own son during a game, for holding up used toilet paper in the locker room to express his feelings about how his players were performing, for putting his hand around the neck of a player during practice, for being, in a word, a bully. That was the dark side. There was also a good Knight—who won more basketball games than any other coach except one in Division I NCAA basketball, who made sure the majority of his players graduated, who raised millions of dollars for the university, who brought in funds to battle cancer, who stood by his players years after they stopped playing. Knight is definitely a complicated man. But when the university could take no more of Darth Knight, they fired him. And suddenly, the man who was considered more powerful than the governor of Indiana was without a job, without a power base, without a reason to get up in the morning. It took a few weeks for this reality to set in. And that's when I arrived.

I flew to Indianapolis, rented a car, drove to Bloomington, and then headed to Knight's home in the suburbs. We spent three hours talking and eating before he invited me to go to Akron the next morning to see his son work a practice as an assistant coach at the university. He also invited his friend, Don Donoher, former University of Dayton basketball coach and a scout for the Cleveland Cavaliers. Donoher would meet us in Dayton. So the first three hours I was alone with Knight as he ignored the speed limit on the highway to Ohio (and talked his way out of a speeding ticket after being pulled over by an Indiana highway patrol officer who recognized him and treated him like an exiled king). Once we got to the topic of the day—his being fired—he couldn't contain himself. I asked about the incident that set it off—how a nineteen-year-old freshman named Kent Harvey addressed him by his last name and how Knight castigated the young man for not being more respectful. It wasn't how one would think his career at Indiana would come to an end, but that's what happened, and Knight blamed the student's stepfather for putting him up to it. The stepfather had it in for Knight, he was convinced. And when I brought it up, Knight went bonkers on me. He punched the steering column so hard I thought we had hit a deer. The steady stream of curses that spewed from his mouth was so ferociously awesome that I was left speechless. His rage was like the crack of a rifle— quick, immediate, forceful, terrifying. I had never seen anything like it. He missed the exit where Donoher was waiting and drove thirty miles up the highway before he calmed down enough to turn around. And that was just the beginning.

He went nuts a second time on the ride back, this time late in the evening, with Donoher driving and Knight in the front passenger seat and me in the back. That time he was complaining how other coaches did similar things as he had but their actions weren't always shown on TV the way his throwing that chair was. I said to him, "Why you, Coach?" And that set him off again. He threw my tape recorder into the backseat and started cursing. Then he asked me for both my recorders. When I refused to give them up, he turned around on his knees, leaned over, grabbed me by my wrists, and tried to wrestle away my bag with the tape recorders inside. "Stop the car, Don!" he shouted. "He's getting out and I'm taking those tapes!" But Donoher didn't stop the car, and I wouldn't release my grip on my bag. Eventually, like an exhausted boxer, he slumped back into his seat and stewed. When we got to Dayton, Donoher left and I was stuck with Knight. We had three hours of driving ahead of us and I wondered if I'd make it back with all my teeth in order.

Somehow I managed to calm him down. I asked him to shake my hand. I told him I wasn't out to get him, I was just there to give him a chance to respond to all the allegations against him. And he began to pour his heart out. I felt sympathy for the guy. He had fallen from a pretty high place in American sports culture; he was a legitimate tragic figure. And when we got back to my hotel, I tried to put up a front, to shake hands good-bye, to walk out without letting him see that my knees were wobbly and my heart was pounding. I knew just one thing: I wanted to get out of Indiana before he came back to ask for those tapes.

One thing I learned from all the radio sports shows that called me was that there truly was a feeding frenzy concerning Knight. I could understand his anger at the media. They smelled his temper a mile away and came in droves to make sure the country knew about it. He couldn't cut himself a break. And because of that, he needed to learn how to control the contempt he felt for so many in the media he believed were out to get him. He needed to humble himself, or open himself up to the idea of therapy. He needed to understand that his brain wasn't working for him all the time, that there was some place inside his head that needed calming, and that there was medication that could help. He needed to learn the ways of a Zen monk rather than a samurai warrior. But Knight is a man set in his ways and he's been used to getting his way most of his life.

I've chosen to feature the full Knight interview here because it demonstrates many of the things about interviewing I've discussed in this book. You will see, by my marginal comments that accompany the text, what I had in mind as I asked my questions or heard his answers. It presented an editing challenge: Does one start with his anger or build up to it? Where does one place the first of his two explosions? How much italicized narrative should one use between brackets to inform the reader about what's going on? Does one end on an angry, threatening note to show what a bully the man was or take it further to show what happened next? And because the unexpected happened in the first hour of our drive to Ohio, this, too, became a challenge. We were no longer two people sitting somewhere having a conversation—we were on the road, another character was going to join us, one had to be open for anything . . . and so this drama, this "play," begins.

COMMENT

ACT I.

Q: Let's get the address out of the way up front: Do you prefer I call you Coach or Mister, Bob or Bobby?

I thought a great title for my book would be *They Call Me a Lot of Things*. From the time I started teaching when I was twenty-one, I've always signed my name Bob Knight. My college coach called me Bobby, still does. But I have never introduced myself to anybody in my adult life other than "I'm Bob Knight."

COMMENT

Knight lost his job at the U of Indiana after he verbally attacked a 19-year-old freshman for calling him by his last name, showing a lack of respect. So I thought it was appropriate to ask him what he prefers to be called before we got started.

COMMENT

I represent the media, this is his first interview since being fired, might as well acknowledge we're in the lion's den and see where his head is at.

Q: Let's begin with the media, which has always been a problem for you. Do you agree with Governor Jesse Ventura, who thinks the media are dangerous, because they carry their personal beliefs and attitudes into the articles they write?

I agree with that completely. I also believe that when something very negative comes out about you in the media, that's only one person's opinion. These guys sometimes believe that they've been ordained from on High to give the general opinion of the total populace, and that just isn't the case.

Q: Since you're in the public eye, isn't that the bargain with the devil you must deal with?

Why should it be? Why should people be unfair? I have as many good friends in the media as anybody in sports has. It's just that I probably have a hell of a lot more enemies than anybody else. The thing that bothers me the most about the media is just simple accuracy. There are as many guys in

COMMENT

Knight's ready to do verbal battle. He's not going to back down from his beliefs. He's letting us know.

coaching that do a lousy job as there are in the media. They are two professions that in that vein are a lot alike. There are not a hell of a lot of really good coaches . . . or writers.

Q: You may not like the media, but you've still got to talk to

them, don't you, to at least try and get your side out?

That depends on whether you want to talk to them or not. "To thine own self be true." Al McGuire talked to me I don't know how many times about dealing with the press: "You've got to be a con man." I tried that for a day or so but it never really worked for me. My wife, Karen, is right about this. In my dealings with the press, I was like the guy who goes into the cathouse and the madam

gets him prepared and looks at him and says, "Who are you going to satisfy with *that?*" And he looks back and says, "Me." That's kind of my sense of humor at times. I'd probably be better off without trying to satisfy me, with my sense of humor. There are things that I have said that are funny to me, but they aren't to somebody in the press. So that's not worked to my benefit.

Q: In the *Sporting News,* Mike DeCourcy wrote: "No one has done more to demean the art of sportswriting than Knight. He may take a perverse pride in having so greatly offended so many journalists."

I'm not sure that sportswriting is an art. But that's fairly accurate. It doesn't say that I'm a bad person, or that I'm a bully. You can't imagine the number of people in professional sports who have come up to me and said, "God, you treat those assholes like I'd like to treat them." And my question is "Then why don't you?"

COMMENT

OK, he's letting us know what he thinks of journalists. You know I'm going to treat him accordingly. Hopefully the reader senses that this is going to be a feisty and fun interview to read.

Q: Why don't they?

They're afraid.

Q: What's the difference between today's sportswriters and those of the past?

Writing was far more of an art in the sports world in the past than it is now. David Halberstam is a close friend of mine, so I've read everything he's written. I was critical to him about his book about the Portland Trail Blazers because he failed to capture what pro basketball was all about. Today you have an awful lot of sports—writers that don't like sports or the people in sports: I can look at a room full of sportswriters and I wonder if any of them can explain to me how to attack a one-three-one trap? Or what to do with the ball against a three-two matchup zone? I'm sure there was far more written about Clemens throwing the bat than there was about the masterful performance that Clemens had as a pitcher.

Q: Should the Yankees' Roger Clemens have been fined fifty thousand dollars for throwing that bat near the Mets' Mike Piazza in the 2000 World Series?

No, absolutely not. The situation between Clemens and Piazza was about as out of proportion as anything could be. I admire Clemens for how tough and competitive and team-oriented he is. There isn't anything more that a pitcher can do to fire himself up than breaking the other guy's bat. And particularly when it's a really good hitter like Piazza. When that bat broke I bet Clemens was at the zenith, at the apex of positive emotion. Clemens just sawed off the bat in Piazza's hands. Obviously they don't like each other to begin with, so that adds to it. I don't think Clemens's vision would have been any wider than the brim of his hat. Clemens picked up the bat and threw it, thinking, "Goddammit is that great!" Had no idea that Piazza was running down the baseline. I thought it was ridiculous. But Piazza is far more attuned with the press than Clemens is. So that enters into the equation.

Q: Is that a lesson to be learned then: to make nice with the press?

That's not what I'm talking about.

Q: Look at your career—you've had ten or twelve incidents over a period of twenty-nine years, yet it's those incidents that are always mentioned in stories about you.

COMMENT

This is what the subject of this interview is going to be. Bob Knight's character.

I buy that. How many times, without ever knowing me, have you seen the chair thrown? My contention there is, if I throw that chair and it hit somebody and hurt somebody, that's a real issue. That chair was scooted across the floor, that's no different than a guy throwing a coat, kicking a water bucket, slamming a clipboard down.

COMMENT

Good, he brought this up first, it's now fair game.

Q: But you've got to admit that chair throwing had a dramatic effect. It certainly lasted longer on videotape than someone kicking a bucket. From the visuals alone, why would you be surprised they keep showing it?

I don't have any problem with it being shown once, but for fifteen years? I was standing in the wings to be introduced

COMMENT

No sense shying away from the subject now that he's brought it up. It's an infamous incident, and it still annoys the hell out of him. Here's why.

on Letterman's show. Here I am as a coach who's had three teams that have won national championships, a team that's won the Olympic gold medal, another that's won the Pan-American gold medal, and as I'm being introduced on the monitor is a replay of me throwing the chair across the floor. I almost turned around and walked out. Of all the things that could be put up there relative to an introduction to me, this seems to be about as cheap a piece of shit as somebody could do.

Q: You're not alone. When Clemens is inducted into the Hall of Fame, that bat-throwing incident will also be shown.

Absolutely. And it meant nothing. He expressed something in a particular way and then, "Oh boy, now we can make a big issue out of this." The same thing with the chair. That chair doesn't come within fifteen feet of anybody. It seems to me that out of that game, the winning sequence was a fuck more important. I think we even got beat in the game. That's where I think that things have changed.

Q: Did you ever go into a game as a player or coach thinking you were going to lose?

Never as a player, that's a major difference between playing and coaching. A lot of players think they're gonna lose, but I happened to play on a really good team and I didn't think anybody could beat us. I was wrong six times. As a coach I have always felt we could win; sometimes, however, there are things that we really have to do well, and our margin for error is nonexistent if we're gonna win. But if in fact we can bring those things about, we can win. In one game it can be, if we don't keep them off the board, we can't beat them. Another game might be, if we don't stop their running game, we can't beat them. So what has to be done to win varies from game to game. In some cases they are very hard things to do.

Q: How hard is it to lose?

It's not at all difficult to lose a game. If you're sloppy in preparation, if you don't pay attention to detail, if execution is not what it should be, you're gonna get beat. Winning is a difficult proposition. Who is there among us who does everything consistently well? I made up a definition of discipline when I was at West Point: Doing what has to be done; doing it as well as you can do it; doing it when it has to be done; doing it that way all the time. Four things. It's not a whip and a chair, it's those four ingredients that makes a disciplined person.

Q: Can you relate to Lakers coach Phil Jackson's remark, that losing made him feel humiliated and worthless, as if he didn't exist?

That's stretching it for me. Losing has always made me feel that there was something else I could have done. What else was there that could have happened? Why did we make these mistakes? What the hell was so-and-so thinking about? What didn't I do in preparation? Losing is a defeat. There's a difference in thinking that you've been defeated than you've lost.

Q: Do you take defeat personally?

Losing has always been far far more difficult to deal with than the enjoyment you get out of winning. Winning is really important, winning fairly, squarely within the rules, but winning. When winning goes outside the rules, then sports become a negative. Winning is a by-product of doing things right. Over the years I've seen teams beat us and it was like they just won the national championship, and then invariably lose the next game they play. Too many people get caught up with the euphoria of winning rather than just accept it as that's what the hell you're supposed to do. On the other hand, losing is not what you're supposed to do. The disappointment, the frustration, the agony of losing is infinitely greater than whatever should come with winning.

COMMENT

I've now quoted from two coaches, a governor, and a sportswriter. Later on Knight will criticize me for this, but I'm letting him know that I've come prepared.

Q: The Heat's Pat Riley has said, "I believe there is winning and misery, and even when we win I'm miserable."

I'm not always satisfied with winning. Sometimes we have won and I've been very unhappy with the effort or the execution. Too many people that coach accept winning as being really good and euphoric. That's not the case. There are times when you are really happy when you win, and the players always need to know that they have done something when they've won, but there are also times when you need to let them know that their play wasn't acceptable. [Vince] Lombardi was always toughest on teams that won.

Q: Has your philosophy been: If my players can handle me, they can handle any kind of adversity?

I've never looked at it that way. What I've simply looked at is: Unless you graduate from college and become completely and totally independently wealthy, you're going to have somebody make demands of you, and you've got to learn to handle demands. I make a mistake if I'm not demanding of kids, because now that kid leaves here and he's out working for Red Roof Inn and he's got a regional supervisor who's very demanding—if he doesn't know how to handle that, he's not going to have any chance at all of being successful. Even beyond that, there have to be demands based on perfor—mance. It's necessary from a coach's standpoint. It's demanded of a coach that he win, and win honestly.

Q: Is it a mistake to take sports so deadly serious?

Sports are the most useful instruments and the best tools at the service academies. Not just intercollegiate, but also intramural, where everybody gets a chance to play—it's the competitiveness that is necessary for our military to stay strong. At Indiana, if they eliminated sports tomorrow it would have no effect on the quality of the institution. Sports is simply the tail of the dog; you cut off the tail and the dog is still in pretty good shape.

Q: Would you agree with Isiah Thomas, who said: "When you go to college, you're not a student–athlete but an athlete–student.

Your main purpose is not to be an Einstein but a ballplayer, to generate some money, put people in the stands."

COMMENT

Knight coached Thomas, who went on to be perhaps his most successful player, so what Thomas has to say about Knight later on is significant. I'm quoting something easier here, setting up the next quote.

If he said it. In many cases the kid is an athlete-student, but that depends on the emphasis that coaches place on the two. We have shown more than anybody in the country that a kid can play and graduate and the team can win. If it can be done here it can be done anywhere.

Q: How do you change the emphasis, though, and make academics the higher priority among Division I schools?

If you want to really promote academics at this level, what you do is tie scholarships to graduation. If a kid doesn't graduate in five years, the team loses that scholarship for two years, or whatever. That's how you make academics really important. But nobody wants to do that because of the tremendously low graduation rates around the country in both football and basketball. There are highly ranked basketball teams that graduate less than twenty-five percent of the players that enter.

Q: You've always seen yourself as a teacher as much as a coach, haven't you?

We graduated over seventy-eight percent of the freshman who entered in basketball. Indiana overall graduated sixty-eight percent of its freshman class. So when this president commented about my dismissal saying we needed to get back to academics, I didn't know whether he was talking about lowering the standard of the basketball team to that of the university or bringing the standard of the university up to that of the basketball team.

Q: You're proud of the high standards you have set for those who have played for you, aren't you?

When I was at West Point I once made the comment at a meeting that didn't go over real well. In fact, a couple of people wanted me fired for it. I said, "We should build an entrance at Thayer Gate that said: United States Military Academy Founded in 1803 and Since Then Unhindered by Progress." My point was there are almost no public-speaking courses taught at West Point. And that's what being an officer is all about. I don't think there's ever a word said about how to dress as a civilian. Or dealing with civilians in something other than a military manner. The psychology of relating to people is so important, and there's so little taught in that area. I taught a class here [at Indiana] for twenty-eight years titled "Methods in Coaching Basketball." And I never once talked about coaching basketball. I talked about how you go about getting a job, how you dress, how you act, how you speak, how to deal with parents, and the peripheral things relative to teaching and coaching. Do you in fact want to be a teacher? What qualifies you to be a teacher? Let's each of you draw up a personality of yourself: What do you do well? What don't you do well? I tried to really touch on things that were going to help these kids to prepare themselves and be able to conduct themselves once they had a job in such a way that they would be effective.

Q: What would you say are your own strengths and weaknesses in these areas?

COMMENT

Never hurts to ask someone their strengths and weaknesses. Self-analysis often proves enlightening.

We all probably overestimate our strengths to some degree and underestimate our weaknesses. In my case, my weaknesses are staying with something. Like [my wife] Karen puts this up everywhere: The horse is dead, get off. Probably as a coach I would stay on a mistake too long. Instead of telling you one time, I might just stay with it. But I'm trying to really impress this upon you. One of the things that I'm always accused of, and it sort of amuses me in the press, is a lack of discipline. Well, nobody's ever seen me drunk or unruly; very few people have ever seen me discourteous. I've been called everything you can be called, screamed at, yelled at, at games and only twice have I ever said anything to anybody in the stands—and one of these people became a really good friend of mine. If you were to check every year's records since I've been here you would find that Indiana has led the Big Ten in fewest technical fouls as a team.

Q: So how did it come to be that you became so much bigger than life? You've very rarely had a player who drew more attention than you did. When other teams came to play you, they wanted to beat Knight more than Indiana. What is it about you?

COMMENT
Just trying to get him to do a little soul-searching. If one can get an answer to this, to what makes Knight Knight, it would make this a successful interview.

I don't know. I'm not those people. People tell me that I just don't understand that, that I have no idea about that whole phenomena. And why, I don't know. One of the things about the press may be an answer to that: one of the strengths that I have had is a lot of the negative press that I've received. Because it has established some kind of an aura about me that set me apart. When I come in to visit you and your wife about your son coming to Indiana, you have some really preconceived ideas about me because you never met me. And when I leave, almost without exception, those ideas are going to be changed. I will explain what I expect of your son. I tell you: Here's what it takes to play for me, and if you don't think your son can do this, you should advise him not to come. The first thing I tell a kid is that we're not for everybody. I've never tried to please everybody.

COMMENT
Here we go—the opening attempt at what got him fired, what changed his life.

Q: You certainly didn't please the current Indiana administration. Do you think you've been treated unfairly by the university?

The administration and the trustees have right from the beginning been very deceitful. Their approach has been one of enormous duplicity. They've just been very dishonest in their presentation of things and reasons. They put a spin on everything they can in an attempt to explain why I've been dismissed as the basketball coach. These people that have made these decisions are the most dishonest people that I've ever dealt with. And yet, I'm not sure that I blame them as much as I blame myself for not having followed my feelings and certainly my wife's feelings, which would have been to leave five years ago. The key positions at the university changed six years ago. In those spots before there were people who I got along with extremely well; they never had a problem with me that wasn't quickly or readily solved. I just didn't fit in with the new people: their approach to things, their self-interest, their own agendas. I didn't think they were good for the university. I have yet to see anything they've done that's been of any benefit whatsoever to either the faculty or the students.

Q: Has what happened to you put a very sour taste to what you accomplished at Indiana in twenty-nine years? Do you feel bitter?

I try not to because of all the good people that were involved and all of the great kids that I've had a chance to coach and the great opportunities that were afforded me personally. Yet it's hard not to feel that way. As an example, on the [Neil] Reed question: two trustees became investigators and they spoke to me for an hour and forty minutes. One of them mentioned seven times the pressure he was under. I said, "What the hell pressure are you under? This isn't your job, you don't get paid to be a trustee. Why don't you coach basketball for a year and see what pressure's like?" The other guy not once took a note on anything that I said. When those two left my office my wife, who sat in, said, "They may be the two most disgusting people I've ever had to sit through."

Q: The tape showing you with your hand on Neil Reed's neck didn't surface for three years. When it was shown, did you feel trapped or vindicated?

COMMENT

Knight knew this subject was coming; my question shied away from being accusatory. I wanted to hear what he had to say about the tape from his POV.

When this practice tape was shown, everything that this kid said was refuted. One trustee from here apparently made the comment: "Now that we've seen that and all that bullshit has been dispelled, let's go on to something that's important." When it went one day beyond looking at that practice tape that's when I should have quit, had I been true to myself. I should have said: "This is enough of your chickenshit garbage here. This thing was discussed and looked at three years ago, now if you people want to reopen it, do it with another coach. This is enough of you people positioning for the press. I don't need this bullshit. Good-bye." That is what I will regret more than anything else in my life.

I explained this to a writer and he quoted me this way: "I knew when they showed the tape that I was finished." That's the furthest thing imaginable from what I just said. What he was quoting me as saying is when they showed the tape, I was all wrong. Well, that's not it at all.

Q: I'll get to the restrictions placed upon you after this came out, but looking ahead for a moment, what happened to the talk of you working for Isiah Thomas and the Indiana Pacers?

COMMENT

Back to Isiah Thomas, to ease into the next question, which is the loaded one.

He said I could do anything I wanted to do with the Pacers, from helping occasionally to being with them full-time. I said, "Anything I can do to help you, I will. All you got to do is tell me. You want me to come to practice, I'll come to practice. You want me to scout a team, I will. You want me to scout your own team—you tell me what you want me to do specifically and I'll be glad to do it. I just don't want to make a commitment to doing anything either on a continual part-time or full-time basis at this point."

Q: Thomas has said about playing for you: "There were times when if I had a gun, I think I would have shot him. And other times when I wanted to tell him that I loved him."

COMMENT

Obviously they butted heads.

COMMENT

And bingo, Knight's response comes through. My answer, which I didn't say, was no, I never wanted to shoot my kids literally, and I don't know any parent who has wanted that. Punish, of course. Shoot? Please. But we're getting to how Knight thinks, and that's what this is all about.

Did you ever feel like shooting one of your kids, literally? So why is that a big deal? Isiah Thomas also with tears in his eyes said, "Coach, don't you ever change."

Q: It's been written that the most stormy relationship you had with a player was with Isiah. Is that true?

I don't think so. Isiah in the final analysis was extremely successful as a player for us. We've had other players who weren't successful and left.

Q: One of the players who left was Larry Bird. How long was he at Indiana?

COMMENT

Bird was one of the all-time great NBA players, and he left Indiana because he didn't care for Knight's coaching. You can't interview Knight without asking about Bird.

He was at Indiana for a month, but he never was here for a practice. He was awed by Indiana. Larry Bird is one of my great mistakes. When he came here it was just a major, major adjustment for a kid coming out of his background—

COMMENT

This is obvious to any basketball fan, but important to hear it from Knight himself.

a small town down in southern Indiana, a real poor kid growing up, his father was an alcoholic, his mother was a cook at a mental institution. I was negligent in realizing what Bird needed at that time in his life. As an incoming freshman I let Larry Bird down.

Q: Did he talk to you before he left?

No, he just left. As I thought things over, I made a mistake in terms of who I had him room with. I had him room with a really sophisticated, articulate, well-dressed kid the same age, Jimmy Wisman, who went on to become vice president of a large advertising firm. Jimmy was everything that Larry wasn't: He was really a nice-looking kid, the girls gravitated to him automatically, he was really good with people, was an excellent student. Just in terms of roommates it was a bad match.

Q: What do you think of Bird's leaving the Pacers as a coach after three years?

Larry Bird's decision to leave was better than my decision to stay here. His decision was a close adherence to his own principles. Going by what Larry Bird did, I would have left here five years ago.

Q: Three years from now, if there's a new administration at Indiana and they asked you back to coach, would you consider it?

I don't think so.

> **COMMENT**
>
> *Note the transition from Bird leaving coaching to Knight possibly returning to Indiana.*

Q: The *Columbia Journalism Review* wrote: "College athletics is a corrupt and corrupting enterprise." It points out how legendary college coaches wield enormous clout—often exercised to hold hostage university budgets, building programs, and academic enterprises. Do you take exception to that?

> **COMMENT**
>
> *By quoting this here it has more weight than if I just asked the question myself.*

I'm sure that there are examples of what they're saying there. The president before this one, when he left, stated publicly that we had raised over five million dollars for the library. Is that corrupt? Is that bad? We've been instrumental in establishing two professorial chairs and refurbishing the golf course. So athletics and people in them can be very valuable assets to a university.

Q: What about academic dishonesty in college athletic departments: like the former tutor for the University of Minnesota who wrote four hundred papers for twenty basketball players between 1993 and 1998? That's not necessarily an exceptional case, is it?

There is a lot of academic fraud in the eligibility process. One of the things that has happened entirely too much is the athletic endorsement and expenditure on athletic tutoring. A school like this one has a tremendous budget for tutoring. I'm not of the opinion that it's not necessary, but what happens there is that a kid becomes almost totally dependent on tutors. Now there's a fine line existing between the tutor and the kid, particularly in work done outside the classroom, and that's where there are problems.

Q: Isn't it true that tutors are often told by coaches to keep the athletes eligible any way they can, which at times leads to cheating?

How the hell would I know what other coaches do? You think coaches talk to each other about how they cheat?

COMMENT

I love this response. Coaches cheat . . . Knight's not defending them.

COMMENT

Bring it home, back to Knight and his players. Go from the general to the specific.

Q: Have you had to face ethical or moral decisions regarding such behavior with any of your players?

I've had kids, parents, coaches ask me what in addition of what's allowed are they going to get to come here? And that's eliminated our recruiting the kid.

Q: It's estimated that gambling on college sports is around seventy-five billion dollars a year. Northwestern and Arizona State basketball players in the past admitted to shaving points in games. How do coaches police such incidents when there's so much money involved?

Shaving points in games goes back to the 1919 Black Sox and probably before that.

Q: We're talking college now, not pros.

We're talking sports. Take drug use: How do you deal with your children with drugs? You constantly try to bring things to their attention that would dissuade them from using drugs. As a coach you constantly try to bring things to the attention of kids relative to drugs, gambling, drinking, not getting a degree. That's part of the coach's job. To develop a sense of right and wrong with kids. What degree of success you have depends on how hard you go at it, how well you emphasize it, and how well you stand for things. I mean, what are you going to do: hire somebody to go with the kid every moment? You give me something else you can do. There's no answer to it.

Q: Did you ever have any drug-related problems with your players over the years?

COMMENT
Sports and drugs: have to ask about it.

We had a marijuana problem in 1978— there were eight kids involved. I brought them in one at a time. I ended up keeping six of them because they were honest with me about what they were doing, and I dropped two because they weren't. There've been some pretty good people that have experimented with drugs, so that in itself is not a reason to discount someone.

Q: How serious an issue is drinking, and also binge drinking, on campus? *Newsweek* devoted a cover story to this issue and asked whether colleges are doing enough to crack down on risky drinking. Are they?

Did parents do enough before the kids came to college? How many parents today buy kegs of beer for high school graduation parties? That's ludicrous to blame the colleges for that.

Q: U.S. Secretary of health and human services Donna Shalala spoke at an NCAA convention in 1998. She asked for voluntary guidelines that say, "No alcohol advertising on the premises of an intercollegiate athletic event. No bringing alcohol to the site of an event. No alcohol sponsorship of intercollegiate sporting events." The NCAA officials dismissed her recommendations. Obviously the beer industry is a cash cow in sports broadcasting. What is your opinion?

I agree with her completely. Because in most states and on most college campuses underage drinking is less than twenty-one years of age. So why are we advertising beer in a basketball arena or on a football scoreboard when a high percentage of those attending are not of an age where they can legally drink? I don't think there's any NCAA sporting event on television where beer should be a sponsor. It shouldn't be advertised in college arenas or stadiums. She used to be the president of the University of Wisconsin, prior to her going into the cabinet. Wisconsin, oddly enough, was the first university in America to serve beer in the student union.

Q: What about the money issue? College athletes don't get paid, but coaches make a lot of money. A team wins, the coach gets more money from a sneaker company or some other sponsor. Can you see how players might resent this?

Yeah, I really can. A very successful coach receives a remuneration that's comparable to what a successful coach receives, OK? Kids in football and basketball, in revenue-producing sports, a whole outline needs to be developed on what the average cost for a student to live on this particular campus or that campus might be per month. And then the kid is expected to earn a part of that, or as much as his schedule allows, and then to be subsidized the rest of it. Because you've got an inner-city or just a plain poor kid who comes to school and on the basis of his scholarship he cannot live as the average student on campus lives. What's the average that a kid spends for clothes, on dates, for recreation? I would see no problem for all of those things put together and then subsidizing that. But it could only be kids in revenue sports.

Q: What do you think of athletes often invoking God when they're interviewed after a sporting event?

I have a great story to tell about that. Broadcaster is interviewing after a game, let's say it's Bob Costas interviewing Bill Smith, who's hit a home run to put his team in the World Series. Costas: You're in the on-deck circle, there's one out, Robinson pops up, you're down two runs, there are two on, it's the bottom of the ninth, now two outs and you're coming to the plate. What's on your mind? Smith: Well, Bob, I pray, I ask God to give me the best swing I ever had. I asked for God's help. Costas: You swung and missed the first pitch, the second was a called strike. What's on your mind now? Smith: Well, I stepped out of the box and I prayed harder. I asked the Almighty to let me have a swing better than Babe Ruth ever had. Let me see the baseball like it was a basketball. And God answered my prayers and we're in the World Series. I watch this on TV and I say to myself: God screwed the pitcher.

COMMENT

Amen.

Let's let the Lord work on cancer, on providing more homes for the homeless.

The first time I ever coached at college, not knowing what the hell I was doing, we were playing at Princeton and before I sent the team out we said the Lord's Prayer. Our trainer put his arm around my shoulders and said, "For whatever it's worth, I just don't think that you and praying mix." And we never said another pregame prayer.

Q: Jesse Ventura said that organized religion was a sham and a crutch for weak-minded people. Did he deserve to be backed into a corner for that remark?

COMMENT

This comment of Ventura's made national headlines. Knight has often been courted to one day run for governor. I couldn't resist asking this just to see if Knight, too, might say something controversial.

I'd have more interest in that if Truman had said it. Or Socrates. Your religion is of no interest to me. I have never understood the fanaticism that grows out of religion, or the total inability of some religions to accept the theories of other religions.

Q: Are you at all religious today?

I believe very strongly in God in my way. The greatest religious statement ever made was "Do unto others as you would have them do unto you." If a person can follow that, then what the hell difference does it make what religion he follows?

Q: When was the last time you prayed?

You don't need to know that, nor does anybody else.

Q: You're a friend of former president George Bush; what do you think of his son?

He's a good guy—he's friendly, down-to-earth, interesting. He cares, and he cares enough to make damn sure he's got good people around him—that's what being a president is all about.

Q: Would you ever consider running for political office?

No. You have to commit yourself to too many obligations for me.

Q: What did you think of Clinton's two terms as president? Are you better off now than you were eight years ago?

No, I'm not. But a lot of people probably are. I have a real problem with Clinton in his not having involved himself in our military effort, however you feel about Vietnam. He evaded the draft. And I think Clinton was dishonest. We should expect a little more from the president of the U.S. than getting a blow job on the presidential seal in the White House.

COMMENT

Ouch! OK, we have seen where he stands politically.

[He interrupts our talk to take a call from former Dayton coach Don Donoher, now a scout for the Cleveland Cavaliers. They are planning to drive to the University of Akron in Ohio the next day to watch both their sons assisting coaching the basketball team's practice. "We'll meet you at the Bob Evans off 75," Knight says. "There's a really interesting guy here with me that's going to come. He wants to know how I feel about God, marijuana, Clinton, Gore, and Bush. This has been like an investigation that's being conducted by the CIA to see whether or not I'm capable of running the Buenos Aires branch of covert operations. And I'm being used as a disguise to really run covert operations in Santiago, Chile. This is a question-and-answer session the likes of which Rockefeller did not put his potential son-in-law through."]

COMMENT

This italicized insert sets up the "second act" of this interview. We began at his home, we talked about various topics, got to feel each other out. Now the reader is going to go for a ride: literally and figuratively. Twelve hours in a car with Bob Knight. This ought to be something!

COMMENT

ACT II.

Q: Well, since you feel like you're under investigation, just a few more political questions. Where do you stand on abortion?

I'm very much pro-choice.

Q: Gay rights?

The Constitution should take care of all of us, across the board.

Q: What about gay marriages?

I don't know. I sure as hell wouldn't want to marry you, but maybe somebody else would. Maybe a guy wants to marry a horse, what the hell would be wrong with that? I'd have no problem with a guy marrying a horse.

Q: The legalization of marijuana for medicinal purposes?

Forget marijuana. Anything that can be used as a controlled substance that can in any way better our outlook and our prospects for good health, as long as it's not injurious or addictive, I don't have a problem with it.

Q: Is it true you've never drank liquor?

I've tasted liquor. But I don't drink.

Q: What about any kind of drug—were you ever even curious?

No. When I grew up kids weren't involved with drugs like they are today. That was over forty years ago. I have never been able to understand how you can ingest or use something that's harmful. Every time I see a guy smoke a cigarette I just shake my head.

Q: How would you describe yourself? ◄ . . . .

COMMENT

This is such a simple question, but it can sometimes lead to interesting self-analysis. In this case, not really.

It's hard to describe yourself. What I have always tried to be is honest, fair, and to help people whenever it was possible for me to do so. That, in essence, is what I've tried to do over the years.

Q: The words often used: brilliant, compassionate, driven, a throwback, impatient . . .

I would agree with impatient. I used to have a sign up that said: God Grant Me Patience, and Please Hurry.

COMMENT

This wasn't a prepared question, just something that struck me as we talked, so I threw it out. And it paid off with his reflection on Gable and his take on the movies.

Q: Has anyone ever told you that you sound like John Wayne with an occasional ring of Jack Nicholson?

Well, my all-time favorite actor is Clark Gable.

Q: Well, frankly, my dear, I don't give a damn.

There's a sardonic aura about Clark Gable that I really like. His demeanor, his facial expressions, it almost conveys to me that he's saying to himself, "Boy, this is a lot of bullshit. I can't believe I'm really getting paid for it." Really good actors like Mitchum, Kirk Douglas, Burt Lancaster—they worked at being actors. I don't think Clark Gable worked at anything, that was his beauty. What you saw was what you got. If you pay attention to Jimmy Stewart and Gary Cooper in a movie, their speech is really studied, almost predetermined. I always got the impression that Clark Gable may be speaking with no script.

Q: Are there any films about sports that you've liked?

COMMENT

If you're talking about films, you have to bring the subject back to Knight's expertise, which is sports.

They're all recent because early sports movies were all terrible. I remember one with Anthony Perkins in a basketball movie, Perkins couldn't chew bubblegum and walk at the same time. He was also terrible in *Fear Strikes Out*—Christ Almighty, didn't even know how to swing a bat. The tip-off in bad sports movies is guys who can't throw or can't catch or swing a bat or a golf club. *The Natural* with Robert Redford was pretty accurate.

Q: Is hitting a baseball the hardest thing to do in sports?

Ted Williams said it was. It's pretty damn difficult to hit an object going ninety-plus miles per hour with another object that has a diameter of three and a half inches. There is one thing that supersedes that in difficulty, and that's the simple act of winning. Winning is worthy of more consideration than an individual skill. What goes into winning is far more important to me.

COMMENT

This might seem like a weak transition, but he was talking about baseball movies and I wanted to get back to his losing his job, and the end of this comment, about what was important to him, allowed me to change the subject in the next question.

Q: Let's talk about something else that's obviously important to you, and that's your being fired from coaching at Indiana.

In a way, this whole thing that's transpired with me really amuses me. Because there's so much bullshit and so much deceit involved in this. When all these people had to do was come to me and say, "You don't fit in with what we want our basketball coach to be. You're no longer what we think is needed here." All I say is "That's fine. Let's settle up."

Q: Aren't you a difficult person to deal with because, perhaps, they're afraid of you?

COMMENT

Knight can be a scary person. His temper is legendary. What does he think of this?

That's their problem, not mine. Why should anybody be afraid to deal with me? I've been in two different institutions and neither one has had the first problem in academics or recruiting violations while I've been there. So what is there to fear?

Q: The *Columbia Journalism Review* wrote: "Bobby Knight is perhaps the most powerful public figure in Indiana and very few people from the governor on down are willing to cross him."

Something like that boggles my mind. How do they determine that? I have never once entered into one single political decision. That's asinine to ever think that. Rarely have I ever publicly gone after somebody.

Q: Because few have crossed you.

COMMENT

He's getting testy here. Get ready for more.

Oh, bullshit.

Q: Can you relate to this from Mike Ditka: "Sometimes our mouths and reactions operate before our brains get synchronized, and that happens to me a lot"?

Everybody says something that they'd like to recall. Given time to think, by tomorrow maybe I would have changed what I said. But I've seen some people who I know are just absolute scumbags in their personal lives write things that judge me. That's why you really have no chance with the press.

COMMENT

He can't stop taking shots at the press. As his comments build, one senses that he might explode. But he's still simmering here.

Q: Knowing that, why take it on? Isn't that tilting at windmills in a way?

Probably. I really tried in this thing with this university to be something that I wasn't back in the spring.

Q: Was that the time when you were saying that you welcomed the zero-tolerance policy?

I never, ever said I welcomed zero tolerance, because it was never explained to me. I simply said that guidelines can be of benefit, period. The whole idea of using things that had happened up to twenty-five years ago, and using them inaccurately, eventually really pissed me off. Pissed me off more at myself for having accepted it than anybody else.

Q: Were you getting any advice at the time? Were you talking to your lawyer?

COMMENT

So why didn't he? His answers trigger follow-up questions.

I talked to some people. And almost without exception they told me to leave.

Q: So you weren't listening to the advice?

What I did in this situation was think about the wrong things.

Q: What were you thinking about?

How this has been a very comfortable place for me to live. I envisioned when I quit coaching to be able to stay around the university, to help in any way they asked, to raise money—there's nobody who could raise more money for this university than I could—without ever interfering with anybody who replaced me as a coach. It was a very comfortable life in an area that I liked around people that I liked. So, OK, they tell me here's what you have to do. And I could do any of those things. I could change in press conferences. What I intended to do was not even have press conferences. I was going to have a postgame radio show where I'd answer questions from two people who knew about the game. But what was zero tolerance? Does that mean one technical foul and we fire you? Or you go speak somewhere and somebody doesn't like your answer and they complain about it, so we fire you? There were never any outlines placed on this phrase. I asked two different vice presidents to define zero tolerance and they couldn't do it.

Q: Why would you agree to something that you couldn't get defined?

COMMENT

Pressing Knight is dangerous. I didn't know this yet, but I'm about to find out.

I'm just telling you why I *fucking* agreed to it! Because of my lifestyle here and how much I liked it here. So, I say to myself, if I have to do this to stay here, and I have to agree to this, now's the time for me to just simply say, OK, I'll do that. And that was wrong. That was a mistake. That's what I'm trying to tell you.

Q: But why aren't you asking at the time for zero tolerance to be explained?

COMMENT

Knight has a way of throwing questions back, which can also throw you off course. Best to keep it focused on him.

I don't know. Do you do everything that's brilliant? Sometimes you don't cover everything. But I certainly tried to find out right away afterward.

Q: The definition of zero tolerance that was printed was: "Any verified, inappropriate physical contact with players, members of the university community or others in connection with the coach's employment at IU will be the cause for immediate termination."

COMMENT

I had this definition with me, knowing I would use it.

What is verified? Explain the word *inappropriate* to me.

Q: Something that is not appropriate.

Who determines that?

Q: That's like asking the definition of pornography. And the usual answer is, you know it when you see it.

COMMENT

A reminder that we're in his car. And now for a little comic relief. This is like the gatekeeper in Macbeth. "Knock knock . . . etc." It's my attempt to balance the interview, it's been getting pretty serious, and it's about to get a lot more so, so this is a break that also reminds the reader that Knight is a man who can be, at times, above the law.

I don't think so. This is the reason why I didn't teach class. I walk into a class, there's a girl standing there, and I put my hand on her back and say, "Excuse me, miss," so I could get through. What if the girl complains about that? *[He looks at his rearview mirror.]* Oh shoot, goddamn it. I've got a cop behind me. If it's a state policeman it might be all right. Aw, it's the county sheriff.

[SHERIFF: I stopped you for doing seventy-five.

KNIGHT: I know. He's doing an interview with me and I was paying no attention to what I was doing.

SHERIFF: Bob Knight? How're you doing?

KNIGHT: Oh, so-so.

SHERIFF: My wife works with your daughter-in-law.

KNIGHT: At the hospital? Oh, great. Sorry you stopped me. He just asked me if I get stopped often and I said, "No, I really don't, because I'm paying more attention to what the hell I'm doing than listening to your bullshit."

SHERIFF: I heard you're going hunting with Colin Powell.

KNIGHT: No, with Schwarzkopf. Going to go over to Spain on a deal that a friend of mine put together. Again, I apologize for you having to stop me. I don't like you guys to have to do that, you've got enough problems without me creating them for you.

SHERIFF: No problem

KNIGHT: Thanks a lot.]

Q: When you say that you never understood what zero tolerance meant—would you have accepted that answer from any of your players?

COMMENT
Back to business.

That wouldn't have come up with players because I would have explained things a lot better. You writers expect things out of the people that you're writing about that you yourself never think about.

COMMENT
Knight obviously dislikes the man who set the policy that would get him fired. This is pouring oil into his smoldering fire. It's time to get to the nitty-gritty . . .

Q: Indiana president Myles Brand said that there were many instances in which you had been defiant and hostile. Did he point these out to you in private?

Never! That's just bullshit. Another thing Brand said was that I didn't follow the chain of command. Twenty years ago my contract was written that I had final approval over everything to do with men's basketball at Indiana University. Now you tell me, where's my chain of command? There is none. I don't have to ask anybody there for a single thing. And I put that in there because I was the only guy who really knew how to run basketball at Indiana and I didn't want any interference with the scheduling, the recruiting, anything. I've had five athletic directors since I've been here and this guy [Clarence Doninger] is the only one I didn't get along with because he's the most incompetent and the least trustworthy person I've ever met in athletics. The guy's a little man, he's a very small person in all respects other than size. I once told him, "When I was at West Point and here, I counted up thirty-nine people that I worked for, and of those thirty-nine people there are only two that I didn't get along with. And you're one of them. What does that say about you and what does that say about me?" If I were to make that statement today, there would have been forty-two people and instead of two there are now five that I didn't get along with. That's pretty good.

COMMENT

This is the university's athletic director he's talking about. Always a highlight when your subject begins bad-mouthing people.

Q: Was your problem with him always about basketball matters?

No, it was never about anything. But it didn't make any difference because he had no say in what we did anyhow, which he resented from the beginning. But the guy had never been in athletics, he's a lawyer, didn't know the first thing about how people think in athletics.

Q: Can you give an example of any specific incident you had with him?

COMMENT

I always like to get specific. Most people talk in generalities. Try to narrow them down, to get examples.

There are a dozen coaches in Indiana male and female that I've worked hard to help recruit. Last year the girls' basketball program needed ten thousand dollars to buy some electronic equipment. I gave them the money. And the athletic director and his assistant wouldn't let them buy it because the money came from me. I made a public comment about that at an Indiana alumni-sponsored luncheon, about what a hell of a state of affairs that was.

Q: Did he defend his decision in any way?

No, he just got enormously pissed off. How could he defend it? Eventually they had to buy the equipment, and that's what it forced him to do, and that's what my intent was.

Q: Did there ever come a time when you physically threatened Doninger?

COMMENT

First ask.

No, what would I physically threaten the guy for?

COMMENT

Then point out it was reported.

Q: It was reported that you did after a game last February nineteenth.

Now you get into this bullshit.

Q: I don't know anything more than what was reported.

COMMENT

And then you get his side of the story.

Then let me tell you exactly what happened. This goes to show how untrustworthy the guy is. The biggest game of the year for us last season was playing Ohio State here. I thought if we could beat them and Michigan State we could win the Big Ten championship. We get in the Ohio State game and we have it won, but we lose it in the end. I walk through that hallway and here's the athletic director, after we've gotten our asses beat, and I haven't seen him once all year. He looks at me and says, "Boy, that was a tough game." And I said, "How the hell would you know?" And I just kept on going. Then I came back and said, "I don't even understand what you're doing here." He said, "I have a right to be here." I said, "I don't care what your rights are, nobody wants you here, nobody gives a damn about you being here under these circumstances." I didn't raise my voice, there was no threatening gesture. The next two days at three different meetings this athletic director tells people about how he knows if the doctor hadn't interfered with me I was going to punch him. That's what I was dealing with.

COMMENT

Getting back to strengths and weaknesses here.

Q: Do you ever wish that you had it in you to be able to ignore the kind of stuff that really bothers you?

You can't imagine how much I ignore. That's a fallacy. I go to a game and some people are all over my ass and I never say anything, I just walk on and off the floor.

Q: Have opposing fans ever thrown anything at you?

COMMENT

I knew the answer, but preferred to ask as if I didn't.

Well, certainly they have. We played up at Syracuse when I was at West Point and they took out nuts and bolts and threw them at us. Would you like to get hit in the fucking head with a bolt while you're out on the basketball floor getting ready for a game?

Q: When Larry Brown resigned from the Pacers he said: "Sometimes being a coach is like being a second lieutenant in a combat zone. Eventually you are going to get shot."

I still haven't had anybody shoot at me.

Q: Have you ever had death threats that you took seriously?

Yeah. A couple of times I've had the FBI come to me about it.

Q: Did they ever tell you to wear a protective vest or anything like that?

Once they did.

Q: And did you?

No. I figured there are a lot of bad shots out there.

COMMENT

Finally, we get to the specific incident that got him fired. Before this I tried to get in a variety of topics and his take on things, because I knew when we got down to this, anything might happen, including him ending the interview.

Q: This freshman Kent Harvey, who called you by your last name and was the catalyst for your being fired, was burned in effigy outside Brand's home; flyers of him were printed with the words "Wanted: Dead." How concerned were you for this young man?

Now you ask me that question. Why not ask me the question that when I addressed the fans the last time I talked to them I told them to leave that kid alone?

Q: Harvey and his two brothers withdrew from the university and they've left the state. What do you think of that?

I have not followed what direction their lives have taken.

Q: Do you feel for the kid?

Not in the slightest.

COMMENT

This surprised—and intrigued—me.

Q: Was he wrong in saying anything about you?

The kid's stepfather used me. He talked about how I said "fuck this" and "fuck that" and "goddamned this" and "goddamned that." The total context of what I said was this, verbatim: "Son, I don't call people by their last names. My name to you is Coach or Mister Knight, and you should remember that when you're dealing with elders." And I walked away. Would it piss you off?

COMMENT

Knight once again attempts to get me to side with him.

Q: What?

Would what was said by the stepfather piss you off?

COMMENT

I preferred neutrality. Though I wasn't sure if he was asking me about the young man or the stepfather.

COMMENT

To me, this was a perfectly innocent question. I wasn't trying to bait him. I had no idea this was the question that would cause him to lose control.

Q: Didn't the stepfather also say that he didn't think that you should be fired over this incident?

[*BANGS the center of the steering wheel with his fist. His rage is sudden, frightening, and unexpected.*] JESUS CHRIST! THIS IS BULLSHIT! I'M NOT HERE FOR A FUCKING INQUISITION! AND IF THAT'S WHAT THIS IS THEN GET THE FUCK OUT AND HITCHHIKE BACK HOME! THE FUCKING STEPFATHER WAS A FUCKING GODDAMN FUCKING ASSHOLE FROM THE WORD GODDAMN GO! HE FUCKING LIED AND HE LIED AND HE LIED! *JESUS CHRIST!* I MEAN THIS IS MY FUCKING LIFE HERE THAT WE'RE TALKING ABOUT! MY FUCKING *HEART* WAS RIPPED OUT BY THIS GODDAMN BULLSHIT!

COMMENT

Believe me, this was scary.

Q: Ok . . .

OK MY *ASS!* IT ISN'T FUCKING OKAY! GODDAMN IT, I DON'T NEED THIS SHIT! I'LL DROP YOU OFF IN FUCKING DAYTON AND YOU CAN GET HOME.

COMMENT

I'm just trying to calm him down now, he's out of control, he's still driving 70 mph, and he would like to punch my lights out. I glance at my tape recorder to make sure it's still recording.

Q: Please, Coach . . .

THIS IS FUCKING BULLSHIT! I DON'T WANT TO HEAR ANOTHER FUCKING
WORD.

*[For two minutes, we drive in silence.
The coach continues to stew.]*

YOU HAVEN'T BROUGHT UP ONE FUCKING
POSITIVE THING THAT I'VE SAID OR DONE
SINCE WE'VE BEEN TALKING. "Isn't this
right? Isn't that right?" I'M TIRED OF IT.
WE'LL GET TO DAYTON, YOU GET THIS CAR
AND DRIVE BACK TO BLOOMINGTON.

Q: Coach . . .

NO, THERE ISN'T ANY IFS, ANDS, OR
BUTS ABOUT IT!

Q: One of the problems that you
have had to deal with is that the
press has not been so nice to you,
or they only report certain things.
There are issues that will remain in the press for the rest of
your life if you don't take the opportunity to give your side.

That's not true. *[Calming down.]* When I was in Puerto Rico in
1979, that's twenty-one years ago, to this day I have still
punched a Puerto Rican policeman and called the Brazilian women's
teams "niggers" and "whores." Seated forty feet away from me
were twelve players representing the U.S. in the Pan American
games, eight of them were black and three played for me. Now how
logical would it be for America's greatest racist to make that
comment under those circumstances? So it isn't going to change.
I've been burned too many times trying to deal with somebody that I
think is going to deal with things honestly. This guy you're talking
about *[Harvey's stepfather]*, he asked me five different times
through letters to allow him to write a book on me. I turned him
down every single time. So now he became a guy on a radio talk

show and never did a day go by when he didn't just rip my ass about something. So he ends up being the stepfather of this kid. I think it was the kid's father, not the stepfather, who was very apologetic about what happened—that the stepfather just tried to crucify me over this thing by making up one thing after another. So you asked me do I feel sorry about these kids? Hell no, I don't feel sorry about them, because their own stepfather did to them what was done to them. There was another coach standing about ten feet away

COMMENT

One thing about Knight, he's willing to return to painful places and elaborate. Points for him.

from this, and a player fifteen feet away sitting in a car with the window down who heard the whole thing. They corroborated what I said happened. And the kid himself and the brothers eventually had to recant what they had said. You don't understand how sick and tired you get of this bullshit.

Q: I'm trying.

You do the things that you know are the right things to do, that enable your school to have a really good basketball program, you don't succumb to any of the temptations of recruiting violations or academic fraud or anything like that, and I'm not sure what else can be asked of a guy . . . The petty bullshit that went on here, the guys that I felt were friends that

COMMENT

He's starting to unload here. This is what one hopes to get in an interview with someone as volcanic as Knight.

weren't, this president's idiotic accusations—another one was: Knight demeaned and insulted our alumni by not speaking at luncheons in Chicago and Indianapolis. Well, my contract has called for me to make four appearances a year on behalf of the university. Over twenty years I probably averaged never less than twenty appearances. So this year, with this set of circumstances that I was confronted with, my attorney said to me, "You just can't expose yourself to this stuff." So I spoke at six things. Now, Brand uses this in his way to support a reason for why

I'm being fired. How would you feel about that one? Another thing he referred to was all the public remarks that I had made criticizing the administration and the board of trustees. There isn't a day goes by that some professor doesn't write a note in the paper how inept this board of trustees and this administration is. Are they going to fire all those professors? Am I denied freedom of speech? To take a word out of the Gettysburg Address, is that not one of my inalienable rights? Instead of just saying we don't want you as our basketball coach, why make up all this bullshit? Why color everything?

And not only that, the total sum of my public remarks about this administration after this stuff happened is one. I was at a fund-raiser for cancer and my wife introduced me saying she never knew anyone who could get from A to B faster than I do. When I got up I said, "I've always taken pride in getting from A to B and eliminating all the hurdles in between except when the Indiana board of trustees might be situated between A and B." That's the only comment I ever made. So where's the whole series of comments I've made? Or the whole series of incidents that have never been explained to me? When this list of sanctions came out, there were only three things that I was ever made aware of and those happened three, twelve, and twenty-five years ago. One of them was the athletic director's secretary getting on TV saying I called her a fucking bitch. What I in fact did was after she had harassed the hell out of my two secretaries who were going to write a letter of complaint to the university about her. I said there's no need to do that, let me go straighten it out. I went down to the woman, whose name is Ginette, and said, "There are two things you need to understand. One, my girls don't work for you, they work for me. If you have a problem with them you come see me about it. I'm tired of you acting like a bitch around them constantly." That was the extent of it. And she goes on TV saying I called her a fucking bitch. So the president wants me to write a letter of apology to her. It was the one time I spoke to him throughout this whole thing. I was sitting with four men, including him, and I made the comment,

"Hasn't everyone at some point had a disagreement with a secretary?" And Brand's words were, "Well, I never have." I didn't say anything. This is when I started to become really disgusted with myself, because I want to stay here, I want to coach this team, I want to live here, and I want to make this thing work. But to do it I have to accept a lot of bullshit that just isn't true. So the way I eventually wrote a letter of apology to her was this: "You and I have a totally different recollection of what I said to you. However, I would imagine that because of all that was involved, I should apologize to you for not having gone through the proper channels—i.e., allowing the girls to go ahead and file their complaint." At no time did I ever apologize for what I didn't say.

Q: Wasn't there also an issue he made of your leaving on a fishing trip when Brand wanted you to stay through the weekend when this was going down?

Brand calls me at ten-thirty on Friday night and I have not heard from the guy in over three months. He asks me to stay on the campus the next day when for six months I've had a trip planned that involved several other people who have paid a lot of money to be involved with a fishing trip with me in eastern Quebec. He wants me to stay so he can give me a phone call the next morning. I said no, I'm not going to do that. I said I made enough changes in my life in the last four months that I'm just not going to make any more.

Q: And that gets reported that you were defiant . . .

That I was insubordinate. I said if there's a phone number where I'm going I'll call my wife with it. The decision to fire me was made on that Saturday morning in two meetings that people have sued about right now.

Q: Because they weren't publicly held meetings?

Yes. I had nothing to do with that. A trustee's wife told my wife that this had taken place on Saturday morning. That afternoon Brand tells the team that nothing is going to be decided until he has a police report on what happened with this kid. The police report did not come out until Tuesday and I was officially fired on Sunday morning.

Q: Michigan State Coach Tom Izzo said he smelt a rat in what happened to you. Pete Newell said he smelled a setup, a trap. Is that also how you feel about what happened?

COMMENT

OK, to be fair to him, I've hit him with some tough shots, now it's time to let those who came to his defense have a say.

The setup was such that I was put into an impossible situation. Anybody with any intelligence knows that zero tolerance is just a prelude to failure. Nobody can operate on zero anything.

Q: Has Brand and his administration hurt the university?

That would have to be determined by somebody else. In my own case, I had a plan where I was going to leave five million dollars over stuff that I would eventually do—write a book, television stuff, whatever—money that I don't need, for the athletic department. And a million of it would go to the football team as long as the coach remained. There's no way I would do that today. I spoke a while ago in southern Indiana that raised sixty thousand dollars for cancer research. That would have gone to the university. I told them I didn't want it to.

Q: What are you looking at in the future?

I don't know what the future holds. I don't know what opportunities there are. I haven't decided what I want to do—that depends on opportunities.

COMMENT

Another way of asking him of his own importance.

Q: How do you think things will change at actual basketball games at Indiana now?

We had the best fans in the world here and that will change, because they'll be allowed to yell and holler and scream and do whatever the hell they want to do with things now. I would never allow that, but that'll happen very quickly now. "Bullshit, bullshit" chants—I never let that happen here.

Q: How much mail did you receive after you were fired?

See that truck in front of us? That probably carried it. I've tried to read and answer everything that's been sent to me that's been worthwhile. And I don't think there's been a negative thing sent.

Q: Did three ex-presidents send you letters of encouragement after your firing?

COMMENT

A reminder that Knight's fall can be considered tragic: which is defined as a fall from high places. If presidents write to Knight, he was obviously in a high place.

I heard from two. But that's nobody's business. I've heard from owners or coaches from fourteen different NFL franchises. I got a really nice letter from the governor of Wisconsin telling me how much he appreciated what I had contributed to the Big Ten over the years. I never once heard from Indiana's governor.

[*We arrive at Dayton; Don Donoher is waiting. Knight asks me to jump in the backseat. Donoher tells Knight he'll drive. Knight apologizes for being late, having missed a turn on the highway because "he got me so pissed off about an hour ago with these fucking questions that I was yelling and screaming at him and missed the fucking turnoff."*

COMMENT

Another attempt at relieving tension. An interview has ebbs and flows. We began with getting to know him, warming up. Then came his explosion. Now comes a bit of calm before the next storm.

DONOHER: You just missed the turnoff and you're blaming Larry.

KNIGHT: I was goddamn up near Meridian before I realized we passed 70. That's on the dead north side, I was so pissed off. It took me goddamn near the Ohio line before I started answering his fucking questions again.

DONOHER: What are you collaborating on?

KNIGHT: I'm not really sure. There is a question remaining whether he will ever live long enough for this article to see the fucking light of day. You know that movie A Bridge Too Far? A bridge in Arnum in WWII, they stretched themselves out too thin and they went one bridge too far. That's what happened with Larry this morning, it was A Question Too Far. I think to a small degree I may have overreacted.

After the two coaches talk sports, legal matters, and bakeries for a while, the interview continues.]

Q: Did you once lose a putter up a tree while golfing?

I one time threw a Ping putter in a tree and came out the next day. It was a huge tree and I climbed it, and sat there while about five groups went through underneath me, and I never did find the goddamn putter. It was kind of interesting trying to keep anyone from seeing me up in that tree.

COMMENT

There's a third person now in the car. Obviously one cannot go back to the jugular, it would be impolite and unrealistic. So I've put aside the tough questions for now, as we continue the drive up to Akron.

Q: How good a golfer are you?

The last two times I played golf I bogied the last two holes to shoot eighty. The six times before that I shot seventy-six four times, seventy-seven once, and eighty-two. But what keeps me from being good is I'm not very flexible. I play a screwy game. I have an eleven and a nine wood because I don't hit irons well.

Q: Did Jack Nicklaus make a funny video for you on your fiftieth birthday?

My fiftieth birthday raised one hundred thousand dollars for our library. There was a skit from Jack Nicklaus on the videotape that was made. It was really funny. He had a putting mechanism set up in his office. He had two balls and a putter. He putted the first one from six feet and it goes right, the second one goes left. He breaks the putter over his leg, throws it on the floor, walks over to his desk, picks up the chair, throws it across the room and walks off camera. Then he sticks his head back in and says, "Happy Birthday, Robert."

COMMENT

This question would never have made it into the interview, except for his response. Woods, to Knight, is not an athlete.

Q: Is Tiger Woods on his way to becoming the world's greatest athlete?

No, I don't think you can equate golf with athletes. An athlete can play anything, that's the difference. There've been some really good golfers like Ben Hogan who couldn't play anything else. Sam Snead was a good athlete. But Hogan, Byron Nelson, these guys weren't athletes.

Q: Do you consider golf a sport?

Yeah. There is athletic ability, hand-eye coordination, flexibility—there's never been a good golfer who didn't have good flexibility. J. C. Snead may be the best athlete playing golf—he played baseball good enough to sign a pro contract; he was a good basketball player. Jack Nicklaus was a good high school basketball player and a catcher in baseball. Until Woods has been able to play for twenty years at the level he plays at now, then Nicklaus will always be the best player, because he played longer well than anybody else.

Q: But isn't someone who plays a sport an athlete?

COMMENT

This is the kind of locker room BS that guys like to talk about. Knight has his opinions, they're worth including because one can see how a reader might take what he says and bring it up at a poker game and stir the pot while the cards are being dealt.

You think a boxer is an athlete? What else can a boxer do but box? Sports are very individual in many cases, but a great athlete can play anything. You take a really good home run hitter—I'm not sure about McGuire, because I think he's a pretty good athlete—but really, what the hell else could Babe Ruth have played? He wasn't going to play football or basketball. He was just a baseball player.

Q: You have a high standard for the word *athlete.*

I have a very high standard. Because that's not the same thing as a player. A great player in any given sport might not necessarily be a great athlete.

Q: So Roger Clemens is . . . ?

A great pitcher. Larry Bird was a great basketball player, but he wasn't a great athlete.

Q: You have a special fondness for Mark McGuire, don't you?

I went over to Saint Louis not long after I got fired and I was standing by the dugout while they were taking batting practice. [St. Louis Cardinal's manager Tony] La Russa is a close friend of mine and I often go down to spring training. McGuire saw me standing there and he came over and stood on the first step, put his arms around me, lifted me up, and hugged me. And said, "Are you doing okay?" That's Mark McGuire.

Q: What about Pete Rose—should he be in the Hall of Fame?

I think so.

Q: Let's talk about the NCAA. What is your take on the way the NCAA is run?

The NCAA tries to encompass far too much. The disparity between schools that play in Division III and Division I is enormous. There should be separate governing bodies for each of the various divisions. It's just too big with too many problems and not enough time to deal with all that's on their plate, with a rule book that no one completely understands.

Q: How much cheating goes on in Division I-A recruiting?

How much is a lot? To me there's a lot.

Q: How many different ways are there to cheat?

How many different ways are there to dress? The majority of recruiting problems are the result of alumni zealousness in terms of winning or of being a part of or wanting to have a hand in.

COMMENT

Focusing here on his expertise. This is one of the great college coaches, his opinion counts more than most.

Q: How would you change college basketball? Would you raise the basket to eleven feet? Eliminate the dunk? Make the dunk worth one point? Move the three-point line back? Widen the court or the lane?

You widen the court, all the action still takes place at the basket. It's a big man's game. Let those little fuckers play second base or play golf. If you widen the lane you take away the strength and the thrust to the bucket. You raise the basket to eleven feet and the shooting percentages drop enormously. You go to see shots made or missed? What's one of the most thrilling things in the game? It's the dunk. And sometimes the dunk is a hell of a lot harder to get to than the three-point shot. As for moving the line back, do you want to see guys miss or see them make the three-pointer?

Q: So there are no changes you'd make to the game?

I might make the trapezoidal lane of international basketball. I think that officiating should be more standardized across the country. There has been a physical play allowed to creep in and prosper in college basketball that shouldn't be there. It takes away from what basketball is all about.

Q: How did ESPN change the nature of college sports?

Television has had far too much control over it. That's also a result of the college's search for the dollar. So now time-outs are two and a half minutes, to get in as much commercial time as possible. That means more dollars. There aren't as many really good, smart basketball players today as there once was. And yet overall, the quality of the player is much better. If you watch an ESPN show like *SportsCenter*, let's say there are twelve things showing, what will ten of them be? Ten dunks. ESPN never shows a back cut and a bounce pass that leads to a layup, that's way too generic, but that's the guts of the game. They don't show a guy drawing a charge. They show a dunk. So kids have a much different idea of what the game is all about today than they had when I played. When I played, there was a much better understanding of how to play.

Q: Do you think players today play better or are at another level than players in the past?

I don't think so. There isn't anybody playing basketball today that's any better than Jerry West or Oscar Robertson or Willis Reed or John Havlicek or Bill Russell. Wilt Chamberlain. Or in golf, nobody's playing any better than Nicklaus or Snead or Hogan or Nelson. But what's happened is, as we become more and more sports oriented as a country . . . There are more teams and more good players in anything. But the great players aren't any better than they were in the past.

Q: Who's the best basketball player ◄········· of them all?

Russell was the most valuable player that ever lived. The [Boston Celtics] won eleven championships in thirteen years. Michael Jordan is the best player, but Russell the most valuable. And I really admired and liked Chamberlain. He was a dignified and gracious man. He gave and

COMMENT

While we all know there is no "best" and "worst," it's still fun to play this game with guys like Knight. Again, it makes for comments readers can relate to, can take exception to, can write letters to the editor in response.

accomplished so much, and yet more was always expected from him. His records are phenomenal. I was a great admirer of Jerry West.

Willis Reed—I started his basketball camp for him when I was a coach at Army.

Q: What about Kareem?

Jabbar was very good, but he wasn't Chamberlain or Russell.

Q: What did you think when Chamberlain revealed that he had slept with over twenty thousand women?

Dick Schaap told me a story of how he was at a sports banquet in New York where he had taken a picture with Chamberlain and Roger Staubach. And Schaap said, "Roger, you know the three of us had sex with 20,002 women. And Chamberlain said, 'Dick, that book's two years old.'" That's one of the great lines I've ever heard.

Q: Did you also admire Dennis Rodman as a player?

I had a lot of respect for Rodman in terms of how hard he played defensively, how well he rebounded, and how much he contributed to teams winning. You can totally disagree with all of Rodman's bullshit and his approach to living, but the guy played on six championship teams and was a major contributor to all of them.

Q: How does a coach deal with someone like Shaquille O'Neal and his inability to sink free throws?

Maybe he's a bad free-throw shooter. There's no panacea to free-throw shooting. Chamberlain may be the greatest athlete that ever lived and couldn't shoot free throws. Maybe O'Neal won't be able to shoot free throws, maybe there's a mental block there.

Q: What do you do if . . . ?

Let me finish, Jeremy Schaap. It seems to me that Jackson got O'Neal playing better and more consistently than anybody ever has, so whether or not he ever shoots free throws well, that's

COMMENT

The reference is to the ESPN interviewer who interrupted him during a TV interview. Knight is being sarcastic. He assumes (correctly) that I'll know the reference.

incidental to what Jackson has done in one year with O'Neal. I'm done, Jeremy.

Q: Are there many coaches in the NBA you admire?

I've got two players who are head coaches in the NBA: [Randy] Wittman and [Isiah] Thomas. They were two kids that I admired greatly as players. They'll both be very good coaches. What Jackson has done—he's a great manager of personalities. There is a combination there that has been extremely good, and Jackson has been good about the combination, and that's Jackson and Tex Winter. Tex Winter is a very good basketball man—he has handled the basketball and Jackson has handled the psychology of managing. It's been a tremendous combination. The best that ever coached in the NBA at doing both of those things was Red Auerbach. There's no bigger Red Auerbach fan in the universe than I am. Van Gundy with the Knicks has done a very good job. Pat Riley has done a really good job. There's a good combination of two people at San Antonio—Hank Egan as the assistant and Popovich as head coach.

Q: Chris Webber said, "When we're on the court, I am not a great person. I'm trying to beat you and I'm trying to mentally harm you." Is that your kind of player?

Chris Webber called a time-out when there were no time-outs left, that's all we need to say about Chris Webber.

Q: What do you think of a professional athlete like Allen Iverson releasing a hip-hop song with lines like: "Man enough to pull a gun/Be man enough to squeeze it." And: "Come to me with faggot tendencies/You be sleeping where the maggots be . . ." "Get money, kill and fuck bitches." "I know niggas that kill for a fee/That would kill your ass for free."

If I were the owner of that team, upon hearing that one time, the guy would be traded.

Q: What things most upset you about a player?

That he doesn't develop a work ethic. That he doesn't pay attention to what's happening, he doesn't see the game as it's developing. And perhaps most important, that he simply doesn't take advantage of the ability that he has and in the end the guy who ends up getting cheated is he himself but in the process he also cheats his teammates.

Q: What's the best advice you've ever received as a player?

Having been told that any play in which you're involved may ultimately be a play that can be pointed to as having decided the game, so make sure that the level of your recognition and your intensity is as great as it can be as long as you're in the game. The players that can most closely develop that kind of approach are always the players that wind up being involved as any game goes down the wire in those plays that can be pointed to as having made the difference.

[We arrive in Akron and watch the team practice for two hours, then go out for dinner. At 8 P.M. Donoher gets back behind the wheel of Knight's Lincoln; Knight sits besides him with one tape recorder between them. I'm in the back with the second recorder.]

COMMENT
Another bit of narration to indicate we have arrived at our destination. The third act, the drive back, is about to begin. Expect more drama than what we've had.

COMMENT
A detail that pays off later.

Q: I haven't asked you about your two passions other than coaching: hunting and fishing. What is it about hunting that attracts you?

COMMENT
These next few questions are just to get him back in the mood to answer questions. Although reading this, it's question/answer, question/answer, there are really hours of break between drives and I'm trying to re-create the experience of spending this long, full day with Knight.

As you get older, if you're going to compete, you damn near have to play golf or tennis. There's a competitiveness in hunting: the bird gets up, are you quick enough to get on it? Can you hit it? There's also a stamina in hunting. Yesterday I walked in the woods for five hours—up steep hills and down. I was hunting for grouse, didn't see any, didn't get a shot.

Q: Is that considered a wasted day?

No. Karen roots for the birds when she goes with me. Fishing I really like—you're more challenged with the fish than with the birds. But I don't care for deep-sea fishing, where the boat fishes. The bell rings and you just grab the rod and try to reel it in. That's not fishing, that's catching.

Q: How long does it take to become a decent fly fisherman?

I can make a guy a decent caster in thirty minutes. The cast is a lot in your mind like the golf swing. Timing is really important. Then you have to learn how to wade the stream, the pressure of the water against you, the slipperiness of the rocks.

Q: When hunting, have you ever gone after big game?

No, I have no interest in shooting anything that's on four legs.

Q: Have you ever regretted shooting anything?

Yeah. It's been a long, long time since I shot a rabbit or a squirrel. Not too long ago this farmer asked me to shoot rabbits, because they'd become a real problem for him. I did, but I didn't really enjoy that. That's just killing to kill something. Tony La Russa, the Cardinals manager, is a really good friend of mine and he hates hunting with a passion. "It takes a real set of balls to be a hunter." He really gets going. My rejoinder to La Russa is: I look at it as though I cleanse the world of bird shit. He and I go back and forth about that.

Q: What's the hardest bird to hunt?

Turkey are really difficult. You've got to get 'em within thirty-five yards of you, and that's hard. Last spring I spent ten days turkey hunting and we never got one.

COMMENT

My first attempt at bringing up his father. Freud said everything we are starts with those early years, and those early years means dealing with parents. I'm just testing the waters here.

Q: Did you hunt much with your father?

He hunted and took me occasionally. We didn't go a lot. I still have his sixteen-gauge gun.

Q: Didn't you once compare basketball to fishing and golf?

Basketball is different because you're playing against somebody all the time. The difference between a lot of mediocre players and a lot of good players is the ability to see the game. Everybody looks, but very few see. The kid who learns to see has an advantage over all the kids who don't see.

Q: What is it about basketball that so distinguishes it as a game?

There are so many facets that a kid can work on by himself. It's an indoor sport. It's fast. It's fun to play. I'm not sure how much fun kids think practicing football or baseball is. But most enjoy basketball practice.

Q: Steve Alford said he understood why people called you a genius—there was a method to your madness. Can coaches be geniuses?

COMMENT

One doesn't always have to throw negative comments his way. It's sometimes as interesting to see how people react to flattery.

Basketball is not nuclear physics or cancer research. I don't know how applicable that word is. Obviously some coaches are a hell of a lot smarter than others. But let's take another word you just used: madness. What response does that illicit? That borders on some form of insanity. So how accurate is the term *madness* in that phrase? Rasputin was mad. What does that imply?

Q: I'd like to ask you to comment on some of the incidents that are usually described in articles about you. Given your earlier reaction to a question that disturbed you, would you be willing to answer these questions? I don't want you to get angry.

That doesn't guarantee that I won't. But before you get into it, you're going to go over the same incidents that have been brought up in anything that's ever been written about me and I'm tired of talking about them. With that, go ahead.

Q: In 1980 you fired a blank shot from a starter's pistol at *Louisville Courier—Journal* reporter Russ Brown. You said you did it "to keep from going nuts."

I fired a blank starter's pistol in a pressroom one time in what I thought was kind of a humorous situation. I don't recall ever saying that I did it to keep from going nuts.

Q: But did you fire it at someone or just in the air?

First of all, you don't aim a pistol that doesn't have a barrel, do you? This is simply a device that makes noise. It's a solid piece of metal.

Q: In 1981, during the Final Four in Philadelphia, did you shove a fan into a garbage can?

You know I have no interest in this whole line. Ground zero. Everything that I have said relative to these things has been documented and redocumented and documented again and I'm not going through it all again. [*A heavy silence fills the car for a few minutes. Then Knight addresses the incident in his own way.*]

COMMENT

He's thought about it, and is coming around . . .

Let me create a situation for you and tell me how you think most people would react to this, OK? A team is playing and prior to the game fans really obnoxiously berate the players on the other team. That day the team that has been berated wins the game. That night their coach is walking to eat dinner and a fan who's obviously under the influence says, "Well, coach, your team played well today." And the coach replies by saying, "Yeah, we just didn't roll over for your team, did we?" And the guy starts screaming at the top of his lungs that the coach was an asshole, in front of probably a hundred people in a crowded restaurant. How do you think the coach would react to that?

COMMENT

He's turned this around. Now he's asking me questions.

COMMENT

I answer, but he doesn't like what I say.

Q: If the fan was inebriated, the best thing would be to walk away.

How do you avoid it when the guy's screaming at you in front of a hundred people? Do you think there are many competitive people that would avoid that?

Q: It's obviously a difficult situation, but if you're a profes—sional ballplayer or a coach, you really shouldn't get into tussles with fans. What do you think Coach Donoher?

COMMENT

A reminder that there is still someone else in the car with us.

DONOHER: Unless you're confronted with it I don't know how you can answer it. I've never been confronted with anything like that.

[Long pause.]

Q: Let's change the subject to Bill Walton, who often bad-mouths you on camera or writes negatively about you. Why does Walton have it in for you?

There are people that when they bad-mouth you, that's really the best compliment you can get. When they agree with you, then you know you're wrong. Walton is a guy I would never want to think well of me, because then I would know that I had something I should really be bothered about. Walton doesn't know me. He never attended a practice or a clinic that I've given. Walton as a basketball player was one of the great players I ever saw. As a person he leaves a lot to be desired. A guy that refuses to try to represent his country in the Olympics is a guy that I've never had any respect for whatsoever. One time he did an interview with me during the NCAA tournament and Walton made some imperious statement: "Tell me who Bob Knight really is. You tell me!" And I said, "What you see is what you get, which is a hell of a lot different than the guy you played for." A friend of mine was standing behind Walton and he said the color just went up Walton's neck.

Q: Speaking of the guy Walton played for, John Wooden is a sacred name in college basketball: Has he always done things by the book?

I don't know Wooden's history well enough, but it seems to me that Sam Gilbert was awfully intricately involved with basketball at UCLA and it's pretty obvious that Sam Gilbert didn't do very much by the book, whatever that entails.

Q: If you get back into coaching, would you consider changing your coaching style?

Most of what has been written about my coaching style has been written by people who have never been to practice. Have you seen anything where players who have played for me through their eligibility have ever complained about my coaching style?

Q: You have a style that you know works, yet there is a perception out there that indicates some changes might be in order.

COMMENT ....> Who's responsible for the perception?

Starting to get testy.

Q: Partly the media. But they're obviously reporting things they've seen.

What have they seen? Give me an example.

COMMENT

Turning the tables again.

Q: They've seen you get angry.

Have they seen other coaches get angry?

Q: Of course.

Has that been given the same attention as me getting upset with anything?

COMMENT

There's that damn chair again. We've seen already how this torments him.

Q: They're not necessarily providing footage of a chair being thrown across a gym floor.

I saw Rick Majerus, who's a very good coach and friend, pick up an ice cooler in a game in Hawaii where we were playing them and throw it on the floor, with ice and water going everywhere. Did you ever see a picture of it on television? No you didn't. I saw John Chaney, one of the great people I know in coaching, tell a guy that he was going to kill him. Have you ever seen that on television, replayed and replayed again?

Q: So the question comes back: Why you?

COMMENT

Obvious question. Again, one I didn't expect to so tick him off.

You know, forget this whole thing. Do whatever the fuck you want to do with this. I don't think you understand that I don't

COMMENT

That's why I mentioned earlier where it was.

need to go through this kind of bullshit. *[Throws the tape recorder into the backseat.]* I'm not trying to defend myself. I don't give a fuck what you write. You come here and bring up all the bullshit that's happened to me over all these years, and why? This whole thing has been ridiculous. You think I've enjoyed this bullshit? Going through this crap? Like I'm on trial somewhere? Like I have to defend myself? *[Slight pause.]* Give me your two tape recorders.

COMMENT

This is a dramatic turn. He's asking me to give up all the work we've done. He wants to destroy the tapes.

COMMENT

Telling Knight no is like waving a red flag before an angry bull. But what choice do I have? I wasn't going to let him bully me.

Q: No, Coach, I'm not going to do that.

Give me your two tape recorders!

Q: I can't.

Stop the car, Don! *[Knight's rage once again erupts abruptly and unexpectedly. He turns around, his knees on the seat, his head now inches from mine, as he grabs my wrists, trying to get my bag with the tape recorders in them.* "Pull over!" *he orders Donoher, who keeps on driving.* "I want you out of here," *he yells at me.* "And I want those goddamn tapes!"

COMMENT

I went further. I said to him, "You're making a mistake, Coach." Because I knew that his behavior was going to be reported, and that it was going to reach a large audience, into the millions. But Knight was truly out of control. His face was in mine, he was pulling at my bag, and all I could think about was if Donoher slowed up, I was going to open the back door and dive out. I wasn't thinking about saving the interview here, but of saving my hide.

COMMENT

Who could have predicted this? He wants to throw me out of the car!

"You don't want to do this," I say.

"Calm down, Bob." Donoher says, still concentrating on the dark road. "Sit down."

We drive on in tense silence for a while. Then Donoher says, "We have a bad situation here. I don't think it's a good idea for the two of you to be in the car together when I leave. Either I can drive Larry back or I can drive Coach back and you can drive his car back."

When we arrive at Donoher's car we all get out. Donoher asks me what I want to do. I say I'll do whatever Coach Knight wants me to do. I'm willing to get a taxi rather than have Donoher have to drive the two hundred miles back to Bloomington. But Knight grumbles, "Get in the car, I'll drive you." And Donoher says, "Stay in the back, don't sit in the front." I get back in the car and Knight gets behind the wheel and says a gruff good-bye to Donoher. As soon as Donoher leaves, Knight says, "I'll take you back but I'll be goddamned if I'll be your chauffeur. Get in the front."

COMMENT

All this happened as described. Talk about drama—when this interview was published, there were sports radio shows that had two guys playing me and Knight, and it went on for weeks.

I leave my bag with the tape recorders in the back and get in the front seat.

COMMENT

ACT III.

But before we start to drive I look at Knight and stick out my hand. "Shake my hand, Coach," I say. He looks at me for a moment, then shakes my hand. For the next two hours, as we drive back to Bloomington, he pours out his heart.

"You don't understand," he says. "You can't understand. How would you like to have had your whole world taken from you for no good reason? Today was the first time in thirty-eight years where I attended a practice without having a team. For twenty-nine years I did things for Indiana, I raised five

COMMENT

One of those moments you never know how you will react or what you're going to do. A short while ago he wanted to throw me onto the highway and destroy the tapes of our conversation. Now I'm getting back into the car with him, and I felt the need to tone this down a few notches. I wanted to humanize the situation, I didn't want him to see me as the enemy, "the media." When he finally took my hand, I held his firmly. I wanted to get back safely, and we still had three hours of driving in front of us.

Once he started to pour out his feelings, all I could think about was my tape recorders were not on, they were in my bag in the backseat. So I was listening hard to remember what he was saying. Because I knew that this was the denouement. If this was a play—and it sure seemed like one—then it had to have a resolution, and Knight was opening up here.

million dollars for the library, I established two professorial chairs, and when I left there was no thanks. Not a word. I'm selling my house, moving to Phoenix. I don't know if I'll ever get another coaching job again. I never made more than two hundred thirty thousand dollars at Indiana and when they hire some new coach it will cost them between six hundred thousand dollars and a million." He begins laying out his woes. How someone at the Mexican restaurant where we ate the night before had goaded him and claimed he had abused him and took him to court, and it took nine days before the judge threw out the case. How the university lied and spun stories about him. He never threw a vase at the athletic director's secretary, she wasn't even in the room when that happened. And about Neil Reed: Did I know that Knight asked his players whether they wanted Reed on the team and they voted him off, eight to nothing, with one abstention? And Reed went to another program and the coach there said he didn't belong. And that Reed's father coached and got in trouble for punching a kid. Did I know any of that? How come we never hear about these things, only about him?

Then he brings up sportscasters who like him, as if to convince me that he is capable of being liked. "Would you say that among sports broadcasters of the last twenty years no one has been better received than Dick Enberg? Only Curt Gowdy has ever done as many things as Dick Enberg has done. Let's say those are the two premier broadcasters. Curt is a very close friend of mine. Here's a guy who has known everybody in sports since 1950 and he would probably tell you that he is as close to me as anybody he's ever known in sports. Why is that? Dick Enberg, who hasn't done college basketball as a regular in a long time, and I've only talked to him once in the last six years, it's my understanding that on the day this thing happened with me, Enberg contacted the president of CBS Sports and told them that they absolutely had to get me involved in basketball on CBS. So why is that, with these two people? I did a thing with Bob Costas on his late-night show that didn't have anything to do with sports, it was a half-hour show and there was so much that he made two shows out of it. When he ended the second show he said what has been my wife's all-time favorite comment: 'There is a man of substance in an age of style.' So that's Costas. It's kind of amazing when you take the time to look at it: There are also some great writers that I've gotten along well with. Two guys who almost never wrote about basketball were Red Smith and Jim Murray—I've got incredible positive articles that both of them wrote about me. If you pick the five best sportswriters in America today, these three would have to be among them: Dave Kindred, Bob Verdi, and Frank Deford. They have always been very positive about what I've tried to do. Bob Hammel is the best and most honest writer I've ever been around. He was always characterized as being a guy that was in my pocket. No one would say, Hammel happens to agree with me.

"I don't think anyone you've ever interviewed has been more forthright or straightforward as I have with the questions you've asked," he says.

"That's why I didn't want to let you destroy the tapes," I say.

COMMENT

I bring up the tapes because I want to go back to recording, but I'm not sure he will agree.

"You can put the machines back on. I won't do that."]

COMMENT

He agrees.

Q: How important is your record of victories to you? And would you like to get the one hundred seventeen you need to break Dean Smith's record?

COMMENT

At this writing the number is less than sixty.

The teams that I have had at Indiana have set every team record there is in the Big Ten for anything. Not one of the records was ever an objective or a goal of mine. And that's not ever going to change with me in coaching.

Q: If you were to coach again, whatever school, whatever division, how would you handle the press when they asked you: What can we expect of you from what we know of your anger in the past? Why should you be coaching again?

COMMENT

After his two vicious displays of emotion, this is a legitimate question to ask as we drive the empty highway in the middle of the night.

From the standpoint of why I should be coaching, it's simply because I'm damn good at it. I really believe that no one has given as much to basketball as I have, because whatever I developed from an innovative standpoint or whatever I borrowed and refined or whatever I'm responsible for, I have in every conceivable way shared it with any coach that wanted it. But how would I deal with the press? One thing that I would eliminate completely is any attempt at humor. In most cases I don't mean anything malicious by it but I can understand it can on occasions be interpreted that way. And probably sometimes rightfully so. Sometimes I've gone overboard . . . but that's past, that's gone. If I were to coach again, the first thing that I would say at the first press conference would be: "You can judge me by what you've heard or read, or you can just simply say, OK, I'm going to see how he deals with me, see if he's fair, if he's honest, if he's cooperative. That's the way I'm gonna judge you people and I hope that's the way you would judge me."

Q: Family members of a high school football player in South Torrance, California, assaulted the coach because they were upset over the boy's lack of playing time. How do you deal with the psyche of guys who warm the bench and their disappointed families?

Parents start getting upset when their kids don't get to play at the Little League level. The parents have a very difficult time understanding that someone else's kid is better than theirs is. One thing that can be done about it is never let parents come to games. That would eliminate a lot of problems.

Q: Twenty-five years ago in *Newsweek,* you said that most of your coaching is negative, that you concentrate on the ways you could lose. Has it always been like that for you?

That's exactly right. To win you have to eliminate losing. You figure up all the reasons why you can lose—sloppy ball handling, poor shot selection, no block out, no help out on defense—those things don't guarantee you're going to win, but they will all guarantee if they're not handled properly that you're going to lose.

I can remember my mom saying time and time and frigging time again, "Just remember, somebody has to lose." And my rejoinder has always been, "Why should it be me?" My dislike for losing was far more of a motivating factor than my wanting to win.

Q: Talk about your parents . . . ◀ .... **COMMENT**

Dr. Freud is in the car.

My dad was an incredibly disciplined person. From 1937 until he died in 1970 my dad owned just three different cars—a 1937 Chevrolet, 1951 Ford, 1961 Rambler. He never had a credit card, never paid for anything on time. If he hadn't saved the money to buy something he just didn't buy it. He was a lifelong railroader, he never made more than eight thousand dollars a year. Yet we never went hungry, we lived comfortably. My mom and dad were married in 1934, and they bought a lot and built the first home that they ever owned in 1955, when I was going to be a sophomore in high school. They'd been married for twenty-one years before they owned a home. My dad had to take out a twenty- thousand-dollar mortgage. He paid fifteen hundred dollars for the lot and the home cost twenty-three thousand dollars to build. On what my mom and dad made, that mortgage was paid off in four and a half years. He was an incredibly disciplined person. He always had a little problem with weight, and he would just lose it when he had to. From where we lived to where he worked was a mile, and he would walk there in the morning, walk back for lunch, walk back, and then walk home at night. My dad told me only two or three things: One was to never gamble. And I never have.

Q: What were the other two?

They're not any of your business.

Q: Was he strict?

Not really.

Q: Did you have any heart-to-heart talks with him?

COMMENT

Revealing.

We talked about important things. I wouldn't say that they were long conversations. He died at seventy-two. He had a really tough time. He contracted acute leukemia, which is basically a children's disease. They tried to convert it to chronic leukemia and had they been successful it might have given him another eight or ten years to live.

Q: And your mom?

She was a schoolteacher—second and third grade. Very smart. I had her as a second-grade teacher. She was very strict. At my mom's funeral there were three ladies in their eighties that I had in the fourth and sixth grades. I told them, "Would anybody imagine today that I was absolutely scared to death of the three of you?"

Q: Your grandmother was an important person in your life, wasn't she?

My grandmother lived with us until she passed away when I was nineteen, and always used the public library. I was one of the few boys that had a library card, which I had from the time I was old enough to read. My grandmother used to go into the country to buy vegetables or visit her sister in Pennsylvania or go to the movies, and I'd always go with her. In 1960 when she was eighty-three I came home from college and found her where she had passed away after going for a walk, sitting in the living room with her coat and hat on. My mom passed away twenty-seven years later in the same room in a chair facing the one where my grandmother died. She was working a crossword puzzle when she passed away. She was almost the same age as my grandmother was.

Q: What were the turning points in your life?

COMMENT

It's late, it's been a long day's journey into night, we've had some emotional outbursts, now it's time to take him back into his past, to get him to reflect on who he was and how he became who he is.

One was having a mother that was a schoolteacher. From the moment I even understood what education was all about I knew there was a real importance to it. However it was obtained, education was very important to success. Education doesn't just come from attending class, it comes as much as anything from reading. In the third or fourth grade I read a whole series of yellow-and-orange bound books on great figures in American history—obviously at that time they were all white: Eli Whitney, George Washington, Thomas Jefferson, Alexander Hamilton. There was a kids' book, one of which I would always get for Christmas, called *The Hardy Boys.* They were two post-teenage boys who solved all kinds of mysteries. I read the whole series. Prior to that was a series of books called the Bobbsey Twins—one male and one female. As I got more into sports I read books by John Artunis and others. In the seventh grade I read the Chip Hilton series, written by a coach, Clair Bee. They were the most fascinating thing I ever read given my age and interests. There were twenty-three books in the series, a dollar and a quarter each, and I bought them.

Q: What other turning points were there?

I had two people I became close to when I was growing up. One was Dave Knight, no relation. He came to Orrville [Ohio] when I was in the sixth grade, he was an assistant coach and a teacher and later became the principal. He got me started playing basketball with the junior high. He took me to all the practices and I played, even though I was younger. He took me places and did things with me. Then I had a neighbor, Don "Doc" Boop, he was a dentist. He was a great sports fan.

I played for a really good coach from the seventh grade through my senior year in high school named Bill Shunkwiler. Then at Ohio State I played for a great coach in Fred Taylor. Then when I coached the first year [at Cuyahoga Falls High School in Ohio] I worked for a great coach named Harold Andreas. All of them were really meaningful to me. I also played for a coach in high school who was horrible, and yet from him I learned a lot about what not to do, which is every bit as important as learning what to do.

The opportunity to go to Indiana was really big in my life because for twenty-four years it was a situation that I could not have asked for anything better.

COMMENT

·····························

For a guy like Knight, this can be an interesting question.

Q: Who are your heroes?

I have interesting heroes. People who have been willing to take a chance and do things. Ted Williams, who helped thousands of people without anyone knowing what he'd done. George Steinbrenner, who does things with millions of dollars to help people. Harry Truman, who had the courage to drop the atomic bomb and live with the consequences. Probably the most devastating decision ever made in world history. [Ulysses S.] Grant. There's a book called *Grant and Lee* written by a British military historian. Until I read this book it was always that Grant was a butcher and Lee a brilliant strategist and tactician. This book completely wipes that thought out. There was no greater error ever made in the American military than Pickett's Charge up Little Round Top in the Civil War. Thousands of men were sent to be slaughtered. Longstreet argued over and over with Lee about leaving and Lee didn't listen. And they were decimated. So Grant became one of my favorite people in

American history. My favorite military hero, though, is John Wood. He was commander general of the Fourth Armored Division, which spearheaded Patton's march across France. People who have been willing to take a chance and do things are heroes of mine.

Q: Ted Williams has a special place in your heart, doesn't he?

Curt Gowdy always said that Ted Williams and I were kindred spirits. His exact phraseology was "Knight is a pup from Ted Williams." He'd been to the NCAA finals one year and was a fan. I had talked to him once on the telephone. My secretary came in and said, "Ted Williams is on the phone." And I'm saying to myself, "Now who's this asshole calling me telling me he's Ted Williams?" So I picked up the phone and he said, "*Goddamn it,* Coach, how long a leader do you use fishing for brown trout in Montana?" And I mean goddamn there was absolutely no doubt in my mind who this was. He was my favorite player as a kid. I saw him hit four ground-rule doubles in a doubleheader in Cleveland stadium once. Even then, I admired him for his independence. I'm not sure that you would be wrong if you picked Ted Williams and me as the two greatest antagonists of the press.

Q: After losing two fights, Oscar De La Hoya said: "I need a Bob Knight in my training camp, someone who is going to be firm with me and push me to the next level." Think you could ever coach a singular competitor like a boxer, gymnast, or swimmer?

I didn't hear that, that's a pretty nice comment. When it comes to psychology and competition, if a guy can coach, then he can direct individuals. Paul Marchand, the coach for [golfer] Freddie Couples, told our golf coach that Couples wants to sit down and talk to me. But I've never had the chance to talk to him.

Q: Do you like boxing?

No.

[We pass a car on fire. Knight stops, gets out, talks to the cop nearby to see if there's anything he can do.]

COMMENT

The second time we had a cop encounter—only this time, he's stopping to talk to the cop, not the other way around.

Q: It's past midnight, Coach; it's been a long day. Let me throw some offbeat questions at you. What's the most extravagant present anyone's given you?

COMMENT

We're winding down now, passing the time until we get back to Bloomington. Sometimes you get interesting, telling answers to offbeat questions.

I've got a fishing rod that the publisher of the paper in town gave me that's really expensive. And a couple of guns that were expensive. I've got some cartoons upstairs, one that Charles Schultz drew. I'm in it, it's a *Peanuts* cartoon. Then Mort Cooper, the originator of *Beetle Bailey,* drew another one.

Q: Do you have a lot of valuable letters as well?

Yeah, I've got some presidential letters and things like that. I got a handwritten letter from President Ford the other day. I just got a book that George Bush signed to me.

Q: If you could have witnessed any moment in history, what would you choose?

COMMENT

These next group of speculative questions are included because I liked his answers. I asked a lot more, but chose to keep these. In a long interview like this, these offer a change of pace and also provide insight into his character.

I would have really enjoyed seeing five loaves and seven fishes feed five thousand goddamn people.

Q: In what period of time would you have liked to have lived?

I would have enjoyed living in the West from 1875 until the 1890s, when your disagreements were settled by whoever had the fastest draw. And I would have worked awfully hard at it.

Q: If you could have been any person?

I'm satisfied with me.

Q: Fought in any war?

The American Revolution. It was a decided underdog taking on the world's most powerful country and winning on sheer determination.

Q: Compose any music?

"God Bless America."

Q: If you were to be successful in another profession?

If I could have done any one thing other than coach it would have been placed in charge of America's antidrug program with the authority to handle it any way I'd want. I would send the military to take out any drug-producing plant wherever in the world it was.

Q: Most terrifying moment of your life?

Two or three times when I've been very close in being involved in major automobile accidents, and in one case I could have been the cause of serious injury or death to others.

Q: Retract one lie you've told?

The one I told myself about staying in Indiana is something that I should do.

Q: What quotation would you like to have authored?

"Nuts." You know where that comes from? It's what [Brigadier General Anthony] McAuliffe said when the Germans demanded that he surrender Bastogne. The 101st Airborne Division was surrounded and the Germans sent a demand for surrender and McAuliffe answered with one word. They told Patton what McAuliffe had said and Patton said they had to get going because a man that eloquent had to be saved.

Q: If you could reverse any sports call, which would you choose?

A call that a guy made against Steve Downing in the 1973 NCAA finals that would have been Walton's fifth foul. Playing UCLA and it ended up being Downing's fourth foul and he fouled out a minute and a half later. We'd come from twenty-three behind to two behind. Walton would have been out of the game with about seven and a half minutes to go. It was a terrible call. And then had another call the same way in a St. John's game, a semifinal game at the NIT in 1970 [when Knight was coaching Army]. Guy goes up to take a shot, four seconds to play, the ball hits way up on the square of the backboard, and the ref gives him two shots. Cost us a chance to play Marquette for the championship.

Q: Change one thing about your childhood?

I would like to have had brothers and sisters.

Q: If you could insure that your son shared one experience that you've had?

To have had parents that taught him as much as mine taught me.

Q: Spend one night alone with any woman?

My wife.

Q: Live the life of any fictional character?

Robin Hood.

Q: Take revenge on any one person?

Right now it would be absolutely impossible for me to devote all the ideas I would currently have to just one person.

Q: If you could be forgiven for one thing?

For those times when my lack of patience or understanding unjustly hurt somebody.

Q: Seattle Mariners' center fielder Mike Cameron said of his manager, Lou Piniella: "It seems like Lou is at peace with himself. It's as if somebody came down and touched him on the shoulder. It's a blessing."

Why am I even concerned about who said what? That befuddles me. We brought up all these people, what Ventura said, what this guy said, most of whom I've never met, some of whom I don't even know. I like your questions much better when you ask them than when Jesse Ventura does. You ask a question and it comes from somebody I don't respect or like, I say to myself, "Well, who gives a shit." Why are you asking me to respond to these remarks?

Q: It's a way of easing into subjects that might be too delicate to ask bluntly. What I wanted to ask you was: When do you think you might be at peace with yourself—or is that even an issue for you?

That is an issue. Everybody wants to feel at peace with himself. But in a competitive environment, however long you're in there, there are going to be times when you're not going to be at peace with yourself.

> **COMMENT**
>
> *I'm being honest with him. Knight's called me on this, the way Marlon Brando once did when I prefaced a question by saying, "You once said." And he said, "How do you know I once said that?"*

Q: If you could choose how you'd die?

Really late in life.

Q: Reincarnated as an animal?

A mountain lion.

Q: If you could ask God one question?

How in the hell did they ever get all that food out of five loaves and seven fishes?

Q: Return to one year in your life, knowing what you know now?

Five years ago. Had I done that I'd have been coaching someplace else the last five years.

Q: What do you think of Al McGuire's remark, that you remind him of Alexander the Great, "who conquered the world and then sat down and cried because there was nothing left to conquer"?

Basketball has always had a great fascination for me. I haven't yet conquered the game, so maybe that's what I'm trying to do.

Q: So retirement's out of the question. You really do want to coach again?

Yeah, I'd really like to coach again. I would like to wind up my coaching career working for people that I really like and respect and who feel the same way about me. I want better final memories than I have right now.

COMMENT

This feels like it should be the last word, so I ended it here, though there was still the matter of getting out of the car once we arrived at the inn where I was staying. When we said good-bye, Knight said "I'm not now really comfortable with very many things." He also wanted me to meet him the next morning for breakfast, but I knew that I had the interview and I didn't want to see him again, because I figured he would ask me not to write about what happened in the car, and I didn't want to get into any more verbal battles with him. I just wanted to get out of Indiana with my tapes. I said that I was glad I finished the ride down with him, and he said, "I wouldn't have had it any other way." I smiled and said, "It would have been a long walk." I thought of including these last few remarks, but the interview should be about him, not about us.

SOURCES

Impolite Interviews, Paul Krassner, Lyle Stuart, 1961.

Actors Talk About Acting, Lewis Funke and John E. Booth, Random House, 1961.

The Egotists, Oriana Fallaci, Regnery, 1963.

Counterpoint, Roy Newquist, Allen & Unwin, 1965.

Conversations, Roy Newquist, Rand McNally, 1967.

Interviews with Film Directors, Andrew Sarris, Bobbs-Merrill, 1967.

Division Street: America, Studs Terkel, Pantheon, 1967.

Conversations with . . . , Henry Brandon, Houghton Mifflin, 1968.

Do You Sleep in the Nude? Rex Reed, NAL, 1968.

Conversations in the Raw, Rex Reed, World, 1969.

How to Talk with Practically Anybody about Practically Anything, Barbara Walters, Doubleday, 1970.

The Great Comedians, Larry Wilde, Citadel, 1973.

Super-Talk, Digby Diehl, Doubleday, 1974.

Working, Studs Terkel, Pantheon, 1974.

Academy All the Way, Grover Lewis, Straight Arrow, 1974.

Off Camera, Leonard Probst, Stein & Day, 1975.

Burke's Steerage, Tom Burke, Putnam, 1976.

Conversations with Marilyn, W. J. Weatherby, Mason/Charter, 1976.

Interview with History, Oriana Fallaci, Liveright, 1976.

The Craft of Interviewing, John Brady, Vintage Books, 1977.

The Star Treatment, Dick Selzer, Bobbs-Merrill, 1977.

Celebrity Circus, Charles Higham, Delacorte, 1979.

American Dreams: Lost and Found, Studs Terkel, Ballantine, 1980.

Intimacies, Alan Ebert, Dell, 1980.

The Playboy Interview, ed. G. Barry Golson, Playboy Press, 1981.

The Playboy Interview: Volume II, ed. G. Barry Golson, Wideview/Perigee, 1983.

The Omni Interviews, ed. Pamela Weintrau, Ticknor & Fields, 1984.

The Courage to Change, Dennis Wholey, Houghton Mifflin, 1984.

Visions and Voices, Jonathan Cott, Dolphin Doubleday, 1987.

American Singers, Whitney Balliett, Oxford, 1988.

Off the Record, Joe Smith, Warner, 1988.

Creative Conversations, Michael Schumacher, Writer's Digest Books, 1990.

Hard to Get, Nancy Collins, HarperCollins, 1990.

Interviewing America's Top Interviewers, Jack Huger and Dean Diggins, Birch Lane Press, 1991.

Who the Devil Made It, Peter Bogdanovich, Knopf, 1997.

Interview, Claudia Dreifus, Seven Stories, 1997.

Scientific Conversations, Claudia Dreifus, Times Books, 2001.

The Gay Talese Reader, Gay Talese, Walker, 2003.

The Paris Review collections of Interviews with Writers, ed. George Plimpton.

The University Press of Mississippi series of interviews with writers and filmmakers.

INDEX

Ali, Muhammad, 239, 358
Allen, Tim, 41
Allen, Woody, 91–92, 96
Altman, Robert, 111
Alzado, Lyle, 56
Amin, Idi, 364
Angelou, Maya, 268
Aniston, Jennifer, 72, 229–230
Ashby, Hal, 91
Ashe, Arthur, 56
Asner, Jules, 49
Auletta, Ken, 37–38, 89

Baitz, Jon Robin, 67
Baldwin, Alec, 24, 104
Baldwin, Neil, 32
Ball, Lucille, 177, 347
Barkley, Frank, 56
Barris, Chuck, 196–197
Barry, Rick, 262
Barrymore, Drew, 84–98, 117,
        162–163, 353, 367–378
Barrymore, John, 86, 98
Basinger, Kim, 24, 125
Beatles, the, 90–91
Beatty, Warren, 16, 25–26, 118,
        128–130, 134, 196, 197, 347,
        358
Belafonte, Henry, 268
Bellow, Saul, 82, 115–117, 132,
        176–177, 191–192, 207, 209,
        245, 257–259, 287
Benet, Eric, 77
Bening, Annette, 24, 25
Berg, A. Scott, 32
Bergman, Ingmar, 111
Bernhard, Sandra, 231, 232
Berry, Halle, 23, 24, 77–81, 128, 143,
        151, 163–164
Bird, Larry, 396–397, 424
Blake, Robert, 353–354
Bloch, Peter, 263–265, 268, 269,
        271–274, 276, 277, 280, 281,
        283–284, 286–289, 291

Bogart, Humphrey, 126
Boggs, Wade, 56
Bonds, Barry, 58, 176, 339
Bowie, David, 196, 197
Boyle, Lara Flynn, 195, 197
Boyle, T. C., 259
Bracco, Lorraine, 128, 181–184
Brand, Myles, 410–411, 417, 419, 420,
        449
Brando, Marlon, 15–17, 23, 24, 33, 38,
        41, 66, 104, 108, 116, 117, 126,
        133, 209–214, 218, 236,
        246–247, 252, 254, 256, 323,
        345–349, 360, 361, 364–365
Brenner, Marie, 115, 293
Brett, George, 56
Broomfield, Nick, 46–47
Brosnan, Pierce, 79, 128
Brown, H. Rap, 234, 244
Brown, Larry, 413
Browne, Jackson, 328–329
Bryant, Kobe, 58
Bugliosi, Vincent, 34–35, 148–150
Bullock, Sandra, 117
Burger, Neil, 45
Burns, Ken, 47
Burroughs, William S., 32
Bush, George, 59–60, 103, 402, 448

Caesar, Sid, 11
Cameron, Mike, 448–449
Capote, Truman, 32, 33, 36, 41, 49,
        61–62, 82, 128, 191–192,
        207–209, 249, 256–257, 346,
        348, 349, 354, 360
Capp, Al, 153–155
Carlson, Tucker, 49
Carrey, Jim, 91, 128
Carter, Jimmy, 99, 103, 193, 349
Cavett, Dick, 41, 66
Cazale, John, 128
Chamberlain, Wilt, 426, 427
Chambers, Marilyn, 49, 54–55
Chan, Jackie, 41

Chaney, John, 435
Clarke, Gerald, 32
Clemens, Roger, 386–388, 424
Clinton, Bill, 135, 403
Clooney, George, 97, 267
Cobain, Kurt, 87
Cole, Natalie, 49
Collins, Joan, 121–122
Conlin, Bill, 379–380
Connery, Sean, 233–234, 312–313, 324
Cook, Kevin, 293, 299, 304, 305, 307, 310, 314–315, 318, 324, 326–327, 329, 334, 335, 339
Cooper, Gary, 405
Cossman, E. Joseph, 189–190, 255
Costas, Bob, 49, 57, 439
Couric, Katie, 49, 60
Cruise, Tom, 68, 315, 330, 332
Culp, Robert, 101–102
Curtis, Jamie Lee, 128
Curtis, Tony, 128

Dana, Will, 263, 266, 269–272, 274, 276–284, 286, 288, 290, 292
Dangerfield, Rodney, 128
Davis, Miles, 49, 185, 240, 323
Davis, Sammy, Jr., 234–235
Dean, James, 174
DeGeneres, Ellen, 49, 159
De Havilland, Olivia, 40, 160
De Kock, Eugene, 31–32
DeLillo, Don, 259, 364
De Niro, Robert, 25, 125, 170, 189, 214–219
De Palma, Brian, 319–320
Depp, Johnny, 120, 121, 339
De Swart, Jan, 159, 365
Diaz, Cameron, 24
Diehl, Matt, 231, 233
Diggins, Dean, 185, 233
Donahue, Phil, 49
Doninger, Clarence, 411, 412
Donleavy, J. P., 117, 347, 348
Donoher, Don, 381, 382, 403, 421, 422, 433, 436–437
Downey, Robert, Jr., 125, 287, 341
Downing, Steve, 448
Dreifus, Claudia, 235–236, 293–294, 299, 301, 303, 305, 307, 308,

310, 312, 313, 316, 317, 319, 321, 322, 324, 325, 327, 328, 330, 331, 333–337, 341
Drury, Chris, 49
Dunaway, David King, 32
Dunne, John Gregory, 114–115

Eastwood, Clint, 24
Edwards, John, 102–103, 128
Eichmann, Adolf, 17
Eliot, T. S., 117
Ellman, Richard, 32
Ellroy, James, 39, 239
Enberg, Dick, 438–439
Englebert, Victor, 133–134
Essex, Andrew, 263, 266, 268, 270, 273, 275–277, 279–280, 282–286, 288, 289, 290
Evans, Robert, 23, 134–135

Fairchild, Morgan, 53, 54
Fallaci, Oriana, 15, 55, 185–186, 233–235, 244–245, 248
Farley, Chris, 49, 321
Fast, Howard, 39
Feynman, Richard, 117, 132, 191
Field, Sally, 128
Firestone, Roy, 55–57, 175
Fleming, Michael, 294, 298, 302, 304, 305, 307, 308, 310, 311, 314, 316–322, 324, 326–328, 330–338, 341
Flockhart, Calista, 231–232
Flynn, Errol, 98
Folsing, Albrecht, 32
Fonda, Bridget, 24
Fonda, Henry, 15, 41, 106, 107, 115, 166–167, 256, 365
Fonda, Jane, 86, 328
Fonda, Peter, 166
Fonda, Shirlee, 106
Ford, Harrison, 24, 135, 170, 195, 203, 231–232, 281, 324, 341
Foster, Jodie, 72, 86, 97, 200–203
Fox, Michael J., 320
Franco, James, 24, 170, 173–175
Fraser, Brendan, 365
Friedan, Betty, 49, 51–53, 287
Friend, Tad, 67

Gable, Clark, 126, 405
Gallin, Sandy, 118
Gandhi, Indira, 235
Gardner, Ava, 36, 40, 41, 125, 127–128
Gardner, John, 207
Garner, James, 128, 161–162
Gates, Bill, 230, 287, 342
Gates, Darryl, 287
Giap, General, 244
Gibson, Charles, 49
Gibson, Mel, 137–138, 150–151
Gilbert, Sam, 434
Ginsberg, Allen, 32, 49, 50, 115, 157–158, 239
Glass, Ira, 42, 43
Gobodo-Madikizela, Pumla, 31–32
Godard, Jean-Luc, 45
Gold, Don, 256–257
Golson, Barry, 256–257, 260–262, 263–265, 268, 271, 273–275, 280, 283, 284, 288, 290
Gooding, Cuba, 56
Gould, Elliott, 23, 41, 108–114, 170
Gowdy, Curt, 438, 445
Grant, Hugh, 178, 267, 353
Grant, Ulysses S., 444
Greeley, Andrew, 238–239, 249
Green, Tom, 84, 86–88, 93–94
Grodin, Charles, 53–54

Haley, Alex, 50, 128, 240–241, 246, 323
Hannity and Colmes, 49
Harvey, Anthony, 112
Hawn, Goldie, 24, 117, 153–155
Hearst, Patty, 24, 99–102, 119–120, 143, 256
Hefner, Christie, 99, 101, 256
Hefner, Hugh, 41, 55, 234
Heller, Joseph, 247–248
Hemingway, Ernest, 133
Hennicke, Slim, 36–37
Heston, Charlton, 46
Hill, George Roy, 348
Hilton, Paris, 347
Hinckley, John, 72, 200, 201
Hirschberg, Lynn, 67
Hitchcock, Alfred, 244–245

Hoffman, Dustin, 26, 207
Hopkins, Abigail, 167
Hopkins, Anthony, 24, 25, 139–140, 167–168, 249
Hopper, Dennis, 174
Huber, Jack, 185, 233
Hudson, Kate, 24
Hughes, Howard, 127–128
Hurley, Elizabeth, 36
Hurrell, George, 50–51
Hussein, King of Jordan, 235
Hussein, Saddam, 364
Huston, Anjelica, 127, 198–199, 352
Huston, John, 39–40, 132, 159–161, 193, 194, 198–199, 351–352, 365
Huston, Ricki, 198, 199
Huston, Tony, 198, 199
Huvane, Stephen, 72

Isay, David, 42–44
Iverson, Allen, 58, 428

Jabbar, Kareem, 427
Jackman, Hugh, 24
Jackson, Michael, 183, 347, 350
Jackson, Phil, 389
Jarecki, Andrew, 231, 232
Jenkins, Patty, 47
Jenkins, Stephen, 231, 232
Jennings, C. Robert, 245
Johnson, Magic, 56
Jolie, Angelina, 24, 186–188
Jones, Grace, 115
Jones, James Earl, 41, 128
Jones, Jenny, 49
Jong, Erica, 245–246
Jordan, Michael, 339, 426
Julian, Hubert Fauntleroy, 255
Justice, David, 151
Juvonen, Nan, 87

Kael, Pauline, 207, 209
Kaplan, Jonathan, 86, 97
Kasten, Fred, 42
Keaton, Diane, 116, 358
Keitel, Harvey, 24, 128, 180–185
Kennedy, John F., 45
Kerouac, Jack, 158
Kidman, Nicole, 23, 24, 193

Kiedis, Anthony, 22, 23, 128, 164–165, 230
Kimmel, Jimmy, 49
King, Don, 237, 238
King, Larry, 49, 60, 347, 350–352
King, Martin Luther, Jr., 246
Kingsley, Pat, 67, 72
Kissinger, Henry, 244, 268, 331
Knight, Bob, 23, 128, 143, 251, 287, 360–361, 379–450
Kofi, Vincent, 357
Koppel, Ted, 49, 60, 136, 352
Ky, Nguyen Cao, 234

Lake, Ricki, 49
Lamb, Brian, 59, 60
La Russa, Tony, 430
Lauer, Matt, 49, 60, 176
Ledger, Heath, 24
Lee, Spike, 287
Lee, Stan, 145, 147
Lennon, John, 323, 339–340
Leno, Jay, 49, 60, 178, 352–353
Leonard, Elmore, 39, 82
Leonard, Sugar Ray, 56
LeRoy, JT, 231, 232
Letterman, David, 49, 60, 85, 196, 352–353
Lewis, Jerry, 36, 115, 166
Lipton, James, 225
Liu, Lucy, 87
Lombardi, Vince, 390
Loren, Sophia, 41, 79
Love, Courtney, 87

Madonna, 29, 86, 353
Mailer, Norman, 32, 33, 49, 54, 65, 106–107, 121, 128, 192, 205–207, 209, 238, 239, 358–359
Majerus, Rick, 435
Mamet, David, 1, 2
Mantle, Mickey, 56
Martin, Christy, 237–238
Martin, Steve, 1, 2, 117, 170–173, 175, 256
Martinson, Connie, 58–60
Marx, Groucho, 113–114
Matisse, Henri, 364
Matthews, Chris, 49

Maxwell, Robert, 287, 340
McCartney, Paul, 176
McDermott, Dylan, 127, 199–200
McGuire, Al, 450
McGuire, Mark, 424
McKenna, Kristine, 295, 297, 299–300, 304, 306, 308, 309, 311, 315, 316, 318, 321–323, 325, 326, 328, 329, 331–333, 335–337, 341–342
McNamara, Robert, 46
McNeese, Gretchen, 245
Meir, Golda, 248
Meisner, Sanford, 199
Mengers, Sue, 134
Merrill, Sam, 247–248
Meyers, Jeffrey, 32
Michener, James A., 82–83, 203–205, 256, 257, 259, 345, 348–349, 365
Midler, Bette, 175
Mile, Barry, 32
Miller, Arthur, 115
Min, Janice, 263, 264, 266–272, 274, 276, 277, 279, 280, 282–285, 288, 291, 355
Mitchum, Robert, 15–17
Monroe, Marilyn, 126, 247
Moore, Henry, 132, 252, 253, 347–348, 365
Moore, Julianne, 353
Moore, Michael, 46
Morgan, Ted, 32, 36
Morgan, Thomas, 33, 34, 66
Morris, Errol, 43, 46
Morrison, Toni, 364
Murray, Jim, 176
Muske-Dukes, Carol, 1

Newcott, Bill, 263–265, 268–271, 273, 276, 278, 281, 282, 284–286, 288, 289, 291, 355
Newman, Paul, 40, 309
Nicholson, Jack, 125, 134, 195–197, 223–225
Nicklaus, Jack, 422–423
Nicks, Stevie, 233
Nolte, Nick, 117, 128
Norden, Eric, 235

Oates, Joyce Carol, 1, 39, 82, 128, 132, 155–156, 176, 259, 289, 346
O'Brien, Conan, 49
Obst, Lynda, 85, 92
O'Donnell, Chris, 170
Olmos, James Edward, 181–184
O'Neal, Shaquille, 58, 339, 427
O'Reilly, Bill, 49
Oswald, Lee Harvey, 45

Pacino, Al, 15–17, 23, 38, 75–77, 116, 123, 125, 207, 209, 218, 220–226, 256, 261–262, 323, 349, 353, 358
Parker, Heidi, 263–265, 268, 269, 271, 273, 275, 276, 278, 280, 282, 284, 286, 288, 290, 291
Parton, Dolly, 23, 115, 116, 249–250, 256
Pauley, Jane, 61–62
Pauling, Linus, 82, 115, 132, 190–191
Pavarotti, Luciano, 23, 49, 256
Pesci, Joe, 208
Peters, Jon, 73–75
Philbin, Regis, 49
Phoenix, River, 320, 332
Piazza, Mike, 386–387
Picasso, Pablo, 364
Pierson, Frank, 73
Pileggi, Nicholas, 33, 34, 36, 66
Piniella, Lou, 448–449
Plimpton, George, 41
Polanski, Roman, 40, 128
Pond, Steve, 295–296, 299, 301, 303–304, 306–308, 310–313, 315–324, 327–339
Pop, Iggy, 196, 197
Povich, Maury, 49
Prinze, Freddie, Jr., 144–147, 170, 175
Pryor, Richard, 41, 173

Radner, Gilda, 353
Randall, Stephen, 263, 266–268, 271, 273, 275, 277, 279, 281, 283–285, 287–292
Reagan, Nancy, 40
Redford, Robert, 405

Reed, Lou, 196, 197
Reed, Neil, 395
Reeves, Keanu, 365
Rensin, David, 286, 298, 300, 304, 306–309, 311–313, 316–318, 320, 322–325, 328, 329, 331–333, 335–337, 342–344
Ricci, Christina, 24, 162
Rice, Anne, 45
Rijker, Lucia, 23, 116, 237–238, 258
Riley, Pat, 389
Roberts, Julia, 231, 313
Robeson, Paul, 268
Rock, Chris, 41
Rockwell, George Lincoln, 240–241
Rodman, Dennis, 56, 327, 339, 427
Romano, Ray, 125, 162
Rose, Charlie, 49, 60, 264, 352
Ross, Lillian, 33
Roth, Philip, 259, 364
Russell, Bill, 426, 427
Russell, Kurt, 24, 115
Russert, Tim, 60
Rutten, Tim, 114
Ryder, Winona, 125, 186

Salisbury, Harrison, 31, 136
Sandler, Adam, 86
Sawyer, Diane, 49, 60, 63, 66
Schaap, Jeremy, 427, 428
Schanberg, Sydney, 49
Schlafly, Phyllis, 51
Scorsese, Martin, 34, 47, 321
Scott, George C., 15, 36, 115, 228, 256
Seltzer, Nancy, 72
Shah, Diane K., 296, 298–300, 302, 309, 310–314, 317, 319, 321–322, 324–326, 328, 332, 334–337
Shalala, Donna, 400
Shaw, Bernie, 99, 102
Sheen, Charlie, 129, 140–143
Sheff, David, 35, 297–298, 301–303, 305, 307, 308, 310, 311, 315–323, 325–328, 330–335, 337–341
Shnayerson, Robert, 252–253
Shoemaker, Willie, 107
Short, Martin, 49

Shriver, Maria, 60
Shue, Elisabeth, 127
Siegel, Joel, 116
Simon, Neil, 49, 239, 248
Sinatra, Frank, 75
Singer, Isaac Bashevis, 330, 345
Slater, Christian, 24, 105, 128,
        177–180, 362
Smith, Emmitt, 56
Smith, Liz, 72
Smith, Ray, 1
Spacey, Kevin, 121
Spears, Britney, 347, 353
Speer, Albert, 235
Spielberg, Steven, 85, 96
Stallone, Sylvester, 128, 147
Stamberg, Susan, 44–45
Stark, Ray, 35, 112
Steinbrenner, George, 444
Stewart, Jimmy, 405
Stewart, Jon, 49
Stone, Oliver, 45, 117, 164, 208–209
Stone, Sharon, 24, 118–119, 246, 359
Streep, Meryl, 128, 170, 189
Streisand, Barbra, 16, 26–27, 41,
        72–75, 86, 104, 111,
        118–119, 189, 193, 252, 253,
        256, 260–262, 348, 349, 363
Sturges, Preston, 91
Sutherland, Kiefer, 23, 24, 259
Svetkey, Benjamin, 196

Talese, Gay, 1, 114, 121
Terkel, Studs, 220
Theron, Charlize, 47
Thomas, Isiah, 390–391, 395–396,
        428
Thornton, Billy Bob, 186–188,
        193–194, 230–231
Towne, Robert, 134
Travolta, John, 108
Truman, Harry, 444
Tyson, Mike, 155–156, 287

Unseld, Wes, 56–57

Updike, John, 39, 66, 170, 259, 364

Valentino, Rudolph, 126
Van Damme, Jean-Claude, 23, 115,
        168–170
Van Damme, Kristofer, 168, 169
Van Doren, Mamie, 49
Ventura, Jesse, 23, 68–72, 134, 144,
        193, 226–228, 248–249, 287,
        402, 449
Vidal, Gore, 39, 207–209
Voight, Jon, 24, 186–188

Walken, Christopher, 117
Wallace, David Foster, 259
Walsh, Raoul, 98
Walters, Barbara, 56, 60, 66, 75, 220,
        347, 353–354
Walton, Bill, 434
Warhol, Andy, 354, 364
Warren, Lesley Ann, 152
Webber, Chris, 428
Weinstein, Harvey, 86
Welles, Orson, 116
Wenner, Jann, 323, 328–329
West, Mae, 35, 175, 347, 357
Wheeler, Susan, 1
Williams, Montel, 40, 49, 168
Williams, Robin, 115, 230, 259
Williams, Ted, 406, 444, 445
Williams, Tennessee, 117, 245
Willis, Bruce, 23
Winfrey, Oprah, 49, 60
Winkler, Henry, 242–243, 256
Winters, Shelley, 49
Wittman, Randy, 428
Wolfe, Tom, 259, 364
Wooden, John, 434
Wuornos, Aileen, 46–47

Yorn, Pete, 231, 250–251

Zappa, Frank, 287, 340–341
Zelasko, Jeanne, 83
Zellweger, Renee, 231, 250–251

ABOUT THE AUTHOR

LAWRENCE GROBEL has been a freelance writer for more than thirty years. He has written for the *New York Times, Rolling Stone, Entertainment Weekly, Reader's Digest, Cosmopolitan, Redbook,* and *Details,* and is a contributing editor at *Playboy* and *Movieline's Hollywood Life. Playboy* called him "the interviewer's interviewer," and Joyce Carol Oates has dubbed him "the Mozart of interviewers." Between 1968 and 1971 he taught in the Peace Corps at the Ghana Institute of Journalism. His book *Conversations with Capote* received a PEN Special Achievement award. He has also received a National Endowment for the Arts grant for fiction. He created the M.F.A. in Professional Writing program for Antioch University and teaches "Life Skills: The Art of the Interview" at UCLA.

Grobel's other books include *Conversations with Capote; The Hustons; Conversations with Brando; Talking with Michener; Above the Line: Conversations About the Movies; Endangered Species: Writers Talk About Their Craft, Their Visions, Their Lives;* and *Climbing Higher* (with Montel Williams).